W9-ASR-138

Presented To

*St. Mary's
College of Maryland
Library*

By ......JOHN..G...WILLIAMSON..............

....

Date ....JULY 1980..........................

THE BORMANN
BROTHERHOOD

Other books by William Stevenson

THE YELLOW WIND

BIRDS' NESTS IN THEIR BEARDS

THE BUSHBABIES

STRIKE ZION

ZANEK!

EMPEROR RED

WILLIAM STEVENSON

THE BORMANN BROTHERHOOD

HARCOURT BRACE JOVANOVICH, INC., NEW YORK

Copyright © 1973 by William Stevenson

All rights reserved. No part of this publication may
be reproduced or transmitted in any form or by any means,
electronic or mechanical, including photocopy, recording,
or any information storage and retrieval system,
without permission in writing from Bantam Books, Inc.,
666 Fifth Avenue, New York, N.Y. 10019

Printed in the United States of America

ISBN 0-15-113590-8
Library of Congress Catalog Card Number: 73-2287
First edition
B C D E

For
INTREPID

CONTENTS

ACKNOWLEDGMENTS AND
A NOTE ON SOURCES

ix

PART ONE
THE PUZZLE
1

PART TWO
THE PIECES
21

PART THREE
THE CONDEMNED
313

INDEX
328

ACKNOWLEDGMENTS AND
A NOTE ON SOURCES

Martin Bormann did all he could to prevent information about himself from reaching his enemies. War criminals sank into a similar anonymity. Their postwar movements were followed by Allied joint intelligence teams, and their findings, particularly in the case of Bormann, became a primary source of information. Some of this material is available in the National Archives, Washington, D.C., and is classified as "privileged." Similar material was declassified by the British in 1972 and can be traced through the Public Record Office. However, the hunt for Bormann and his Nazi brothers continued into the period still covered by countries' various official secrecy acts. A report involving espionage and secret-police operations is bedeviled by difficulties of this sort. Some sources cannot be plainly identified; some informants risk the vengeance of Nazi self-protection gangs.

I have mentioned in the text those authorities who can be identified; I am, of course, most grateful for their help. Listed here are some of the individuals to whom I am also indebted. I have added the names of those libraries from which came most of my background information and many of my leads. The mention of film libraries as well may seem a trifle eccentric. In the case of an elusive personality like Bormann, I found a new method in use among investigative agencies utilizing old newsreels. These conveyed in an uncanny fashion the man's true dimensions. I would like to thank the film archivists who helped catch Bormann flitting through old and scratched film. He was examined frame by frame until we became familiar with small gestures and other mannerisms which he would have difficulty changing.

It is the practice in any historical survey of this kind to support certain assertions with detailed references to the writer's authorities. I have quoted from documents which at the time they were written were secret and confidential. Time changed their grading. To avoid embarrassment, however, I have not referred to documents that are not yet open to public inspection in the United States and Britain, although I have seen parallel documents in European archives, where their authenticity is beyond doubt.

In the case of individual accounts, Thucydides said it all when he commented upon the difficulty of chronicling the Peloponnesian War. The stories of battle commanders did not tally with the facts. General impressions were misleading. Eyewitnesses had to be double-checked because "many suffered either from partiality for one side or the other or else from imperfect memories." So far as I have been able, I have taken into account here the imperfections and fallibilities of human memory. Most direct quotations come from transcripts of tape recordings or from shorthand notes.

The full verbatim account of the Nuremberg trials provided much information on Bormann and those who escaped through his foresight. Rather than refer to the many sources now available, which would tend to bewilder anyone pursuing this investigation further, I suggest consulting the twenty-three volumes of reports on the trials published by Her Majesty's Stationery Office. It also confuses the issue to refer to the numbered Nuremberg trials documents, because not all were put in evidence; and of those put in evidence, not all were accepted by the court; but a tendency exists to regard any such documents as established evidence.

The long bibliographies that were a feature of books on the Nazi period tend nowadays to overlap to such an extent that it seemed more practical to refer to recent publications covering most of the existing literature. The opening of British Foreign Office files covering the war years and the relaxation of secrecy restrictions on certain Allied intelligence operations have also made clear inconsistencies and contradictions in earlier reports. This has been particularly true of Bormann himself, whose monstrous influence has become apparent only in more recent times.

The help given to me varied, naturally, because some individuals and libraries had more material to offer than others. Lord Russell of Liverpool, who was legal adviser to the British Commander in Chief in occupied Germany in the early postwar years, does deserve special mention because he was for a long time a voice crying in the wilderness. His experiences during the war-crimes trials led him to write *The Scourge of the Swastika,* and by the end of the 1960's he was disturbed enough to obtain the full text of the neo-Nazi National Democratic party manifesto and to gather the records of Nazi war criminals who, by one device or another, had cheated justice.

The late chief of the U.S. Office of Strategic Services, General William J. Donovan, left personal notes, which some of his friends and former agents have been kind enough to let me see, believing that he would have wanted this. The wartime chiefs of American and British secret agencies contributed personal accounts that had a bearing on the preparations for escape undertaken by thousands of leading Nazi figures in the midst of Germany's military campaigns.

Some German sources might prefer not to be acknowledged. I gained useful insight into the mentality of Hitler's military commanders from a book published in 1941 by a general staff officer of the First Panzer Division, called *Tanks Between Warsaw and the Atlantic.* The author, twenty-five years later, became Supreme Commander of all NATO forces in Europe. He was General Count von Kielmansegg. The memoirs of other German personalities have been consulted, but with reservations. And it is important to note that East Germany's own use of former military commanders under Hitler is still a closed book. I have restricted myself to an account of events that, in the main, occurred in areas open to public scrutiny. One can only hope that in time it will be possible to give a fuller report on how the Soviet Union also made its private arrangements with men guilty of crimes against humanity.

In thanking the individuals listed alphabetically below, I hope it will not be thought they were responsible for conclusions other than those directly quoted, nor that they have broken the long silence imposed by the various secrecy acts.

Professor Niels Bohr: He provided me with introductions to the Academy of Sciences of the Ukraine, USSR. Professor Bohr died, in 1962, dedicated to the belief that secrecy with regard to the escape of Nazi war criminals was an impediment to mankind's progress. He had worked under Nazi rule in Copenhagen until August 1943, when, aware of Germany's growing interest in his development of atomic energy, he escaped.

Colonel André Dewavrin: He parachuted twice into Nazi-occupied France on missions for the British secret service. He became expert in unconventional warfare and a source of up-to-date information on the movements of Nazi war criminals.

Alexander Foote: This Englishman, recruited into Soviet intelligence service, worked in Switzerland in association with the legendary "Lucy," the Russian espionage expert with a direct line to the German high command. Foote kept a record of Nazi preparations in Switzerland for postwar financing of escape agencies, and before he died he delivered the details to British intelligence.

Welles Hangen: The National Broadcasting Company's Far East bureau chief, who disappeared and was one of many American correspondents listed as missing in the wars of Indochina, was the New York *Times* correspondent in Moscow when we together tackled the Soviet bureaucracy on the question of Martin Bormann's alleged service as a Russian agent.

Iser Harel: He is the former chief of Israel intelligence, the Shin Beth, or National Security Office, which controls Sheruth Modiin, the military intelligence department.

Richard Hughes: The doyen of Western correspondents in Asia, Far East expert for the *Times* of London and the *Economist,* he provided me with some little-known facts about the Soviet spy Richard Sorge. It was through his initiative while he was in Moscow that the British spies Guy Burgess and Donald Maclean were produced for the first time to confirm that they had indeed returned to their Soviet masters. Hughes is a veteran in investigative reporting, combining experience in police methods with a considerable knowledge of Nazi and Soviet affairs. His many years of active and concentrated interest in the travels of Nazi war criminals provided guidelines for this book.

Hermann Langbein: Secretary of the International Concentration Camp Committee, which documents and tries to secure the punishment of Nazi war criminals, he asked me in 1972 to publicize some of the grosser examples of prominent Germans in public life today whose trials have been delayed by various excuses; "Possibly one can still change the practice of German Law Courts which at the moment permit a defendant to simply choose a busy barrister who then keeps asking for postponements of these trials. . . ."

Paul Leverkühn: The German military intelligence director of Mideast operations, he provided some details of how Nazi Mideast spy rings became ODESSA escape routes. He had been a close admirer of Admiral Canaris, his chief, less for that man's reluctance to go to war with the West than for his bitter anti-Communist feelings. He defended German supreme headquarters senior commanders at their trials, including Field Marshal Fritz von Manstein, and in this role developed an undying hostility to Dr. Otto John, who exposed Manstein's dishonesty.

Milton Shulman: Now of the London *Evening Standard,* he was a Toronto *Star* correspondent who, as a qualified barrister, interrogated senior German Army commanders on behalf of British military intelligence in the war's aftermath. He had made himself expert on the German Army as a major in Canadian military intelligence.

Jacques Soustelle: French Governor-General in Algeria under De Gaulle, he worked for the Free French in Latin America against Nazi operations there during the war.

General Leandro Sanchez Salazar: Formerly chief of the Mexican secret service, he guided me through many of the problems of dealing with police forces in Latin America.

Südwestfunk, of Hans-Bredowstrasse, Baden-Baden, West Germany: A documentary by this company, broadcast in July 1972, drew public attention to the case of Dr. Josef Thümmler, the Gestapo chief of Katowice and President of the infamous Auschwitz Summary Court. The West German prosecutors declared themselves unable to assemble the material from Poland that would make a case. The producer of the documentary, Henning Roehl, then went to Poland and obtained the material documenting the alleged atrocities. Thümmler was pensioned off by his employers: Zeiss-Werken.

Bickham Sweet-Escott: Some of the frustrations of piecing together a puzzle of this nature were conveyed by Mr. Sweet-Escott, of Special Operations, who wrote in his book *Baker Street Irregular* that there were no real secrets, "least of all from the people who work in the huge wedding-cake skyscrapers which house the Soviet Ministry of Foreign Affairs." He cut through a great deal of the bureaucratic red tape with the observation that professional historians in their own parts of Europe had managed to re-create an account of events in spite of the inaccessibility of the official records kept by Anglo-American governments, "without whom there would have been no resistance to the Nazis." An earlier book he wrote on British secret operations was based upon what published material then existed. The typescript was sent to the British War Office for clearance under the Official Secrets Act in late 1954. Half a year later, he was informed that the strongest objections were taken to the book and he would be liable for prosecution under the law if he went ahead and published. Eventually, after many arguments, and with the help of friends in high places, he was able to bring out a somewhat censored version. Such are the vagaries of military security.

Kurt Tank: One of Hitler's weaponry experts, he first drew my attention to escape routes when I found him in India. Tank was an aircraft designer who worked in Cairo on the Egyptian-built He 300 fighter under the direction of "Herr Doktor Mahmoud." Tank became controller of production in Bangalore, India, of the first Indian jet fighter, the Hindustan HF 24. It was in Bangalore that I talked with him about escape routes he had followed, first to Argentina.

Sir Robert Thompson: Chief of the British Advisory Mission in Vietnam and formerly director of counter-terrorist work in Malaya and Borneo, he provided expertise on escape and evasion techniques.

James Wei: Special adviser to Generalissimo Chiang Kai-shek, formerly of Yenching University, and a keen historian, he kept records of Hitler's military commanders who during the war made inquiries about future work and later came to Taiwan on arms missions. A man of many talents and great intellectual resources, he was director-general of the Republic of China information services and took an amateur interest that would put professional detectives to shame. His knowledge of Latin America and the movements of war criminals, through his country's embassies and missions in that area, proved profound and accurate.

Vice-Admiral A. G. N. Wyatt: Hydrographer of the British Royal Navy, he charted U-boat movements at war's end.

Marshal Georgi Zhukov: Russian suspicions about escaping Nazis were described by this Soviet military leader, who in World War II was in over-all command of Soviet forces in Germany when Stalin refused to stop investigating the possibility that even Hitler got away. He had studied in Berlin during Soviet-German military collaboration, 1923–33. He was kind enough to discuss the mystery surrounding the Berlin escapees and later, from Stalingrad, sent further notes, which were intended for his memoirs.

Archives were more accessible by 1973. Those given here are an indication of the immense amount of material available. Unfortunately, many documents only confirm the confusion among Nazi officials whose day-by-day accounts often contradict each other. Evidence given at trials has to be read with due regard for the defendants' anxiety to please their captors. Military trials held by Yugoslav, Czech, Polish, Norwegian, Russian, and other tribunals nevertheless cast a fresh light on events because in some cases the verbatim reports have only now become available. The Russian documents were not printed except in brief excerpts, and so their contents have been obtained at second hand. The German trials of war criminals have been preserved in court copies of the charges and the summing-up speeches.

The phrase "Third Reich" is used here in the sense of Germany's hopes and ambitions of that time for a Thousand-Year Reich. The National Socialist regime came to be called the "Greater German Empire" after the proclamation of the Third Reich in 1933. This confusion of terms sometimes misleads the student. Librarians usually file material under "Third Reich" in chronological order from 1933 to 1945, and the subsequent fate of believers in a thousand-year empire has to be pursued through cross references. A source of postwar information is, of course, the Central Office for the Elucidation of National Socialist Crimes at Ludwigsburg, West Germany.

The Ludwigsburg Office is to bring its activities to a close in 1980. Now, so long after the end of the war, as the Chief Prosecutor for that office has said, the chances of satisfactorily clearing up cases are steadily deteriorating. A comprehensive report on the prosecution and punishment of war criminals and of persons who have committed crimes against humanity was requested by the United Nations General Assembly in its resolution 2583 (XXIV) of December 15, 1969. This was answered in a statement by the Federal Republic of Germany on July 9, 1970, which showed that the West German authorities had sentenced twelve convicted war criminals to death and 6,215 to varying terms of imprisonment, which under German law can be shortened considerably on grounds of good behavior. The reader is referred to the Bonn statement, which sets forth the total figures and an explanation of the difficulty in pursuing investigations and securing convictions.

Two indispensable sources, the first of which is found in a few specialist libraries, were the ten volumes on *Nazi Conspiracy and Aggression* published by the U.S. Government Printing Office in 1946, and *Mein Kampf*. The U.S. Nazi party, in its monthly *White Power* and in the *National Renaissance Bulletin,* regularly advertises *Mein Kampf* as "the bible of National-Socialism."

Amnesty International, of New York and London, is an overworked but resourceful documentation center which has assembled material on fascist-type police methods in Latin America. For many reasons, not the least being the danger in which informants stand if identified by police agencies in their own countries, Amnesty does not publicly identify sources. It does keep a most careful watch over the credibility of those who seek help through its intervention. The organization is voluntary and relies upon the sense of obligation shared by leading legal authorities in those countries where the phrase "secret police" is still offensive. Much of the background to reports of Nazi war-criminal organizations has been assembled by Amnesty researchers, working sometimes in conditions of danger.

The Hispanic and Luso-Brazilian Councils, at Canning House, Belgrave Square, London, have the largest library in Europe specializing in Spanish, Portuguese, and Latin-American affairs, and work in close liaison with government institutions in the United Kingdom and abroad.

The Central State Archives of the USSR contain relevant documents under Sovietskiye Organy Gosudarstviennoy Bezopasnost (Soviet Organ of State Security) and transcripts of trials before military tribunals of the USSR Supreme Court and the Supreme Court of the German Democratic Republic.

Officials of the Supreme Court of the (East) German Democratic Republic made available transcripts of trials: and the editors of *Neue Justiz* in Leipzig helped in tracing Nazi documents recently assembled from places of hiding in East Germany.

Documents surrendered to the American security forces in 1945 by General Gehlen were microfilmed, and copies are stored in the National Archives in Washington, D.C.

The collection of the Institute für Zeitgeschichte in Munich includes summaries said to come from the original diaries of Admiral Canaris; the location of the originals is as yet unknown to the general public.

The Institute of Jewish Affairs of London works in association with the World Jewish Congress to advance education in the field of human relationships, and its excellent team of researchers produces background papers on the causes of racial and religious stress.

Military archives at Freiburg, in Breisgau (Bundesarchiv-Militärarchiv), of the Federal Republic of Germany contain originals of records from Hitler's supreme headquarters (Oberkommando der Wehrmacht).

No serious work on the postwar history of Nazi war criminals can ignore the detailed case histories assembled by Simon Wiesenthal, of the Vienna Documentation Center.

Visnews, the international film-news service of London, provided access to newsreels of the Hitler period in which Martin Bormann makes his rare appearances.

The Wiener Library of London rendered invaluable service.

There is no work of importance on the political science of the totalitarian era that is complete without reference to this unique center. Founded in Amsterdam in 1933 by Dr. Alfred Wiener, a refugee from Nazi persecution, the library was transferred to London in the long hot summer of 1939, a few weeks before Britain declared war on Hitler's Germany; and it became virtually part of the British Ministry of Information, from which a large quantity of intelligence and secret operations derived their inspiration. The library contains among many thousands of documents some 5,000 files relating to the "final solution" as recorded in the papers of the German Foreign Office, the chancellery of the Nazi party, and local Gestapo offices.

Other prime sources of information were the Archives of Radio Free Europe, in Munich; Partisan warfare papers in the Yugoslav State Secretariat for National Defense; Ernst Kaltenbrunner's reports to Bormann for Hitler on the July 1944 plot; The Hoover Institution on War, Revolution and Peace, Stanford University, Palo Alto, California; "Kontraobaveshtayna Slushba" ("Counterespionage Service") in Volume 4 of Voyna Encyclopedia, published in Belgrade; National Research Council archives of the Canadian government in Ottawa; National Film Archives, Ottawa; U.S. Office of Naval Intelligence reviews from 1946: National Archives and Record Service of the U.S. General Services Administration, Washington, D.C.; Royal Canadian Mounted Police security-service archives, which include the report of the Royal Commission on the Canadian spy case involving Igor Gouzenko and the use of forged passports.

The military museums of several nations yielded film and documents which helped bring into focus Bormann's friends and enemies. These museums include that of the Yugoslav People's Army in Belgrade, the Norwegian Museum of Resistance to the Nazi Occupiers in Oslo, Canadian Army Headquarters in Ottawa, and the Imperial War Museum in London, which contains perhaps the only surviving copies of film shot on Hitler's movie camera by Bormann. Interfoto MTI of Budapest was able to turn up photographs of Bormann with Himmler taken shortly before the chief of secret-police groups was sent to command the Rhine and Vistula armies. There is an unmistakable gleam of joy in Bormann's eye as he says farewell to his last enemy.

Because several of the researchers on this project must remain anonymous for their own protection, others agreed with me that it would be unfair to name some and not all. This is an inadequate way of thanking all of them. Motivated by a strong sense of justice, they checked and double-checked my work. Any mistakes are my own. One who need not remain anonymous, although his old comrades in arms will remember him as INTREPID, is Sir William Stephenson, who made this journey through a terrible chapter in history possible.

PART ONE

THE PUZZLE

CHAPTER 1

The man in London's Festival Hall coffee shop said: "Nobody *wants* to believe I shot Bormann."

"Are you still certain it was he?"

"Absolutely."

A waitress banged past with a tray of rattling mugs.

"Things don't change much, do they?" he said, glancing at the steaming urn. "Just like an army canteen."

He was a big man. I could imagine the lightweight Sten gun between those thick hands.

"You mean you're absolutely certain it was Martin Bormann?"

"Do I look daft enough to say it was if it wasn't?"

"No." I turned my head. The Thames glittered in the sunlight. Big red double-deck buses lumbered past London Bridge.

"I mean, I've nothing to gain."

Nobody ever had. Thirty times some honest individual had come forward with enough evidence to warrant an investigation. Thirty different investigations leading nowhere.

"You see," he said, "the real truth is, they don't *want* to find him."

"They?"

"The lot back in power in West Germany. The letter I got from the State Attorney's office was written by an ex-Nazi. Found his name in the Brown Book."

"More coffee, luv?" asked the waitress, in that aggrieved voice of the Cockney who thinks you've had more than your tuppence's worth already.

"Yes," the large man said obstinately. "We do want more coffee."

"Orl right. Keep yer shirt on!" She disappeared, a teaspoon hanging on a string from her waist like a jailer's key.

It was eleven o'clock on the morning of June 19, 1972, and I was talking to Ronald Gray, former member of the British Army Intelligence Corps; trained gunman with the 33rd Armoured

3

Brigade; mentioned in American dispatches for his counterintelligence work in Korea; Identity Card No. 001237, signed by U.S. General James Van Fleet; later served with Her Majesty's Admiralty Criminal Investigation Department; now living at West Wickham in Kent and a regular traveler to Germany. I had done my homework.

"What's the Brown Book?"

"A secret Russian book. Lists all the names of the *Bonzen*, the Nazi party bigwigs, Gestapo, SS, what war crimes they committed, and how they're back in every key job in West Germany today."

"It's not secret, this book. You can buy all four hundred pages in East Berlin."

"Oh." He looked down at his clasped hands. "Well, it was secret when I saw it."

A stubborn man. Well dressed, without show. Conservative tie. Shoes polished with the dedication of a good soldier. When I came into the coffee shop, at the time he had designated, he was nowhere to be seen. I had never met him before and had no idea whom to look for. I slid into a booth by the windows and suddenly he was there. A fast man on his feet but slow and stubborn if he felt like it.

It could have been just another story. Except that Gray told it differently, not knowing that his observations were a curious confirmation of reports he could not possibly have seen. He was certain he had shot Bormann. I guessed that he was intended to believe he had witnessed the death of Adolf Hitler's puppetmaster. There had been a gun battle and then, in the light of a winter's moon, he thought he had seen Bormann's body weighted and dropped into Flensborg Fjord.

The town of Flensburg is in the northernmost tip of Germany. Escaping criminals find it fairly easy to cross from there into Denmark and then to proceed across the narrow strait between Copenhagen and Malmö, in southern Sweden. It is also in that most authoritarian of all states, Schleswig-Holstein, full of gloomy castles and dark memories. Flensburg was the last refuge of the last government of the Third Reich under the "weekend Führer," Grand Admiral Karl Doenitz. It was the last name on the map before German armies, pouring in in panic from the Russians, fell into the fjord. It was the northern retreat for escaping Nazis; an alternative exit to the Alpine Fortress, which covered the mountains that sprawled over three frontiers to the south.

In March 1946, when the picket fences of Germany were

4

plastered with scraps of paper informing homeless citizens that this or that relative was in such a camp or such a hospital, Ronald Gray crossed the frontier near Flensburg on a regular British Army courier route. In his pocket he carried photographs of major Nazis wanted on charges of war crimes. The chief among these was Martin Bormann.

Gray recalled that in those days nobody knew what had happened to Bormann. He was regarded as the evil genius. It was many years before he was recognized as a conspirator of even more grotesque size. He was hated by Hitler's henchmen. He was also feared by them. He had been seen escaping from the Führer's bunker in Berlin after the suicides of Hitler and of Bormann's remaining enemy, Joseph Goebbels. Some thought Bormann had, all along, worked for Stalin. He had been the secret promoter, they said, of every move that guaranteed a Russian victory, so that, in the guise of rolling back the German armies, Stalin had seized half of Europe.

Others among Gray's colleagues said Bormann was in Washington quietly dictating an account of how a civilized nation had gone berserk.

The Russians suspected that Bormann had always been working for the British. The British had a sinking feeling that they had depth-charged (accidentally, of course) a German submarine bearing Bormann to his Brotherhood abroad.

Gray was not bothered in those days by misgivings of this kind. He knew that among Flensburg's attractions was the presence of U-boats whose commanders subscribed to Plan Regenbogen (Rainbow), which called for scuttling their vessels rather than surrendering—a plan that would, however, cover the escape of some. He knew, too, that Bormann was aware of the illegal traffic between these coastal waters and Sweden during the war; the scientists vital to developing Germany's atomic bomb had been among those who slipped out in that fashion while the Nazis still controlled Fortress Europe.

Gray was trailing his coat in the hope of drawing out any members of the escape organizations, which the Nazis, ironically, based upon Allied spy routes. Allied soldiers with multiple re-entry passes had been approached with offers of money to help escapees. Gray traveled three times a week past British military police, German border guards, and Danish customs men. His face was familiar—familiar enough that an agent for the SS and Gestapo "welfare organizations" might try to bribe him.

At the end of Europe's worst winter, Gray was approached by a young German girl, Ursula Schmidt. She had been asked to make contact with him, she said, by a group of refugees in a wooden barracks at Flensburg. For 30,000 Danish kroner, about $10,000, they wanted him to take someone across the border. Gray agreed. He told me that he borrowed the uniform of Captain Ronald Grundy to disguise the fugitive. On the night of the escape, he drove in a British Army truck to the Flensburg rendezvous and collected a thickset man muffled in castoff clothing.

The man struggled into Grundy's uniform jacket, pulled the peaked cap over his eyes, and told Gray to drive on. It was nearly midnight. The border guards recognized Gray and the truck and waved them through. Gray drove another three miles. His passenger ordered him to stop. He got out and stuck black tape in a star over the nearside headlight. At that moment, said Gray, he recognized Bormann. He was, he told me, frightened. And added, revealingly: "I saw this wasn't going to be one of those thank-you-and-good-by jobs. I was supposed to be paid on delivery. I was going to be lucky to get away alive."

The passenger made Gray drive through the Danish village of Rinkenaes, and then ordered him to stop. His manner was curt now. To their left ran a railroad. On the right glimmered the waters of Flensborg Fjord. A flashlight winked in the light mist, reflecting on a thin layer of ice. Gray's client got out onto the road, took off the British jacket and cap, and suddenly broke into a run.

"Then I shot him," said Gray.

We were looking through the windows at the river boats. A pretty girl walked along the embankment, followed by a Thames Television van, a mobile camera, and about a dozen figures whose identities were concealed by long hair and sunglasses. A quiet summer's day, Britain on the verge of going into the European Common Market, Willy Brandt about to take West Germany into a new relationship with the Communist East . . . and here was Bormann, back to haunt us. The skeleton in everybody's cupboard.

"You shot him?"

"I stood in the middle of the road with the Sten and got him on the run at a distance of about a hundred feet."

I did not doubt Gray's honesty.

"And then?"

"The rest of the gang fired back. I rolled into a ditch. They grabbed the body of Bormann and went on shooting."

6

"What gang?"

"Well, we knew it as Die Spinne, the Spider."

"You knew the name then? Or you read it since?"

He shifted his large bulk. "I knew the name. One of the escape organizations. The Americans and the British could never get the ringleaders."

He took up his story again. He had hidden in the ditch, afraid to move. He saw two men lift what he believed to be Bormann's body and haul it to the bank of the fjord. He heard splashing noises and then a silence. He got up, walked to the edge of the water. There was a fitful moon, layers of mist, and lights glowing in the distance. Standing there, he saw a small rowboat silhouetted against the brighter northern sky. The boat rocked unsteadily. Two men stood upright, holding what he believed to be a weighted sack. The sack went overboard with a splash that Ronald Gray can hear to this day.

A curious story. Gray was not acting with the knowledge of regular British military authorities, and yet he was never charged with breaking regulations. He said nothing publicly until 1965, when he was outraged by the prospect of an amnesty for German war criminals. He got in touch with West German judicial authorities. And after that, according to his version, he got the runaround.

Checking parts of his story was easy enough. Captain Grundy was now a Liverpool advertising man. Ursula Schmidt had married Robert Brookes, a Welshman, and now lived in Rhyl, although she frequently visited her family, who had moved from No. 41, Bismarckstrasse, Flensburg, to a new home in Bad Godesberg.

Did Gray run escapees across the border with tacit British Army approval in order to catch ringleaders? The War Office knew nothing of such a game. Then why was he not put on charges? No answer. His record since then made it clear that authority had every confidence in him: he was in Berlin in 1948, on a renewed British Army contract, engaged in intelligence work.

And the State Prosecutor in Frankfurt, where the main work was done for years to bring war criminals before West German courts? He was, at the time, Joachim Richter, according to Gray, who made several trips to the Frankfurt office. Gray claimed that his sworn testimony, his letters, and his later submissions were all "lost." He had inquired into the background of the small staff. He believed that for many reasons none of them wished to pursue inquiries into Bormann's fate.

"*Your* Bormann?"

"The man I saw dropped into the fjord. They could easily drag for the skeleton, even now. But any kind of Bormann. It's possible I was meant to see a 'dead body' dropped into Flensborg Fjord that night. It's possible I've been wrong. I don't understand, though, why *nobody wants to investigate my story!*"

Gray had impeccable references. He was not a man obsessed. He was in his late forties, good-humored, physically very fit. He liked West Germans, had fought against Communist forces in Korea. He had suffered no personal losses from Nazi bestiality. He read Communist publications from East Germany with an open mind, but his adult life had been spent in a disciplined Western environment.

He was telling what he believed to be the truth.

The mystery of German official disinterest is a matter for conjecture. But it is a fact that the Cold War dampened interest in Nazi war criminals. There are qualified observers who say the Cold War was started deliberately by the only Nazi spy chief to be taken straight from Hitler's side to ours; and these observers are far from being Communists.

Gray's story happens to fit into a reconstruction of events following the night Martin Bormann slipped out of the Führer's bunker in Berlin. The refusal to give it credence is understandable. In 1959 the West German government felt obliged, for reasons of diplomacy, to open an office that would co-ordinate investigations into crimes committed during World War II. Its title is "Ludwigsburg Central Office for the Elucidation of National Socialist Crimes." It lacks any power to prosecute. Its job has been somewhat romanticized as being the pursuit of the guilty. Not all guilt, however. Not guilt involving torture. Only Nazi crimes of mass murder.

It was born late. It depended on the co-operation of the state authorities, most of whom ignored its representations. Its investigators were regarded with distaste by other police agencies. Its lawyers knew that the judicial system was infiltrated with former Nazis, and therefore their own careers were unlikely to prosper if they looked too closely into *that* can of worms. Five years after it opened, twenty years after Bormann disappeared, the man in charge of the Ludwigsburg Office was found to have been a member of the Nazi party, a storm trooper, and a judge in Hitler's people's courts.

8

As somebody pointed out to Gray, he was lucky to be alive. He was sticking his nose into a very strange business indeed.

Why, then, pursue it? I had asked that question a hundred times since the mystery of Martin Bormann first began to plague a world anxious to forget and perhaps afraid to look too deeply into a recent chapter in the history of that part of the human race which has prided itself upon being superior and civilized. I had asked the question, not because Bormann interested me, but because the mystery fascinated so many others. It was partly because Bormann represented secret power; and in our disheveled human condition today, we suspect that the trappings of democracy are more of a dangerous camouflage than before, that real power begins where secrecy begins.

Martin Bormann, we see now, possessed that secret power.

He possessed it to such a degree that he was able to escape the gallows.

The lady in Jacob's Well Mews said: "Don't fall for the temptation of the treasure hunt."

I murmured something about being too old for treasure hunts.

She nodded. "The treasure hunt is chasing up every story that Bormann's alive."

"I don't collect such stories. I haven't time, resources, or even the inclination to chase them."

She glanced down into the narrow lane behind Oxford Street where crumbling old gardeners' cottages have been converted into smart but discreet offices or the kind of cozy mews flats occupied by actresses. Her whole professional life was concerned with democratic institutions in Germany. She betrayed no signs of damage, even though she had lost an uncountable number of relatives in the camps. She was surrounded by the records of torture, mass killings, and medical experiments on captive humans. She journeyed frequently to Germany and she was determined to believe the best: the West German schools were making a real effort to look at their own people's recent past; the courts were doing their best to see that justice was done. She refused to lapse into the role of a mild but implacable Jewish monomaniac who would never rest until every German accused of genocide had been brought to justice.

"All we know for certain is that there have been false trails without number because there is a sinister romance surrounding his name. Who has the slightest idea of what Bormann looks like? You may say there are photographs and descriptions. And I reply

9

that these are the pictures and details that fit anybody and everyone. Come into the street, and I will point you out twenty Bormanns in the space of twenty minutes."

Out of the mews and across the street is London's famous old Spanish Catholic Church. Farther along George Street is one of those unobtrusive London hotels that never have to advertise: Durrant's. Here in wartime stayed the secret agents who had business with the Baker Street Irregulars (the British Special Operations Executive), just around the corner, before parachuting into Nazi territory. Here I met Dr. Otto John for the first of our discussions. He was one of those tortured Germans, or so it has always seemed to me, who are torn between their perception of what is right and their instinctive loyalty to their own people. He had twice been called a traitor by General Reinhard Gehlen, who tried in postwar West Germany to ease his rival out of the top job concerned with internal security. John had crossed into Communist East Germany, had been taken into the Russian interior by his opposite numbers in the Soviet secret service, and then had escaped back again into the West.

He smiled resignedly when I mentioned the analogy of the treasure hunt. "You mean the lost Nazi treasures, the forged banknotes, the stolen art treasures, and Bormann's hoard of gold coins?"

"I don't mean anything. This is all incidental. Did you just get fed up with what you discovered as Bonn's head of security? Is that why you crossed over to the Russians?"

He shook his head. We were drinking gin-and-tonics in an elegant back-room bar. "Let's talk generalities," he said. "The Nazi war criminals exist but who judges them? Certainly the Communists can get convictions. They drag these creatures into court when the case is already settled, and then shoot them. But in a free society? You need witnesses. Not silent witnesses. I mean men and women able to use the power of words still. There were few enough twenty years ago. Even then, those who could have said 'I saw this,' 'I heard that' were often unable to speak. What remains now? Files. Millions of words, and cellars filled with documents, and a few dedicated Germans honestly trying to secure justice. The German authorities know the identity of major war criminals, they know where they are, they know their abominable histories. But these days, the Bonn government would be wasting votes to go after them, even if it could. The public is not concerned any more. The few Germans who want justice done, they cannot get a legal grip upon the guilty, and the guilty know it. The guilty are beginning already to boast of their actions, and say they acted for the good of the nation. They cannot be brought to trial for lack of compelling evidence."

Dr. John was a German liberal who hated Nazism and was convinced that he must act against it. He conspired against the rule of Hitler and failed. His brother was shot in the aftermath of the July 1944 bomb plot. He spoke out against Konrad Adenauer's regime after the war and failed again. He had been in prison or internment in Germany, in Portugal, in England, in Russia, and now in effect he was exiled from his homeland again. He had given information to the British secret service during the war before making the dangerous trip back to Berlin, where, since 1942, he had been in touch with men who wanted to destroy Hitler and all his works. His friends of the resistance—those who survived—helped him gain office as head of BfV (Bundesant fuer Verfassungsschutz, the Federal Office for Protection of the Constitution). The former opponents of Nazism were resolved to prevent this post from falling into the hands of ex-Nazis. And former Nazis were equally resolved to get John out. The most talented of the old Nazis was Gehlen, who, as head of the new German secret service, used his position to rescue old SS and other Nazi comrades.

John's experience with double-dealing and betrayal was not likely, I thought, to make him talkative in this year when East Germany was finally recognized as a separate and independent nation. But there comes a time when a man no longer cares about consequences to himself and becomes wholly concerned with truth. That doesn't make it any easier, of course. Who defines truth? For what the comment is worth, I felt that Dr. John's struggle to keep life in focus had just begun in the autumn of 1972. The lady in Jacob's Well Mews took a cold and intellectual view of events; perhaps because it was her only protection, her only way of remaining sane. John was, and probably always had been, an emotional person whose "defection" to Russia and back again seemed to be a consequence of his own horror at what his people had done and might be doing again.

"Is it really so hard to get an extradition order against a notorious Nazi?" I asked him.

"Yes. I was—I am—a lawyer. I know."

"It's not enough to say 'I accuse'?"

"That's what the Nazis said."

11

"Then Bormann has little to fear from the law?"

"Even Hitler would not be prosecuted in West Germany once the statute of limitations ran out." He glanced around the lounge: leather-upholstered chairs occupied by straight-backed tweedy Englishmen and frail ladies in floppy hats. "Bormann could walk in here now and I wouldn't be surprised. He could wear his name around his neck and offer evidence of his identity and I wouldn't be surprised if he was asked politely to keep his voice down."

CHAPTER 2

In the latter half of 1972, certain European and American newspapers published a series of reports by a serious, respected writer who claimed to have discovered Martin Bormann alive in South America. Bormann, who leads all lists as the most wanted of the condemned but unexecuted Nazi war criminals, seems capable of provoking headlines at the drop of an allegation. Within weeks of those published reports, investigations by other journalists and authorities cast substantial doubts on the authenticity and value of the evidence supporting this "discovery." This was not the first claim since his disappearance more than a quarter-century ago that Martin Bormann has been found "alive." It will not likely be the last.

Hardly had the journalistic ripples of the 1972 "live" discovery of Bormann quieted down when the first of the 1973 "dead" theories surfaced, this one in a West German newspaper. A skeleton, one of two unearthed accidentally in West Berlin by a labor crew in December of 1972, was studied "for more than a month" by Dr. Heinz Spengler, Director of the Institute for Forensic Medicine. He based his conclusion, the story continued, on "comparisons of the skull with photographs of Bormann, discovery of a mended collar bone break such as one Bormann had suffered, measurements of the skeleton, and correspondence of the skull's dentures with a sketch of Bormann's teeth made by his dentist." This would seem a reasonable scientific procedure conducted over a substantially long enough period to reach an authoritative finding. Or, on reflection, does it seem reasonable?

In all my searching I have been able to find no fully detailed physical description of Martin Bormann. Few photographs of the man exist. Such recollections of Bormann's height as have been noted by those who knew him vary by as much as four to six inches. His actual dental records do not exist; the comparison made in this recent instance relies solely on the memory of a dentist who had not seen his patient for almost thirty years. Yet such evidence seems to have persuaded Dr. Spengler to venture the unqualified statement "There is no longer any doubt. One of the skeletons is the remains of Bormann." That is not the first time skeletal fragments purporting to be the earthly remains of Martin Bormann have been discovered.

The puzzle of Bormann's fate persists now as it has over the years, over the decades. Thousands of trained professionals —military and diplomatic intelligence agencies of at least ten nations—have attempted to pick up the trail that started in the flames of crumbling Berlin as the city fell to the Allies in May 1945. Independent investigators—journalists in search of history, unofficial groups in search of vengeance—have joined the strange, unending pursuit. Bormann's whereabouts has been publicly reported, always without eventual confirmation, always without concrete proof, in places as distant from Berlin as mainland China and South America. Rumors and theories, perhaps feeding on one another, have sent him over the northern borders of defeated Germany into Scandinavia, or south into the lonely mountain passes of the Alpine Fortress. Tales, unsubstantiated, have him escaping by submarine, plane, boat, truck, or foot. The search for Martin Bormann has not yielded its quarry.

Ronald Gray's brief crossing of the uncertain path has provided him with a bizarre, frightening memory and a gnawing question that evades an answer. Bewilderment.

One professional investigator, hardened by hard fact of a hideous, endless variety, warns against getting caught up in a single foolhardy obsession. Cool logic, cold comfort.

And one soul, a benevolent spy, bent by the weight of spent idealism, self-doubt, guilt, and the realization of the human capacity for deceit, muses on whether civilized society can be long spared its blind, mannered suicide. Skepticism forged into cynicism.

Is that where the puzzle of Martin Bormann leads—to some miserable way station on the road from confusion to despair? Is it the stuff of sporadic news stories, the framework for occasional retrospective articles, the germ for novelists of international intrigues? Yes, it is surely all of that. But it is more, much more. This is a puzzle that, in its way, is a mirror to the darkest reaches of the mind of modern man.

Gray was one of many men drawn unwillingly into the mystery. I was another. Martin Bormann crossed my path near the end of World War II and has kept crossing it year after year. He was like some ghost plucking at my sleeve until I would hear what he had to say. Vanity might lead me to say I recognized, even in the last days of the war, something of its grim importance. I did not. It was easy to hunt for a single man, far easier than to see the significance of the terrors he wrought and the insidious hold he had on the future.

Martin Bormann vanished when he was forty-five years old. That is a simple statement. Other guilty men vanished with him. That is also a simple statement. Did they escape because most of humanity was too stunned by the enormity of their crimes, because it was assumed that nobody would conceal such monsters? As the years passed, it became apparent that they escaped because there were carefully laid plans, brilliantly conceived to give them immediate sanctuary and eventual survival. What seemed so simple when Ronald Gray had his strange encounter at Flensburg had now become complex beyond words. The puzzle broke into fragments, and these in turn broke into smaller pieces. And there was outwardly no visible shape to it.

This must sound, at this stage, a generalization, an oversimplification. Nothing about Bormann will prove to be simple in the end. Each piece in the puzzle, regardless of how it is expanded, explained, rationalized, provokes new questions, deeper profundities. This is the way Bormann cast his shadow during my years of travel with British naval intelligence, as a writer and a foreign correspondent, and as a producer of television documentaries. These activities gave me the opportunity to look and listen and ask questions in distant parts of the world, in Communist as well as Western societies. Others would have done as I did given such opportunities to search and to find. There was never any special merit in this. I had the opportunities. I do not know just when opportunity turned into obligation. This is not, then, a book I chose to write; it had to be written.

I have tried to separate fact from comment. I have sometimes found my journey to be among liars and cheats, where "facts" could be bought by the gross. But there were also documents and authorities whose testimony could be trusted. There were documents available by 1972 to prove just how successfully the Bormann "plan for the future" infiltrated our lives. In London there were files that should have stayed secret under a thirty-year rule. These were opened by the British Foreign Office so that historians could catch some of the sweep of the Nazi period of open oppression. In the Public Record Office in London it was possible for scholars to look at the 1939–1945 war in its entirety. (The situation was different in Washington, where I was told intelligence material had never been declassified and was not likely to be.)

The declassification of British documents made it possible for many men of authority to speak. I was surprised by the number of Americans and Europeans who had honored their promises to British security to keep their knowledge of Nazi operations secret. Some were willing and eager to talk now, because they believed that even honest documents can "lie."

One Englishwoman was the only survivor of six girls parachuted into Nazi-occupied France. The other five girls were tortured to death. The survivor traced their stories through interviews. She discovered that the girls, all former classmates of hers, were sacrificed deliberately in order to maintain the credibility of other Allied agents, of greater consequence to London. She found that the official documents in the case told a more palatable story. They disassociated the British government from a coldly calculated plan. The girls had been provided with information that it was intended the Nazis would extract from them on the rack. Perhaps the stakes were so high, the consequences so grave, the necessity so clear that this horror had to be employed to counter the known viciousness of the enemy. Does the designer of this scheme, a blurred footnote in the history of British espionage, sleep with nightmares?

Another girl, a German, helped put together pieces of the puzzle. She was a child when Bormann disappeared. She grew up with a sense of horror about her own people. She searched for documents, and concluded that society had perfected a method of piling fact upon fact to produce distortion. She went after other escaped war criminals. She convinced me, without herself once expressing the thought, that a woman's intuition could be more dependable when it comes to separating truth from falsehood. Her name was Beata Klarsfeld, and each time I crossed her trail, she lightened my gloom.

But the gloom was inevitable. The story was complicated by a personal desire to get away from it. Why should we be forced to rake through this bloody garbage? None of it made sense. Most of it made Western civilization look like a deepening nightmare. And there was so much of it. The persecution of the weak and the helpless was preserved in permanent records. Yet there is too much to grasp; from this overflowing fountain of misery, how can one continue to drink and remain sane?

The files on the German SS filled six freight cars for the Interna-

16

tional Military Tribunal at Nuremberg. Five million pages of type-written records were produced by the prosecution hearings against twelve major war criminals alone. In twelve subsequent American trials at Nuremberg, another 24,000 pages were made public and a further quarter-million pages were left unpublished. The story they told should have shocked us out of a complacent belief in our Western civilization. They told of the great nation called Germany which had contributed so much for so long to culture and scientific progress and how it brought back slavery on an unprecedented scale; planned the mass murder of entire populations of children, old people, the sick and infirm, Jews, Gypsies, and Slavs; plundered Europe from one end to the other with careful calculation; and trained in schools, with chalk and blackboard, the men and women whose specialty in the middle of the twentieth century was to be the brisk disposal of millions of human lives.

There were documents in plenty and yet somehow they must have overwhelmed us. The documents set forth, beyond all possible contradiction, the behavior of the German people once they became members of their own totalitarian state.

Yes, there were documents all right. Hans Frank kept thirty-eight volumes of his diary while he was Governor General of Poland and using that position to kill and loot wherever he went. He recorded everything. His house was crammed with art treasures, from landscapes by Rembrandt to gilded chalices. His German troops were authorized to kill any non-German who showed hostility. Frank kept detailed notes of events that were regarded by his fellow pro-consuls as routine: children scattered the ashes of the cremated on the death-camp roads to make them less slippery; Greek boys were freighted to Silesia for experimental castration; girls were sewn together to make Siamese twins; slave workers had their testicles exposed to X rays, which burned and mutilated them; prisoners of war, soldiers and civilians, captured in the "barbarian" territories of Russia and East Europe were shipped by numbers to labor camps where SS doctors performed experiments under what they called "controlled" conditions.

The whole effect was surrealistic. The documents sent ten men to the gallows on October 15, 1945. The relatively modest series of executions horrified many civilized observers. It came as a purge for Western society. Hitler was dead. Ten of his henchmen had been executed. Now, surely, the night had passed.

Two men condemned by the International Military Tribunal were Göring and Bormann. Field Marshal Hermann Göring crushed and swallowed a phial of potassium cyanide two hours before he was due to hang. Bormann not only cheated the gallows; he also contrived to miss his own trial. He was the only defendant whose case was heard *in absentia* and who was sentenced *in absentia*. In retrospect, this was entirely in keeping with the mystery that surrounds the man. Nazism never died on the gallows. Bormann and his companions never intended to see their life's work destroyed.

The German Brotherhood (Die deutsche Gemeinschaft) was explained to me first by one of the Latin-American intelligence agents managed by Sir William Stephenson, Winston Churchill's personal representative in charge of secret operations during World War II. In putting together the pieces of the Bormann puzzle, I received enormous help and encouragement from "Little Bill," as he was called, and his American associates. His great comrade in wartime was General William J. Donovan, chief of the Office of Strategic Services. Stephenson said, when I went to him with my last bits of the puzzle in 1972: "Nothing deceives like a document."

His man in Latin America repeated the warning. "The spirit of Nazism binds groups of men who keep no membership lists, who seldom refer to each other by their real names, and who manipulate and operate like the old German Brotherhood which gave Bormann a stranglehold on Hitler. There's no documentation for those sort of people."

There is, instead, this man Bormann, who covertly governed the Third Reich. For more than twenty years, this stocky peasant with the pug nose and the obsequious habits of a butler brought together into his misleadingly soft and plump hands the strings that manipulated the Führer. Long after Hitler was dead, historians continued to misinterpret his role and his character. This is the measure of the man. He never cared for the visible trappings of power. He wanted the reality of it. He moved in Hitler's court, a shrewd and unobtrusive figure who was looked down upon by the thin-lipped generals with their bogus tradition of aristocracy. Foolish men like Joachim von Ribbentrop, hungry for titles and honors, disregarded him. Intellectual snobs like Albert Speer continued into the 1970's to speak of Bormann as a crude and vulgar peasant. Crazed ideologists like Alfred Rosenberg, apostle for a Nazi religion, said he was illiterate.

Nazi strategists had plotted for many years to set the West against Russia. They continued with that plan after the war ended. Members of the Bormann Brotherhood became hired agents of Western intelligence. How that came about is one of the pieces in the puzzle. Each piece seems outrageous enough. The cumulative effect becomes as difficult to grasp as the Third Reich itself. The Nazi experiment to produce a master race in Germany had failed, and so the Germans had proved themselves unworthy. The experiment must be resumed elsewhere. Farsighted Nazis had prepared for this, but they were also concerned about the legalities.

At the time of the Nuremberg trials, a great new sense of moral purpose had started to sweep the Western part of the world. The Cold War required some temporary expediencies, however. We told ourselves that the means justified the ends. The Soviets told themselves the same comforting story. And both sides plunged into a wild competition to buy Nazis with professional experience in war and military science. So, little by little, we drifted into that very climate of opinion upon which Bormann and his brothers counted. They began to come out into the open, so quietly that few of us noticed.

Bormann himself became an inconvenient symbol. He was a reminder of the past, whereas the West had accepted the small compromises: the fact, for instance, that by 1970 there were 176 German generals in a revived West German Army, and that every single one of them had served under Hitler as a senior officer. By the 1970's it was possible to buy the memoirs of the "Hangman of Lyons," who had taken refuge in Latin America. He was a member of the Brotherhood and he felt safe enough to tell the world that he did nothing more than his duty as a Gestapo chief when he sent orphaned children to the gas chambers.

A chronological account would fail to give cohesion and understanding to so complex a narrative. So I have felt free to rove in time and place. My purpose is to move back and forth and to fill in as many elements of fact and motivations as can provide a balanced view of an unbalanced world, a panorama of mania that defies the imagination of a reasonable individual. And I have tried to put the pieces together as best I can, but without pretense that I would solve the puzzle.

Before I set forth the pieces, there is one more thing to be said. Martin Bormann kept careful note of everything, and when he left the burning corpse of Hitler, he took with him more than a thousand typed pages, headed "Notes of fundamental interest for the future: To be preserved with the greatest care." This is the real dimension of the puzzle. This is the measure of its meaning.

19

PART TWO

THE PIECES

CHAPTER 3

There was never an exact description of Martin Bormann.

The most detailed was given me by the late Walter Schellenberg, former chief of the Nazi foreign intelligence service: "Scar on left cheek, thin strands of hair, balding, between five feet three inches tall and five feet seven inches."

The discrepancy of four inches seemed extravagant. Schellenberg shrugged. "Everything about him was inexact. Some say there are thumbprints in police records from when he was jailed for murder, but I say the records are in Communist hands. Some say there are SS tattoo marks giving his blood group under one arm. I say he never went through that procedure because he was given purely an honorary SS membership and rank by Himmler, who wanted to curry favor."

This exchange took place in Switzerland just after Hitler's former spy chief had conferred in Spain with Hitler's former SS commando chief, Otto ("Scarface") Skorzeny. It was the year 1951, at Pallanza, on the shores of Lake Maggiore. There was nothing about Schellenberg to provoke any feelings one way or another. He had contributed to the British study of Bormann at a peculiar stage in his career; and now he was eager to prove that he had never served Hitler, only Germany. He offered more of his personal impressions of Bormann; and these, too, were much the same as the information filtered through Anglo-German contacts in the Iberian peninsula during the war.

"I studied Bormann's technique with Hitler and realized he controlled the Führer. He did this by making himself indispensable. This was long before the war, mark you, and I remember thinking I would refuse to make myself a slave to any man just to control him. But in those days I didn't understand where Bormann was going. . . .

"You see, Bormann had a cast-iron memory and the constitution of an ox. He looked like an ox. He was stocky, with round and powerful shoulders and a short bullish neck. His head was pushed forward and cocked to one side all the time. He seemed like one of those women wrestlers in Berlin, moving sideways in the mud, waiting to trick an opponent. Shifty eyes, always ready to cut you down. Very nimble for such a heavy man. Short, fat fingers like a certain kind of sausage you see hanging in bunches. The fingers were covered with black hair along the back. Women liked him, you know, because he had so much hair.

"He remembered everything. He knew exactly what to say, and when to say it, but only in regard to Hitler. He was like a devoted and intelligent wife, removing from the Führer any responsibility for small daily worries. There was something funny in this relationship though, as if he also provided the Führer with a sense of physical strength. Hitler, you know, looked awful in bathing suits. Bormann was like a pig in a potato field, and in Germany this is not such a bad way to look. In my diaries, I wrote how Himmler made such a contrast—a stork in a lily pond."

SS Lieutenant General Schellenberg was a dapper little Nazi technocrat who was cut out of Bormann's plans for survival because of his own secret contacts with Western intelligence and his attempts, while fighting was at its height, to bargain in neutral Sweden for his own life. He was absorbed into a British secret-service net and spent five postwar years in what had been a lunatic asylum outside London. This asylum provided the perfect cover for the long-term interrogation of such men.

Schellenberg had made a permanent enemy of Gehlen when the latter was head of the Wehrmacht's Fremde Heere Ost (Foreign Armies East) intelligence service, which specialized in Soviet affairs. Gehlen had played on Western fears of Communism, and overnight became the chief of his own organization, which spied for American intelligence. These were all posts Schellenberg thought he was better suited to fill; and in his jealous rage he disclosed what purported to be a conspiracy to make use of the Gehlen Org as a channel of escape for war criminals. Many of Gehlen's agents, subsidized by Western intelligence funds, proved to be notorious Gestapo and SS killers. This piece of the puzzle is examined later.

What Schellenberg gave me was a glimpse of the shape and personality of Martin Bormann when he was operating at his peak. The outline can be filled in with some of the detail of Bormann's early years. A psychoanalytical report by Allied intelligence focused on his loss of his father at the age of four, and his sense after that of being unwanted within the family. He had been born on June

24

17, 1900, in the small Lower Saxony town of Halberstadt. His father was a trumpeter in a military band. The widow remarried, a banker, and the boy was conscripted as a cannoneer near the end of World War I. He never saw action.

He joined the Society Against Presumptuousness of the Jewry after eight months' military service and an even briefer postwar search for work. He found what he later called an estate-management job, having attached himself to a family of local landowners. There is no record of why the twenty-year-old youth became fired by anti-Semitism. A number of writers of the time were preaching a secular neo-Teutonic Aryanism. A Cistercian monk, Lanz von Liebenfals, as far back as 1900 had used the swastika as a symbol of his Order of the New Templars. The monk produced books and pamphlets which are said to have influenced Hitler, too: certainly, they met, and Liebenfals later took credit for some of Hitler's proposals for a "final solution to the Jewish problem."

Bormann had a strong affinity to the peasantry, and this seems to have drawn him to the monk's vision of a master race springing out of the good earth. "The race can only flourish on the land," wrote Liebenfals. The Germans of pure Aryan blood would purify and strengthen themselves through direct contact with the soil. The Jews polluted the pure Aryan blood because they were alienated from this blood-and-iron influence. Therefore the Jews must be destroyed. He set forth the manner of liquidating the Jewish people in details so revolting that intellectuals could never take him seriously. Bormann did, and his actions later surpassed anything the monk conceived in flights of hate-ridden fantasy. What was manifest at the start of this century as a mad monk's muddled and malevolent fiction became within thirty or forty years fearful reality. Other theorists were writing a pseudo-scientific version of mankind's evolution—men like Richard Wagner, whom Hitler idolized. Bormann grew up in a society saturated in mysticism masquerading as a new order, a properly scientific view based upon Darwin's revolutionary ideas of how man evolved from ape.

The prospect of Germans proving to be a master race was attractive in those years of defeat. It became an obsession with Bormann, and, like any religion, it provided him with an excuse to pursue purely selfish ends. His love of money, his greed for power, were commented upon by Gerhard Rossbach in an interview many years later. Rossbach had led a Freikorps, a group of armed volunteers supported by the German Army, which had been restricted in the number of regular soldiers it could keep on the books by the

Versailles Treaty. Bormann became treasurer of the group after it underwent several changes of name to evade the law. The mission of the Freikorps was to weed out weaklings said to have caused German sufferings. The groups were also used to fight Bolshevik forces on the eastern frontier. But the young German republican government also saw them as a threat to its own existence. They were declared illegal in 1920, but were more active than ever by 1923, when the French executed Leo Schlageter, a Freikorps soldier, for industrial sabotage. The incident took place in the industrial heart of Germany, which was under French and Belgian occupation. The German economy was falling apart. The execution brought to a climax all the feelings of resentment and frustrated nationalism.

Rossbach's organization, masquerading as the Union for Agricultural Professional Training, recalled at that time one of its former members, Walter Kadow, who became the first recorded victim of Bormann's talent for destroying those he regarded as rivals. Kadow, a young schoolteacher, borrowed 30,000 marks (a paltry sum when translated into present terms, about four dollars, but a great deal to a family which could buy groceries for a week with such an amount) from the group's treasury, of which Bormann was the guardian. Bormann announced that he would make Kadow work until he had paid off the money, but he also whispered to the group's strong-arm section that Kadow had betrayed the Freikorps soldier shot by the French. When the teacher returned to headquarters, he was taken at night into the forest and beaten until his teeth fell out and his arms and legs were broken. His throat was then cut. To cap the night's work, two bullets were fired into his head.

Years later, the Führer's Order of Blood * was awarded to Bormann for this object lesson to traitors. But in July 1923 there was still some measure of morality abroad. Bormann was placed under investigative arrest in Leipzig, and eight months later stood trial, along with other members of the Rossbach group, for Kadow's murder. From the trial records, Bormann emerges in his classic role: he had only told the others what to do, provided a car and weapons, and he denounced Kadow as a traitor and a Bolshevik. (Kadow was never shown to be involved in the Freikorps soldier's execution; nor had he displayed interest in left-wing politics.)

Bormann got away with murder. He did it with the style that

* The Nazi Blutorden was struck for those who had served time in the Weimar Republic's jails.

became his trademark: "I've signed nothing; you can prove nothing." The man who kept voluminous notes on the activities of others was nimble in keeping himself out of documents. He left no fingerprints because he handled no weapons. Even the thumbprints about which there was to be so much speculation were later extracted from the records of the State Court for the Defense of the Republic of Leipzig.

The court sentenced Bormann to a year in prison. His puppet, Rudolf Franz Höss, who was to have studied for the Catholic priesthood, got ten years' hard labor. Höss betrayed no bitterness at taking the rap for Bormann; he could never pin down in precise detail how it was that Bormann manipulated the affair. His jail sentence was terminated by a general amnesty, and he was rewarded by a series of promotions, which led ultimately to the post of commandant at Auschwitz. Thus he became the SS Report Leader at Dachau concentration camp when he should have been serving time himself. Bormann continued to take a protective interest in his career as a mass killer.

By this early age, Bormann had developed principles that would guide him through life: never be directly responsible for controversial decisions, never leave your imprint on anything, never forget to advance the interests of those who can help you and those who can hurt you. Many of his victims were advanced by him into situations from which death was the only exit. He carried his fear of leaving any tracks behind him to the extreme and induced Hitler to sign the order that Bormann must not be photographed.

Hitler at this time was serving fourteen months because of the failed Putsch of 1923. The Nazi party had been declared illegal, but the ban was lifted in 1925 and Hitler, free again, revived it. By then, Bormann had joined another anti-Semitic group, the Frontbann, which was a successor to the German Fighting Union. These militant groups shared the same aims: make Germany the most powerful nation, crush Communism, destroy Jews.

Bormann was a hired hand, in charge of peasant farmers who rented their land from his employers, when he became Nazi party member 60/508. He served as press chief of the party in Thuringia, and then as business manager. Here he learned to make more skillful use of party funds; here he learned that power resided in the Gau. There were forty-one such administrative regions into which Germany was divided by the Nazis. A Gauleiter was a dictator in his region.

A joint intelligence study made by American and British experts following the wartime flight of Rudolf Hess showed just how clever Bormann had been to concentrate on power within the party. The barons of the Third Reich were these forty-one Gauleiter,* and the 808 Kreisleiter, 28,376 Ortsgruppenleiter, in charge of towns or sections of large cities, 89,378 Zellenleiter, over Nazi cells consisting of several districts in each city, and, underpinning this structure, several hundred thousand Blockleiter, who were small gods in their own neighborhoods.

Hitler had a sentimental regard for these subordinates, and he maintained it against pressures from other power groups, including the military. A year after he became Chancellor of the German Reich, he said at the National Socialist German Workers' party rally in Nuremberg: "The state does not command us. We command the state." The Nazis were the only legal party by then, and in effect the Führer's statement placed the party in supreme command. All party matters were handled by the Office of the Deputy Führer, Rudolf Hess, who explained all this in considerable detail after his flight to Britain, which owed its inspiration to Bormann.

How did Bormann advance from being an ex-convict in 1926 to Reich Leader and Chief of Staff to Hess by 1933, shortly after Hitler came to power?

For one thing, he married the sturdy, pure-blooded Aryan, blonde daughter of the man who kept party discipline: Walter Buch, Chairman of the party "court." The girl, Gerda, was fanatical in her devotion to German folklore and her hatred of all forms of religion. She met Bormann in 1928 when he became a staff officer of the Supreme Command of the Brown Shirts, the storm troopers who beat down anyone who spoke against the party at Nazi rallies. Hitler was a witness to the marriage, and shortly afterward Bormann became leader of the Aid Fund of the Nazi party, and placed large numbers of key party officials in his debt by the discreet distribution of loans.

Bormann's wife had studied at the feet of Julius Streicher, who preached the central ideology of the movement: Jews were the cause of the disaster that had befallen Germany. He had been tried for offenses that ranged from sadism to rape. As Gauleiter of Nuremberg, he had ceremoniously launched the demolition of that

---

* The word meant simply the leader of a political region under Nazi control, but it became synonymous with brutal chieftains who drew their power directly from the Führer. In practice, this meant, in later years, that the power came from Bormann.

city's main synagogue. He had seen the halo around Hitler's head and soon became a trusted disciple and mouthpiece. Through his writings and his publications he gave a theoretical structure to the policy of stamping out the weaker races in order to strengthen the fit.

By 1930, Bormann had a son named Adolf, in honor of Hitler. And he had Gerda's wholehearted support in his efforts to help unmarried German girls procreate out of wedlock. Gerda was to bear him ten children, but she thought "the Bull" should produce more in order to outpopulate lesser breeds. She thought the Slavs should become slave workers: their fertility was undesirable. She wrote: "Every single child must realize that the Jew is the Absolute Evil in this world."

The Jew as the source of all evil haunted Adolf Hitler, who feared that his own blood was "tainted." This led to the brutal murder of his niece and mistress. The details were lost at the time, for the Nazis were already on the march and violent killings became the order of the day. Forty years passed before the full story unfolded. This was understandable enough. Students of the period were concerned with a scholarly review of documents, events, and speeches dealing with the larger issues of world politics and the clash of ideologies. The professional police investigators who might have looked into the murder were never allowed to see the evidence, and lost interest. It was only when Bormann's disappearance became a matter for serious conjecture, and intelligence agents began to dig into the ugly details, that an incredible episode in Hitler's life came to light. This explained exactly how Martin Bormann was able to gather into his hands all the strings required to make Hitler dance to his tune.

CHAPTER 4

Bormann's power over Hitler began with the murder of Hitler's niece, Angela ("Geli") Raubal, who catered to Hitler's perverted sexual needs. She was still in her teens when her uncle first lay on his back and required her to crouch naked over his face and urinate on him. This activity spread into other forms of obscenity, until the girl protested to friends: "He's a monster. Nobody can imagine the things he wants me to do."

Drawings made by Hitler showed Geli "in positions and in detail which would not be allowed by a professional model," according to Ernst ("Putzi") Hanfstaengl, the future foreign press chief. These drawings got into the hands of a Munich dealer, who sold them to Bormann for money drawn from the Nazi party funds under Bormann's control.

On the evening of September 18, 1931, the noise of the Bavarian capital's Oktoberfest drowned a gunshot in the luxury apartment on Munich's Prinzregentplatz where Geli lived on funds paid out of Nazi coffers by Bormann, who was already Hitler's personal paymaster.

Among the investigators called to the spot was Heinrich ("Gestapo") Müller, then on the local detective squad. Müller paid the minimum regular contribution to one of Bormann's devices for raising money, but he was otherwise unwilling in those days to stick out his neck for the Nazis. He was ambitious, however; "bent on recognition from his superiors under any system," to quote from the political appreciation of Senior Criminal Inspector Heinrich Müller in the Munich–Upper Bavarian Gau files of the period.

Müller found the girl lying dead beside what turned out to be Hitler's revolver. Her naked body was bruised and her nose had been broken.

What happened next has been described by Gerhard Rossbach. He told me, in his Hamburg home, thirty-five years later, that Bormann arrived at an understanding with Müller which resulted in the girl's body being shipped back to Vienna in a sealed lead coffin without further questions.

Rossbach, who was a Nazi intelligence agent in France and Turkey during World War II, was known to Western intelligence as an old man with a considerable and reliable memory for detail. Until his death, at the age of seventy-four, on September 1, 1967, he was consulted regularly by the U.S. Central Intelligence Agency and historians. His account of Geli's murder tallies, in matters of detail, with the recollections of Dr. Otto Strasser, who, after having lost a power struggle with Hitler, found refuge in Canada until the war was over.

Hanfstaengl, another of the few men who knew Hitler and Geli well in those days, agreed that the girl was pregnant at the time of the murder. "She could not have been put in the family way by Hitler," said Strasser, somewhat prudishly. "He was not capable of normal intercourse."

Geli was regarded as an oversexed and foolish girl who talked too much. She told Brigid Hitler, the wife of Adolf's half-brother Alois, that she was pregnant by a Jewish artist whom she wanted to marry, and apparently made the same statement to Hitler in a moment of alcoholic indiscretion during that Oktoberfest mood of mass hysteria. On the night of the murder, she seems to have told Hitler that she wanted to get away from him and return to Vienna. There must have been a fearsome quarrel, because the contents of the apartment were scattered and broken. The news that his mistress had enjoyed normal sexual relations with a Jew undoubtedly struck at every vulnerable point in Hitler's make-up.

He was a man easily made to feel sexually humiliated because of his own genital deformity. He lacked a left testicle, a condition known as monorchism, which led to feelings of inadequacy and those self-punishing encounters with women that characterized his sex life.

He had also at this time chosen, as a major theme of the speeches that were winning him such ovations, the subhuman and corrupting nature of the Jews. The purity of the Aryan blood had to be protected against the syphilitic rottenness of inferior races. He regarded Jewishness as a disease, and his obsession with syphilis had first become evident in *Mein Kampf*.

His mistress may have been taunting him without fully understanding the danger she was in. She must have known his fear of impotence (which later imposed upon his physician, Dr. Theodore

31

Morell, the necessity of adding pulverized bulls' testicles to the regular pharmacopoeia of dexedrine, pervatin, cocaine, prozymen, ultraseptyl, and antigas pills poured down the Führer's gullet). She had certainly shared in bizarre scenes like those described by the actress Rene Müller to her film director, Zeitzler. "I spent an evening at the Chancellery and expected to go to bed with him," Rene said, according to Zeissler's account, given in Hollywood to OSS agents in 1941. "We got undressed and then Hitler fell on the floor. He began screaming accusations against himself. He begged me to kick him. He made so much noise I did kick him, hoping he'd quieten down. The more I kicked, the more excited he became." (Rene committed suicide soon after, and Zeissler fled to the United States.)

Geli had apparently caused him to fly into one of the rages that filled his associates with fear and later led to those acts of insanity performed on his behalf by Bormann: an order to dispose of another hundred thousand Jews or a decision to fling whole armies into an obvious Russian trap at Stalingrad or a request to bring the Duke of Windsor to chat about the monarchy. His career would have come to an abrupt halt if the case against him for the brutal killing of twenty-four-year-old Geli had gone to trial.

Heinrich Müller would not have risen to the dizzy height of Gestapo chief, with the rank of general, if he had not had the wit that night in September to scoop up the incriminating evidence in Geli's flat: the letters which made it clear that she planned to leave Hitler and that she had been having passionate and normal affairs with men he regarded as inferior, including his own chauffeur and bodyguard, Ernst Maurice; his personal revolver, which was demonstrably the murder weapon; intimate notes exchanged with the young Jewish artist; a reference in her diary to Hitler's godfather, Prinz, "that Viennese Jew."

Was Hitler's godfather a Jew? The police dossier opened new avenues for speculation. Bormann took possession of all papers in the case, and after Inspector Müller got his reward and became Gestapo chief, a series of special Gestapo reports on the family background revealed that Hitler's grandmother had been a servant in the household of Baron Rothschild and that her illegitimate son, Alois, father of Adolf, was generally supposed to be the result of an alliance with one of the Jewish aristocracy. Certainly there was no disputing the fact that Alois chose a Jewish godfather for his own son. This information proved dangerous to those who came into possession of it without Hitler's approval. But Bormann himself looked into the matter, and Müller produced the Gestapo investigative reports, dated 1935, 1938, 1941, 1942, and 1943, on Hitler's family history. In those years, Hitler could destroy anyone within the Nazi empire who said he was one-quarter Jewish. It was a different story in 1931, however, when he was preparing to become the first dictator to make use of mass propaganda based on the Big Lie, the biggest part of which was his bombastic autobiography, *Mein Kampf,* and its racial-nationalist (*Voelkish*) philosophy. The German peoples were the creators of culture above all other races, with the Nazi party above them and Hitler at the apex. It was inconvenient, to say the least, during this critical year of 1931 to have Hitler suddenly identified with the Jews, whom he had made the scapegoats for all Germany's troubles.

Geli may have known of Hitler's secret fears in this matter. Those who were to reminisce about those days—Hanfstaengl, Strasser, Hermann Rauschning, Konrad Heiden, Winifred and Friedelind Wagner, Ernst Röhm, and the host of young women captured by some strange quality in his eyes and voice—all agree that Hitler had never confided in any friend except Geli; and that after her death, Bormann inherited the perilous role, though if there were perils, there were also compensations.

Bormann disposed of Geli's corpse with crafty dispatch. She was declared a suicide in Munich. She was buried by a Catholic priest in Vienna. Suicide and consecrated ground are not usually compatible among Catholics. But Bormann probably stopped awkward questions with the same Nazi party funds with which he silenced Müller and took over the police files.

This concealment could have destroyed a less cunning man, for the knowledge was dangerous. Bormann was clever enough, at the time, to perform the dirty work while playing the role of Hitler's most obedient servant. This was intensely satisfying to Hitler, eighteen months before he came to power. He regarded Bormann as a bull-like symbol of brutal masculinity; and although Hitler never left evidence of homosexual activities, his private confusion concerning his sexual role and his instinctive disgust with normal sexual relationships aroused in him an admiration for someone as musky as the younger Martin, at that time in his prime, a thirty-one-year-old sexual primitive.

Bormann swept clean the area around Hitler's pedestal while preserving every scrap of dirt. Once the Munich police, through Müller, had closed the records on Geli's death, Müller himself appeared to be in Bormann's pocket. All the subsequent investigations into Hitler's real family history (as opposed to the romanticized "official" version) were conducted by Müller for Bormann. Most astonishing of all, Hitler's timid and hidden side, the second half of the split personality, knew about and secretly hungered after the Gestapo reports, which followed the realization of his dreams: himself at the apex of the Third Reich and the Jews crushed beneath Germanic superiority. It was a strange obsession. Hitler had to know if there was Jewish blood in his veins, as if he carried a picture of the Judas in his soul who betrayed the Christ within him again and again. Hitler and most of the men around him were Catholics, and during the war the Führer received communion. When he first came to Berlin and saw its luxury, he said that he thought himself Jesus Christ driving the money-changers from the temple. The persecuted Jews were to become the visible manifestation of Christ Crucified.

The murder of Geli, now that it can be reconstructed, shows Bormann instinctively playing on Hitler's fear of the Jew as an image of his own darker self. The reality of his family background was forced on him by his niece. Geli was the daughter of Hitler's half-sister, Angela Raubal. She had worked as housekeeper for a time in the alpine farmhouse that became famous as Eagle's Nest. Geli went to live with Hitler in the Munich flat, a safe eighty miles away from her mother. The girl chattered more than was good for her; she confronted Hitler with allegations about his grandmother, Maria Anna Schicklgruber, and the Rothschild affair.

The tension she created apparently came to a boil during that 1931 Oktoberfest. There was, it seemed, a violent quarrel over Geli's Jewish lover in which she retaliated by demanding to know how Hitler could revile the very race of people whose blood he carried. She spat out the gossip, common in Vienna, that Austria's Chancellor, Engelbert Dollfuss, had ordered an investigation into the family's history.

The scene is not hard to visualize. We know now that Hitler suffered from masochistic and perverse tendencies that made him grovel at women's feet, eat dung, and drink urine. We know now that he made the Jew a symbol of everything he hated in himself. We have the evidence of other women—Unity Mitford, who tried suicide later, Rene Müller, who did kill herself—that he begged to be punished and humiliated in the bedchamber and then exploded into supermasculine outbursts: "Brutality is respected. . . . The plain man in the street respects nothing but brutal strength and ruthlessness. Our people will be free when they learn to hate, hate, and hate again."

When the paunchy, skinny-legged Hitler exposed all his physical ugliness to Geli, begged her to humble him, and then met with defiance and some unpleasant truths, he reacted in the same way that he was to react three years later, when Dollfuss was assassinated, on his orders, by Austrian Nazis because it was suspected he had all the facts of Hitler's ancestry.

Geli died brutally. Her brother Leo accused Hitler of responsibility. But Leo Raubal was living at the time in Vienna and he was never able to reopen the case. Nevertheless, he threatened so often to bring Hitler to justice that he died violently in the Balkans, where he was sent on military orders and where he was killed in 1942 in circumstances never explained. A son of Hitler's brother made the same accusation but not the same mistake: William Patrick Hitler denounced Uncle Adolf from the safety of New York, to which he fled in 1939. The murdered girl's mother left Hitler's employ and married a Professor Hamitsch, in Dresden, where years later she said that Martin Bormann extracted from her a promise never to discuss the dropped charges against her half-brother. The whole family specialized in intermarriage, and Hitler's relatives may have preferred not to wash dirty linen in public anyway, especially since his relations with Geli added incestuous undertones to an already squalid affair. Still, faint squeaks of disgust escaped from the Hitler-Schicklgruber tribe from time to time. His full sister, Paula, changed her name to "Frau Wolff" and took a job addressing envelopes for an insurance company. After 1945 the Bavarian Free State confiscated Hitler's property and tried to return to Frau Wolff the contents of her late brother's pockets. She could not be traced, but in the attempt, a carbon copy was discovered of a deposition she had made to the Vienna criminal-investigation agency. Dated October 1931, it stated that her life was threatened by members of the German Gymnastic Association, which provided camouflage for young Nazis and future SS troops. The threats, she said, followed a comment she made that her brother Adolf was a murderer but also mad and ought to be locked up. The original of this report had been removed. It quoted Hitler's sister as saying that Geli would be alive still if someone had only warned the poor thing.

A young Englishwoman could have warned her. Winifred Wagner was a daughter-in-law of Richard Wagner, whose doomsday music and tribal operatic themes so thundered through Hitler's head that

35

he showed an unbalanced respect for the man he called "His Excellency Baron Richard von Wagner, Privy Counsellor and Chief Conductor." This exaggerated respect for titles was typical of Hitler and might have been mistaken for some form of self-ridicule, the stuff of Gilbert and Sullivan. With Hitler, it was no joke.

He permitted Winifred a few glimpses of his perverted tastes. She and her three small children were taught to call him "Wolf," a name with which the entire Schicklgruber clan seems to have had a grim obsession.

Winifred was expected to marry Hitler after she became a widow. She supported his political views and therefore confided little of her misgivings about him as a man. But one of the children, Friedelind, later told Allied intelligence agents that he had asked Winifred to whip him and that he treated her sometimes like his mother, asking her to punish him. He had a cottage built on the Wagner estate and appointed Bormann to manage it after Winifred's husband, Siegfried, died. Bormann was given the task of building up the annual music festival, founded there at Bayreuth by Richard Wagner. For a long time in the 1920's and early '30's, Winifred's home was the one place where Hitler was seen to relax without the customary guard of blond young thugs, but always with Bormann in attendance.

Winifred did make some mild observations, however, which seem to have been authenticated by many independent sources. She disliked, for instance, the way Hitler responded to "the musk-ox figure" of Bormann. She thought Hitler got pleasure from Bormann's undisguised sexuality. She had heard Hitler once call him "Bubi," which was a term of affection used among homosexuals. She sensed a desperate battle between a soft and indecisive personality within Hitler and another force, "like that of a beast," which responded to Bormann's oppressive and silent presence. But it was Friedelind who spoke openly of Hitler's love of pornography and other strange matters. Winifred contented herself with an occasional comment, in letters to her family in England, suggesting that Bormann was at least open in his disregard for Wagnerian music whereas Hitler "tries very hard to comprehend, so hard that sometimes I could wish he were (with regard to *his* equal ignorance) more frank."

She might have saved Geli from moral corruption and death if she herself had been more frank. Geli was seventeen when she came with her mother from a Vienna back street to join Hitler. She was treated at first like any favorite niece of a rich uncle. Winifred arranged for singing lessons, and Geli, taught by two of Germany's most distinguished music professors, was to become a Wagnerian soprano. She was a bridesmaid at Bormann's wedding in 1929. Hitler was then forty years old, a critical age in those days for a bachelor whose dreams of glory were still unfulfilled and whose sexual frustrations were perhaps further complicated by the spectacle of Bormann embarking upon a normal family life.

The whole atmosphere reeked of "furtive unnatural sexuality," wrote Hermann Rauschning, who later broke with Hitler. "Surreptitious relationships, substitutes and symbols, false sentiments and secret lusts—nothing in [Hitler's] surroundings is natural. Nothing has the openness of natural instinct."

Another girl sucked into this "evil emanation" was Henny Hoffmann, whose father was a party member. Henny would be called today a hundred-dollar party girl. In a drunken moment she told her father some of Hitler's bestial habits. Her revelations were of a nature that might well disgust the most profligate young rake. Heinrich Hoffmann used the information to blackmail Hitler into appointing him the party's official photographer, with exclusive rights that made him a millionaire. Henny married the notorious homosexual Baldur von Schirach, who was sentenced at Nuremberg for war crimes including the deportation of Austrian Jews to liquidation camps. (Hoffmann survived to make another postwar killing with his photographs; and in 1966 a West German literary agency offered Schirach, no longer in jail, $150,000 for his memoirs.)

The Munich detective squads were long accustomed to savagery that went unpunished. Heinrich Himmler, who became an SS Field Marshal, had wriggled out of well-documented charges that he had murdered a Munich prostitute with whom he lived and from whose earnings he drew a percentage. This was a period of political killings in the medieval tradition, and it had enabled Bormann to serve only one year for his part in the murder of Kadow. This ancient view of Germanic justice was lenient toward soldiers who claimed that they had carried out the sentence of impromptu military courts against traitors. Bormann persuaded Müller, or the Inspector allowed himself to be persuaded, that the murdered niece had been a threat to Germany's New Order; and having provided an argument to satisfy moral objections, Bormann produced more tangible inducements. Müller, already widely known for his soaring ambition, was promised power and a title to dazzle this former sergeant-pilot turned policeman.

Geli's funeral was attended on Hitler's behalf by Ernst Röhm, the Brown Shirt leader, and Himmler, the bespectacled ex-teacher who was head of the Black Shirt SS Guards. "Butcher" Himmler was already beholden to Bormann, and so, it seemed, was Müller; but Röhm could and did talk, and he was accordingly executed by yet another summary military court some three years later.

Otto Strasser, although a notorious gossip, swears that his brother Gregor spent several days and nights at Hitler's side after the murder, fearing he might commit suicide in what appeared to be his paroxysms of grief. There were terrifying scenes when Hitler would wake up with convulsive shrieks for help. Gregor, who was then high in Nazi party councils, reported that Hitler sat on the edge of his bed shaking so that the whole room seemed to vibrate, yet unable himself to shift position. Once, his lips turned blue and he pointed to a corner of the bedroom crying: "It's him! He! He! He's been here. . . ." His voice became guttural and, in Gregor's own words, "Horrible sounds emerged and strange words which were not in any language known to man."

Borman noted these indiscreet stories. He had witnessed such scenes himself but took care not to confide them until very much later, and then only to his wife. He drove a wedge between Hitler and Gregor Strasser, Otto told me in Montreal. Three years later, Gregor was murdered, too. The weight of circumstantial evidence, gathered through the years, indicates that Bormann was again the mastermind. This was always the view of Otto Strasser, who recovered his German citizenship in 1954 and left Canada to pursue his own investigation into Bormann's past.

Even without such secondhand observations, it seemed to expert analysts during and after World War II that the murder of Geli Raubal was a pivotal moment in Bormann's career. She might have prevented Hitler's subsequent incurable paranoia. She was a normal, if highly sexed, girl, who had a variety of lovers. She could have used her influence on Hitler to relieve some of his frustrations and redirect his energies into less destructive channels. After her death, Hitler turned her room in the Munich flat into a shrine, where fresh flowers were placed each day beside a statuette made in her likeness. He locked himself in her room on the anniversary of her death and meditated for hours. Her room in his Bavarian "fortress" was left untouched during the remodeling of the Berghof into the palatial quarters that befitted his image of himself as an emperor.

This imperial phase began with Geli's death and lasted almost twelve years, until the catastrophic military defeat at Stalingrad, which was interpreted by Hitler as another public exposure of his own lack of real manhood. He then withdrew from the public appearances that throughout 1931–1942 were reported by chroniclers of the time as nothing less than sexual orgies, in which Hitler worked up the crowds until they reached an orgasm of roars and shrieks and fainting women.

The man who stage-managed these public appearances was Bormann. His work behind the scenes was described to me in 1972 by the former opera star who became Göring's wife. Göring himself told a press conference shortly before he committed suicide that "Bormann stayed with Hitler night and day and gradually brought him under his will so that he ruled Hitler's whole existence."

Bormann made sure that Hitler never again found the satisfactions offered by Geli. The Führer lost his mysterious empathy with a crowd if there was the briefest introduction of sexual relief in his private life. He was introduced, through Bormann, to a young and asexual physical-fitness enthusiast named Eva Braun, who remained until the end as Hitler's official mistress. Eva was part of the window dressing. When she realized her role, she became increasingly frank in expressing her hatred of Bormann, who was seldom absent when she and Hitler were together. Others have recorded the strange insistence with which Bormann kept at her side. He permitted Eva a limited role as a kind of substitute mother: a role played by many women in the Führer's life, a role that required them to listen for hours while he talked about himself. When Hitler decided that Eva must die at his side, he placed center stage in the death scene a vase of red roses, which had been his mother's favorite flower and which he had always associated with her funeral.

In speculating on how Geli might have redirected Hitler's spermal energies, we should not forget the state of mind then existing in millions of Germans. The vast stadiums were filled with crowds which came of their own volition. Hitler, according to his associates, spoke often of handling these crowds as though seducing a woman: the masses responded in a typically feminine way, he said, and they enjoyed what he was doing to them. They were not being raped. They were eager participants in orgies that happened to be on a scale larger than that familiar to a later generation in the form of mass gatherings of young people drugged in other ways. The pimp who stood aloof from Hitler, the drug pusher himself, was Bormann. He had the mind of the animal trainer who starves a beast before shoving it into the circus ring.

CHAPTER 5

The mind of Martin Bormann had its own peculiar twists. He was a practical psychologist with a peasant's natural instinct for sizing up another person. He had a contempt for the pretensions of society but he knew how to make use of them. His exploitation of Hitler's sexual aberrations from the Geli Raubal period was single-minded, ruthless, and largely invisible to anyone excluded from the bedchamber. He was manufacturing a monster, and Geli had endangered his work. She knew how to satisfy Hitler, she was willing to do it, and she could have been persuaded to continue in this role if Bormann had so wanted. But a placid Führer was the last thing he needed.

Much of this became known through studies that were assembled, after Bormann disappeared, under the title "The Life Past & Future, Mind & Conduct of Nazi Party Reich Minister Martin Bormann." They were the result of a technique pioneered by Anglo-American intelligence experts, based upon several older methods of examining an enemy at a distance. This technique is known today as prosopography, from a Greek word meaning the representation of an absent or deceased person as if he spoke and acted in our company. It grew out of the work of professors of ancient history like the Oxford don Ronald K. Syme, who could make a Roman emperor come alive by a painstaking study of the people around him. A long-range psychoanalysis of Bormann was conducted by teams of specialists, and their work was based upon interviews with those who had known him intimately.

One of these was the mistress of Martin Bormann himself. She was entirely different from Geli and found nothing in common with Eva, who could suppress her own sexual instincts for the sake of the comparative fame and fortune that went with playing mother to Hitler. Bormann's mistress vanished into Communist East Germany after the war. She proved eventually to be a great help in producing the final study on the mind of Bormann, which brought into closer focus the interplay between the Führer and the Secretary.

She believed Bormann used his familiar trick of whispering gossip into Hitler's trusting ear so that he became suspicious of Geli. At the same time, Bormann encouraged the girl to have other affairs, and was a kind of liaison officer between Geli and her lover. He was the confidant of both, and he built up the misunderstandings and tensions that led to murder. His control over Hitler increased twofold. He had disposed of the girl who could pull some of the strings that made Hitler dance. He had disposed of the evidence that Hitler shot the girl.

These were matters of which Bormann's mistress had no direct knowledge. She was too young to have moved in early Nazi circles. She did have a strong memory of her conversations with Bormann, however; and it was unlikely that she would have known certain details from any other source. These details conformed with what Allied investigators discovered more than thirty years after Geli's murder.

This mistress of Martin Bormann was known as "M." She materialized out of the shadows like some member of a conspiracy to keep alive the memories of the past.

She was living quietly in East Berlin when the District Attorney's office in the Western Zone bowed to political pressures and agreed to have yet another ceremonial digging up of an area said to have been turned into a mass grave by the Russians. The Red Army, fearing the spread of disease, had ordered the burial of thousands of bodies that littered the Berlin streets on the day Bormann vanished.

M since then had returned to her profession as an actress. During the night of July 20, 1965, she slipped out of her apartment and crossed into the Western Zone, with every intention of going back. She was an attractive, middle-aged, and slender woman, who had been allowed to live in the decent obscurity denied her by Mr. and Mrs. Bormann. They had immortalized her in some of the strangest love letters known to literature. Her seduction was described by Bormann in a letter to his wife:

"I kissed her without further ado and quite scorched her with my burning joy. I fell madly in love with her. I arranged it so I met her again many times and then I took her in spite of her refusals. You know the strength of my will against which M was of course unable to hold out for long. Now she is mine and now— lucky fellow—now I am or rather I feel doubly and unbelievably happily married. . . . What do you think, beloved, of your crazy fellow?"

Mrs. Bormann replied at once: "I am so fond of M myself that I simply cannot be angry with you." She considered it a thousand pities that M should be denied children, and Martin ought to be able to order the situation "and see to it that one year M has a child and the next year I have a child, so you will always have a wife who is serviceable."

M had come out this night in 1965 wondering if her lover's remains might be among the skulls and bones shoveled from the clay of a public park near the Lehrter railroad station. A forlorn hope, no doubt. Identification would have to be made in a forensic lab. In any case, one of the minor mysteries that surrounded the great central puzzle of Martin Bormann's fate was that the authorities tended to contradict each other. There were several dentists who claimed to remember Bormann's teeth. There were police who said they knew Bormann's prints were lost, and other, more majestic, figures of the law, the prosecutors, who themselves differed about the existence or even the value of thumbprints or fingerprints which might or might not be authentic. Bormann had been erased from the public records, his tracks smoothed over, even his photographs rarely seen. He carried this passion for secrecy to the point where he referred to his mistress as "M" even in his letters to Gerda, whom he called "Mommy" most of the time.

Others shared with M something more than idle curiosity in this ghoulish spectacle of police raking over the remains of those killed inside the Russian Iron Ring of twenty years ago. There was General Gehlen, who had moved into the villa Bormann once occupied. Also watching were Gehlen's chief and, according to him, only enemies, the Russians. The British secret service, which had its own ideas about where Gehlen really thought his enemies lay, was also represented. A man from Vatican intelligence was there, sent by the Prelate Volmy, who led the Roman Pontificate in "ideological countermeasures" against Communism in Latin America. There was an observer for Father Martin Bormann, Jr., a Catholic missionary who had just narrowly missed death in the Congo. Father Bormann was the eldest son of the man they were digging for.

An old man pottered through the rubble. Albert Krumnow, a retired mailman, thought he remembered burying bodies here on Russian orders, about five hundred meters from the present Sandkrug break in the Berlin Wall. He may have been encouraged by the reward of 100,000 marks (about $25,000) offered by the Frankfurt

Prosecutor's office for information leading to Bormann's discovery. The old mailman had come forward to say that he recalled finding papers on one body which identified it as Bormann's. Why had he waited so long? And where were the papers now? An investigator from the Vienna Documentation Center, listening to the vague replies, reported later that the old man had been duped by the Brotherhood, which was taking over the task of protecting ex-Nazis and preserving the spirit of their philosophy.

M returned to her flat on the other side of the Berlin Wall. Behind her, and along the banks of the River Spree, men in white overalls still picked gingerly among clods of earth. Rusted helmets, the pitted barrels of rifles, shrunken boots, and rotted webbing were separated from the bones that emerged seemingly without end, glowing in the darkness. She said later that she believed these false alarms were deliberately sounded by the Brotherhood to divert attention from their operations abroad. "But," she said with a shrug of thin shoulders, "I really cannot pretend to know about these things."

Her real name was Manja Behrens. She had irritated Gerda Bormann because of her timidity, not because of her affair with Martin. She had read Gerda's letters proposing that her husband impregnate M and then his wife, turn and turn about, so that one or the other would always be carrying a good Aryan child. This and other matters made Manja Behrens choose the East. It was a puritan reaction, for the actress had had strong religious beliefs at one time; a rejection of what seemed to her to be a continuation of corruption in the plump and sex-obsessed West.

Three weeks after the digging near the Lehrter Station, she heard that none of the exhumed bones could be identified as being her lost lover's. The news came as no real surprise. She had made a similar but more secretive journey during the night of September 25, 1963 to the German military garrison at Kreuzberg, in West Berlin. There, a group of gravediggers had brought out of the cemetery a worm-eaten coffin. A marker, placed by the family, said that here were the last mortal remains of Heinrich Müller. Müller was second on the list of the 160,000 most-wanted war criminals in the eleven states of West Germany. At the top of the list, of course, was Bormann.

When reports that Bormann had escaped from Berlin were published prior to 1963, the case of Gestapo Müller was quoted as a convincing example of how the two most wanted men could not really be expected to have broken out. He, too, had supposedly crossed through Russian lines. And yet, *look!* Here was his grave, properly registered and marked in accordance with military rules and regulations.

Now, in late September, it turned out that the grave contained none of Müller's bones. What appeared to be a single skeleton was made up from parts of three different men, and, according to scientific tests, none of the bones could have been Müller's. Someone had deliberately and with calculation prepared a fake corpse and given prominence to the grave of the wanted man. For eighteen years there had been a regular Sunday charade of placing flowers on the grave of the man who wasn't really there. If Gestapo Müller had friends who would bury his past in order to keep him alive, then the same might well be true for Bormann.

M was always an intelligent observer, without pretensions; and like the girls of her generation, she did not ask questions of the male, who was dominant. During the long wait after Bormann vanished, she was treated well by the East German government, and in return she repeated what she had seen and heard. Her testimony was the more effective because it came from a young woman accustomed to discipline and in the habit of keeping her imagination under tight rein. Gerda Bormann's judgment that M was somewhat stupid and afraid can be disregarded: it is the remark of a wife breaking through the crust of dogma. It can be said that M's recollections confirmed what others said about the way Bormann won power over Hitler.

The three years that followed the death of Hitler's niece were busy ones for Bormann. He was sidling into a central position backstage where he could exercise full control of his puppet and remain unseen. He was not at all sure of his power and he could not afford to draw the fire of his rivals. The job to which he aspired lacked glamour and the glitter of high military rank. He needed to manipulate the weak and indecisive Deputy Führer, Rudolf Hess, get rid of him, and then take his place, with a more clearly defined authority over the Nazi party machine.

His success was recognized only in 1941, and then not by his enemies at home in the Third Reich but by Germany's enemies in the West. Hess had flown by himself to Scotland, where he parachuted into that war camp with an extraordinary tale. He was interrogated by Winston Churchill's personal investigator into the mystery, Lord Beaverbrook, who disguised himself as "Dr. Livingstone." From this encounter stemmed the first of the long-range studies of Martin Bormann.

In 1934, however, Bormann was regarded as a nonentity by all except Hitler. Few knew his name. Fewer knew what he looked like. He stabbed in the back Hitler's right-hand man of that time, Ernst Röhm, in what became known as the "Night of the Long Knives." The details of how this was done, and how it led to the wartime flight of the Deputy Führer, emerged only from the long and difficult investigations launched as a result of Beaverbrook's recommendations to Churchill and the subsequent request sent to Roosevelt for American co-operation.

Röhm had been working in Bolivia. During his absence, in those three years after Geli's murder, Bormann had made the necessary moves to place himself behind Hitler and in control.

Bormann solidified his mastery of the party machinery and released a swarm of memos. These were never self-incriminating. Nothing went out over his signature that might be used against him by his enemies. And he saw enemies everywhere, even and especially among those with whom he formed temporary alliances. The paperwork was designed to impress and flatter the Führer. Private notes and dossiers of confidential reports were to provide Bormann with the stuff of blackmail. He kept all the personnel files and saw the confidential reports of all the intelligence organizations, which gave him an advantage over the chiefs of those same agencies, who seldom got to see the secret accounts of their rivals. He decided on promotions and demotions within the party, whose supremacy he guarded. Above all, he dogged Hitler's footsteps, anticipating his wishes, interpreting his dreams, soothing his days, and softly and unobtrusively directing the long mealtime conversations that led, for some guests, to an early grave or a sudden more earthly elevation.

Bormann learned to construct private agencies. These balanced on friendships which in turn depended upon favors given and received. The Gauleiters and the body of men beneath them were increasingly a source of strength. They provided him with unparalleled experience in maneuvering individuals. His influence extended into the armed forces, by nature and tradition hostile at first to this outside interference. He probed police organizations and put key men into his debt. The complicated machinery of the Nazi apparatus—political, military, and security—was always clearly laid out in a mind that thrived upon this kind of nutrition. He had an extraordinary memory for the tiniest details, which baffled outsiders.*

A crisis arose just when Bormann had settled into the saddle as Chief of Staff to Rudolf Hess. The way he handled the crisis is illuminating. It shows him getting a firm grip on agencies that might have become hostile. It reveals his total disinterest in human loyalties. It provides a brief guide to Nazi interest in South America in the 1930's, and Bormann's own familiarity with a region that always aroused romantic German visions of "partnership" with allegedly backward nations. The partnership required from the inferior natives of Latin America a willing supply of cheap labor to gather raw materials that would feed the Ruhr factories.

This crisis, in the spring of 1934, began when Bormann realized that Hitler meant to crack down on the Brown Shirts. It made no difference that Bormann himself had served four years on the staff of the Supreme Command of the SA (Sturmabteilung) storm troopers and on the face of it was on close friendly terms with SA leaders. He began at once to pass information on the SA to his father-in-law, party disciplinarian Walter Buch, with particular emphasis on the SA Chief of Staff, Ernst Röhm.

Captain Röhm had trained the army in Bolivia, an important South American source of tin and a primitive mountain state in the high Andes whose economy was dominated by German firms. Previously, German General Hans Kundt led a group of German military advisers for the Bolivian Army, which absorbed almost half the national budget, despite the country's extreme poverty. Röhm had been sent by Hitler to build the army more in keeping with Nazi ideas than with old General Kundt's staid imperial concepts. The two men had little difficulty reaching a compromise. They dressed the troops in Nazi-style uniforms, drilled them in the Nazi salute, hung the Führer's portrait in the canteens, and prepared the way for a German-equipped air force. They agreed that an Italian military mission, preaching fascist theories, would help dampen any suspicion that the Germans had taken over while simultaneously making sure they did. They selected a proper pro-Nazi president

* Allied intelligence experts got into a tangle with just the police machinery. When Bormann escaped, there was a main office of Reich Security, under Heinrich Himmler, which covered security police, the Gestapo, the SD (Security Service) terrorist police, and subdivisions such as Adolf Eichmann's Bureau IV A, 4b. There were more than one hundred Reich Security agencies, and Bormann knew them all, whereas it is doubtful if Hitler or anyone else was fully conversant with their activities.

for the future, an up-and-coming Bolivian whose father was a German doctor: Germán Busch.

Röhm was a snub-nosed, stocky Bavarian with a battered florid face. He was a monarchist, and gained influence during the struggle against Communists when the Bavarian monarchy was overthrown in the aftermath of World War I. He organized a so-called home guard similar to the Freikorps. In Munich he met Hitler in another of the secret societies that kept popping up in Germany: the Iron Fist. He boasted to Hitler that he had helped execute Rosa Luxemburg and Karl Liebknecht, the two German Communists who are remembered in East Germany today as revolutionary martyrs (but not in the West, where the Bonn government in an official bulletin described the man who ordered the killings as "the well-known Freikorps leader, Major Pabst, who prevented the Bolshevizing of Germany"). The murders were on a par with political killings characteristic of the period. Other Freikorps groups were obliged to disband for less. But in the case of the two Communist leaders, shot on January 15, 1919, it was ten years before an open court looked as if it might act against Pabst and his group. By then, Röhm's own secret army had grown into the Nazi SA storm troopers. Pabst became a Nazi hero.*

Röhm came back from Bolivia full of what his troopers would have called "piss and vinegar," cocky and ready to take on any helpless crowd of little old ladies. His forces grew in number to three million bully boys, and he was all set to take over the professional army.

The regular German Army, seeded with young aristocratic officers, was not as virtuous and above thuggery as its survivors have since protested. Bormann, at a disadvantage because his career as a cannoneer lacked the luster of service at the front, knew this. He saw the danger of an alliance between the army and Röhm's Brown Shirts. His strategy was based on the superiority of the party over all other elements.

Since the murder of Hitler's niece, Bormann had cultivated groups of men in Munich who either were serving in the police or

* Major Waldemar Pabst died on May 7, 1970. The death notice in *Die Welt* described him as a Royal Prussian major, former Director of Rheinmetall-Borsig AG, and quoted from Revelations: "They may rest from their labors; and their works do follow them." Pabst told the story of the murders only in 1962, when he wrote: "It was not easy for me to take the decision to have them done away with [but it was] absolutely tenable from the moral and theological viewpoint."

were known to the police as reasonably successful criminals. There was a watchmaker convicted of embezzlement: Emil Maurice, whose brother Ernst had intimate knowledge of the murdered girl. There was Christian Weber, a former stableboy. They called themselves "headquarters guardsmen" and formed their own protective squadrons, known as the SS (Schutzstaffel). They wore black ski caps with a death's-head button and black-bordered swastika armbands. They were led by Heinrich Himmler, the Police President for Bavaria, who was very much aware of the real influence exercised by Bormann behind the scenes.

In the early hours of June 30, 1934, the opposing SA leaders were caught in their beds and swept into makeshift prisons, where, during the next three days, they were shot one after another in accordance with a mysterious list of condemned men which Hitler saw only after the massacre. The list was a subject of endless controversy and speculation.

This Night of the Long Knives led to Captain Röhm and 921 others being trapped and subsequently killed, in ways more amateurish than might be supposed from reading accounts of the purge. Bormann issued a tidy if emotional version through the Table Talk Notes that supposedly conveyed Hitler's thoughts.* Once again, however, this was Bormann's filtered version. In public, Hitler said fifty-eight were executed. All through the reports of that period runs the thread of Hitler's uncertainty of what was happening.

General Kundt dispatched urgent and earnest pleas from Bolivia for information on Röhm's fate. The German military mission was then caught in an awkward posture, which had nothing to do with events far away at home. Bolivian troops were fighting for an unimportant piece of land claimed by neighboring Paraguay. The forces of Paraguay included an artillery officer, Alfredo Stroessner, son of a German brewer. (Later on, as President of Paraguay, and dictator of the toughest of totalitarian states, Stroessner provided sanctuary for Nazi war criminals with the same enthusiasm as that displayed by Bolivia.) Now, Bormann, acting as always in the name of the Deputy Führer, assured Kundt that Röhm's "gang of fairies" had gone down to defeat.

Bormann had wiped out the biggest threat to his own secret authority. He must have known that he could handle the regular army, and he was confident that he could outwit the SS under

---

* The Bormann-Vermerke was authorized by the Führer; its final form was to be corrected, approved, and preserved by the only reliable interpreter of Hitler's thoughts, Martin Bormann.

Himmler. These forces recognized the over-all superiority of the Nazi party as already laid down by the Führer. But Röhm had seemed ready to challenge party omniscience. He was shown to have been at the center of a conspiracy that in retrospect Hitler could regard as a direct attempt to defy party rule. The source of evidence was Bormann's own police file; and the interpretation placed upon Röhm's actions was Bormann's, too. He was never caught among the gunmen, naturally.

The mysterious hand that placed Röhm on the list of those to be summarily executed was thought to be that of the leader of the rival SS. It was an obvious deduction. But Himmler always denied this in private; and from that date he was seen to be in fear of Bormann.

The Führer and Bormann were reduced frequently to malicious laughter over the strange posturings of Heinrich Himmler and his Secret Inner Order of the SS. Himmler never ceased to look like what he was: the myopic son of a greengrocer with a wild concept of a new aristocracy that would govern Germany and then Europe and finally the world. He held mystical gatherings in a monastery, where his inner circle of twelve disciples bestrode chairs on which each name was engraved on a silver plate.

Himmler was a child in the hands of an expert wet nurse like Bormann, and he was comfortably kept in place without knowing it. He became "Uncle Heinrich" and godfather to the fourth Bormann child, conceived after the blood purge. In return, he made Bormann an SS Gruppenführer, a major general. This did not mean, as overenthusiastic Nazi hunters have sometimes assumed, that Bormann went through SS procedures, which would have marked him for life and left details of his physical appearance on the record. It is one more small indication of Bormann's effective control over Himmler that he never participated in SS ceremonies and treated the title as purely honorary. When the SS columns marched past Hitler's reviewing stand, Bormann was up there looking down. Newsreels of the year 1937 show him in attendance on Hitler; and an examination of the film, frame by frame, starkly demonstrates his separation from the only other person who might stand between him and Hitler: the Führer's Deputy, Hess.

Other personalities filled the scene, but Bormann's genius lay in his perception of what really mattered in a bureaucracy. Hermann Göring could occupy himself with air-force matters; Goebbels and Ribbentrop and Schacht and Speer and a host of specialists could plunge into great adventures (which is how they saw the testing of the Nazi war machine in the Spanish Civil War and the annexation of Austria, the planning of the final Arch of Triumph and the logistics of reducing the Slavs to slaves). Bormann knew he must remain at the center of the spiraling interests of Hitler's henchmen. He showed contempt for the symbols of power, which diverted his competitors.

Himmler must have guessed what was happening. But there was little time to consider these things. Much later, he said in some bewilderment to Walter Schellenberg, the spy chief, who had become his personal adviser: "Again and again, I have to come to terms with Bormann although it's my duty really to get him out. The Führer has become so accustomed to Bormann, it's very difficult to lessen his influence."

The number-two man was always thought to be Field Marshal Hermann Göring. He testified at the International Military Tribunal at Nuremberg, however, that after Deputy Führer Hess went, Bormann exerted the real influence: "The most decisive influence during the war . . . disastrously so, was that of Herr Bormann."

Göring was asked: "Do you think the Führer is dead?"

He replied: "Absolutely. No doubt about it."

"What about Bormann?"

"I hope he is frying in hell!" replied Göring.

His widow was just as vigorous in her denunciation twenty-six years later. Emmy Göring, at her modest home, No. 16 on the eminently respectable Buercleinstrasse in Munich, quoted the Field Marshal on the eve of his suicide: "Bormann destroyed each one of us in turn. He got Heydrich assassinated and he maneuvered Himmler into an impossibly ridiculous situation. With the Führer dying, he got rid of Goebbels and had me arrested as a traitor. He got the Deputy Führer to fly to England because Hess was the only real obstacle."

The flight was made on the night of May 10, 1941. Hess was in his late forties. He was born in Egypt, in 1894, and his early boyhood was spent on the banks of the Nile. He was a brooding figure, whose thoughts about purity of race became part of *Mein Kampf,* much of which he wrote at Hitler's dictation when they were both in prison. When he planned his flight, Germany was gorged with victories in Europe and was preparing for the invasion of Russia, which Hitler said would "make the world stand still." A man with, theoretically, heavy party responsibilities, Hess knew the details of the impending attack on Russia, which was at that time the most ambitious military adventure in history. Yet he was able to practice flying a fighter plane for hours on end, over a prolonged period.

Obviously, his strange behavior could not pass without comment. His flight and the preparations for it should certainly have been known, in considerable detail, to Göring. The chief of the air force maintained always that Hess had received outside help for the hazardous journey. Hess told others that he wanted to keep his hand in as a pilot. But who told Hess to make the flight? He was a man who listened to the disembodied voices conjured up by his imagination, and for years he had studied Egyptian astrologers. At the same time, he was intensely practical. He had to arrange for the conversion of a Messerschmitt 110, a fighter that did not have the normal range he required. He had to provide the combat plane with an extra fuel tank for each wing tip and a third under the fuselage. He had to fly by his own navigation, without normal radio aids, without navigation lights, through savage skies filled with night fighters, for this was at the height of the Battle of Britain. Before this journey even began, he had to make long and careful preparations, which included thirty practice flights and the secret acquisition of maps and equipment.

About the only feature in this whole escapade that had not been meticulously planned was the role of the young Duke of Hamilton, Hess's goal. It had been supposed by Hess that he could communicate directly with the King of England through the Duke, and negotiate a peace treaty that would release the Nazi war machine to concentrate on the Soviet Union. The Duke was hardly the man to play ball. He was flying a single-seat Hurricane converted for night fighting, and his job was to shoot down German aircraft attempting to fulfill Göring's prediction that the Luftwaffe would wipe Britain from the map within another month. The Duke's companions were suffering the highest casualty rate of any fighting service. And their particular assignment was the protection of Scotland, where Hess expected to be welcomed at the Duke's hearthside.

It has been said that Hess was mad. There is no proof of this in conversations and letters of the time. None seem any more lunatic than what passed for social intercourse in Hitler's circle. Later, Hess behaved less rationally, as might be expected of a man doomed to spend the rest of his life in solitary confinement.

Today, Hess is the sole occupant of cavernous Spandau Prison in Berlin, where he is watched by armed troops supplied in rotation by the Four Powers, entirely at Moscow's insistence. It was Stalin's recurrent nightmare that the Nazis might form a secret alliance with Western capitalism against the Soviets; and the flight of Hess was regarded by the Russians as having a far deeper significance than being merely a political maneuver by Bormann to place himself in power.

The maneuver was carried out with so little attention paid to the change in Bormann's position that its significance was unnoticed by most of the Nazi chieftains themselves. It was signaled in terms of utmost discretion in a directive from Hitler:

"The former post of Deputy to the Führer will henceforth bear the title of Party Minister. It is directly subordinate to me. It will be directed as heretofore by Party Comrade Martin Bormann."

The text was drafted by Bormann. The terms did not alert those enemies who might have stopped his progress if they had recognized that the peasant who seemed concerned only with serving his master was in reality manipulating him.

With Hess gone, his name struck from the party record by Bormann, the focus of power was clear. Hitler's Deputy had made his office a center of party activity. As his successor, Bormann made it the party chancellery. And it was the party, his minions were reminded, that ordered the state. At the age of forty-one, Bormann had *official* power that gave him personal direction of the Nazi party, an instrument he had forged and used to bring Hitler to power. The Führer was busy playing the Supreme War Lord and admitted later that he lost sight of party affairs. The dramatic launching of Hess into the blue was a personal triumph for Bormann, who could now appoint or dismiss every party official, advance or ruin careers in any organ of government or in the political and military ranks, and who now answered only to Hitler.

His glee at the removal of his rival loomed larger in his mind than the enlargement of the war. This was evident in his letters and notes of the period. To one of his next victims, Himmler, he wrote: "Hess wanted to shine because he suffered from an inferiority complex. In the opinion of the Führer these are in fact the real causes. Only now has it become known that R H has been treated again and again for impotence even at the time his son was produced. Before himself, before his wife and before the party and the people, R H believed that by this undertaking he could prove his virility."

This technique of quoting the Führer to support his own positions would continue until Hitler's own usefulness had ended. It was many more years before the method was identified. Nazi business was conducted in secrecy, of course, and after the war there was simply too much documentation. Bormann's small slips of paper sank to the bottom of the pile. Thus the view prevailed that Bormann depended upon the Führer and lost his own sense of identity when Hitler died. Everything he did, as pieced together from those harmless slips of paper and fitted into the larger pattern of Nazi affairs, proves the very opposite. Bormann used others until they became a nuisance or a threat. He used Rudolf Hess for "finger exercises," exploiting the same kind of delusions that enveloped Hitler. The Messiah complex of Hitler was clear in his identification with Saint Matthew as a voice crying in a wilderness; and himself as Saint John the Baptist carving a path for those to come. There were similar sicknesses in the mind of Rudolf Hess. These would have become evident during the years when Bormann worked with him.

Bormann's skill in turning the weaknesses of others to good account is evident in the way Hess was led into his strange flight. The preparations and the aftermath show the ruthlessness, the crafty manipulation of others, the capacity to become part of another personality which would make it possible for Bormann to embrace the dogma of another faith without necessarily believing it. He needed to be rid of Hess. He played on the man's credulity with regard to the British. More than anything, he exploited the man's bizarre faith in soothsaying, old prophesies, and visionary revelations.

His instrument was a crackpot genius, Karl Haushofer, who was Professor of Geopolitics at Munich University when Rudolf Hess enrolled in 1920 as a student. Haushofer believed in premonitions and the influence of the soil upon a nation's character. The Germans were the destined master race thwarted by the Jews. Germany would control Europe from the Atlantic to the Urals. Astrology would bring Germany and Japan together. Much of this crept into *Mein Kampf*.

Incredibly, Haushofer had been an army general in World War I and the German military attaché in Tokyo. His mysticism, and his sometimes shrewd guesses, had won him the attention of credulous Germans, including Hitler. When the next war came along, he pressed on anyone who would listen his theory that conflict with Britain was wrong for a number of mystical reasons. His influence on Hitler was exercised through Hess; and Schellenberg later testified that it was generally recognized that Hess should be stopped from communicating this mixed bag of ideas. (Hitler, if exposed to the prophesies of such men, listened with superstitious attention to

53

such a degree that the British finally lured away and hired his personal astrologer, Louis de Wohl,* who worked under Allied secret-service instructions in New York from 1941. His job was to harmonize the predictions he wrote in a syndicated column with world events, and to slip in from time to time predictions of Hitler's inevitable disaster. Another soothsayer, in Cairo, was bribed to put Hitler's planet, Neptune, in the House of Death. It was hoped to drive Hitler, over a period of time, to suicide.)

Bormann, instead of cutting Haushofer off, diverted his visits into long private chats with Hess. When Hitler continued to prepare for war against Russia, Bormann saw to it that Haushofer concentrated on Hess. The Professor, guided by the stars, wrote to the Duke of Hamilton, whom he supposed to have some special influence with the King. The Duke never replied to the letter, sent through neutral channels, or took it seriously. Meanwhile, the Professor confided to Hess that he had had three dreams on three separate nights in which he saw the Deputy Führer piloting a plane and later walking in a great castle with tartan tapestries on the wall.

It cannot have taken the Deputy Führer long to get the message. He went first to discuss the whole idea with Hitler in October of 1940; Bormann's brother Albert escorted him to Hitler's presence. There followed an odd conversation in which Hitler resisted the suggestion that he put off the offensive against Russia until peace had been secured with Britain, in accordance with the Professor's premonitions. In the months that followed, Albert kept Martin informed of the growing disparity between Hitler's inspirations and the secondhand predictions from Hess.

Ilse Hess, the Deputy Führer's wife, had a four-year-old boy who was unusually like Martin Bormann, although nothing was ever said about the matter. Rudolf had a reputation for homosexuality, and Bormann nailed the coffin more firmly with his theories of how Hess demonstrated his masculinity, which was not normal. Ilse was puzzled by the way Bormann seemed to promote the Professor's ideas in private while deploring them in public. She said later that Bormann was a scheming careerist who had wormed his way into her husband's affections—an interesting thought. At all events, there was remarkably little effort made to prevent Hess from

* He was Hungarian and responded to the financial inducements conveyed through British agents. One of these, Ben Levy, a British playwright and Member of Parliament, had to climb the back stairs of a New York hotel to pay him each week in greenbacks.

practicing flying and from making relatively long flights for those days, each lasting two hours or more.

Hess made his flight, and was astonished when he was clapped into a British prison. There he talked rationally, if obsessively, to Beaverbrook about the coming conquest of the world by Russia. Otherwise, Beaverbrook reported to Churchill, the man was absolutely sane: "He may have unsound ideas about himself but he is not mad."

Churchill cabled Roosevelt that there were no signs of insanity in the Deputy Führer, who seemed in good health. He then speculated on the new role of Martin Bormann. It was agreed that there was an intelligence gap that needed filling here: nobody knew enough about Bormann to make any kind of assessment. He was a cipher. Further talks with Hess only confirmed a deepening suspicion that Bormann had calculatingly led him into his strange mission.

Whatever Mrs. Hess might have said later about Bormann, she let him spend a great deal of time with her son, Wolf. They developed a strong and intimate friendship, and after the war, when Bormann had disappeared, a watch was kept on young Wolf Hess by Allied intelligence, as was done with the Bormann family.

Bormann's savage action, after the mess was cleared up with Hitler's statement that his Deputy suffered from hallucinations, was typical. Hess's young adjutant, Captain Karlheinz Pintsch, who lived near the Hess household outside Munich, at Pullach, was invited to lunch with the Führer. Pintsch went, carrying a letter Hess had asked to have delivered to Hitler. Lunch was the usual Spartan affair, and afterward Hitler glanced at Bormann, whose brother Albert was already standing by the door. With a quick nod, Martin rose and told Pintsch he was under arrest. Two bodyguards crashed through the door and took him away. He was sent to the Russian front, where he was captured and tortured. Years later, when he finally returned, he described these events and said it was clear in retrospect that Bormann had wanted to silence him quickly, since he might have known too much about Bormann's part in a conspiracy fatal to Hess.

In the aftermath, Mrs. Hess was evicted from her Berlin quarters on the third floor of Wilhelmstrasse 64. She was told to list all possessions that were in her husband's name; and his house in Harthauserstrasse was confiscated. The blame for these actions was placed upon Bormann. Years later, police files showed that the orders were issued by Gestapo Müller.

. . .

When Beaverbrook reported to Stalin his impressions of the Hess peace mission, there was a long silence. The proposal that Nazi Germany should unite with Britain against Russia "really knocked him for six," the press baron said later.

The Russians suspected that Bormann persuaded his nominal chief to make the flight; that Bormann was a British informer; that although the Hess mission failed, it put Bormann into direct contact with British intelligence; and that Bormann remained a British agent until the end of the war.

From that time onward, Gestapo Müller was never far from Bormann's side. There was talk that Müller was "looking after Stalin's interests," a rather heavy-handed line of Germanic humor which referred to Müller's police training in Russia. The gossip stopped with the abruptness of a strangled cough, and the Gestapo men responsible for these ill-advised "froth-blowing" jokes were victims of another piece of Nazi fun. They were sent to battle fronts from which it was unlikely they would return, under the Nazi term *"zum Verheizen,"* the slang for "incineration."

CHAPTER 6

The stocky watchful figure moved onto the platform behind Hitler, then moved jerkily to join a cluster of jack-booted generals.

"Okay, run it in reverse."

The girl in the London archives pressed a button, and the figures flickered on the screen again.

"Now roll both projectors."

On another screen appeared an old man walking along a jungle path.

We watched the two films projected side by side: one grainy and scratched, the other in vivid color. One showed Bormann at a Nazi rally. The other showed a German farmer on the banks of a tributary to the Amazon. Both figures betrayed similarities of gesture. By running the film frame by frame, it was almost possible to synchronize the movements of a pudgy man aged forty-one and a leathery peasant aged seventy-two. Uncanny.

"You're on to *something*," said Norman Clark, foreign manager of the big London news-film agency Visnews. He had been my foreign editor on the liberal *News Chronicle*. Now we stood in the vaults where the agency stored millions of feet of rare wartime film. He left me as the film editor wrestled with another of the 35-mm. cans. It was going to take hours to hunt through this film rescued long after the war from hiding places in the Bavarian alps.* Above us, roses bloomed in the back yards of semidetached houses.

Bormann flickered in and out, a few brief seconds here and there, never identified on the dope sheets, never more than the same slightly bookish figure with a slim briefcase and a fixed smile.

And always behind Bormann came the same dapper little man in gray jacket and black riding breeches that I had learned to

---

* An epidemic of Nazi films broke out in 1972, mysteriously recovered from unnamed "Swiss caves," as the result of an agreement among U.S. television companies to pay royalties. The British so far still refuse to meet the financial demands of the purveyors.

recognize as Gestapo Müller. He was a surprisingly handsome figure in that mob. Even in old newsreels, one caught the characteristic flash of eyes that seemed everywhere at once.

Here were the two men in the front seat of Hitler's Mercedes, driving to the heart of that region where so many Nazi leaders later vanished: the Alpine Fortress. The potholed road climbed between steep slabs of rock. Now the men stood before huge bronze doors. Obviously this film had been shot to record the entrance to the Führer's impressive retreat. A long tunnel struck into the flank of a mountain. At the far end, an elevator plated with copper waited to lift Bormann, Müller, and the cameraman up through several hundred feet of rock to the home of the Reich Chancellor.

In the postwar analytical study of Bormann's influence over Hitler, the stunning approach to Eagle's Nest had been likened to a return to the womb. The top of the vertical shaft opened into a great gallery of Roman columns, a circular hall with windows all around, giving a sense of floating in the golden glow of an alpine twilight.

Bormann had supervised the construction of this eyrie since he first got his hands on the Berghof and began lacing the landscape with barbed wire, pillboxes, and blockhouses. Did he consciously cater to Hitler's sexual fantasies? I doubt it. He seemed more like a man with an instinctive way of manipulating others.

The film I was watching went back thirty years. Bormann's power was then real. Hess had gone. Of a lunch in a Berlin restaurant, one of the guests later recorded: "We were talking about Hitler's grave mood. Bormann said to him, 'You are burdened with worries and the successful conclusion of the great campaign depends on you alone. Providence has appointed you as her instrument to decide the future of the whole world. You have studied every detail of the task. I am certain, Mein Führer, you have planned everything thoroughly. Your mission will surely succeed."

At dawn the next day, June 22, 1941, three million German troops struck eastward toward Moscow and the Caucasus.

The chronicler of that moment when Bormann patted his Führer's head was the rising star in the foreign intelligence service, Lieutenant General Walter Schellenberg. Two months later, he was observing the struggle between Bormann and the next on the list of victims; a struggle that seemed more important than the terrible battles foreshadowing defeat in the east.

The new rival was Heinrich Himmler, whose SS empire functioned as a law to itself. Bormann looked for an ally inside the SS apparatus and found him in the preposterous figure of Ernst Kaltenbrunner. Even Himmler had confessed privately his fear of the giant Austrian, who had gone to school with Adolf Eichmann and been blooded alongside Otto Skorzeny in Austria. Bormann had been subsidizing Kaltenbrunner since prewar days, and when Himmler saw him in 1938 to bail him out of debts incurred from drinking and whoring, the scarred giant had roared with laughter. He was in Bormann's pay already, and the SS chief's prissy lecture on how to live within one's means struck Kaltenbrunner as hilarious.

Before the conflict with Himmler reached its climax though, another competitor was removed from the scene. SS General Reinhard Heydrich was the overlord of a system of terror in May 1942 that had no precedent. He was known as the "Butcher of Prague," although officially the title was "Reich Protector." He was also supreme boss of the gangsters and thugs of the Gestapo and other forms of security police. On the twenty-seventh day of that May, the Protector was being driven in his open green Mercedes from Prague to his summer residence when two agents, parachuted from Britain months before, rolled grenades and fired Sten guns from a point of ambush. Heydrich the Butcher died after days of agonizing pain from splinters of steel and horsehair driven upward into his spleen and liver.

An investigation was led by Gestapo Müller. The pieces of grenade were of English origin. He traced back the movements of the agents and concluded that the killing was a consequence of information squeezed out of the lately departed Deputy Führer. The killing was of the greatest advantage to Bormann, and again the question was raised: had the Führer's secret master planned this operation, too?

Schellenberg thought so. He noted in his diary the lamentations at Heydrich's funeral. Admiral Wilhelm Canaris, director of military intelligence, was in tears. Himmler lectured the assembly: "Intelligence achievements in this special sector cannot compare with those of the British secret service." A state funeral oration was delivered by the Führer, and Schellenberg wrote that he could not help feeling the whole spectacle was like something in a Renaissance painting. Meanwhile, all the people in the Czech village where the assassination took place had been herded into their local church, which was then set on fire. Anyone who tried to escape was shot dead.

Now, a man who would become Bormann's monstrous ally moved into the slot vacated by the slaughtered Heydrich. The new man was that scar-faced giant and veteran of the early bully-boy days, Ernst Kaltenbrunner.

The Brotherhood was closing ranks. Another ally, Erich Koch, was made Reich Commissar of the Ukraine. He was a fellow pallbearer with Bormann at the funeral of an early Nazi martyr, Leo Schlageter, whose execution had led to the Kadow murder. Graduates of that group shared mutual fears and needed each other for favors received or given. They had embraced Kaltenbrunner, a member of the original German Brotherhood in Austria, and widened their scope because this brought into the secret fraternity such young adventurers as Otto Skorzeny, who later became Hitler's freebooter, with a license to kill and the freedom to collect and store away all the weaponry and wealth to help the Brotherhood survive any disaster.

And disaster was clearly on the horizon. This was the time of the Battle of Stalingrad. It was a turning point in the war, and Bormann recognized this, long before others, caught in the detail of military operations or the bureaucracy of slave labor and mass liquidation.

The bull-necked Koch had been put into the Ukraine to whip the Russian civilians into line and feed the German factories with able-bodied men and women. He was helped by another Bormann appointee, Fritz Sauckel, who shipped three million workers to stoke the fires of the Ruhr. Five million Russian soldiers were captured and treated as slaves, with a total disregard for the usual rules of war. Out of this number, four million died from neglect, ill-treatment, or the conditions in the camps. Among those who died slowly and in black misery was Stalin's son Jacob.

Revenge came in the winter of 1942. A trap was set at Stalingrad on the basis of information leaked from Hitler's court. The source of this information was close to Bormann.

At Stalingrad, the armies of two rival ideologies clashed in a struggle for possession of a city that was not originally considered a prime military objective. Hitler's plans were to strike for the oil of the Caucasus. Behind his armies, the Slav population was to work German farming colonies in the Ukrainian granary of the Thousand-Year Reich. The Russians shared bottom place with the Jews in that outrageous philosophy which put the master race, the Germans, at the pinnacle of human evolution.

All this and more was known to Stalin in the greatest detail. He diverted Hitler from his Caucasian objective by planting the idea that Stalingrad had great symbolic meaning. He then drew into the Stalingrad area the best of Hitler's Blitzkrieg forces. Finally he circled the entire battlefield and moved through the long winter nights a vast assembly of tanks, artillery, and men. In his speech on the twenty-fifth anniversary of the Revolution, November 7, 1942, Stalin had made the cryptic statement: "There's going to be a holiday in our street, too." He was referring to the street and the city named after him. Less than two weeks later, the trap closed there.

The historian writing after the event has information denied to the generals conducting a battle as complex as Stalingrad and of such a vast scale. A German field marshal captured there, Friedrich von Paulus, did not suffer afterthoughts. Nor was he under the usual compulsion to rewrite history in order to exonerate himself. He remained in the Communist camp. He was denied any opportunity to compose his memoirs. He had nothing to gain from distorting the facts: indeed, he had a great deal to lose, including his life. He conveyed to the West his conviction, many years later, that someone with an intimate knowledge of Hitler had kept Stalin informed of each stage in the Russian campaign.

The catastrophe at Stalingrad unmanned Hitler totally. He shared his table now with nobody but Bormann.

The following month, thinking perhaps to lift Hitler out of his gloom, Bormann decreed "preparatory measures to solve the Jewish problem in Europe." He was again demonstrating his natural instinct for pacifying his man: in this case, Hitler, whose outstanding defense mechanism was what we call now "projection," by which the ego protects itself by attributing unpleasant impulses to others. The Jew was a symbol of everything Hitler hated in himself. Now, the turning of the tide against the Nazis at Stalingrad was blamed on the Jews. He recovered his self-esteem in Bormann's ordinance: "For 2,000 years an unsuccessful battle has been waged against Judaism. Only since 1933 have we started to find ways and means in order to enable a complete separation of Judaism from the German masses. . . . A complete removal or withdrawal of the millions of Jews residing in the European economic space is therefore an urgent need in the fight for the security and existence of the German people. Starting with the territory of the Reich, proceeding to the remaining European countries included in the final solution, the Jews are being deported to large camps which have been established . . . where they will either be used for labor or transported still further to the west."

In this way Hitler recovered a little of his courage. Beaten in the field, he smashed the helpless in their homes. By the end of that winter, Bormann had purchased a formal recognition of his power with the lives of those who were driven to the death camps. He had saved the Führer's face, and his reward was his formal appointment, on April 12, 1943, as Secretary to the Führer.

Hitler never again performed his public act of talking to a massed German audience as if he were seducing a woman. This change in behavior told Bormann that the marionette would not again be jerked into life. He needed the Führer to put the seal of approval on his own maneuvers within the Nazi movement, but already he mentally divorced the movement from the nation where it was born. This was clear in his notes, his letters, and his actions, which always gave the lowest priority to the fate of Germany. It explains his personal orders toward the end of the war that would have reduced Germany to total ruin and the German people to corpses. He was concerned instead with a future based on Nazi philosophy, financed by Nazi loot, supported by a personally loyal Brotherhood of the kind that flourished before Germany had seemed to offer an imperial base for the creed of the superman.

Stalingrad robbed Hitler of that singular quality which provided a means of control over the masses. Before, he had aroused in massed German males the sense of virility required by men who manifest all the characteristics of the feminine-masochistic type, wanting to display their manliness by being bullies while simultaneously groveling under harsh orders. He was no longer capable of doing this, and Bormann wisely removed him from the stage. When Hitler did appear before his generals, they later described him as a quivering caricature of the man who thought of himself once as the new Emperor Barbarossa. Nothing the Führer did passed unobserved by Bormann. He monitored every action and listened carefully to the monologues delivered to the closed circle of the court. Accounts of Bormann during the last two years of the war fortify the belief that he was waiting patiently for the collapse of Germany and the moment when the dying Führer would hand over the documents making him the legitimate heir to the movement.

The figure of the Führer was vital in those dying months. Bormann was surrounded by enemies who held superior rank *outside the party*. Their hatred for him echoes down the years. He needed to strengthen his position by making the Führer issue the required orders. As Secretary he had acquired that hidden and secret power which is always the more terrifying for being anonymous. He could initiate or interpret orders, and his voice would be the voice of Hitler. The people obeyed because they feared and worshipped that abstract authority.

Already it had become evident that some powerful men recognized and respected his greater power. Gestapo Müller, still doggedly inquiring into the precisely timed execution of Heydrich, learned from witnesses that the Reich Protector before his murder was once kept waiting outside Hitler's office. Despite his impatience, Heydrich recoiled when the Führer emerged with Bormann, who immediately tugged Hitler in another direction. Schellenberg (who had been told now to concentrate entirely on secret-service activities abroad) recorded that "Heydrich, though convinced of his own power, showed he was afraid."

Bormann was master of Wolf's Lair, the East Prussian head-quarters which impressed Albert Speer as being virtually an animal cage for the Führer. The visitor had to penetrate a series of security rings of electrified barbed wire and get permits to travel through a forest patrolled by wolfhounds before he was granted an audience with the Secretary, who would then convey the nature of his business to Hitler.

Bormann had his eye on Speer, who could slip through Hitler's defenses on the basis of their old friendship and long talks about architecture. The War Production Minister said, with that arrogance which led so many Germans to underestimate Bormann: "He stood out by his brutality, his lack of culture. A subordinate by nature, he treated his own subordinates as if he were dealing with oxen. He was a peasant."

The peasant's control was enough to drive the German military caste out of its collective mind. He told General Alfred Jodl: "Never remind a dictator of his own errors. This is a psychological necessity. Otherwise he will lose confidence."

Jodl admitted later to the tribunal which hanged him that, as chief of land operations, he followed that dictum. Had he contradicted Hitler, he would have been in trouble with Bormann for disturbing the Führer's meditations.

"The more absurd the Führer's ideas, the more rapturously you should welcome them," Bormann advised another visitor, who was thunderstruck by Hitler's plan to sabotage the big Russian industrial center at Magnetogorsk, far beyond the Urals. "All you should do is make showy preparations. Keep giving assurances that plans are going forward full speed. Then, gradually, drop by drop, spread the notion that certain outside factors may defer the glorious consummation of this affair. The sense that things may be deferred should seep through in such a way that the author of the project finds himself wondering at his own earlier enthusiasm and begins discreetly to shelve the whole thing—if he hasn't already forgotten about it."

Some of the crazier schemes originated with Bormann or were palmed off onto the Führer during sessions around the fireside. At the time, they seemed to Allied observers to be part of the childish gangsterism of the Bormann crew. Gangsterism there was, but conceived with an eye to the future. When British commandos tried to kidnap Field Marshal Erwin Rommel, the first intelligence reports were snapped up by Bormann.

He was building a picture of international Nazism. Spy chief Schellenberg was expected to send him a copy of all operations abroad. In this way Bormann knew the Nazi networks in the Mideast and Latin America, and the large German espionage bases in the Iberian peninsula. He knew the names of Nazi agents and sympathizers, including that of an Egyptian named Anwar Sadat, who was destined to become the President of the United Arab Republic. With the benefit of hindsight, one can see that the self-appointed guardian of an ideology, with his Brotherhood watchdogs, would require a thorough knowledge of those territories where Nazism had taken root or would find friendly accommodation. He had at his finger tips all the details required for moving money secretly through the channels arranged for German espionage funds, for moving special cargoes like the dismantled rockets shipped by U-boat to Japan, and for establishing fortified camps abroad for survivors of the coming collapse in Europe.

There was nobody to supervise his requests for this information. It was held to be either information required by Hitler or, if it seemed too trival, a matter of petty detail occupying the fussy mind of the Secretary. He was regarded with amused contempt by middle-rank Nazis and by those chieftains not directly engaged in a power struggle. This was his strength, of course, this contempt he invited by his deliberate display of coarse manners and lack of refined knowledge. He created fear in men like Himmler, who recognized the peasant cunning and who said: "He would wreck a scheme to end the war by twisting it into a compromise with Stalin." He doubtless rejoiced in the aristocratic superiority of the chief of the General Staff, General Heinz Guderian, who spluttered: "Everything had to be done through this sinister guttersnipe."

Guttersnipe . . . peasant . . . a pig rooting for potatoes—these were useful terms of camouflage for a man who had disposed of Röhm, Streicher, Hess, possibly Heydrich, and who was moving in for the kill against Himmler, Goebbels, and Göring; a man who built up party funds in the years of early starvation with schemes like compulsory insurance for all Nazis, who found a way to charge royalties whenever Hitler's profile appeared on postage stamps or posters or government bills, and who trapped the slippery Himmler in the end by getting him appointed to the hopeless and humiliating post of Supreme Commander of Army Group Vistula, which horrified the soldiers and made Himmler radiant with dreams of glory never to be fulfilled.

Long before the July 1944 plot to kill Hitler, Bormann had taken control of the routes to freedom and the large stores of wealth established abroad. The truth was best expressed by the Führer himself when, nearing his end, he screamed at his personal photographer, Heinrich Hoffmann: "Whoever is against Bormann is against the state."

CHAPTER 7

Martin Bormann began to plan for a Fourth Reich after the German defeat at Stalingrad. He called secret meetings in 1943 of those industrialists who financed Hitler's rise to power ten years earlier. They listened to Bormann because he had demonstrated a superior talent in the money game, in conspiracy and the shuffling of secret funds. It was not Bormann's fault that the Führer had lost his ability to hypnotize the masses. Bormann proposed the distribution of liquid assets to safe parts of the world; the accumulation of gold and other treasures in the Alps; and the assembly of bodyguards of devout Nazis into an Alpine fortress with escape routes into nearby countries. Out of this grew notorious organizations, among them ODESSA, for the protection of Nazis and the preservation of the faith. The full story took another thirty years to surface. The clues floated into public view at long intervals.

Bormann's preparations had been known to the wartime Allies. In 1946, a few details leaked into an American Treasury report. British and U.S. Treasury agents were on the trail but they wanted to maintain total secrecy. They were in competition with the Soviet Union for the capture of the Fourth Reich's hidden leaders and funds worth 800 million American dollars. By 1973 the situation had changed. Bormann's financial wizardry at war's end virtually made sure that Nazi funds would be inflated into a vast fortune. Gold was now regarded as the only safe source of wealth, and some ninety-five tons of it were thought to be still in Nazi hands. This was a great deal in a world where only 75,000 tons of gold were known to be cumulatively in private *and* public ownership. The situation had changed politically, too. Once covert Nazis were challenging their enemies to come and get them if they dare. Some hungered to prove that they had been right all along, and that National Socialism was the best antidote to Communism. Others had prospered in lonely places, having used Bormann's funds to pile up their fortunes: these men wanted to spend their money freely in their declining years. If Martin Bormann was alive, he was more likely now to be challenged to come into the open. In these new circumstances, the professional Nazi-hunters saw no value in further secrecy. It was possible for the public to get an over-all view, to put together scraps of history. Then the exposure of ODESSA and its brother organizations began.

ODESSA was no longer an intriguing fiction; it was a hard reality. It was an organization for the protection of former SS and Gestapo men who became, in their turn, the guardians of the party and its philosophy. ODESSA had branched into new adventures as postwar society became more tolerant of men involved in war crimes. It began to change as more and more of its children crept back into German public life. It became the parent of new organizations that took up the campaign to put into key jobs those who believed in National Socialist ideals. All owed their financial existence and took direction from the Brotherhood strategists. There were groups like Comradely Aid (Kameradschaftshilfe) to take care of military experts; the Salzburg Circle to train defendants awaiting trial for war crimes; Action-for-Comrades to filter into the police agencies those who sympathized with any campaign to disown Hitler in order to make National Socialism again acceptable.

All had roots in the talks that began in 1943 and reached a climax at Strasbourg the following year, twenty days after the plot to kill Hitler failed. In the Hotel Maison Rouge on August 10, 1944 were gathered the heads of industrial dynasties once again in need of Bormann's talents. The War Ministry and the Ministry of Armaments were represented. Ostensibly, they brooded upon the need to dispatch abroad the blueprints of secret weapons. In truth, nobody there believed in either Hitler's magic or the wild promises of secret devices for mass destruction. Technical men like Willy Messerschmitt had produced such great aircraft as the Me-109. They were not fools. They knew they were beaten. (Messerschmitt later slipped into Spain and built up a small hardware business while continuing to design new aircraft.) The concern for the safety of Germany's industrial secrets concealed the real purpose of the conference, making it possible to enlist the co-operation of German intelligence and police agencies abroad, whose more dogged and dogmatic servants would have been outraged to learn that industrialists were preparing for postwar economic operations. In truth, each industrialist was to set himself up abroad, unobtrusively, and with party aid. In return, the party (which here meant Martin Bormann) would expect to draw upon financial reserves later.

The Strasbourg conference was documented in detail. The files were discovered by American counterintelligence. The information was distributed among Allied government agencies concerned with the recovery of stolen goods. Some of the contents leaked out through the Italian Government Recovery Office, which sought stolen art treasures and discovered that Bormann had arranged for them to be stored inside the Alpine Fortress. Other details were disclosed after President Juan Perón's overthrow in Argentina, when Sylvano Santander, later appointed ambassador to Spain, took charge of investigations into Nazi-financed commercial enterprises in Latin America. The Czech government exposed a part of the mystery when divers lifted out of Black Lake a number of sealed boxes containing similar information and other Nazi documents. But Prague, regarded in those days as Communist and untouchable, found willing listeners mostly in countries like Yugoslavia. The government there was fascinated to receive from the Black Lake boxes a list of 1,800 Yugoslavs who had been secret Gestapo agents.

All these bits and pieces interlocked. ODESSA's sources of money were made clear. Bormann had directed an intricate plan for the distribution of funds through foreign companies which were listed by the U.S. Treasury Department in a 1946 report. The list covered 750 different business enterprises scattered from Switzerland to the Mideast and Latin America. There were 200 in the Iberian peninsula; 35 in Turkey; 98 in Argentina; 214 in Switzerland—"a technical network," as it had been described at the Strasbourg conference, manned by self-professed experts in industrial processes. Research institutions had been established near lakes and hydro-power plants so that the "engineers" of a new Fourth Reich had the camouflage of scientific inquiry to cover their hoarding of material and funds. ODESSA's early days were financed by the sale of discarded U.S. and other Allied weapons, transport, and scrap metal through Mideast import-export agencies.

Valid German securities, issued in the 1930's and still convertible three or four decades later, were moved out of the Third Reich through the network of foreign companies under secret German control. These were worth, in 1944, about $100 million. The postwar federal government would not cash these securities without proper identification of ownership. This position had been anticipated by Bormann. Many a minor SS officer has told of being required by his superiors to write his signature and bank account number on blank sheets of paper for the purpose of eventual withdrawals. These bank accounts were to be used by prominent Nazis and businessmen who, as recorded in the captured documents from the Strasbourg conference, might expect to spend some time in jail on charges of war crimes. The whole point of the conference was to face realistically the period of Allied occupation. The wives and children of major war criminals would be looked after. Less obvious figures from Hitler's past would rebuild the party's foundations, abroad if necessary, in Germany if possible.

The machinery was set in motion to concentrate and conceal the sources of future wealth. A network of railroads brought "subhumans" from all over Europe to the death camps. The same brisk efficiency organized traffic in the other direction. Art treasures, jewelry, precious stones, gold teeth, and loot were freighted into the Alpine Fortress. A German company, Degussa, melted gold fillings into gold bars. The Reichsbank's special department for stolen goods (not, of course, identified in such frank terms) took charge of assets that would be difficult to convert immediately into liquid cash. The concentration camp at Oranienburg processed the gold and crated the jewelry. Everything was funneled into the Altaussee region of Hitler's Bavarian retreat. There, the myth of a last Nazi military stand was fostered. The Alpine Fortress was, of course, a natural piece of camouflage. There were 17,500 residents registered there in 1944, and a year later the U.S. occupation authorities counted 80,000 adult civilians. They were not soldiers fighting to the end. They were the families of German notables, and men already traveling the secret escape routes. The confusion was majestic. The Gestapo chief Ernst Kaltenbrunner dispatched from Berlin to this region, according to British Treasury agents, fifty cases of gold coins, two million American dollars, two million Swiss francs, five cases of diamonds and other precious stones, and a quantity of gold bars, all buried in the grounds of the house where he finally took refuge. Josef Pucherl, a local farmer, dug up two iron boxes containing more than 10,000 gold coins some time after Kaltenbrunner's capture.

The Organisation der SS-Argehörigen (ODESSA) did not function well in the beginning. Bormann's own accountant, an economist of eccentric imagination, Dr. Helmut von Hummel, had to bury some $5 million worth of gold coins near Hitler's retreat before himself going underground. He had failed to make contact with "Haddad Said," in reality SS Captain Franz Roestel, an escape organizer who later commuted on Brotherhood business between Spain and Uruguay. By then, the escape lines were fairly secure. They linked distribution centers, and each line was knotted at fifty-mile intervals with wayside sanctuaries. The staff at each station knew only about the next station up or down the line. Die Spinne (The Spider) took its name from this system. The main threads ran between Hamburg and Rome by land, and between Hamburg and Genoa by sea. Almost inevitably, they overlapped Jewish escape lines. Much of what is known now about ODESSA and its more sophisticated partner, Die Spinne (used for large-scale operations only), comes from Israeli dignitaries who were experts in the early postwar years at moving thousands of survivors out of Europe. Thus Ante Pavelić, the Nazi chief of the Croat breakaway state, escaped along a route overlapping a Jewish line to Rome. There, the Catholic church had given refuge to half of the surviving 8,000 Jews of that city at the same time that help was also provided for Nazi escapers.

The confusion and urgency of the times had been foreseen by Bormann. Refugee camps were utilized to make contacts. What might have surprised him was the speed with which this primitive start developed into a more intricate system. By 1955, German prisoners released from Russia were directed to lawyers who would protect their interests. ODESSA had branched into legal activities to test public acceptance of returning Nazis, and subsidiaries like HIAG used political pressure at home and abroad to take the heat off the fugitives. HIAG, for instance, led the Bonn government to permit former SS officers to join the new federal army, and to keep the same rank as they had held under Hitler. HIAG, an acronym for the German title of Mutual Aid Committee of Soldiers of the former Waffen SS, showed how much things had improved when it put on a public platform General Kurt ("Panzer") Meyer, the SS commander who was sentenced to death by a Canadian tribunal. On May 20, 1960, Meyer was not only a long way from execution, but also out of jail and addressing HIAG's mass meeting thus: "SS veterans will continue to fight for the things for which our dead have fallen." Nobody questioned his implied argument that the dead Canadians (whose massacre led to Meyer's death sentence) had fallen for the wrong cause.

Such a bold reversal of values shocked those who had fought against fascism. It demonstrated how rapidly and luxuriantly National Socialist ideas revived under ODESSA's protective wings. The evidence had always been there that Martin Bormann and his henchmen were capable of infinite ingenuity. The new growth was no more astonishing than that of AHSDI, the Adolf Hitler Fund of German Industry. It placed at Bormann's disposal in 1933 an unknown fortune contributed by German industrialists. Each year they gave more, and each year Bormann built up the Third Reich a little more extravagantly. Within a decade, AHSDI provided the financial resources for the Führer to govern Europe and hammer at the Kremlin doors. ODESSA's secret rise was slower; its changes less vivid.

"The Nazi regime in Germany has developed well-arranged plans for the perpetuation of Nazi doctrines after the war," reported the Research and Analysis branch of OSS in March 1945. "Some of these plans have already been put into operation and others are ready to be launched on a widespread scale immediately upon termination of hostilities in Europe."

This prediction was based upon deciphered radio communications between Germany and secret stations in South America. The messages were intercepted by British intelligence from a base in Bermuda, in concert with American code breakers. Most of the traffic was between Berlin and Buenos Aires. The outward-bound messages were relayed by the powerful German Navy transmitter at Bordeaux, in occupied France. "Little Bill" Stephenson's headquarters in New York processed an immense amount of secret traffic, totaling over one million code groups a day. Intelligence on Nazis in South America was gathered mostly by Stephenson's network for reasons connected with U.S. foreign policy in that region. He sent to General Donovan as much information as he could, knowing that the OSS had gathered "the most brilliant team of analysts in the history of intelligence." In return, reports were passed to the British by American intelligence men: notably, Allen Dulles, then heading OSS in Switzerland, who on one occasion collected some 2,000 microfilm photographs of German diplomatic correspondence during a period of eighteen months. Much of this correspondence was directly concerned with South American plans and thus provided independent confirmation of what Stephenson's radio intercepts had disclosed.

The German postwar plans, as seen by the OSS analysts, were summarized thus: "Nazi party members, German industrialists and the German military, realizing that victory can no longer be attained, are now developing postwar commercial projects, endeavouring to renew and cement friendships in foreign commercial circles and planning for renewals of pre-war cartel agreements.

"German technicians, cultural experts and undercover agents have well-laid plans to infiltrate into foreign countries with the object of developing economic, cultural and political ties. German technicians and scientific research experts will be made available at low cost to industrial firms and technical schools in foreign countries. German capital and plans for the construction of ultramodern technical schools and research laboratories will be offered at extremely favourable terms since they will afford the Germans an excellent opportunity to design and perfect new weapons."

A modified version of this report found its way into State Department and Foreign Office files:

"We are in possession of photostat copies of several volumes of German plans which include a propaganda program directed at removing Allied control measures by 'softening up' the Allies through a subtle plea for 'fair treatment' of Germans. Later the program will be expanded and intensified with the object of giving rebirth to Nazi doctrines and furthering German ambitions for world domination. Unless these plans are checked they will present a constant menace to postwar peace and security."

Secret contacts had been made with influential Germans who might be persuaded to help the Allies in the climactic months of the war. There was a difference, however, in the motives of such Germans. This may seem elementary now; then, it was less acknowledged. There were German military commanders who wanted badly to escape the consequences of defeat and who had already convinced themselves that they had all along fought Bolshevism. There were Nazi party officials, Gestapo and SS chiefs, and large groups of defecting German intelligence agents who wanted to get out of the ruins of the Third Reich to rebuild the faith abroad and rekindle it inside a reborn Germany when memories had faded. Important to these hard-line Nazis were the voluminous notes taken by the literal-minded evangelist of the movement, Martin Bormann. These Bormann Papers, as they were called later, were regarded with the same possessive awe as the great religious documents of the past or the works of Marx and Lenin.

It was known that Bormann had prepared these papers long before he left the burning ruins of Berlin. "George Wood," a senior German Foreign Office man, supplied this kind of information to Allen Dulles, along with data on German intelligence nets that might provide transport, shelter, and safe haven. Similar informants reported that the Führer himself had authorized Bormann to take charge of a special staff of stenographers and typists who would set down fresh installments of the thoughts of the first leader of the National Socialist movement. Thus the faith would be preserved.

Before a full-scale hunt for Bormann could be mounted, however, the conflict between Russia and the West produced a new set of priorities. In this political climate, attention shifted away from escaping war criminals, who were favored already by the physical conditions of ravaged Europe and the structure of various Nazi agencies Bormann had counted upon to help his escape and the safe evacuation of his papers and financial resources.

There were eight million men and women who belonged to the Nazi party when Germany capitulated. Bormann was among the hundreds of more highly placed Germans who had the right to wear the death's-head insigne, the black uniform, and the runic double-S flash as an honorary SS officer.

The word "honorary" was not the invention of some Nazi wit. To belong to the SS *was,* in that fanatical atmosphere, an honor. The SS guarding the Reich Chancellery were men chosen for their tall slim figures and their blond, blue-eyed beauty, from which Hitler was reputed to get a certain satisfaction. The SS ran the death camps and held the key positions in the farmers' advisory bureaus and departments on racial policy. The SS chieftains were the watchdogs over science and health, with the key to the scriptures of the Führer. They were "a new form of religious sect," said Eichmann's aide in butchering the Jews, SS Major Dieter Wisliceny. There were SS sections devoted to German archeology, baby farms, and collecting skeletons ("preferably undamaged" was the proviso in a request to Professor Hans Fleischhacker* regarding Jewish specimens, which "should be done to death without harm to the skull"). There were SS institutes for alchemy and astrology; for the adaptation of horses to the steppes, but not, oddly enough, for the experimental uranium pile in the Black Forest. The SS ran night clubs in foreign capitals. Their business enterprises were in parts of the world conveniently located for the more farsighted Nazis, those who were later wanted for war crimes.

Their leaders were planning escape long before the end. Bormann called for another 6,000 boys aged fifteen years to be mobilized in February 1945 while the Grand Master of the Order of the SS, Heinrich Himmler, was secretly meeting Count Folke Bernadotte, of Sweden, in the attempt to save his own skin. Werner Naumann,

---

* Fleischhacker did not change his name after the war, as most of his colleagues did, and was lecturing on biology almost thirty years later in Frankfurt.

the Nazi Secretary of State for Propaganda, made a speech in Munich praising a twelve-year-old "soldier" for his loyalty, while Naumann himself was actually in Munich to arrange to go underground.

General Karl Wolff, head of German police and SS units in Italy, and others with bargaining power there were making deals with the Allied secret service in Switzerland for the capitulation of the German Army in Italy. "Wolff is a rabid SS follower of Himmler," wrote Field Marshal Viscount Alanbrooke in his diary. "It just does not seem plausible." But it was. Wolff sold out in return for assurance from Allen Dulles that he would not be tried for war crimes.

"All German males in a house displaying the white flag will be shot!" was a decree issued while Himmler was trying to curry favor with the Allies by an offer to liberate death-camp prisoners. Bormann, while stuffing valuable official Third Reich papers into sealed bags, proclaimed: "Carry on the good fight, or die. Only scoundrels will leave their posts. . . ."

There was a variety of escape organizations. Those for SS members were organized with the help of German intelligence abroad; and SS leaders could travel pretty much as they pleased, being answerable to nobody. They could ship money and valuables by Lufthansa, the German airline, or by way of neutral cities like Madrid; and they had their own claims upon the cargo and passenger space in U-boats and shipping in general. The leader of India's anti-British conspirators, S. Chandra Bose, had been brought to Germany by U-boat for talks with Hitler in 1943, at the request of Schellenberg, acting in concert with Himmler. Japanese Rear Admiral Iso Kojima traveled to Germany by U-boat in 1944 and returned with passengers selected by SS Major General Wilhelm Mohnke and a quantity of gold bullion.

The SS were the chief target, or so they suspected, of Allied revenge. They were also the natural channel for passing along to future generations the Nazi mystique. Bormann had kept a record of Hitler's secret speech to the officers' class of 1939, in which the Führer spoke of a development extending over another hundred years, at the end of which, by careful breeding, an elite would exist to rule the world. "Those who see in National Socialism nothing more than a political movement know scarcely anything of it," he said on another occasion. "It is more even than a religion: it is the will to create man anew."

Because the inner workings of this secret society were hidden from the public eye, the SS had a reputation for the mysterious, the sinister, and the incomprehensible, which gave freedom to provide for its own survival.

Bormann was perfectly in tune with the double-mindedness of the SS empire. Fine phrases concealed the behavior of gangsters. Citizens were bullied into actions that were below the dignity or beyond the courage of an SS man. There were 45,000 Gestapo watchdogs to see that orders were obeyed in the streets; 65,000 agents who looked for enemies within the state; 2,800,000 regular police led by senior SS commanders. There were 40,000 guards to terrorize inmates of twenty major concentration camps and 160 slave-labor camps. The Armed, or Waffen, SS had 950,000 in uniform at one time. Another 100,000 SS security-service informers made sure that every German displayed in word and deed (thoughts were more elusive) unquestioning loyalty. To prevent any secrets leaking to the public, no SS man could go to an ordinary court of law.

But Bormann had his own power to counterbalance Himmler's empire. He had created this immense and secret power within the party since he took control of the central administrative machinery and the treasury. The barons and liegemen of the Third Reich were his party functionaries. They formed a pyramid, with several hundred thousand block leaders at the base and the forty-one Gauleiter at the top. The Führer's mystical powers flowed down to them through Bormann, and nobody else. These party functionaries would continue to follow his directions: they were cogs in the administrative machine, and he had always kept them well oiled.

Moreover, he had already browbeaten those senior military figures who might be helpful, and others, such as Göring, he could override. Foreign intelligence networks were at his disposal, for he need only get the Führer's approval to make arrangements that would benefit himself.

Yet the secret power residing in the SS was necessary to Bormann's personal plans. After Hitler's defeat at Stalingrad foreshadowed the end of Nazi Germany, his most eager allies were the SS formations. They knew already that the Allies considered the SS to be a criminal organization. Himmler, isolated in his own world of self-delusion, thought he could negotiate with the Allies for his safety, using methods that seemed normal after a lifetime within the SS structure. He would barter, use blackmail, appeal to emotions, evoke the specter of Bolshevism. He would buy his freedom with the lives of condemned Jews, perhaps; or establish a working relationship with General Dwight Eisenhower, whom he seems to have regarded as purely a *Junker*-type general (even the name had, to his ear, an East Prussian timbre). Others, from Kaltenbrunner down, had heard the warnings of what would be done at war's end to punish them. The Moscow Declaration signed by Roosevelt, Churchill, and Stalin vowed to pursue the guilty "to the furthest corners of the earth."

Bormann's most willing helpers, and the most ingenious, were clearly to be found in the SS, which included 200,000 *foreigners*. These were the SS men who could provide temporary refuge in their own homes in Austria, Belgium, and, most useful of all (because of proximity to neutral Sweden), Denmark. Most SS men were terrified of exposure. They had no need to wait for the Allied judgment at Nuremberg: "The SS was used for purposes which were criminal, involving the persecution and extermination of the Jews, brutalities and killings in the concentration camps . . . slave-labor programs and the maltreatment and murder of prisoners of war." The SS had liquidated 2,500,000 Poles, 520,000 gypsies, 473,000 Russian prisoners, 4 to 5 million Jews. Another 100,000 "incurables" had been gassed under the "euthanasia" program. Thus more than a million men formed an "army of outlaws," and their racial fanaticism was not likely to be changed overnight. The most devout among them, from Bormann's viewpoint, were likely to be the most reliable.

CHAPTER 8

"The youth of a people of eighty millions has bled to death on the battlefields of Europe while you enriched yourself, feasted, robbed estates, swindled and oppressed the people. Our young officers have taken the field with a faith and idealism unique in the history of the world. By the hundred thousands they have gone to their death. But for what? For the German Fatherland, for our greatness and future? No. They died for you, for your life of luxury and your thirst for power."

General Wilhelm Burgdorf sprawled across a bench in front of the most powerful man in Nazi Germany: Martin Bormann. The time was 4:30 A.M. on April 28, 1945. The place: a bunker under the Reich Chancellery in Berlin. Both men had been drinking all night. Between them and the world outside were sixteen feet of concrete topped by six feet of solid earth. When bombs exploded, the bunker quivered as the shock waves were transmitted through the sandy subsoil of the city.

Nobody had dared talk to Bormann in such terms. Not even Adolf Hitler, asleep in another of the bunker's eighteen tomblike rooms.

"My dear fellow," said Bormann after a pause, "you don't have to be personal about it."

This odd exchange was recorded later, in a book, by a young military aide, Captain Gerhard Boldt. He was astonished. Bormann never drank when Hitler was around. And as for General Burgdorf, he had deserted the traditional officer caste to become the kind of rabid Nazi who normally fawned upon Bormann, the Führer's alter ego.

Two days later Hitler was dead and the way clear for Bormann to become legally the Führer of a Fourth Reich. The proper documents had been drawn up. He had reached the climax of a long climb through the central core of power. While others, no less ambitious, fought for positions of eminence, Bormann stayed with the hard and unobtrusive tasks at the heart of the whole machine: the party. He had what he needed most: responsibility as Party Minister for the future of Nazism. He had volumes of notes on which to build the faith; but more to the point, he had the duly witnessed statement of the last German Emperor that he was the successor to the throne. He could afford to smile at a drunken general.

Burgdorf in his maudlin state had talked of some higher ideal. This same Burgdorf gave Rommel the poison with which he killed himself, on orders conveyed by Bormann after the July 1944 plot to kill Hitler. Idealism had a different meaning in Bormann's lexicon. While Hitler fussed over the smallest detail of conquest and extermination, Bormann made himself the richest individual in the land, Göring notwithstanding. He did this for the sake of the movement, beginning in 1933 when Germans stormed the new ruling party with sycophantic schemes to make themselves and the new bosses rich. They came to sell the franchise for "Heil Hitler!" stickers, Christmas trees bent to resemble swastikas, or soap carved into busts of Hitler. They were always met by an unsmiling Bormann, with his fat palm turned up to receive this manna.

Now he was saving for a new Reich. He had decided that the first empire must be consumed by fire to be rid of a leader now found unworthy. This, at any rate, was how he presented himself to Captain Boldt. The young veteran from the Russian front wrote later how Bormann said: "We who have stayed here and kept faith with our Führer, we shall when this fight is victoriously ended be invested with high rank in the state and shall have huge estates."

He had trucked out of Berlin a great quantity of papers recording the history of the dying Third Reich. He had also sent some loose change to Mrs. Bormann and the children, hiding in the Alpine Fortress: 2,200 gold coins worth at that time roughly the price of Monaco. The last documents had been squirreled away into his underground office, a cold gray tomb whose cement walls sweated at night.

Someone shrewder than Boldt was watching these preparations. Gestapo Müller worked quietly in a street nearby. He had heard reports of Burgdorf's outburst, and within hours had left on a mission of his own.

There were no great difficulties in moving about Berlin. The defenses consisted of two understrength Wehrmacht divisions and what was left of the SS volunteer division Nordland, to which was attached a French battalion whose men fought one action within a few blocks of the Reich Chancellery. There was a separate command under Mohnke, who was later hunted for a massacre of Canadian prisoners, and it was to Mohnke that Müller made his way. Neither of them was seen after the burning of Hitler's corpse.

Later, a check on Müller's activities prior to his disappearance showed that he helped Bormann store documents and valuables, and held long talks with the mistress of the hulking Kaltenbrunner, who shared with Eichmann certain hopes for the future. The lady's name was Countess Gisela von Westrop, and she had been gone from Berlin a long while by the time the facts were known. Some said she fled to Switzerland or the Alpine Fortress.

It occurred to more than one observer in the preceding months that Bormann seemed to be shipping an unusual quantity of personal effects to his "Beloved Mommy," at Berchtesgaden. But it was a time when even the weightiest dignitaries asked no questions, not wishing to know about the deals being made, for example, with the advancing Allied forces.

Goebbels had a shrewd notion of treachery afoot. Hitler had married his mistress, Eva Braun, in a macabre ceremony before killing her and himself. Bormann had ordered the necessary gasoline, once more anticipating the Führer's wishes. After the suicide, he had carried Eva outside to burn her corpse, and Goebbels was shocked. The dead girl was in the arms of a man she had always regarded with fear and loathing. Goebbels himself poisoned his six children and then, with his wife, Magda, waited for an SS orderly to shoot them both dead. "I do not intend," he had said, "to run around the world like an eternal refugee."

Bormann did intend to travel. He donned the uniform of an SS major general, his honorary rank, and crammed some papers into a leather topcoat, including Hitler's last will and testament, of which he was executor. This blamed "international Jewry" for everything.

He left the Führer's bunker on the night of May 1, 1945. By then, the Russians had learned of Hitler's presence in Berlin. They lobbed shells into the Reich Chancellery grounds but they seemed to be in no hurry. There was opposition from the improvised army of sailors, Hitler Youths, and aged home guards, stiffened by SS troops. There was no resistance from the bombastic Burgdorf; *that* General was shot dead by an unknown hand.

Hitler's former adjutant, and brother of Martin Bormann, Albert, waited in a wooden cuckoo-clock chalet near the Führer's bomb-scarred retreat eighty miles southeast of Munich, in the Alpine Fortress, where SS and fanatical young Werewolves were advertised as ready to wage guerrilla war. Nothing stirred. The story of a secret resistance in the mountains extending from Eagle's Nest to the borders of Austria, Switzerland, and northern Italy was a propaganda operation that delayed Allied entry into Berlin, 320 miles to the north. If all went according to plan, Martin had won the extra time he needed to gather up documents that would revive their fortunes.

Unknown even to Hitler's most intimate friends, Martin Bormann already held legal possession to the Berchtesgaden estate. Registered in his name was a complex of eighty-nine buildings worth a considerable fortune. Furthermore, he was the properly registered owner of Hitler's birthplace, the house of Hitler's parents, and all the properties Hitler had given, so he thought, to Eva Braun and other favorites.

The "gold-rush town" atmosphere Bormann had created around Berchtesgaden was obliterated by Allied bombing a week earlier. The wooden chalet where Hitler had retreated like a bogus peasant, with its cushions embroidered with swastikas by adoring ladies, was destroyed. So was the mansion on the mountaintop, likened to a stranded steamship by the same critics who resented Bormann's construction projects all through the valley.

Plodding toward what remained of Eagle's Nest, his head full of plans to recover that glory, went Dr. Werner Naumann, the Nazi propagandist, who eight years later was accused of conspiring to restore the Nazi regime. His purpose was to get in contact with those who wanted to escape abroad: SS officers, Gauleiter, and bureaucrats sharing the spirit of brotherhood with Bormann. He was also bringing Albert Bormann the glad tidings that brother Martin was on his way.

Ernst Kaltenbrunner was heading in the same direction, disguised as an International Red Cross doctor, if disguise was possible for a man nearly seven feet tall with a face slashed with scars. He knew of plans to use escape routes through the Alps, but he was not sure if his old friend Martin Bormann could help. He had a rendezvous with Adolf Eichmann, the bureaucrat who took the view that the subhuman breeds should be exterminated.

His fellow Austrian Otto Skorzeny had already gone to earth in the region. Earlier, when Kaltenbrunner had been asked what to do about syphilitic prostitutes, he had said (with all the majesty of the law behind him as Heydrich's successor): "Bury them." It had been Skorzeny's task to obey the order. Now he was burying SS documents instead.

General Reinhard Gehlen, in this same part of Bavaria, was also burying documents. His were the German intelligence files on Russia, which he later sold to the Americans for more than mere money.

Hitler's ghost would have found the situation not altogether discouraging. The torch might yet be passed on. All his thoughts were preserved in the voluminous files kept by Martin Bormann. The last leader of the Hitler Youth might be the first of a new era: Artur Axmann had also escaped from Berlin and was heading toward the mountain retreat. So was Bormann's personal assistant, SS Colonel Wilhelm Zander, carrying a trunkload of documents from the party chancellery, which he concealed at a lake forty miles south of Munich and somewhat short of the great assembly area around Berchtesgaden.

At the other end of Germany, far to the north, near the biggest U-boat yards, test pilot Hanna Reitsch was reporting events to a bewildered Grand Admiral, Karl Doenitz, who had made neither head nor tail of the confusing cables sent him by Bormann. Her report made several things clear. Until the very end, Bormann was functioning in a conspiratorial role. He had delayed the dispatch of messages, he had distorted the meaning of Göring's distress signals from the Alpine Fortress, and he had continued as if there was a future for a Nazi government in which he would remain supreme. He had destroyed his last two rivals, Himmler and Göring, in the eyes of the Führer even during the preparations for Hitler's suicide. Hanna Reitsch had been ordered by Hitler to make sure "a traitor does not succeed me," and by that he had meant Himmler. She had flown out of Berlin in a small Arado 96 training plane, with Russians firing from all sides.

She ran into Himmler as she left Doenitz's command post, and demanded point-blank to know if he had been in contact with the enemy offering proposals for peace without the Führer's orders. Himmler agreed that he had. Hanna Reitsch said: "You betrayed your Führer and your people in the very darkest hour? High treason, Herr Reichsführer!"

Then she stamped away to write her notes. The most vivid picture in her mind was Bormann in the bunker scribbling "in his everlasting exercise books and bits of cardboard," as if to record the momentous events for posterity. She thought he planned to escape so the papers might take their place "among the great chapters of German history." Hanna Reitsch contributed one of these chapters herself, both in her aviation career and in her subsequent testimony before Allied interrogators.

In the nearby streets of Hamburg shuffled the former Foreign Minister, Joachim von Ribbentrop, still suffering delusions of grandeur at the same time that he tried to find employment in his old trade as a wine peddler. He called himself "Reiser" and wore dark glasses, a black ambassadorial Homburg, and a striped black suit. In his pocket was a letter he had composed to Winston Churchill, part of which is worth quoting as a reminder of these ingratiating and even self-abasing characters. Ribbentrop had made plain his hatred for the British, yet he wrote now, in his abominable English, "to place myself at the disposal of the British Commander in Chief. . . . I do not know if the old and noble English custom of fair play is also applicable to a defeated foe. I also do not know if you wish to hear the political testament of a deceased man." He was offering to convey the Führer's last message, blithely ignoring the fact that this had been given to Martin Bormann. He sought an audience with Churchill to convey Hitler's message, entrusted to him "personally and verbally." He had wanted to join the fighting in Berlin but the Führer said no, he must await further instructions in a safe zone. And so here he was, ready and eager to discourse at length on matters of consequence. "In spite of all disappointment and embitterment about the repeated English rejection of the German offers the English-German collaboration has to this last hour always been the political creed of the Fuehrer." He had always considered England his second home. When Germany was winning the war, the Führer and he had never wanted to violate English prestige and esteem. And he took up the refrain that was to haunt the Allies: he had had no idea of what was going on inside those concentration camps. He had once caught some rumor concerning ill-treatment of Jews and of course he had gone straight to the Führer, urging "immediate change. The Fuehrer kept the report . . . and gave me clearly to understand this was a question of the interior authorities."

There were two exits for escaping Nazis, unwittingly provided by Hitler at the humble suggestion of Bormann.

South of Berlin was the "last bulwark against Bolshevism," as Hitler saw it. This was the Alpine Fortress, centered on the Führer's lands at Berchtesgaden. The real master of those estates was Bormann, and the notion of turning Eagle's Nest into a fortress was his. The monster created by Frankenstein (as one Communist spy called Hitler *) was about to destroy his master. He needed this last extravaganza to cover his tracks.

Northwest of the Führer's bunker was Project North. This was the Kaiser-Wilhelm-Kanal at Kiel, on the tip of Germany nearest Sweden.

The first area was in fact the hub of escape routes into Switzerland, Austria, and northern Italy. From it flew captured American bombers on secret missions. So far as Hitler was concerned, they were dropping agents behind enemy lines. In reality, they were delivering major Nazis to sanctuaries like Spain.

The Kiel area provided access to U-boats and other vessels at the naval bases around Hamburg. In Hitler's last hours, it was the headquarters of Grand Admiral Doenitz, actual successor to the Führer. Doenitz was performing in one of the war's great charades. It began on an old steamer, the *Patria*. It ended with comic-opera cabinet meetings in a Flensburg schoolroom, where each day's business began with the new Minister of Food measuring out a thimbleful of rye to each of his colleagues.

Göring, skulking in the mountains at Berchtesgaden, gulped paracodeine tablets and worried about his magnificent art collection of some 1,300 paintings, which came in part from property confiscated from Jews sent to the gas chambers, and which was worth the equivalent of $180 million. This valuation was made in May 1945; a quarter-century later the figure was many times greater.

So much that was taken for granted by May 1945 was to prove infinitely more valuable in the 1970's. A long war had just ended. Allied interrogators moved in a daze through the motley collection of Very Important Prisoners. In the schoolroom where Doenitz conducted the new German government in the style of the old imperial cabinets, there was an argument about appointing a Minister for Churches. Nobody mentioned synagogues, for there was nobody there who would admit then or later that he knew the fate of the Jews. There was another debate on reshuffling the Cabinet. Nobody mentioned that there had not been a German

* Leopold Trepper, Resident Director of the Rote Kapelle, the Red Orchestra, the Russian espionage apparatus in Nazi Europe. Admiral Canaris called any spy ring uncovered in Germany an "orchestra." Secret radio transmitters were "pianos." The organizers were "conductors." Espionage circuits then were given an additional name, usually from their locality.

Cabinet meeting for the past twelve years. Somewhere along the line, messages had been received that Hitler was dead; that Eva Braun had become Mrs. Hitler and was dead, too; and that Martin Bormann had broken loose, a piece of news that must have briefly tightened the muscles in the Grand Admiral's face before he got back into one of the dignified limousines requisitioned from the Führer's stable. The beautifully polished Mercedes moved at a stately pace between mud-spattered British scout cars and canvas-shrouded cannons of grubby British tanks. The distance between the school-cum-cabinet and the Grand Admiral's villa was all of five hundred yards. Fortunately, he had an invitation from the Duke of Holstein to move into quarters better suited to the successor to the Führer of the Third Reich: a castle that had been in the Duke's family for three hundred years, and that would lend a suitable air of pomp and circumstance to the leader of a government dealing with grave matters. Hitler's personal photographer had sent one of his best assistants to capture on film the deliberations of President Doenitz and his chief of the high command of the armed forces, Field Marshal Wilhelm Keitel. They were all living in a dream.

On May 21, 1945, two days before the arrest of the entire Doenitz government (which had been simply overlooked by the Allies during the three confusing weeks after Hitler's suicide), an odd-looking man with a black eye patch walked out of Flensburg. The man carried papers that identified him as Heinrich Hitzinger. On his right and his left walked a military adjutant of the Waffen SS. All of them wore ordinary field-police uniforms, with forged documents in the pockets. They were hoping to make it through Allied control points to their new destination, some five hundred miles south—the alternative named by their late Führer, the Alpine Fortress.

The man in the middle of this trio was in fact SS Field Marshal Heinrich Himmler. He had gone through a discouraging encounter with the Grand Admiral, who cocked his pistol and told the Field Marshal there was no place for him in the new Cabinet. Furthermore, Doenitz quoted a message from Bormann saying that Himmler had been talking treason with the Swedes. The whole episode had dampened Himmler's spirits to the point where he delayed his departure by several days. Not very hopefully, he had looked for Gauleiter Erich Koch, who was to have arrived aboard an icebreaker from East Prussia with plans, if it came to the worst, to board one of the U-boats commanded by dissident captains. (Koch, as it happened, had reached Flensburg, but was hard to spot behind an enormous mustache he had grown since the days when he whipped the Ukrainians into line.)

The sad little procession, now augmented, faltered at a checkpoint between Hamburg and Bremerhaven, where other U-boats waited for an opportunity to slip away. Himmler knew there were plans for escape among Bormann's friends, and he hoped some of them, like Koch, would overlook the fact that Bormann wanted him destroyed as the last of a long list of enemies. Yet thoughts of escape were tempered by Himmler's earlier conviction that "Europe in the future cannot manage without me. It will still need me as Minister of Police. After I've spent an hour with Eisenhower, he'll appreciate that fact."

The former king of the concentration camps was in some such reverie, it seemed to the first British Army Intelligence Corps sergeant who screened the group. The sergeant did not recognize Himmler, and it was only in retrospect that he decided the man was mentally a million miles away. This could well have been the case. Himmler is quoted by Count Lutz Schwerin von Krosigk, Doenitz's Foreign Minister, as being convinced the long-awaited war between the Bolsheviks and the Western Allies would break out any moment, whereupon the Nazis would become the tremor in the scales "and achieve what we could not achieve in war." Schwerin von Krosigk, one of Germany's innumerable counts, had once regarded Himmler as the destined savior of Germany. At this later stage, he tried currying favor with Eisenhower by stating virtuously that he and Doenitz were planning to conduct an investigation into concentration camps.

The British sergeant shunted the group aside. They now wore a mixture of civilian and military clothing in which the coarse gray uniform jackets of the German Field Security Police stood out. If they had worn plain German Army togs, all might have gone well. The Field Security Police, however, had become part of the Gestapo and were on the list of indicted organizations. Two of Himmler's companions were SS Colonel Werner Grothmann and Major Heinz Macher, who both caught attention by a peculiarity of gesture: they behaved as if they gave orders rather than took them.

They had trudged about ninety miles. They were picked up and trucked to British Interrogation Center No. 031, on Lüneburger Heath, where Field-Marshal Bernard Montgomery had his headquarters. The officer commanding the center, Captain Thomas Selvester, stared hard at "a small miserable-looking and shabbily-dressed little chap." Himmler had shaved his mustache and was still wearing the black eye patch. Nevertheless, Selvester made him fall out and sent for Montgomery's intelligence chief, Colonel Michael L. Murphy. "You're Himmler," said Murphy. The man removed his eye patch and put on the familiar rimless spectacles.

In reports of the catastrophe that followed, few details have escaped the dead hand of official secrecy—perhaps for good reason. Himmler began to talk, and somebody's clumsiness silenced him forever. Neither Murphy nor Selvester was under any illusion about the problems in dealing with Nazis who remained fanatical to the end. The danger was always that they might kill themselves before talking. So Himmler was handled gently at first. Captain C. J. L. Wells, of the British Army Medical Corps, found a capsule of cyanide in one of Himmler's pockets, and he said quietly that it might be best to have the prisoner stripped.

Himmler was in a state of nervous agitation. But the calm efficiency of his captors encouraged him. He was explaining his importance to the Third Reich, and his hopes for the future of a new Germany, in which doubtless he would have a big part to play. It was Bormann who had caused his difficulties. Bormann had tricked him into the role of a tin-pot war lord. The bitterness came vomiting out. Himmler had been betrayed by Bormann.

This outburst began before anyone had time to strip Himmler. Guards stood back, listening. Himmler said he was aware of secret arrangements made by the "Bormann clique." Cowards had been preparing places of sanctuary abroad, and of course the rank and file followed. What else could you expect when the leaders ran away? The files on a million SS men alone were at this moment being systematically destroyed. His audience stood silent, aghast, disgusted, aware that the rat was cornered and would betray everyone. A month ago he had been an ersatz war lord. Now he was having a tantrum. Hitler's head of the SS, commander in chief of the Replacement Army and an army group in the field, this chief of a police force so complicated that his captors had not yet unraveled the machinery, was once again the Bavarian schoolmaster's son, shrieking for attention, demanding to be properly recognized. The combination of a violent temper and one of the most heavily burdened consciences in Christendom (for Himmler had not formally broken with the Catholic church, and in the church's eyes he remained a member) produced an avalanche of words, out of which, with luck, some hard facts might be extracted.

Bormann had disappeared from the Führer's bunker twenty-three days ago. The denunciation by his archenemy was about to begin. A British officer of exalted rank was called. He was a man unaccustomed to dealing with vermin. Himmler was in a state of hysteria. What he needed at this point was recognition: a handshake, an attitude of "We're all brothers of the same military caste," some hint that he had been right to suppose the enemy understood better than his friends what a fine upstanding *soldierly* man he had always been. Probably nobody can be blamed for what happened. The Briton of exalted rank bawled out the doctor for not stripping the prisoner according to regulations. Guards grabbed Himmler to remove his clothing. Then would he stand naked, a gray and wrinkled little man who had rejoiced for so long in his jack boots and ankle-length military greatcoat.

He turned his head, and his lips were drawn back. Dr. Wells pushed a finger into Himmler's mouth, probing between the rotting teeth. To get a better grip, he pulled him by his thinning hair, twisting his head around into the light. What Wells had seen was "a small black knob sticking out between a gap in the teeth in the right-hand lower jaw." It was a special capsule encased in hammered silver which had turned black. Himmler bit down, and potassium cyanide squirted from the crushed Zyankali vial.

A grim struggle followed. Himmler was forced to the floor and rubber tubes were thrust down his throat. Emetics were pumped in. The contents of his stomach were pumped out. It took fourteen minutes before the commander of the organization that had destroyed six million human beings, and maimed or mentally twisted millions more, jerked his legs for the last time. The damp air was heavy with the frightful odor of potassium cyanide and sweat. The poison began to turn the corpse green. The face, captured in an official photograph, was that of a rabid fox. Later it relaxed into the features reminiscent of the shortsighted nonentity in another photograph, one showing a younger Himmler in a group of untidy men crowding an ancient panel truck bearing the legend STOSS-TRUPP-HITLER/MÜNCHEN 1923.

The man who had fancied himself a reincarnation of Henry the Fowler was dead. Henry, a medieval Duke of Bavaria, had himself crowned without the formal offices of the Catholic church, and Himmler had studied for the priesthood but rejected any formal loyalty to non-Germanic authority. Henry the Fowler had advanced against the subhuman Slavs, and so, in his fashion, had Himmler.

Montgomery's intelligence chief, looking down at the corpse of the Grand Inquisitor surrounded by a grisly litter of enamel basins and rubber tubes, swabs and bile, clenched his fists in despair. "That was the one man who could have told us where Bormann went to earth."

Another man who might have been in a position to tell was caught in Misery Meadow, on the other side of Germany, in the Alpine Fortress. This was General Reinhard Gehlen, who had buried the microfilms and dossiers with which he demonstrated to Washington within a few more weeks his theory that the real enemy of all right-minded people was Bolshevism. This magnificent distraction began on the very day Himmler killed himself. Its repercussions caused the Western Allies almost at once to slacken their hunt for Nazis and begin to recruit German professionals for the war predicted by Gehlen.

American intelligence officers were hopping around the mountains "like fishermen in a shoal of big fish driven into the shallows" said Victor de Guinzbourg, the U.S. Army's Counter-Intelligence Corps sergeant who netted Gehlen and went on to greater things as an army intelligence colonel. Hermann Göring was caught. Julius Streicher, the worst of the Jew-baiters and publisher of racial pornography, was found lurking near the ruins of Hitler's mountaintop mansion. The former overlord of Italy, Field Marshal Albert Kesselring, gave up with his Army Group G, which Bormann had taken care to let everyone know would "circle the Redoubt [the Alpine Fortress] with steel."

One American spotted a man whose description had been given by Hitler's masseur: "A tough, callous ox. A block of wood. Coarse, hard-bitten, capable only of thinking when he's drunk. A giant, built like a lumberjack, heavy chin, thick neck, straight line down the back of his head. Looks like a big grizzly. Small brown eyes that move like a viper, all glittering. Bad teeth, some missing so he hisses." The masseur, Felix Kersten, knew the details only too well, for he had worked over that Gestapo killer's thick body: it was, of course, Ernst Kaltenbrunner. He had shaved off his mustache, for a disguise.

His mistress, Countess Gisela von Westrop, had bags stuffed with fake dollars and British pound notes manufactured by the death-camp inmates whose sentences were suspended so long as they kept up production of counterfeit money in the biggest criminal operation of its kind in history: Operation Bernhard. At the time, Kaltenbrunner's captors were unaware of the use this hoard would serve, for the Countess carried only a minuscule part of it, along with gold and jewelry from Kaltenbrunner's gas-chamber victims. She was allowed to go, but more was heard of her later, for she was on her way to Swiss banks where more liquid assets had been thoughtfully provided for the escape organizations of which she was the "social secretary."

The fishing continued. Robert Ley was trapped; he was the head of the Labor Front, who deported millions of slave workers, who promoted a "death ray" invention, and who nearly persuaded Hitler to release a new poison gas over London. And out of the woods came a leader of the Werewolf hunting units, Otto Skorzeny.

The prison cages at Augsburg stood athwart one of the lesser escape routes to Italy. They were crammed with a motley collection of German VIP's: field commanders, air-force chiefs, top SS and Gestapo leaders. Above them loomed one of the great castles of Austria, and such was the natural innocence of Allied soldiers that none cared to disturb the frightened inmates behind its ivy-covered walls. This was a pity, for it might have impeded the plans of the prisoners below if the castle had been occupied in the way it most assuredly would have been if a victorious German army had conquered this region instead of easygoing Texans of the 307th CIC unit, mostly thinking about when they could get home. Inside the castle was Bishop Alois Hudal, the cleric who planned to bring Martin Bormann out alive.

On the night of May 23, when Himmler was crunching on the cyanide capsule, the wife of Martin Bormann was being questioned in a remote area of the Austrian Tyrol bordering the Italian city of Bolzano, where she had been tracked down. Earlier she had taken another name and escaped to this spot with the children in a bus disguised as a large ambulance. A few miles away, Captain John C. L. Schwarzwalder, of the 307th, listened solemnly to the small German who said: "I am a general and chief of the intelligence department of the high command. I have information of the highest importance for your Supreme Commander. . . ." To which the young American replied: "You *were* a general—you *were*, sir." Reinhard Gehlen gave a stiff nod. He would be a general again if he could drive a bargain for fifty-two huge containers he had buried in an area around the small chalet where he had been hiding at Misery Meadow. Inside the containers were the details of his networks of secret agents still active behind Russian lines—bands of the White Russian Army of Liberation still operating with other armed groups of Ukrainian nationalists—and priceless dossiers of military, economic, industrial, and political intelligence on the Soviet Union itself.

All SS files had been buried or burned. The Russians, by the time they began hunting, were prevented from seeing photostats of German Army and police files for the good reason that some of those names were on fresh lists of Western hirelings.

Bormann's favorite from the old days, Rudolf Höss, of Auschwitz, was also trapped in time. Of the SS leaders who failed to escape, the majority in Western hands were treated with leniency. Only about 50,000 were estimated to have had direct involvement in fearful crimes. Of the thirty senior SS and police commanders who were Himmler's personal stooges in each military region, sixteen eventually went free. Out of twelve Gestapo and Kripo* bosses, eight survived. Out of six divisional heads in the Reich Central Security Office (RSHA), three survived. Out of eight commanders of liquidation missions in Russia, three survived. By the 1970's, most of the major figures sentenced to long jail terms had been released. The biggest criminals had submerged into the millions of German soldiers and ex-prisoners swarming through the confusion of postwar Europe. Others waited to go, or were already on their way, to travel stations en route to Spain and Latin America.

There were, of course, a thousand eyewitness tales from within a thousand yards of Lake Toplitz, where it was rumored ODESSA's agents had concealed in the cold waters a sealed trunk crammed with incriminating documents that could be used to silence ex-Nazis who collaborated with foreigners. (A small example of what this "collaboration" meant in practice was given more than two decades after the war's end at a German Embassy party in London when the outgoing Ambassador's wife warned the staff never to forget they were among enemies.) Those hard-core SS men who were held in Allied camps became the despair of their "re-educators" because they recited democratic dogma without convincing their captors that they understood what a free society was all about. Allied lawyers who tried to segregate SS men in order to be fair, and who sought retribution for crimes that could be proved, were to find the task all but impossible. They were bedeviled by the presumption that the SS constituted a state within a state. During ten years of Allied war trials, the defendants

* Kriminalpolizei, or Criminal Police, which with the Gestapo (the Secret State Police), and the Security Service (SD) were part of the RSHA.

who were not SS men perpetuated the myth. The idea took hold that Himmler's SS was a kind of gigantic secret-police organization, and it became convenient to an older generation of Germans to cling to this faith. It was said that Heinrich Müller organized the political police of the Weimar Republic into the Gestapo after studying the Russian systems, ignoring the fact that the CHEKA, or GPU, or MVD, or whatever ghastly set of initials applied, were instruments of a revolution. There was never a revolution in Germany. The SS was there to prevent those very changes which the Nazi "revolution" was supposed to produce. The German industrial and financial monopolies were run by the same men as before. The civil service was unchanged. Hitler's ministers strutted in the black uniform with the silver death's-head insigne because there was a widely shared enjoyment of the SS mystique.

Himmler was the Ignatius Loyola who, declared Hitler, created a Jesuit Order for him. Those who entered the SS, or gladly took honorary rank, were admitted to an all-powerful secret society. In the words of Albert Speer in an interview with me in 1972: "The SS cannot be understood and Bormann cannot be understood unless you recognize that 'politics' and 'government' meant to most Germans the rule of occult forces. The struggle between Himmler and Bormann was in part a fight to become chief of the lords of the nation, head of the secret society of carefully selected noblemen."

A graphic description of this mentality was given to me one quiet summer's day in a London club by the former chief of intelligence liaison among British secret services, Colonel Charles H. Ellis, who drafted the plans for an American intelligence agency after the war. Ellis still kept, even in his seventies, the impish sense of humor that distinguishes good intelligence agents. (As he himself has said: "They're no good if they think they should make a career in intelligence, to begin with.") He was recalling the atmosphere in Hitler's Berlin when he was working there. He came home one night and sensed a subtle change in the manner of his landlady. "My husband," she declared with a new hauteur, "is a block master." Her man could hold his head up now, for he had been admitted to the outer circle of the secret circles around the Führer. He had entered into the "popular togetherness" of *Volksgemeinschaft*. As he told this anecdote, Ellis slipped into German. He was an inoffensive little Australian, mild and benign of manner, unfailingly courteous to waiters, with no time for pretension. Suddenly, as he gave this imitation of his German landlady, his back stiffened, his blue eyes flashed, and the guttural German accents rolled out across the somnolent club lounge. It was not a conscious imitation. He was simply quoting from the original. The effect around us was electric. Heads snapped back. One of the hovering waiters scuttled over to see what disaster had fallen. I caught a glimpse of what *Volksgemeinschaft* really meant.

There was, in a prewar British edition of *Mein Kampf,* a definition of *Volksgemeinschaft* that sought to stifle any alarmed criticism. The word meant "folk community" and applied to the whole body of the people, without distinction or class. "*Volk*" was a primary word that suggested the basic national mood after the defeat of 1918, the downfall of the monarchy and the destruction of the aristocracy. It was "the unifying coefficient which would embrace the whole German people."

The Brotherhood has the same mystical (and conveniently vague) meaning. "Brotherhood" was a word used in the hushed way ODESSA was discussed in the 1960's, like another phrase whose meaning could be adjusted to suit the audience: Third Reich.

Out of Argentina, in 1961, came the first solid piece of evidence that continuing wild rumors were not entirely unfounded. The man in charge of the "Jewish problem" for the Gestapo, Adolf Eichmann, was taken by Israeli agents and made to stand trial in Jerusalem. There, the former Argentine Ambassador to Israel stated that Bormann had escaped to Argentina and then migrated elsewhere in Latin America. Five years later, Eichmann's son Klaus wrote an open letter calling upon Bormann "to come forward for that part of the guilt for which you are responsible and for which my father stood in your place during the trial in Israel." Klaus was no longer living in Argentina, but his brother Horst Adolf Eichmann was. Horst Adolf had reported to the Attorney General in Frankfurt (who, for various reasons, was most involved in the Bormann case) that he had talked frequently with Bormann. Now, suddenly, he said he'd been wrong: Bormann had died in Berlin. When he was pressed to explain this contradiction, he replied: "When you live in Latin America, where there are still influential Nazi circles, you take into account that these Nazi circles will one day strike. . . ."

CHAPTER 9

The first piece of this puzzle to come my way was a brief conversation in the summer of 1945. It had to do with the disappearance of Martin Bormann, a figure unknown to my small naval unit, preparing to transfer operations to Asia. We had just been converted from the seagoing version of the Spitfire to the gadget-packed Hellcats on loan from the U.S. Navy. A large number of U-boats were thought to have broken loose, and Stalin had all but accused the Western Allies of concealing the escape of Nazi leaders. The Russians seemed to know more about German underwater traffic than we did.

"The greatest manhunt is under way from Norway to the Bavarian alps," Winston Churchill assured Moscow. President Roosevelt had cabled Stalin a bitter protest against his unfounded suspicions about Allied negotiations with Nazi leaders even before the war ended.

We were eight pilots trained for lone-wolf missions, and were waiting to join carriers in the Far East. There seemed little sense to scouring the water around Britain when the war there was over. We thought at the time the decision was just another example of naval bureaucracy at work.

"How do you find this Bormann with high-altitude cameras?" one of us asked the chief pilot.

"Tie a professor to the end of a cable and dangle him over the Atlantic."

"Bormann's escaped in a U-boat?"

"Maybe."

"What's all this professor stuff?"

"Take this and you'll see. It's a proso profile of Bormann." The chief pilot, who was known as "the Fish," being descended from Admiral Sir John Fisher, gave us folders. The material in the folders was impressive. We learned that a proso profile was a method of building up a portrait of someone who was dead or missing. It never occurred to me that bits of the portrait would drift into my hands for the next two decades and more.

The first Bormann profile threw some light on why the Russians were restless and suspicious. The last will and testament of the Führer was among the important papers missing with Bormann. These were documents that might revive someday the whole Nazi mythology. Furthermore, a Russian commission stated there was irrefutable evidence that some Nazi leaders escaped from Berlin in a light plane for Hamburg, from where "mysterious persons" had departed by U-boat.

Our search of the high seas led to one incident, at least, when a German submarine traveling on the surface in the Bay of Biscay was attacked by a Royal Navy torpedo-bomber. The U-boat commander had ignored signals to wait for surface craft and began to crash-dive. The vessel was in the vicinity of San Sebastian, where Albert Speer's personal aircraft had crash-landed a little earlier with Léon Degrelle, a Nazi war criminal, aboard. Moreover, Nazi agents had been picked up from this Spanish port during the war. So the naval plane took no chances and sank the submarine. The whole affair was tactfully forgotten, because the Allies had no wish to cause Franco Spain any embarrassment, nor were they anxious to let it be known that they were aware of escape routes in Spain. This was a time when all sides were anxious to avoid further unpleasantness. It was also a time when the German submarine fleet could move with its customary cunning.

There were 398 U-boats in commission. All were capable of spending more weeks at sea. Many were within reach of American havens. Others could move from their patrols between Norway and Scotland. Several did. For example, Captain Heinz Schaeffer, commanding the specially equipped U-977, moved underwater by day and surfaced at night. Skirting the British Isles, he made for Argentina.

In the twilight of the war, this cat-and-mouse game had many strange twists. Schaeffer gave British waters a wide berth because U-boat intelligence reports had defined several new minefields just before the war ended. These were said to consist of deep mines designed to catch U-boats, which no longer had to surface to recharge batteries, thanks to the snorkel air-breathing device. The truth of the matter was that Britain had a shortage of such mines and the vessels to lay them. Naval intelligence in London therefore fed false information to a double agent known as "Tate." He reported, piece by piece, these nonexistent minefields. Altogether, there was only a small area protected against U-boats. At war's end, nobody bothered to mention that the whole thing was another hoax. As a result, U-977 took longer than it should (fourteen weeks) to make landfall along the Argentinian coast. Admiral Doenitz had ordered all his captains, in a message dated May 7, 1945, to "refrain from any act of war." What was known, however, was that Doenitz, before the victorious Allies ordered him to broadcast the surrender, had told his submarine commanders "never to give up."

Several U-boat commanders chose to follow the never-give-up order. Doubtless Stalin, in his mood of suspicion, smelled Allied collusion. He was not then aware that the U-boats conducted a war by standards of their own.

Schaeffer had already accomplished a transfer of men near the Norwegian coast prior to making the long journey to Argentina. He was surprised, on his arrival, to find himself placed under arrest, though he was told that this was a technicality. Argentina had come into the war at the last moment, to mollify the victors. Because of this, Argentina's profascist government could give safe haven to Nazi refugees. It did not work out this way for U-977's commander, however. His movements had aroused the keen interest of American intelligence. He was flown to Washington and questioned hard about reports that he had carried high-ranking Nazis. This he denied.

He was then flown to England, where he joined other U-boat prisoners in Hertfordshire. There they lived in an old mansion surrounded by parkland. If any were thought to have useful information locked inside their heads, they were given civilian clothes and taken on night-club jaunts by chummy British Navy officers, who took the line "We're all brothers of the sea. . . ."

Commander Schaeffer was in time released. Nothing was ever made public of what he revealed.

Otto Kretschmer, whose U-99 had been sunk, was entertained by Captain (later Admiral) George Creasy. The conversation was light but the drinking was heavy. Much later, a rueful Kretschmer said he was surprised by the detailed information the British appeared to have on all German submariners, including their personal histories. He was also slightly appalled by what he himself had contributed to that knowledge in the heady atmosphere of good comradeship.

There has never been a public disclosure of how many U-boats did in fact reach Latin-American havens, often to be scuttled after their crews shifted the cargoes ashore. Otto Wermuth, for instance, was loitering in U-530 off Long Island when he got the order to surrender. He chose to follow Doenitz's earlier instruction, and so he, too, sailed into Argentinian waters, two months after the war's end. Officially listed as "Fate Unknown" are five Nazi submarines whose movements are veiled in obscurity: U-34, U-239, U-547, U-957, and U-1000. A far greater number were said to have been scuttled during the winter of 1946, and there is no record of just how many in fact went down, or how many discharged cargoes before going down. The total number scuttled, 217, is impressive.

Submarines of great endurance were being used, toward the end of the war, to carry strategic materials and to drop agents along the American coast. The big snorkel-equipped U-boats traveled as far as Japan and back.

The Doenitz concept of "wolf packs" was developed while the Admiral still directed the world's largest underwater fleet through his communications center in the French harbor of Lorient, looking out upon the Bay of Biscay. When he was obliged to lay down his arms, he did not lay down orders stopping the traffic of these vessels. Though he was saved from trial by the tributes of American and British naval commanders, he nevertheless had conducted a type of submarine warfare that killed a great many innocent people. He had been expert at it for forty years. He disowned Plan Regenbogen, by which submarine commanders were to scuttle rather than surrender, but cringing and cunning were the earmark of his trade.

There is evidence today that the Soviet Union knew of plans to make use of cargo submarines to move "valuable documents" gathered by Bormann. It also had details of a new type on order. The military version had a range of 31,500 miles at ten knots. A mercantile version carried a cargo dead weight of 252 tons. There were to be thirty old U-boats modified into the new type, and these were registered with the German naval high command. There were seventy registered military versions. All would have been capable of moving large quantities of men and material across the South Atlantic. Officially, they were never built.

The Russians had the registration numbers and became doubly suspicious when told by Allied naval intelligence that the vessels did not exist. One hundred large German submarines had vanished into thin air. Yet Stalin had been told by no less a statesman than Churchill that the Germans were pushing ahead with construction of even more advanced types of U-boat. Soviet distrust persisted for a long time after the war because it seemed inconceivable that the hundred vessels, all properly registered, had no more substance than the blueprints in the shipyards.

Their disbelief is another indication that their highly placed spy at Nazi party headquarters was someone with an over-all view of confidential matters but without sufficient detailed knowledge to pursue inquiries into specific areas. He was good at passing over bulk material but lacked either the time or the expertise to evaluate all of it. The new long-range submarines did not get built because Allied bombing slowed down work in the yards. Thus no written order was given to stop construction, and no piece of paper found its way to Berlin to that effect. Admiral Doenitz was informed, at his naval headquarters, that bombing had disrupted the building program, and that was that.

The Russians did know the plans of Bormann and other leading Nazis to move large quantities of party files and papers by submarine to safety in Latin America. The so-called "Bormann Papers" were regarded by the Soviets as potentially dangerous. They could provide the textual foundations for a future rebirth of the National Socialist movement, and this represented a grave threat in a way little understood in the West. The war between Germany and Russia had been a clash of ideologies. The Russians did not regard the end of the war as an end to the ideological struggle, and for them the missing Bormann Papers, like the missing submarines, presented a mystery that would *have* to be solved.

Bormann cast his shadow on me again after Commander Ian Fleming was released from British naval intelligence at the end of 1945. Fleming's wartime attention had been concentrated on another prominent Nazi: Otto Skorzeny, thought to be part of the Brotherhood. Another flier joined us one day for lunch. Fleming was busy at that time with the foreign-news service known as Mercury. The pilot, Terence Horsley, was then editor of a newspaper associated with the Mercury project. He had piloted the wood-and-string biplanes the British used throughout World War II to hunt German submarines. These Swordfish had a top speed in a dive of ninety miles an hour, but Horsley enjoyed pottering around in them because he was a keen bird-watcher. "If you point 'em into the wind, you can hover by the cliffs and spot the nests."

Fleming cut him short. "What happened to that report on escaping U-boats?"

Horsley's eyes swiveled over to me.

"He's taken the oath," Fleming said impatiently. It was my first indication that he knew about the spy planes and the secrecy oaths we were placed under.

"It's not complete," said Horsley. "Some U-boat commanders struck out on their own. Others went under orders to South America. Then there was Plan Regenbogen. . . ."

I felt out of my depth in this discussion. Then I heard Horsley saying: "Fisher bought it. Crashed in the sea off Newfoundland."

"He was your boss, wasn't he?" Fleming asked me.

I nodded, mute.

"Chip off the old block," said Horsley. "Must've been his grandfather . . . that's right. Old Admiral Fisher. Reckoned we were one of the Ten Lost Tribes of Israel."

"That's what Bormann used to say," I murmured.

They turned their gray wise faces toward me. They must have been in their mid-thirties, but they looked ancient and fierce. What did I know about Martin Bormann?

I repeated the words to my naval unit of the younger Fisher, who had just crashed.

"Did you join the manhunt?" asked Fleming.

"Just watched for U-boats. There was talk of Bormann escaping by air, too. I read up on him but we never got a look at the full report which followed."

Fleming slipped a cigarette into an ivory holder. "The men who know about that are in New York. One's General Donovan of OSS. The other is your namesake, Billy Stephenson. . . ."

I should have paid more attention. I was distracted by Fleming's story of how his brother, Peter, had written a novel in which Hitler's deputy was supposed to fly to Britain. It had appeared *before* the Deputy Führer made that mad dash to Scotland. Peter claimed he had no prior knowledge. But he was a wartime agent with Special Operations Executive, and I began to wonder if someone, somehow, had put the idea into the head of Hitler's henchman. It seems curious, all these years later, to discover that the flight of Rudolf Hess did in fact play a vital part in Bormann's career.

CHAPTER 10

Two hundred thousand copies of a public notice were posted throughout Germany on October 22, 1945, part of which read: "Martin Bormann is charged with having committed crimes against peace, war crimes and crimes against humanity, all as particularly set forth in an indictment. . . . If Martin Bormann appears, he is entitled to be heard. . . ."

This proclamation provided for Bormann to be tried in his absence, and it was the work of the International Military Tribunal, made up of the United States, France, Great Britain, and the Soviet Union. The Deputy Chief Prosecutor, Sir David Maxwell-Fyffe, made this statement to the President of the Tribunal: "There is still the clear possibility that he is alive."

Bormann was found guilty of war crimes and crimes against humanity. But the Tribunal added that his sentence could be altered or reduced if he wished to reopen the case and bring forward any facts in mitigation. Thus the door has been left open for him.

A difficulty at the trial was that the role of the Führer's Secretary could not be documented. All his personal records, his thousands of pages of notes on Hitler, and the party papers for which he was responsible had disappeared. The prosecution's case was put on January 16, 1946 in these words: "Every schoolboy knows that Hitler was an evil man. The point we respectfully emphasize is that, without chieftains like Bormann, Hitler would never have been able to seize and consolidate total power. . . . Bormann was in truth an evil archangel to the Lucifer of Hitler."

The real Lucifer was, of course, Bormann himself. In those days it was hard to perceive his role when the documentary evidence was missing. Furthermore, the political climate had changed drastically. The Devil was once again back in Moscow, and Bolshevism was the anti-Christ.

An astounding readiness to wipe from memory the previous five years of horror was symbolized by the conversion of Bormann's

99

wife and children to Catholicism. It took place quietly and promptly as soon as the war ended. Gerda had written only a year earlier to her husband that she hoped the children would remember how Christianity and Jewry got a foothold in Germany. She had always matched Martin's violent outbursts of hatred for the churches. Now, in the summer of 1945, she placed Adolf Martin Bormann and his brothers in the hands of priests who became known later as members of the Vatican Line, an escape route for wanted Nazis. The eldest son dropped the name Adolf which he had been given in honor of Hitler.

Gerda was ill, and shorty after died from cancer. Her decision helps to make comprehensible what must seem otherwise quite incredible. The mood in Germany favored Nazis who went underground. Allied attempts to denazify officialdom were regarded even then by many Western observers to be quite futile, but it was a period when fear of Communism had replaced the Nazi bogies. Bormann, as the guardian of Nazi philosophy, preserver of the flame, really had little to fear from his own people. They stuck to the safe rationalization that they had behaved like loyal citizens who naturally obeyed the laws of their country.

The threat of war between the Western Allies and Russia had been promoted for years by the Nazis. Their vision of ultimate conflict with "barbaric Bolshevism" produced the first reference to an Iron Curtain.

It was uttered by Hitler's former Finance Minister, Count Schwerin von Krosigk, on May 2, 1945, when he was trying desperately to win Allied recognition for the government of Admiral Doenitz. Schwerin von Krosigk was an unctuous figure who had never forgotten Hess's saying before his departure that the two Germanic nations, Britain and Germany, were fighting each other to the enormous satisfaction of the Bolsheviks. The Count, a former Rhodes Scholar who seems to have learned nothing about the English during his time at Oxford, calculated that Hess had made some impression on his British hosts. "The Iron Curtain moves closer," he declared in a broadcast. "People caught in the mighty hands of the Bolsheviks are being destroyed."

The term was picked up from the German broadcast. Churchill used it when he cabled President Harry Truman on May 12: "An Iron Curtain is drawn upon their front. We do not know what is going on behind." A year later, he dropped it into a speech in the United States. It demonstrates the infectious nature of the fears deliberately released by Hitler's followers in order to win Western sympathy.

Thousands of Hitler's obedient servants, keenly aware of the Allied "unconditional surrender" posture, heeding the Moscow Declaration to pursue war criminals to the ends of the earth, moved fearfully through the ruins of German cities. Some knew where to go. Others had little more than the names of "safe" households. It dawned on the fugitives even before midsummer of 1945 that the Western Allies really had no stomach for revenge, though some popular Allied sentiment favored drumhead courts-martial for a few top Nazis, a proposal voiced by Secretary of State Cordell Hull and supported by Churchill and Secretary of the Treasury Henry Morgenthau; they wanted the worst Nazi criminals taken out one morning and shot.

Lesser criminals, when discovered, often met with indifference. "I sometimes wonder if we should have had some more impressive arrangements for ending the war," wrote Eisenhower's chief of intelligence, Sir Kenneth Strong. "The Germans terminated their campaign in the west in 1940 with much ceremony and a formal signing of armistice terms in the identical railway coach used by Marshal Foch in 1918 when he received the German capitulation. But the feeling of us all at the time was to get the job over as quickly as possible and end the slaughter. There was still a war to be fought in the Far East after the Nazis had been finished with."

A crusade against Communism was what Martin Bormann counted upon. Though he had little time for Schwerin von Krosigk, who was still an active Catholic, he respected what he thought were the Count's contacts at the Vatican and in the Anglo-Saxon world.

Now, the re-creation of Red bogeymen seemed to be away to a good start. The Count, in his broadcast, predicted that the proposed conference at San Francisco would never establish a world constitution "if Red incendiaries take part." He predicted that a Bolshevik Europe would be the first step to a Sovietized world. By the time he was obliged to announce unconditional surrender, the German defeat sounded less shameful. The German military leaders, exploiting Allied ignorance about an arrangement whereby German members of the armed forces were not allowed to join the Nazi party, declared they had been fighting *against* Communism and not *for* Nazism. Singlehanded, they had tackled the Bolshevik hordes. It seemed almost heroic. "Be led by the light of the three stars, the true pledge of the real German character," cried Schwerin von Krosigk. "Unity and Justice and Liberty!"

Some of the stuffing was knocked out of this posture. The British refused to let German commanders evacuate their troops from the path of the advancing Russians. Argentina declared war on the Axis Powers just as the conflict was ending. Pope Pius XII suddenly recovered his voice and condemned the Nazis. On the very last day of fighting, he took another prudent step forward and said that fascism was a bad system in the wrong hands.

Three weeks after the capitulation of German forces in Norway, however, Nazi commanders there continued to behave as if their military courts were preparing for another war, in which they would be fighting with the Allies against Russia. At German naval defense headquarters in Oslo, a judge court-martialed a young sailor for telling his commander: "I'm a free man now, you Nazi dog."

The judge who sentenced this imprudent youth was Hans Filbinger. He later became a prominent figure in West German political life. When I saw him again in 1972 he was much more confident about defending Nazi courts-martial, which after the war still sentenced men to death for desertion. Filbinger's judgment on the sailor was actually dated June 19, 1945 on the official copy. It would have been interesting to hear yet another justification for Nazi punitive measures so long after the surrender, but this was not the purpose of my inquiry. More to the point was the fact that if conditions favored Nazi drumhead trials, then conditions must also have provided a friendly climate for escaping war criminals, even several weeks after Bormann vanished.

Filbinger was in Oslo when Schaeffer, of the U-977, put ashore a small group of men and then left for Argentina. Did Filbinger recall, I asked, why this vessel had put in to Norwegian waters first? No, he did not. Did he know that war criminals had escaped to Norway? Well, it was possible. After all, he said helpfully, there was the case of Degrelle.

Thus, in an infuriatingly casual way, I learned how a close associate of Skorzeny and the Brotherhood got away to the sanctuary of Franco's Spain.

Colonel Léon Degrelle, the Belgian fascist who commanded the SS Army Corps / West, had left Himmler near the Danish border and followed one of the escape routes into Norway. There he sought help from Vidkun Quisling, the Norwegian whose name became a synonym for traitor. The thirty-eight-year-old disciple of Hitler found that Quisling was equally anxious to escape retribution, and just as frustrated. Degrelle then went to Josef Terboven, the Reich Commissar of Norway, who later shot himself. Terboven said he had asked Sweden to provide the Belgian with asylum. The answer was No. "I tried to get you a submarine which was leaving—" Terboven waved vaguely out to sea. "Japan, perhaps, or is that too far? Perhaps I'm thinking of the other place. Argentina. But it seems impossible to get out of harbor. There are too many Allied warships in the vicinity." He suggested Degrelle try to hitch a ride in the private aircraft of the former War Production chief, Albert Speer. The plane was in Oslo, apparently to take Speer to safety if he could make his way from the Flensburg escape hatch. The crew were anxious to leave, fearing Norwegian resistance troops might spot the plane. Its range was somewhat less than the distance to Spain. Did Degrelle want to take the chance?

He grabbed it. The plane left at midnight, slipped across Allied occupied territory, and ran out of fuel at San Sebastian. It made a forced landing on the beach. Degrelle got in touch at once with Madrid, where he was welcome and where he remained.

Filbinger offered no explanation for the presence of Speer's plane in Norway, or any instructions given the crew to airlift important German escapees to freedom. In fact, captured U.S. Flying Fortresses were operating alongside German Condors with a Luftwaffe squadron in special "guerrilla support roles" which gave the commanders a license to do pretty much as they pleased.

Though a majority of hunted men could vanish into the faceless crowds, the intimidating atmosphere cowed many Germans. Fear was abroad: some of it a hangover from years of police oppression and some of it a consequence of the last-ditch propaganda on the Werewolves.

The long-range escape planes were part of the German Air Force's special Werewolf detachment. They were supposed to be used to drop young Werewolves behind Allied lines. They also figured in Martin Bormann's escape plans. Enterprise Werewolf was another of his agencies. He was politically and administratively in control of the Volkssturm, a peculiar people's army made up of very old and very young men and women armed with Czech rifles and *Panzerfaust* one-shot bazookas.

The first of the Volkssturm units was inspected on October 21, 1944 by Himmler. "New resistance will spring up behind [Allied] backs," he proclaimed. "Volunteers will strike like werewolves." The name, which later created fear and uncertainty, was thus mentioned publicly for the first time.

When Germany began to suffer invaders on its soil, trusted men were needed for the huge task of shifting documents and treasure to safety overseas. A crucial appointment, in Bormann's private maneuvers, went to the flamboyant giant who first loomed into his presence in 1940 as a member of the first SS Division, Hitler's bodyguard: Otto Skorzeny. He was put in charge of the Werewolf organization, which provided, along with his other unconventional operations, a cover for the movement of key men and party properties. General Reinhard Gehlen was charged with military direction of Enterprise Werewolf (a responsibility he denied having undertaken, in conversations with me in 1972).

Gehlen and Skorzeny were to provide captured Allied uniforms for the resistance fighters. They were to organize and supply isolated groups, which would carry out orders best summarized in Himmler's letter to the SS Police Chief West, General Karl Gutenberg: "Educate the population not to collaborate with the enemy, by execution of the death penalty behind the front."

Whatever Hitler's addled brain thought this would achieve, the guilty men around him saw a perfect means of escape amidst confusion and fear. SS and Gestapo chiefs who were planning to go underground would have at their disposal Allied uniforms, transport, food, and arms. If need be, they could demand help from their countrymen under Allied occupation. And they could expect to get it, because a campaign was under way to strike terror in the hearts of collaborators. Werewolves would punish acts of disloyalty to Hitler.

The passionate devotion to the Führer among many youngsters was to be fully exploited. Young Werewolves would cover a withdrawal into a "national redoubt" around Hitler's mountaintop home at Berchtesgaden. It was popularly known as the Alpine Fortress, and the U.S. Seventh Army reported it was to be defended by 200,000 veteran SS troops and Werewolves. It covered 20,000 square miles of Bavaria, Austria, and a small part of Italy. It was, of course, to become the hide-out for men escaping abroad.

The atmosphere of bewilderment and terror helped the guilty to get away. This is well illustrated by the curious and frightening Werewolf murder of the Chief Burgomaster of the old imperial city of Aachen.

Aachen was the first German city to be occupied by a foreign invader in a hundred years. Officials who helped the enemy had to be publicly punished. It was the symbolism, as always, that counted. Radio Werewolf hammered the theme "Rather dead than Red" (a phrase that lived long after). Bolshevism was the real enemy; the Nazis had always resisted the Bolsheviks; therefore any German who helped the enemies of Nazism was helping the Bolsheviks and was a traitor. A climate was being created that would favor the concealment of wanted men.

On March 29, 1945 it was announced that the Chief Burgomaster of Aachen, Franz Oppenhoff, had been executed by order of the German people's courts. He was killed by a girl from the Union of Hitler Maidens and a sixteen-year-old boy. They were part of a Werewolf unit parachuted from a captured Flying Fortress of Werewolf Squadron 252. The boy was known as a P-man, in honor of SS Lieutenant General Hans Pruetzmann, who had exported children from the Baltic states for "Germanization" and then terrorized Russian civilians from his post as SS Police Leader to the Southern Army Group at Kiev. Another of his claims to fame was that he was responsible for exterminating 200,000 Jews before the end of 1941.

Oppenhoff's fate had nothing to do with his personal beliefs. These, however, indicate the mentality of dignitaries regarded as "non-Nazis." A new elite had emerged in Aachen before the city's capture. As described by CIC agents, it was: "Shrewd, strong-willed and aggressive, made up of technicians, lawyers, engineers, businessmen, manufacturers and churchmen. . . . In the last ten years under Hitler their earnings ranged from 7,000 to 200,000 marks yearly (representing an upper-middle-class bracket). None of them suffered under the Nazi regime or ever, by word or deed, opposed it."

From this elite, the U.S. Twelfth Army selected Oppenhoff to become chief burgomaster under American control. He was backed by Bishop Van der Valden, who, according to Captain Saul Padover, a professor of history and a member of the Twelfth Army's psychological-warfare section, "endorsed Oppenhoff's view that the American Military Government would give them time to reconstruct the economy without interference from political parties and trade unions. . . . If the United States knew its own interests, it would join Germany against the Soviet Union," according to the Bishop and Oppenhoff.

Oppenhoff, a right-wing Catholic lawyer, said: "Germany can be divided into two categories: those who obey and those who command." There had been chaos before Hitler, with forty political parties at each other's throats. "Heaven help us," the new Burgomaster told Padover, "if Americans permit the existence of political parties."

This was the German singled out by the Nazis for execution. The effect can be imagined. He had recruited men who sounded equally fascist. They certainly offended Padover's sense of democracy: "One or other repeats the slogans and clichés that Germany was dishonored by the Versailles Treaty, that the latter was too harsh . . . that the poor Reich is without space and must expand. . . . Nazi sympathizers, party members or German nationalists are appointed by military governments as the only available specialists. They look extremely presentable and have professional backgrounds similar to those of American Military Government officers. They place their likeminded friends in secondary positions. Our initial indifference to the politics of the situation leads in the end to a political mess."

The Werewolves demonstrated that the Nazis would never be guilty of such laxity. (Fifteen years later, a Werewolf leader was arrested in Hanover: Gunter Welters was charged with promoting neo-Nazi activities. Other Werewolf leaders persist, but seldom get caught. They were handled more firmly during the Allied occupation. In the Communist East, they were simply shot.) Their first prominent victim, ironically enough, could have been expressing their own political instincts when he told Padover that an authoritarian system like that of Mussolini or France was best suited to the German "cadaver-obedience" mentality.

Gehlen's plans for Werewolf read now like the paper plans of a desk-bound general, but he said they were based on his secret intelligence on the Polish resistance to the Nazis. More to the point, he proposed secret hide-outs for German Army weapons and preservation of important documents which would enable the military caste to reconstitute itself. He maintained later that these more prudent and less militant preparations were directed against the Bolsheviks, whom he had always known to be the ultimate enemy. For weeks, however, military trucks conveyed other papers vital to perpetuation of a Nazi myth, including the final Table Talks of Hitler as set down at Bormann's direction. Microfilm copies were deposited in banks, from which they were rescued only years later, the originals having by then served their purpose.

Nazi propaganda had been exploiting a proposal by Henry Morgenthau to turn Germany into an agricultural nation. "This means the destruction of German industry!" Radio Werewolf huffed and puffed. "Germans will starve or be forced to migrate as working slaves. The Jew Morgenthau sings the same tune as the Jews in the Kremlin."

While small boys joined his P-men, SS General Pruetzmann made his dash for safety in the rags of a refugee. Gehlen had already provided himself with false documents: "A simple matter for my intelligence organization. They forged the orders. We faked a Gauleiter's signature. Hitler had strictly forbidden us to evacuate families but it was vital for my future mission that I transfer my wife and children to the Alps." He had started to make arrangements back in midwinter. With Skorzeny operating on similar errands, he buried in the Alpine Fortress the papers that served him so well when the Americans arrived.

Martin Bormann at this time stayed in the Führer's bunker. His ally Erich Koch, no longer boasting of how he would handle Ukrainians with vodka and whip, had requisitioned an icebreaker to flee through "that flooded field" the Baltic, for a rendezvous with an escape submarine at Kiel, where Bormann was presumably to meet him.

The Werewolves and the Alpine Fortress, the convincing reports that Skorzeny was out to kill Eisenhower, and the broadcasts threatening to hang and bury collaborators in the middle of the night, all combined to confuse and distract attention from Berlin, where Hitler in his bunker was not quite as embattled a figure as he seemed. Reports about an Alpine Fortress could not be ignored by Eisenhower, who wrote later: "If the German was permitted to establish [it] he might possibly force us to engage in a long-drawn-out guerilla type of warfare. . . . The purpose of the Werewolf organization was murder and terrorism." He received from Chief of Staff General George C. Marshall, in Washington, a proposal for "rapid action which might prevent the formation of organized resistance areas. The mountainous country in the south is considered a possibility."

Churchill feared any diversion from Berlin, and there were sharp British objections to a change in plan that would alter the shape of Europe. Eisenhower cabled that his decision was to concentrate upon reducing the Alpine Fortress before it became a Werewolf stronghold.

Werewolf schools were reported all over the place, and CIC estimates put the number of youngsters training under SS officers at some 5,000 in one particular week. A booklet appeared that reinforced a general sense of apprehension: *Werwolf: Winke für Jagdeinheiten (Tips for Hunting Units)*. In reality, Chief Werewolf Pruetzmann was now bargaining through the Danish underground with British contacts in the hope that he might be given a safe-conduct in return for the betrayal of his friends.

The *Vogelfrei* legends, revived by the Werewolves, were particularly welcome to Bormann. The word meant "bird-free." It derived from the medieval-style courts of revenge, which declared that anyone found guilty became like a game bird during the open season for hunters. The young Martin Bormann after World War I had busied himself with such tribunals, taking vengeance against the "November criminals" who negotiated in 1918 with the Allies. The medieval vigilantes swore on pain of death to hold and conceal their holy cause "from wife and child, from father and mother, from sister and brother, from fire and wind, from everything upon which the sun shines or the rain falls, from everything between heaven and earth." Anyone found guilty, and not present at the ritual trial, became "bird-free," and any member of the court could kill that person without penalty. In the debased form of the post-1918 Freikorps such as Bormann had joined, there was no pretense of chivalry; the knights were ill-tempered soldiers, the victims were selected less for betrayal and treason than because of their supposed resistance to the demands of the roving gangs. Early Nazis revived the folklore and honored the composer of a ballad to the Werewolf, which in German mythology was protected by the Devil and had the power of turning from man into wolf and back again.

A Reorientation of Strategy, by General Omar Bradley, took all this seriously enough to advise that "the plans we brought with us over the beaches" had been rendered obsolete. "All indications suggest that the enemy's political and military directorate is already in the process of displacing to the Redoubt [the Alpine Fortress] in Lower Bavaria." Air cover, according to a SHAEF (Supreme Headquarters Allied Expeditionary Forces) Intelligence Summary of March 1945 showed at least twenty areas of underground activities and numerous caves around Berchtesgaden. Allen Dulles reported from his observation post in Switzerland that fanatical Nazis would make a last-ditch stand there. He had evidence of frenzied preparations under Major General von Marcinkiewitz to construct a mountain fortress.

Goebbels's broadcasts and those of Radio Werewolf flooded the nation with hysterical warnings: "God has given up the protection of the people. . . . Satan has taken command. Horrible, unmentionable things are happening to our women and children." There were secret recognition signals for boys and girls (some as young as nine), and the *Wolfsangel,* a runic letter to be painted on buildings occupied by those marked for vengeance. Goebbels gave speeches of incredible asininity: "We Werewolves consider it our supreme duty to kill, to kill and to kill, employing every cunning and wile in the darkness of the night, crawling, groping through towns and villages, like wolves, noiselessly, mysteriously."

Bormann diverted Allied military operations in a maneuver of magnificent deception. The bogus fortress was a flight of imagination. It provided cover for the large numbers of Nazis who were planning for the future: those who would conceal negotiable securities ranging from priceless police files to stolen foreign stocks and bonds before going into prison camp as military prisoners; those who would hide until they saw which way the Allied winds blew politically; those who knew without a doubt they were doomed to hang if caught. All these figures flocked to the area, knowing they could take their time. It would be weeks, perhaps months, before Allied search parties became a menace. Many of the trails could be traveled only by mule or on foot.

For years afterward, Eisenhower continued to demand a full-scale inquiry into the whole affair. While he was Allied Supreme Commander, the panic reached such proportions that he was obliged by his security men to stay inside the Paris compound of SHAEF because "Scarface Skorzeny and SS Air Troops are on a mission to kill you." As Eisenhower's intelligence chief commented later: "There were reports of German gunmen parachuting down as priests and nuns. Paratroops *always* seemed to come as priests and nuns."

By this great diversion, Bormann made it easier for the Russians to overrun the area around Berlin. This was later given as a reason for suspecting that Bormann all along worked for the Russians. Gehlen, after his retirement as West German intelligence chief, insisted that Bormann intended Berlin to fall into Russian hands. It is worth remembering, however, that Bormann was not alone in being skilled at deception. He had property in the area of the Alpine Fortress that shortly became the residence of Gehlen's new spy network. It was there that Gehlen concocted the report for the Americans that his fear of a Russian spy in Hitler's inner circle had been confirmed by Admiral Wilhelm Canaris, the "Grand Prince of Espionage" and onetime director of German military intelligence.

Bormann as a Russian spy was a diverting thought and also a good ploy. As to the Admiral, there is evidence that he collaborated in some way with the British; but it can be safely assumed, from what is known today, that he never identified Bormann as the spy in Hitler's camp. He did claim that the Kremlin was receiving top-level intelligence and this worried him. Canaris was never a traitor.

He warned the British of invasion plans after the fall of France in the hope of preventing a direct clash with a traditional enemy which he did not underestimate. He was hoping, even at that late stage, to form a Western alliance against Russia. The secrets of his overtures are locked in his diaries, which are yet to be made public, though some of the contents have filtered into the public domain.

The decision to remain with the Führer was made by Bormann because he understood better than anyone the need to keep within the bounds of German law. The later intelligence studies of Bormann's mind make clear his meticulous approach to quite startling concepts. What first appeared to be lunatic schemes were seen, in retrospect, to have been carried off with such cool detachment that he got his reputation for being insensitive and a rural clod. He put in the order for the gasoline required to consume the bodies of Hitler and Eva with the same attention to detail that he put into getting the Führer's written order that he was to be Nazi Party Minister. All the appointments of others meant nothing. He had demonstrated his control over propagandist Goebbels, and so accepted with his usual equanimity the appointment of that demented little man as Reich Chancellor; he knew Goebbels would be dead within a few more hours of Hitler drawing up his will.

It was inevitable that Bormann would stay to make everything legal. He was hated by almost everyone who saw him operate; but it was the kind of hatred that gives birth to fear and then to obedience. Once he had the Führer's seal stamped upon him, there were still a few last intrigues to be carried out in tidy fashion. The last effective enemies had to be conquered. Death for Hitler, certainly. Death for Goebbels, who had become Bormann's lackey and served no further useful purpose. Himmler's disposal was arranged ("Fresh treachery afoot!" Bormann cabled Hitler's successor, Doenitz, even before Hitler was dead. "Himmler offering surrender . . . take instant and ruthless action. . . .") Death for archenemy Göring ("Are you familiar with Reich Leader Bormann's intrigues to eliminate me?" wailed Göring to Doenitz). There were precious notes to be packaged and sealed, and all the records Bormann had kept of this first stage in the saga of the National Socialist reformation of the world. He was seen by Hanna Reitsch "recording the momentous events for posterity" before spiriting the accounts out. There were scores to be settled, knots to be tied, before Bormann crawled out of the rubble.

The rubble today in Berlin is called the "Collected Works of Hitler." These are mountains of rubbish (Monte Klamotten), sev-

110

enty million cubic meters of ruin. Eight million Germans perished in the war. The stench still lingers in Berlin. East and West zones smell to high heaven of operatic tragedy and boiled cabbage.

An earnest inquirer can still discover there some surprising modifications to conventional history—Artur Axmann, for instance.

Axmann was, when discovered again in 1972, a plump and clearly most successful "businessman." He lost an arm fighting the Russians and is hardly enthusiastic about Communism. Nonetheless, he pours scorn on revised versions of the Battle of Berlin, in which it is said the Russians walked into a virtually undefended city.

Axmann is the single authoritative eyewitness quoted by those who say Bormann died under fire in the early hours of May 2, 1945. Yet a respected authority on Nazi Germany, Hugh Trevor-Roper, commented at the time that "whether we believe Axmann or not is a matter of choice. . . . If he wished to protect Bormann his natural course would be to give false evidence of his death."

That was said when Axmann appeared as the only person claiming to have seen Bormann's dead body.

But now he is not positive at all.

Artur Axmann, a Berliner, was leader of the Hitler Youth thrown into the defense of Berlin. Events when he was thirty-two years old still have the familiarity of a neighborhood event. The names of places that assume a particular significance in all the histories written about this period are, for him, part of everyday life. They are incidents along the block where he lived.

His description of the bombardment of Berlin and the crossfire that night is vivid and detailed. There was never any question, he says, of taking a casual stroll out of the Führer's bunker, even if the Russians had not yet zeroed in upon it. "You need to have been a soldier to understand the Russians weren't fooling around. They were moving into a city that symbolized everything they hated, with as much obsessive ferocity as we attacked Stalingrad—not for its strategic value, but for what it represented. The Russians had heard our broadcasts that Hitler was in Berlin. They knew also that the British and Americans believed reports of a last stand in Bavaria. They took their time moving in, but they had no mercy. They shot everything that moved."

So Bormann could have been killed? At fifty-nine, Axmann was less certain. He thought he saw Bormann lying dead alongside Dr. Ludwig Stumpfegger. The two men, he thought, were bowled over by an explosion on the bridge over the railroad tracks to the Lehrter Station. Now he recalled only that he passed two unconscious men in the dark of night among many dead and dying. He had since been told that Stumpfegger broadcast from Russia. So he was not sure about anything. He had made his way to the Alpine Fortress, knowing there would be nothing in the way of fortifications but having been instructed to join one of the Hitler Youth units hiding in the mountains. He was less fortunate than others, who found safety in Italy; but then, he was not intent upon fleeing Germany altogether. His record was clean, and he could serve the cause better at home. When he moved down to an American military base, he was prepared for the interrogators. The story of Bormann's death put them off other lines of inquiry.

Doubt was cast on his story when, in 1965, an attempt was made to uncover Bormann's body. Axmann had said he lay dead beside Hitler's personal surgeon, Stumpfegger. Berlin Post Office No. 40, the Lehrter Station branch, had notified Frau Gertrud Stumpfegger of her husband's death on the railroad bridge. Four mailmen were said to have buried him, along with a shorter and thickset man, in Exhibition Park. Finally, the park was dug up. Nothing was found to corroborate the report; certainly there was no evidence of Bormann's decayed corpse. A repeat performance in 1973 produced skulls and bones, which by that time were regarded with a jaundiced eye by the general public.

It boiled down to this. Axmann, a fervent Nazi with a responsible position in the Hitler Youth, the successor to Bormann's homosexual old crony Baldur von Schirach, went hotfoot to the Alpine Fortress, some four hundred miles by road through extremely dangerous territory occupied by enemy armies. He traveled fast, knowing Hitler was dead and Germany on the point of surrender. He headed where others were gathering—men wanted as major war criminals. By the time these guilty men had assembled, the Allies knew there was no mountain fortress with Hitler directing guerrilla armies in a new campaign that might last years. Hitler was dead in Berlin. Bormann had vanished. Allied soldiers relaxed. By the time Artur Axmann came out of hiding, there was a general willingness to believe his account of Bormann's death.

Axmann knew about the escape routes through the Alps. He knew the Werewolves and the Alpine Fortress were planned to have a maximum effect as propaganda to deceive the enemy. He knew Bormann would head in the opposite direction, toward northwest Germany and the big U-boat pens near Flensburg. Axmann had done nothing so wrong that an Allied tribunal would punish him, and so he had no need to run away. He was far more useful as a decoy.

He became a remarkably prosperous businessman considering his late start. So did Schirach, who served twenty years for crimes against humanity and came out of Spandau Prison straight into a lucrative publishing enterprise. Both these Hitler Youth leaders had behaved with unswerving loyalty, and they got their reward.

Martin Bormann can hardly have foreseen the use made of another bit of real estate in the Bavarian retreat which fell into his hands after the departure of Hess to England, and which was taken over by an Allied mission after his colleagues were hanged. This was the "White House" and the surrounding settlement at Pullach, about six miles south of Munich. Bormann's family used the old Hess house to entertain. The settlement provided rest and recreation for officers in charge of Dachau concentration camp when the sounds and sights became too much for them.

Into it moved General Gehlen and his intelligence staff after Bormann disappeared. The so-called Gehlen Org was financed by the West and directed against Soviet interests. The irony was complete. The Brotherhood had a friend in Bormann's old mansion. Over the front door the German eagle held in its claws only a few remaining bits of the swastika. The graceful young men on their pedestals in the garden had turned a moldy green since Hess admired them. But on Gehlen's dining-hall wall there survived the bosomy blondes who, true to the official Nazi vision of German womanhood, placidly wove daisy chains or clasped sheaves of wheat to their big breasts. Over Hitler's former intelligence chief's house now flew the Stars and Stripes. On a brass plate on the gates appeared the disarming words SOUTH GERMAN INDUSTRIES UTILIZATION COMPANY. Guards dressed as Bavarian gamekeepers, with leather shorts and embroidered suspenders, patrolled the high walls and the new electrified fencing. Inside, the former Hitler Youth training center became a training school for spies.

When Pullach was built for Hess in 1936, it was surrounded by a wall about a mile long. By the end of Gehlen's first year, entirely at the cost of the United States, a large staff toiled over Russian secrets and Bolshevik conspiracies inside a fortress built to Gehlen's architectural sketches. Some defectors from this agency thought they saw in Gehlen at this time an echo of Hitler: not just the physical resemblance, but the grandiose schemes. There were three levels of underground bunkers. Strongrooms were embedded in steel and concrete. Houses were modernized for the staff, who were discouraged from going outside except on business, and whose families had no contact with the local villagers. Doors and gates around the Pullach compound were operated by electric relays. Closed-circuit television not only scrutinized visitors but, later, also recorded them.

When the Gehlen Org became part of the federal German government, it continued to receive most of its money from American sources. The Free Europe Committee financed propaganda over Radio Free Europe, and the sponsors came from some of the largest and most respected of American business enterprises. Gehlen's liaison officer with this new toy was a former SA Brown Shirt leader, Peter Fischer, who went under the alias "Major Fiedler." During the war he had worked radio deception techniques to catch British agents sent into the Low Countries by air. His boss then was SS Major Josef Schreieder, who boasted that no Dutch resistance worker escaped his clutches.

Radio Free Europe was conveniently close when it began operations in 1950. It occupied a park in the heart of Munich. In time it grew into a chain of radio transmitters beaming anti-Communist information sandwiched between attractive programing into just about every part of the Soviet and Chinese Maoist countries. When uprisings did take place against Communist oppression, the rebels would say later that agents from Pullach and the promises of RFE broadcasters had led them naturally to expect support and, eventually, a democratic paradise. Doubtless those who escaped did find help in resettling. It was cold comfort for rebels against Russian overlords. But most of the Gehlen-type operations were all talk and little action. Risks were taken with other people's lives in truly bureaucratic style.

Gehlen's prominent employment by the West cannot have seemed to the Russians like a friendly gesture. Behind him were the U.S. Council Against Communist Aggression, the Congress for Cultural Freedom, American Friends of Russian Freedom, and other "citizens'" committees. He even had his agents attend world conferences of Moral Re-Armament.

The murderously infantile approach of Germans to secret-service work was captured by Walter Schellenberg's description of his own wartime office: "Microphones were everywhere. They were hidden in the walls, under the desk, even in one of the lamps, so that every conversation and every sound was automatically

114

recorded. . . . My desk was like a small fortress. Automatic guns were built into it which could spray the whole room with bullets. All I had to do in emergency was press a button and both guns would fire simultaneously. At the same time, a siren would summon the guards to surround the building and block every exit. . . . On missions abroad, I had an artificial tooth inserted which contained enough poison to kill me in thirty seconds. To make doubly sure, I wore a signet ring in which a gold capsule was hidden under a large blue stone. The capsule contained cyanide."

The Nazi spy chief's filing system was a masterpiece of intricacy and detail, and set the Gehlen Org a very high standard. There were background notes on the psychology and mannerisms, the friendships and family origins, of every Allied personality whose name appeared in field reports or foreign intelligence summaries. "We had files on every agent, co-worker, member of the staff and motives for collaboration," said Schellenberg. "We could pick out a name in Istanbul and in a moment produce, by cross-indexing, all his contacts and all his human failings." He described, in his Swiss exile, a complex rotating chain of index files which brought to any researcher in a moment all the information relevant to a problem.

This system, crude by today's computerized credit-rating banks, nevertheless was taken over by Gehlen. And the contents were ransacked before the war's end by ODESSA. Obviously, the lucky ones were already in Schellenberg's employ. They had access to gadgets that, for those days, were highly sophisticated.

When Schellenberg realized that his archrival, Gehlen, had no plan to bring him into the new American-German secret service, he talked more freely to his British captors. He told them a great deal about the facilities and gadgets available. They included a radio transmitter about the size of a cigar box with a small telephone-type dial with three buttons. The agent turned the first button and dialed his message in code, which was automatically transferred to magnetized tape inside the box. Then a second button was turned; a light glowed; and when it was brightest, the sender knew he was beamed directly to the contact receiver. The third button activated the high-speed transmission of the wire tape, which Schellenberg claimed took three-fifths of a second to complete, too fast for any direction finder to lock onto it.

Such gadgets were useful for escapees moving through enemy-occupied Europe. The files gave the names and addresses of "friends" in neutral areas.

CHAPTER 11

Bormann at one time asked Walter Schellenberg "to prepare a special brief on the administrative structure of the Roman Catholic Church," and especially "its policy in South America."

His curiosity about networks in Latin America was no greater than that of Washington. Nazi maps of a Greater German Empire in that region, to be shared with colonizers from Franco Spain, had been studied since the first threats were made that bombs could be dropped on American cities from bases to the south. Diplomatic and economic pressures were applied on Nazi-minded governments. The movement of Nazi funds was interrupted wherever possible, and when financial transactions were conducted through American institutions, J. Edgar Hoover was able to get action through Treasury and Federal Bureau of Investigation agents. But the end of the war in Europe resulted in a dismantling of intelligence agencies, or, at best, their struggle to survive.

Anything to thwart Nazi fugitives was done on the same informal basis that characterized the early days when New York lawyer William J. Donovan and the Canadian chief of British intelligence, William Stephenson, worked together to build up a wartime alliance directly responsible to Roosevelt and Churchill. Now Donovan was fighting to have his OSS transformed into a peacetime intelligence organization. Stephenson was closing down Latin-American operations from the regional office in New York's Rockefeller Center. He was diverted briefly to rescue the defecting Russian cipher clerk Igor Gouzenko, who brought with him a full disclosure of the Communist spy rings extracting the secrets of America's atomic bomb. Attention was thus drawn away from the remnants of Hitler's successors.

Yet what frustrated Donovan and Stephenson was that they knew the German networks as well as the Nazis' own spy chief, Schellenberg. They had been warned that "we'll set up bases in Mexico,

116

Argentina, Brazil . . . and in French Canada," by Admiral Canaris.

Canaris, for his own reasons, had leaked information to the Western Allies. But he was hanged as a traitor by Hitler, and his warnings vanished under more urgent files.

After Stephenson withdrew to Bermuda, which had been his spyglass on Latin America, he discussed again, with me, the recurrent nightmare of Bormann. Stephenson's network of communications, which at one time employed 3,000 cipher clerks in the cavernous basement of the Princess Hotel, was much reduced. He was in touch with the international police agency, Interpol, and recognized that it labored under severe restrictions so far as war criminals were concerned. He raised the question of who would have provided Bormann with the specialists in unconventional warfare needed to guard his person. There was only one such German specialist of any note, and that was Scarface Skorzeny. The SS escape organizations had their trained men, of course. The Nazi political theorists, the guardians of the flame, required a military arm. This was in keeping with the traditional Freikorps, and students of German history were sure that the 1945 defeat had not eliminated this instinct to form armed mutual-aid groups.

During Christmastime in 1945, "the most dangerous man in Europe," as the Americans had once called him, SS Major Otto ("Scarface") Skorzeny, was allowed out of prison camp to visit his family in Munich. He was followed by Allied agents, who thought he might get in contact with Bormann. Nothing happened.

Skorzeny was a giant of a man with a chalk-line scar scribbled from the left temple to the corner of his mouth, above a massive chin. He had slate-gray eyes and dark springy hair. This was the man then already suspected of being director of an escape agency, Die Spinne (the Spider).

He saw himself, as he said after he did finally escape to Spain, as the counterpart of the OSS's Donovan. "I was interrogated by the General, and in this way I met the American who performed the same function in his army as I did in mine."

This disarming attempt to equate the job of Hitler's secret and personal supercommando with that of Donovan did nothing to soften OSS feelings toward him. It was typical of the man's insensitivity. But Donovan had no illusions.

In this role, Skorzeny had talked privately and frequently with Bormann. The chief of Hitler's special forces found himself "in control for forty-eight hours of all German forces at home and in occupied Europe." The confusion following the plot against Hitler in July 1944, he said, "made me realize what can be done to seize power by a resourceful individual."

He was the ideal man to prepare for the survival of Bormann's chosen few. He talked about the "Skorzeny Concept" of air-borne privateers, hit-and-run raids, and unconventional methods of controlling nations by using a few toughs to grab the levers of power. He had plans to bombard New York with rockets fired from U-boats, and he persuaded rocket engineer Wernher von Braun to let Hanna Reitsch try riding a V-1 rocket as a preliminary to striking London with human bombs. He wanted to kidnap the King of Italy during a political crisis. His actual wartime exploits fell short of his promises. Nonetheless, he did hoist Mussolini out of a supposedly impregnable mountain position, where the dictator was held prisoner after Italy capitulated. (As late as November 1972 he was still displaying, this time to admiring South African colonels, a gold wristwatch inscribed with Mussolini's "M" and the date of the rescue: "12.9.1943.")

He was provided with the means to prepare SS escape routes by an order drafted by Bormann in July 1944. This called upon "all personnel, military and civil," to help Skorzeny in any way and with anything he wanted. It was signed by Hitler and stated that "Skorzeny has been directly charged with secret and personal orders of utmost importance."

The fullest use of this order was made by General Gehlen, then of Foreign Armies East, who was preparing already for the mass transfer of his intelligence files on Russia. He had used Skorzeny a great deal in the fast few months to build up a picture of secret operations behind Russian lines. And he could use him to buy freedom when the Third Reich fell. Scarface Skorzeny was a means to survive, and more.

There were many things about Skorzeny that made him attractive. He would be bait for the Americans when the time came for Gehlen and the rest to switch sides on the grounds that they had always been fighting Communism. Skorzeny had strong views about the Bolsheviks and the Russians: "All of them, from the Arctic to the Black Sea, have been tarred with the same racial brush. They are just orientals with a callous fatalism," he wrote after the war was long finished. From ODESSA's point of view, he was useful because he had tested escape routes through Italy, and had set up training programs in which each of his commandos became

118

proficient in a variety of skills. They could drive locomotives or steam rollers and could repair anything that moved, including the one-man torpedo. He had Bormann's license to plunder every arsenal and supply depot. He stole weapons for his special forces and made each man expert as an industrial saboteur, parachutist, underwater swimmer, and escape artist. His glider troops for the rescue of Mussolini were provided with maps pinpointing the Catholic havens where they could hide if they were forced to return overland; their disguise was to be the familiar robes of the priesthood.

In November 1944, when secret contacts were being developed between German agents and the West with an eye to escaping postwar retribution, Skorzeny got an assignment that would insure him a friendly reception in Franco Spain, the most promising territory from which the postwar traffic could be directed. He was told to set up a resistance organization behind the Russian lines and to make contact with anti-Communist partisans. The groundwork had been laid two years earlier, in Operation Zeppelin, in which Soviet prisoners were trained to become saboteurs behind their own lines. Now Gehlen envisaged a new non-German intelligence network: the Secret League of Green Partisans.

In all these enterprises, it was the form that mattered and not the content. Scarface Skorzeny got little from this period on the Eastern front except dysentery and bladder trouble. Yet, like Gehlen, he made it all sound impressive later. The "hoop of steel" which he was to throw around Hitler and the Alpine Fortress never proved more than a pipe dream, though it sounded frightening enough that urgent cables flew among the Allies about this last desperate stand. At war's end, Skorzeny and a few SS officers did retire into the region near the Austro-German border. But there was no mountain fortress, none of the thirty divisions of crack troops, no stocks of food and ammunition to supply the "defenders of the Alps."

Instead, there were "incredibly important party documents" to be hidden from the enemy. The President of the Reichsbank and Minister of Economics, Walther Funk, wanted protection there for himself and all the state treasures. Adolf Eichmann was to rendezvous there on the first stage of his long journey through the Argentine to a gallows in Israel. Skorzeny himself had been told to surrender to American troops. This would be safer than risking death as a scarfaced giant of a fugitive in a manhunt. And he could count upon early release.

This in fact happened. First, his old friend and admirer General Gehlen made his deal with American intelligence. Then Skorzeny went through a brief trial for war crimes, from which he was acquitted (largely with the help of testimony by a British secret-service agent), though he was still wanted in Denmark and Czechoslovakia. He remained in Allied hands until he was advised of the time to escape. On July 27, 1948 he walked to a railroad stop, took a train to Stuttgart, and next day was back in the vicinity of Eagle's Nest, where his daughter had been brought secretly to meet him. He spent months "climbing, felling trees and getting back into condition." Then he rejoined his wife, the daughter of Hjalmar Schacht, Hitler's former financial genius. By then, Schacht had been freed by the Nuremberg court, although the Russians voted for finding him guilty.

Why had the British intervened in Skorzeny's case? Why, for that matter, was Schacht afforded British protection from any reversal of a West German denazification court's decision to free him soon after Skorzeny's escape? Schacht, though cleared of the Nuremberg charges, had been classified "a major Nazi offender" and sentenced to eight years in jail. He was released in 1948, however. Before the court, which was in the French Zone, could change its mind, Schacht was in the British Zone, where the legalities were observed in a more accommodating way.

There were other odd circumstances, as Schacht himself told me in Indonesia three years later. When he left prison, he had only two marks and fifty pfennigs in his pocket. Almost overnight, he was directing a major West German bank, of which he soon became President. By the age of seventy-four, he was master-minding a resurgence of foreign trade through private channels.

A major part of that foreign trade was in the Mideast. After King Farouk's overthrow in Egypt, an appeal went to Gehlen to help train security forces there. Here was a long-awaited opportunity to restore German influence in the Mideast, where the Nazi secret services had taken a bad bashing, although remnants still survived and were being used for ODESSA stations. Gehlen and Schacht quickly agreed that there was only one man for the over-all direction of this new challenge: Otto Skorzeny.

Skorzeny had been in touch with forcibly retired German generals and other comrades, seeking support for the bold proposal that he raise several military divisions to help the Americans fight the war in Korea. It is interesting that in the conversations of which there is any record, it was always an American war and it was always a case of the more experienced Germans showing the Americans how to win it. This canvassing started in 1950, when Skorzeny was scarcely out of detention camp, and it clearly had the tolerant interest of the Western occupying powers. Germany was full of ex-soldiers with no place in civil life, and Skorzeny proposed to bring them to Spain for training.

He took the view that the Korean war might be orchestrated with another in Europe, so that his "four or five crack divisions" could be utilized there. How much of this was scaremongering designed to stampede the authorities into making concessions? Skorzeny's record was one of maximum noise. He boasted of great adventures, and he did have a schoolboy enthusiasm for unconventional methods of warfare. His performance was not nearly as impressive as made out. He had rescued Mussolini and also Franco's brother-in-law, Ramón Serrano Suñer, from seemingly impregnable prisons, but, without wishing to diminish these accomplishments, it must be said that he did have a tendency to launch wild schemes that came to nothing. His projected operations in the Mideast during the war never amounted to much because of almost incredible inefficiency and the misjudgment of the Arab temper. Nevertheless, he had his own peculiar vision of what Germany could do in the Arab world and he swallowed the reports given him by his least admiring fan, Walter Schellenberg, who journeyed to the office in Madrid that Skorzeny opened in 1950 for business as a kind of consultant in unconventional warfare (with "engineering" as the professed purpose of the enterprise). Schellenberg wanted a reconciliation because he believed he saw a grand design forming: Gehlen and the Org taking in American money on a scale that for Europe was quite magnificent, and Skorzeny in Spain preparing an operational arm of a restored foreign intelligence service beyond the confining limits of the Soviets. The Communist threat was simply the quickest and most convenient way to get Yankee dollars.

Franco, however grateful for getting back his brother-in-law, knew something of President Juan Perón's problems in Argentina with the boisterous members of the Brotherhood. He told Skorzeny that a defense project in Spain was, of course, always interesting. However, the Americans were dealing directly with Spain in the matter. Perhaps Skorzeny would like to get official American support, particularly for his plan to fall back onto Spanish North Africa if the Russians overran Europe?

Skorzeny then turned his attention to reviving old Nuremberg connections, and through his father-in-law made the biggest postwar deal between Spain and West Germany, for the delivery in 1952 of five million dollars' worth of railway stock and machine tools.

Skorzeny played the part of a Spanish grandee in Madrid. He met "customers" at one of the best restaurants, run by a former pet of Göring. It was here that most of Franco's Cabinet lunched.

Skorzeny was lecturing in Spanish universities on the new warfare and "the strategy of wide spaces where long front lines no longer exist. Between major war theaters will be a wide space for lightning strokes to throw down a slower adversary. Other conflicts may well start with a series of assassinations and kidnappings." He was doing excellent business that spilled over into Brotherhood affairs in Latin America. And he still had his youthful romantic notion of Arab warriors.

The job in Cairo, as Gehlen and Schacht had agreed, was tailor-made for him. He went as General Mohammed Naguib's adviser, and when that gentleman was pushed aside for Gamal Abdel Nasser, continued under the new firm. A German military mission had grown out of the large numbers of former SS men sent to Egypt by ODESSA. Other Nazis were brought over from Argentina, where they had been recruited by the Brotherhood's much-decorated representative, Colonel Hans-Ulrich Rudel.

Did the Americans and British, knowing Skorzeny's projected role in Bormann's postwar plans, deliberately let him go? He was far from stupid, but he was bombastic and indiscreet. He might be expected to lead the hunters to Bormann, or help the Allies define the size of the Brotherhood's conspiracies. His salary was subsidized by Allen Dulles, using the CIA's unaccountable funds, after Dulles persuaded him in 1953 to help build Egyptian security forces. By then, of course, John Foster Dulles was also in the act, and the brothers in this period were swept away by the concept of a liberated Arab world standing strong against Communism.

CHAPTER 12

Nazi influence in the Mideast was the last thing I anticipated when I flew to Cairo after Nasser took over the Suez Canal in 1956. I was living in Hong Kong and covering Asia, where events were having their effect on all the new nations of Africa and the Arab world. I had in my passport the key that opened many doors in those days: a visa into Maoist China. The former wards and colonies of the West welcomed a white man who was in turn welcomed by the New China.

The first sign of something odd came when I went to see General Naguib, the revolutionary leader who was under house arrest. Police agents requisitioned my car and hustled me into a suburban barracks. The drill seemed vaguely familiar. A friendly Egyptian Army sergeant said wryly, when I asked: "The Germans won. Our real boss is one of Rommel's old staff officers, General Farnbacher." This was the former Waffen SS General Wilhelm Farnbacher.

Later, after being released on my promise not to go near that area again, I heard the usual gossip when foreign correspondents flock to the center of a crisis. At the Metropolitan Hotel there was talk of a German military mission, of SS men and Wehrmacht officers who said they were never Nazis (because, of course, as army men they could not join the party). They worked under Arab names. That seemed to imply some sense of embarrassment at least.

At the old Gezira Sporting Club I found an Argentine diplomat who was one of the post-Perón radicals. Would he feel like talking about Nazi survivors? Indeed he would. He had a list of 240 names—the real German names of men who had fled from the prospect of Allied justice. He had the travel details of German professionals recruited in Argentina, where they had found sanctuary while that country endured the dictatorship of Perón.

I cabled Iain Lang, the Foreign Editor of the London *Sunday Times,* asking him to check some of the more prominent names.

123

Back came several potted biographies, including that of a high official of Goebbels's Propaganda Ministry and Himmler's Central Security Office, Franz Bünsch. He was the author of *Sexual Habits of the Jews,* a piece of German racist pornography published at the height of anti-Semitic viciousness. He collaborated with Eichmann on the "final solution." Now he was working in Nasser's Ministry of Guidance under an Arab pseudonym.

When this kind of information comes the way of a reporter, it is good tactics to share it with a colleague. The prospect of confronting Bünsch was slim. It was unlikely I could take notes. I would need a reputable witness. A respected Western writer in Cairo was Ann Sharpley, whose boss was Lord Beaverbrook. She had come to a position similar to mine in her own investigations: there were several hundred Germans with Gestapo, SS, or Nazi propaganda experience. Their anonymity was protected by a security system established by Otto Skorzeny. Worse, Gestapo-trained Egyptian agents were looking for ways to trap Western journalists. These *agents provocateurs* would employ Nazi methods of incriminating their victims. Two correspondents for London newspapers had been warned by the British Embassy's security man that they were in danger. Their "secret" negotiations with an Egyptian Army major for a news story on the Suez defense system would be climaxed by the handing over of military maps, whereupon they would be arrested for spying. One of the reporters hopped on the next plane home. The other, Donald Wise, then with the *Daily Express,* dropped his contact but stayed to brazen things out.

Yet there were Egyptian officials ready to risk their lives to help. An official of the Ministry of Guidance suggested we look for another prominent ex-Nazi, Professor Johann von Leers, masquerading under a Moslem name. He directed radio propaganda against Israel.

The shock of coming face to face with this man still impresses me. It is one thing to put together the circumstantial evidence leading to a certain conclusion, and quite another matter to confront reality. It is one of the most exciting moments in any investigation when all the abstract calculations prove to be visibly exact.

It was a Saturday morning. An anonymous voice on my phone recommended that I go to the ministry. I picked up Ann. We took the precaution of telling two colleagues to start inquiries if we were not back by a certain time. At the ministry the anonymous caller finally made himself known. After sending his watchdog colleague out for coffee, this Egyptian official said quickly: "Go to the office of ———— on the fifth floor."

There the door with that Arab name on it was open. Inside sat a pink-cheeked, white-haired man with bright-blue marblelike eyes. We stepped inside, Ann closed the door, and I said: "Von Leers!"

He sprang to his feet. "Yes?"

"What are you doing here?" "I am a specialist in Zionist affairs." "How did you get here?" "From Argentina in 1954." "You are wanted as a war criminal." "That is right. I have been three times arrested by Americans in Germany before I make my escape. . . ."

The questions and answers fell into the familiar pattern of an interrogation. Ann and I concluded later that the man had been questioned so often by Allied experts that he responded automatically. After the first brisk exchange, we took him back to the mystery of his easy escapes from one Allied camp after another; and further back, to his work for Hitler and his belief in the Zionist menace. I cannot say what created the mood. It seemed as if he had been expecting us all his life.

Ann put her questions quietly, without emotion, a soft woman's voice talking to a child. Only I knew the suppressed rage inside her. Perhaps this plump little man was really not listening to her words so much as responding to the strength behind them. My own questions were brief and deliberately curt, with a touch of panic. I was certain the police would burst in. We had penetrated all the barriers to talk with a Nazi war criminal now held in respect and paid a large salary, plus all expenses, plus the cost of bringing his German wife and children from Argentina.

Incredibly, he continued to talk. There was indeed a Zionist conspiracy, and always had been. Nothing would cure the human race of the Jewish disease except massive surgery. . . . Israel was the cancer that must be cut out. . . . "But in attacking Israel, aren't you providing Russia with a door into this region?" I asked, pursuing his argument that Nazi Germany recognized the true enemy long before the rest of what he called the "civilized world." "Ah, the Russians!" he murmured. He began to rock back and forth, crooning: "First they arrive singing Arab songs and then slowly the melody turns into words and music for balalaika. . . ."

Ann recalled for me in 1972 her own impressions. She said: "He was instantly recognizable as a German despite that Arab name on the door. His manner was nervous and yet welcoming, as if he was bored and glad of the diversion. Without asking who we were, he went into a half-hysterical flood of confession, reminiscences, excuses—and fear. . . . He compared world dictators. Hitler had been too impatient. Perón, for whom he'd also worked, was too impatient. Nasser also. But 'Uncle Joe' Stalin could take his time."

We were arrested that afternoon. By then, however, our dispatches were out. Authority decided to put us on the first available plane, and we were expelled that same night.

We were relieved to get off so lightly. During the previous week, I had received a cable advising that "Mike" considered I should leave Cairo immediately for my own safety. "Mike" was Lester Pearson, the Canadian Foreign Minister at that time. He told me later that the threats which disturbed him most had come from known Nazis, whose opinions about "Jew lovers" were voiced in the presence of Canadian intelligence officers. Threats had been made to both Ann and me in a more direct fashion. We were invited out for dinner with an Egyptian journalist whose job was to keep on good terms with foreign correspondents and also to report to his government. The evening was full of bonhomie until the host turned deadly quiet and said with soft precision: "I have been asked to tell you that if you persist in looking for dirt to dig up, your body will be rolled in a carpet and dropped on the doorstep of your embassy." It took us several seconds to realize that the words had been carefully rehearsed and were not meant as a joke. By the time we were expelled, the threats were taken so seriously that the foreign press corps came out to the Cairo airport to make sure we boarded an overseas flight and were not escorted straight through the customs hall and out the other side.

Professor Johann von Leers was a doctor of philosophy and professor of history in Nazi Germany. He had described Hitler as "absorbing the powerful forces of this Germanic granite landscape into his blood through his father." The Professor wrote little else but variations on the theme of blood and iron. In his conversation with us, he claimed to have been held in "Jewish" concentration camps after the war—American Jews, he added helpfully. On further questioning, however, it developed that he was held in Russian and East German camps, too.

Since then, it has been possible to trace the Professor's movements in greater detail. He was sent into West Germany with Communist help, and, ironically, moved immediately into the Vatican Line. He was regarded by the Brotherhood as a distinguished theoretician in racial matters, and he was able to collect his family in Italy and move to Argentina. Within months, he was on his way to Cairo. His propaganda themes were curious because, on close examination, they promoted ideas that were far more helpful to Communism than anything else: "The Germans will unite again. Their natural friends are the Arabs. The Arabs must unite under Nasser. Israel is an abnormality which must disappear. Zionists are responsible for ninety percent of the press attacks against Nasser. The Egyptian song is a modest song until Father Khrushchev joins in with his Russian balalaika."

One thought he left with me was "Escape. Always escape. Always leave yourself a line of escape."

And another: "Otto Skorzeny is a commando adventurer. He makes business here, in South America, in Africa, wherever our Brotherhood functions. When he comes here next, I will introduce you." But, of course, he never could.

When last heard from, Professor Leers still piped the same tune from Cairo. I have always had the feeling that his escape route now, however, is back to his original home: East Germany.

An encounter of this nature delivers a sharp jolt. It is not like attending the public trial of Eichmann, nor is it the same as facing such men in interrogation centers. It left me with a sense of wonder foreshadowing my 1972 conversation with General Gehlen.

Gehlen sent, under his direct orders, a variety of German "experts" to Cairo in the postwar period. It is claimed he did this after Nasser took over because Washington regarded the new Egypt as a valuable ally. The facts are different. Long before King Farouk was overthrown in January 1952, a steady stream of ex-SS and ex-Gestapo men moved to Cairo and other Mideast centers. By the mid-1950's there were so many in Egypt alone that Gehlen sent a liaison officer, former Deputy Reich Leader of Hitler Youth Hermann Lauterbacher. Another resurrected Nazi to join the Cairo clique was a former colleague of Bünsch. Both had worked under Eichmann in the Central Security Office's "Jewish department." Ex-SS Captain Alois Brunner, supposedly hanged by the Russians, had escaped to join the Gehlen Org and was posted for his own safety to the station in Damascus. There he functioned as director of the Syrian-German trading company Otraco, under the name of George Fisher (spelled sometimes Georg Fischer). He shared an office in Cairo with the stepson of Gehlen's aide, Major General Hans-Heinrich Worgitzky. This was Gerhard Bauch, whose cover was the German heavy industry concern Quandt.

The list goes on. This brief glimpse of mass killers is enough to tell us something about their protectors.

To return to Schacht and Skorzeny, let it be said that the frosty banker in the frock coat and the scarfaced adventurer who shrewdly married his daughter were a curious pair.

Schacht had the golden touch that made him attractive to that other great opportunist, Martin Bormann. They met in 1931 to discuss Hitler's finances.

After that 1931 meeting, Schacht wrote to Hitler: "Your movement is carried internally by so strong a truth and necessity that victory in one form or another cannot elude you. . . ." He thereupon set about drumming up funds. He had Gustav Krupp and other leading German industrialists contributing large sums to Hitler by 1933, when Bormann had full control over all Hitler's income. This was the Ruhr barons' way of saying "thank you and keep it up" while the Nazis crushed Communism, socialism, the free trade unions, and Jewish competition.

Schacht bled the Jews in several ingenious ways. He regarded as the most rewarding of his fiscal measures the price exacted for every Jew who migrated to Palestine. The World Zionist Organization paid, per head, the sum of 15,000 Reichsmarks, which represented a quarter of Schacht's annual salary as President of the Reichsbank.

By 1951, when we talked in Indonesia about his new schemes to make Germany proud again, he had been in and out of twenty-three prisons without visible signs of remorse. He was scouting for Krupp.

His son-in-law was in Spain. Skorzeny himself described one of his lines of business, ADSAP (A Directorship of Strategic Assault Personnel), thus: "Terms of reference would enable it to straddle the watershed between paramilitary operations carried out by troops in uniform and the political warfare which is conducted by civilian agents. It would be the primary task of the Director to plan operations within the widest scope of the highly diversified force at his disposal. In this planning the Director should make full use of all current military and political intelligence for the selection of targets and the assessment of priority. Some of these targets might change from time to time following realignment of policy. Others would retain their importance. The methods of attack would be constantly under review. A large part of this force must be in a state of readiness day by day for specific tasks."

And Schacht? The old man's business was not all that different.

CHAPTER 13

"Horace Greeley and the Brotherhood getting up to mischief in our backyard," said a cable I received in Saigon in 1951. "If you have time between wars, wouldst intercept our Horace in Djakarta?"

Horace Greeley was part of the name given Hitler's banker by his father, who had emigrated from Schleswig-Holstein to America and then gone home again.

The note came from Black Hole Hollow Farm, near Saratoga, New York, where Ian Fleming was staying with Ivan Bryce. He was still managing Mercury's foreign-news service, but he was also talking business with the North American Newspaper Alliance and, in particular, with one of the important figures behind the wartime scene in Washington: Ernest Cuneo, an international lawyer with special interests in the Latin countries. They were all former colleagues of Donovan and Stephenson.

Doctor Horace Greeley Hjalmar Schacht had flown to Indonesia at a time when the victors over Nazi Germany were diverted to fight in Asia. His timing was good. His old enemies were in no shape to worry about the new republic of Indonesia, the wealthiest underdeveloped country in the world, at that time happily kicking out Germany's competitors. The new revolutionary leader was Sukarno. He drew toward him opportunistic Germans, as did other demagogues rising to power on a wave of anticolonial sentiment. The British were fighting terrorism in Malaya and they had land, sea, and air forces engaged in Korea. The Americans were carrying the burden of the Korean war, and took the full impact of Red Chinese armies crossing the Yalu River there. The French were trapped in Indochina. The Western alliance with Russia had foundered in the conflict between Communism and Western interests.

Schacht thought that conditions were ripe for a German return to the Afro-Asian world. Moreover, Chancellor Konrad Adenauer wanted to utilize what few years remained to Schacht. Men of similar backgrounds, regarded as war criminals by the Allies in 1945 and still wanted in some cases by German courts or different governments in Europe, were earmarked for a great revival in German capitalistic enterprise. The groundwork had to be laid, however, outside the purview of the Allies or the Russians.

This was the larger role the Brotherhood was called upon to play. It gave the fugitives a vital sense of righteous anger against their "persecutors," similar to Hitler blaming the Versailles "betrayal" for his aggressive policies. As time passed, notorious figures appeared within the inner councils of a new crop of dictators created by the withdrawal of traditional Western influence from the Third World. One of the brashest of the Brotherhood was to help the former Gold Coast colony, Ghana, collapse into financial ruin. In 1951, it was Sukarno who was courted with the seductive idea that his Moslems should look to German "experts" for help in creating a vast Islamic crescent from Australasia to the Arab nations of the Mideast. Gehlen credited his West German intelligence agency with predicting Sukarno's later downfall (promptly followed by the appointment of a former Nazi storm trooper as Bonn's Ambassador to Djakarta: Dr. Hilmar Bassler, who had been responsible for propaganda to East Asia as a member of Hitler's Foreign Ministry, and who worked with Japanese forces occupying Indonesia).

Djakarta was in utter chaos when the fastidious figure of Dr. Schacht appeared on the scene. The economy suffered from galloping inflation, which reminded him of 1923, when he became President of the Reichsbank and stopped the catastrophic inflation that followed World War I. His remedies were less easily applied to Indonesia. Indeed, knowing and appreciating Indonesian lack of precision, I wondered how Schacht could survive five minutes of discussion with Sukarno. They were totally different. Sukarno was a sex symbol to millions of followers. He did everything on impulse. Schacht was a frosty old man who had always looked at life through spectacles he adjusted to reflect the light back into the eyes of his interlocutors.

The banker was reluctant to be seen at all by a reporter. On the other hand, he was not long out of his last prison, and, like all the others I met in this period who had the same background, he was not anxious to provoke hostility. Also he may have had some impression that I was on good terms with the new Indonesian leaders. From West Germans at the time you could get the most embarrassingly effusive co-operation. Kurt ("Panzer") Meyer, the general who led the Hitler Youth SS Tank Division, had first given me the introductions to Skorzeny, which led to this meeting. He had been under sentence of death for the massacre of Canadian prisoners of war and he was eager to oblige.

I met Schacht at the Hotel Capitol, overlooking the filthiest of Djakarta's canals. There was no protection from swarms of malarial mosquitoes and the stench of sluggish chocolate-brown waters sprinkled with garbage and human excrement. His narrow head balanced on a scrawny neck, his thin mouth pulled down at the corners, he regarded me warily. Below the open-sided hotel restaurant, women loosened their batik sarongs and splashed their firm breasts in gestures that deepened his expression of disapproval. Further along the banks, men and boys urinated in graceful arcs. The air was heavy. The overhead fans crackled, and sparks of electricity showered down. I quoted an Indonesian saying that applied to the clogged canal: "Good germs eat up bad germs if you just leave things alone." He smiled faintly.

There seemed no point beating around the bush. What, I asked, did he know about a so-called Brotherhood?

He looked startled. I said quickly there was no intention of publishing his replies. There had been a continuing interest in such groups, I said; the Circle of Friends, for instance.

He stiffened at this mention of Martin Bormann's source of additional funds, created by Schacht's successor and chief architect of his downfall: Walther Emanuel Funk.

I said: "Funk has told interrogators that the Circle of Friends broke up automatically, but the Brotherhood functions now to support Bormann."

His blue eyes, shaded by beetling brows, shifted behind the rimless glasses. A trickle of sweat ran down his gaunt chin. I had been sweating all morning in the tropical heat, but Schacht, dressed like a Dutch colonizer in open shirt and shorts, white and starched, had shown no previous sign of discomfort.

"Funk said that?"

"So it is reported."

"Funk always was a fool." He drew back. "The Circle of Friends was a source of money, no thanks to Funk."

"And the Brotherhood?"

"Die deutsche Gemeinschaft. I know nothing. I am here on business. The war is past."

"Funk is still in Spandau Prison."

"And I was in Ravensbrück, Flossenburg, and Dachau," he snapped, naming the three concentration camps where Hitler had once held him.

131

"Funk was sentenced to life imprisonment at Nuremberg." I stopped. Funk had escaped the hangman because of a strong feeling among the Allies that the real guilt lay with Schacht.

He looked away. "There was only one Brotherhood. In Vienna. It had no membership lists and nobody was known by his real name."

"Your son-in-law was a member."

"Did he tell you that?"

"No, but he was part of that crowd. Their aim was to liberate the German people from Jewish influence."

"I had nothing against the Jews." Yet it was only sixteen years ago that this man had warned in a 1935 speech: "The Jew can become neither a citizen nor a fellow German." Now, he cocked his head like an intelligent secretary bird. "Are you Jewish?"

"No. Nor married to a Jewess," I added, reminding him of another Brotherhood prohibition.

"What is your purpose?" he asked stiffly.

"Your son-in-law says Russia can be beaten. Communism in China or Russia can be beaten if we learn from the last war."

"Ah. You think Indonesia will go Communist?"

"Yes. In its own peculiar way."

"Perhaps this can be stopped?"

"In the same manner as in Africa or, shall we say, South America?"

"I go there from here. Conditions are better now, is it not true?"

"Better for what?"

"Free enterprise."

He slapped at a mosquito. Around us, Dutch traders leaned on folded arms over the small round tables, or lifted mugs of beer to perspiring faces. Soon most of them would be deported, their commercial operations taken over, their assets seized, their families moved into camps. The words "free enterprise" echoed dismally in the moist air. Schacht had financed the rearming of Hitler's Germany in ways that were illegal under the statutes of the time. He had been deeply involved with a complicated arrangement by which the Soviet Union helped Germany to get around limits on the production of weapons. It seemed to me that his career was based upon exploitation of other people's free-enterprise systems. In the United States he had been partly successful in the early 1930's in reassuring American Jews that their coreligionists had nothing to fear from Hitler. Now it was convenient for him to forget his undercover campaign to drive Jews from German life, forget the big

132

trade deals with Stalin and the "New Plan" to control everything the Reich bought abroad.

"Chancellor Adenauer says your experience in South America can be applied here."

Schacht nodded. "It could be done. Only here we must watch out for the Russians."

"And in Argentina?"

"The Catholic church is too strong to permit Communism. We have good relations there. In Bolivia also. So much in Latin America is badly developed. . . ." He began to talk about the bilateral barter agreements through which more than half of Nazi Germany's trade had been channeled. If things had worked out differently, Argentina and her neighbors would have been prosperous partners today, under a Nazi heaven.

"Perhaps this is still possible?"

"Not yet." He shrugged. Some of his earlier animosity began to melt in this unreal atmosphere. A cool breeze had sprung up, bringing a cleaner perfume of frangipani and spices. Schacht cocked his head. "You mentioned the Circle of Friends?"

"Yes."

"A foolish group of men. They can only do harm."

I realized suddenly that he was talking in the present tense.*

"These are the people who got the Nazis a bad name," he went on. "They lack the sense to keep out of the public eye. Strauss makes too much noise and gives propaganda material for the Communists. They talk about neo-Nazism and then the young students and the dupes of Communism take up the cry. We should move more slowly. Too many foreigners blame us for Hitler."

"But you had a great regard for Hitler."

"His ideas were good at the start. He was led astray."

"By whom? Göring? Bormann . . . ?"

"Not Bormann," he said quickly, and then compressed his lips.

. . .

* The Circle of Friends later came into the open in its new form. By 1970, it issued regular bulletins in support of Franz Josef Strauss, of the Bavarian Christian Social Union (CSU). An example from a bulletin issued in Cologne, October 1970: "We have appealed to all who sympathize with the National Democrats [the most prominent of neo-Nazi groups] to vote to strengthen the position of Franz Josef Strauss. He is the coming man. He does not succeed nor replace Adolf Hitler but he has the leadership qualities. The German Army's officer corps awaits the strong man: Strauss. German youth needs strong and stern leadership. . . . The press must be strictly curbed. . . . We must seize power in one way or another—even if the elections are not in our favor. Germany is at stake."

133

An old newsreel gives a flashback to Schacht in the mid-1930's. It is the year when he boasted to German industrialists: "I have Hitler by the throat." The old film shows him walking alongside the Führer with a proprietorial air. He wears a black banker's suit, the three-buttoned jacket tight around his waistcoat, a conservative tie knotted carefully but scarcely visible within the confines of a three-inch-wide stiff collar. His eyes are narrow slits, and he balances a large monocle in one of them. His silver hair is parted straight down the middle. His arms hang stiff at his sides. Slightly in front of him, a little to his right, prances Hitler, with one arm stretched rigidly at the horizontal. They march among crowds kept at a safe distance by troops in jack boots. Schacht's eyes swivel in Hitler's direction, and one imagines him saying, as indeed he wrote at this period: "Eating keeps body and soul together, drinking separates them. A clean body means a clean mind. A man's character can be judged by the way he cleans his shoes."

It is the year 1933. Hitler has become Reich Chancellor at the age of forty-four. Schacht is Minister of Economics at fifty-five, with special responsibility for rearming Germany. He certainly should feel as if he has a collar around Hitler's throat, and a chain.

Behind him, however, is the ponderous Martin Bormann. This is one of the rare occasions when Bormann does not sidestep behind someone else to dodge a camera. Schacht struts. Bormann plods.

Bormann is in fact Hitler's personal banker, not Schacht. The royalty income from *Mein Kampf* is $300,000 for 1933, at that time an incredible fortune for any book. Millions of marks are rolling into the industrialists' secret Hitler fund. There are the salaries of Hitler's state offices, and his income from various business and party enterprises.

Schacht, on the other hand, is thinking in terms of billions: how to control national economies in faraway places; how to tax Jewish emigrants and force their settlements to take German products; how to finance the munitions makers with the blocked assets of political enemies abroad; how to pay for raw materials in the local currencies of countries like Argentina. All the old arrogance, for which he was notorious during the German occupation of Belgium in World War I, all the smug superiority, is back. He cannot help but strut.

Bormann is in nondescript uniform, somewhere between the world financier and the party thugs. The others walk with the jerky motion that is characteristic of old newsreels, yet Bormann seems to have overcome even the technical obstacle of clumsy cameras.

The son of a post-office clerk has become a Reich Leader. He was an ordinary gunner at the time Schacht was using military force to squeeze the Belgian industrial lemons. He was a convict while Schacht composed pretentious maxims in his presidential office at the Reichsbank. He did the accounts on a farm while Schacht was hobnobbing with the Governor of the Bank of England.

There is another newsreel of about the same period in which Schacht trips and performs a quickstep before regaining his balance. Bormann's face loses its impassive expression. Unholy joy illuminates those porcine features and then vanishes.

Bormann was then Chief of Staff to the Deputy Führer, Rudolf Hess. There were ambitious young men on all sides, and vain old men like Schacht in front. All of them aimed their efforts at Hitler, whose personal favors seemed the best and quickest route to promotion. The working parts of the state machine were, however, in the Office of the Deputy Führer, where Bormann worked his quiet little intrigues. He made himself indispensable to Hess, and also to the lesser party members who called Hess "Fraulein Anna" because of his homosexual tendencies. There were some favors Bormann was not prepared to grant up-and-coming young Nazis; but if those favors were to have a cumulative value (like interest on a bank deposit), he was ready to bring Fraulein Anna and the aspirants together.

His hold over Schacht was partly that of a younger man handling funds acquired by a stiff-necked and unimaginative banker twenty-three years his senior. In a study of Germany's rearmament, made for Churchill on a personal and highly confidential basis by William Stephenson, who was in the Ruhr constantly during this period, the point is made that Schacht rather late in life was suddenly gripped by Hitler's message. Convinced by *Mein Kampf,* he traveled abroad to tell the financial world of the political and economic brilliance of National Socialist theories. At a dinner given by David Sarnoff, of the Radio Corporation of America, in New York in 1933, ten of the dozen guests were Jews from what Schacht called "influential circles." He told them that he did not take Adolf Hitler too seriously; the Jews in Germany had nothing to fear. Bent upon raising money for the Nazi party, he adjusted his words to suit the audience. He told Roosevelt that without the discipline and nationalism of the party, Germany would fall to Communism. He stood before the United States as a banker, and therefore a man of probity, and spoke over a nationwide radio hook-up and addressed some forty audiences in different American cities, repeating his message that

135

there was a close similarity between Roosevelt and Hitler, and it should be easy for their governments to collaborate.

Back home, he told a women's club in Berlin about the historical justification for exterminating Jewish influence. The problem was nothing new. Jews had been out of place in German society for many centuries. There was a "folkish incompatibility." Meanwhile, he was being described in the New York *Times* as "humane and courageous" for a speech in New York and articles that painted quite a different picture of Hitler and Nazi aims. In the presence of this elegant and persuasive snob, some U.S. editors gave him a good press at a time when American newsmen in Germany were trying to convince their editors that concentration camps did exist, and that Jews were already persecuted and officially slated for extermination.

Bormann saw in him just the right man to come to the financial rescue, and to delude the frock-coated gentlemen of the Bourse, the City of London, and Wall Street: a man who would never endanger his family for the sake of a principle. His wife at that time was a formidable lady, frantic to whip up support among the women for the Führer. She carried a picture of Hitler dressed as a Knight of the Holy Grail, and she placed over her bed a portrait of him surrounded by a shining halo of tiny Christs. Later, when Schacht, in his arrogance, failed to make Hitler do things his own way, he resigned as Minister of Economics and Plenipotentiary for War. It was not because he had lost enthusiasm for National Socialism, he said. He was tired of "going to bed with Hitler." His marriage broke up at the same time, and he took for his new wife a girl thirty years his junior.

This young woman was another protégée of Martin Bormann. He knew most of the weaknesses of the leaders around Hitler, and he played on them. In the case of Schacht, it was vanity. Schacht had a passionate love of work. He would spend all night on a plan to default on transfer payments on American loans in order to finance the rearmament program. His first wife showed small regard for this dedication, little understanding of his brilliant solutions, and no patience with his egotism.

The girl who now worshipped at the high-buttoned boots of Schacht had been purposely discovered by Bormann, who recognized in the financial wizard a likely rival. The banker showed unmistakable signs of wanting to make Hitler dance to his own tune and there was room for only one puppetmaster. Bormann pulled the strings with such self-effacing skill that, like others, Schacht never suspected that inarticulate flunkylike figure. Schacht suffered from the same intellectual arrogance, the same social snobbery, and the same disinterest in humbler mortals that afflicted so many of the men around Hitler. Bormann was at his most dangerous when he was still vulnerable, and he remained so deep in shadow that he was scarcely noticed.

Bormann knew enough about higher finance to recognize Schacht's enormous value. He learned enough to realize that you don't have to be a financial expert to pile up a fortune, any more than you have to be qualified as a mechanic to drive a car. What mattered was who you knew.

Immediately after Hitler became Chancellor, a meeting was called of twenty-five leaders of the Reich Association of German Industry. Krupp, the President, led the way in raising three million marks. It was intended to be split between the three parties in Hitler's coalition government. Instead, it went to the man who handled all Nazi party matters, Reich Leader Bormann. The German People's party and the German National People's party never got a sniff of it. The money was delivered by the Reich Association's treasurer, Schacht, to Bormann.

These arrangements were tidier than what Gustav Krupp called "wild collection drives" by Nazi troopers. Krupp admired Hjalmar Schacht and listened to the banker's advice that a "Hitler Donation" should be levied within the German trade associations. This should be, said Schacht, with infinite precision, 0.03 percent of salaries and wages. On paper it looked an infinitesimal figure. It could be explained in terms of a few pfennigs a month to those workers who got so far above their station as to ask questions about where it went. Other critics would be plainly identifiable as Communists if they dared keep up a protest against such a miserly sum. Actually, it produced a half-billion marks during the Nazi period, for Hitler to use in whatever way he liked. There was no need to account for it. Other members of the high command later received similar contributions. But not Bormann. He never asked because he never wanted to be in anyone's pocket. They were all in his. All monies were handled only by him. He kept meticulous records of those who paid into the fund and those who received from it gifts which he distributed. Krupp always found Bormann most obliging in these delicate transactions. And the Krupp family learned, after Hitler died, that this obliging and humble manager had documented some

137

embarrassing balance sheets. Krupp's profits shot up, for instance, doubling themselves in the three years following Hitler's rise to power. It was Bormann who kept the accounts.

On January 30, 1937, Schacht received the Nazi Golden Badge of Honor. The following year, although he had resigned as Minister of Economics, he remained President of the Reichsbank and continued to make speeches abroad that were designed to quell fears and keep the business rolling in. After the *Anschluss* with Austria, he told a Viennese audience that Hitler's hand was forced by the countless perfidies of other nations, and then called upon all present to swear allegiance to the Führer.

Later, at the Nuremberg trials, Schacht said he broke with Hitler when it became evident Germany had gone too far economically in preparing for war. Documents and transcriptions of telephone and other conversations in Allied hands told another story.

Schacht wanted to fashion the Nazi party in his own likeness. He did not fully understand, as Bormann did, the function served by Hitler, who could lead the generals and the people into any crusade. Schacht preferred to build an empire and win control over foreign economies by stealth and cunning. His talent for treachery was useful in the early days; and Bormann appreciated his skill with money and his way of enslaving individuals and whole communities by making them economically dependent upon Nazi leaders. The Schacht Plan, by which nations were obliged to have their raw materials processed in German factories through complex military and economic arrangements, became a model for twentieth-century imperialism, and was adopted by the Soviet Union within its own sphere. But Schacht was personally ambitious, as many of his contemporaries attested, and he began to poke into party affairs with a knowing finger. If anyone was equipped to recognize Bormann's own plan for economic control of the party, it was this expert in financial manipulation.

When Bormann's position was threatened by someone who could conceivably exercise greater power, that was always the time when he resorted to playing the simple peasant, while whispering confidences into the willing ears of a court eager for gossip. Mrs. Göring has described how he set her husband against Schacht by his technique of speaking privately to one rival and then the other. He was never blamed by Schacht for the suicidal quarrel he engineered between the two men. It began with the appointment of Göring to the job of Commissioner of Foreign Exchange and Raw Materials, which brought him into head-on collision with the man whose expertise in this field had won him international renown, if not respect.

Göring summed up his own idea of fiscal policy in these terms: "If the Führer says two and two make five, they make five." It was not Schacht's idea of arithmetic. Nor was it Schacht's notion of utilizing human resources until they were exhausted of all convertible energy when Göring plunged headlong into extermination programs. Schacht wanted to close the ring cautiously around the Jews, and he was aware always of public opinion abroad and the harm it might do to German trade. Göring, as head of the Four-Year Plan, bluntly instructed security chief Reinhard Heydrich to accomplish "the desired final solution of the Jewish question." If things had been left to Schacht, he would have disposed of Göring first, and all the crude leaders who failed to understand that a totalitarian state could achieve total domination by more subtle methods. He was offended by the clumsy investigative methods of the secret police, which Göring had founded: the Gestapo tapped his phone, opened his mail, and reported back to Göring without bothering to conceal their activities. Göring set up the first concentration camps in such a way that foreign newspapers reported their existence long before the war. Schacht was a National Socialist who took the whole thing seriously. He believed in Hitler, saw the necessity for secret police and death camps, had complete faith in the superiority of the Germanic race, and merely wished Hitler would submit to his advice.

David Sarnoff, after that New York dinner, said to Schacht: "Doctor, you've been a very good sport." It was the sort of thing that people say in decent society when they meet visitors who seem to share similar standards of behavior. It is hard to look into a manly face, return the steady gaze of frank blue eyes, relax in the company of a gentleman, and call him a liar. One is nervous of seeming a bigot. "There are always two sides," one is told from childhood. However . . .

One of his good friends who followed his example and sidestepped the Bormann hatchet was Konrad Adenauer. As Chancellor of West Germany from 1949 to 1963, he disarmed suspicious newsmen with the legend that he was an anti-Nazi resistance hero. In other words: "a good sport."

Just about the time it seemed that Schacht had meant no harm by his postwar travels to South America and the Mideast, Adenauer said in a Columbia Broadcasting System interview in February

1963: "I was always an opponent of the Nazis." All the old misgivings flared up again. I remembered a letter published in East Germany, later authenticated by the Chancellor, and written originally on August 10, 1934. It was a begging letter from Adenauer to the Prussian and Reich Minister of the Interior asking for payment of his pension as Lord Mayor of Cologne. The pension was restored, and it was still being paid him at war's end (when he cultivated his own garden with French slave laborers). The ten-page letter was an attempt to prove that he had always been friendly to the Nazi party: "I have always treated [it] in an absolutely correct manner; in so doing, I found myself at loggerheads with ministerial directives. . . . For years, contrary to the decrees of the Prussian Ministry of the Interior I made available to the Party the municipal sports grounds and allowed the Party to hoist its swastika flag. . . . I urged that municipal advertising should be given to the [Nazi party newspaper in Cologne] Westdeutschen Beobachter."

Then came a cringing explanation of how the party might have got the mistaken impression that he was hostile. He described an incident that resulted in the Nazis removing him from his post, "from which it is extremely painful to be dismissed on the grounds that I am 'nationally unreliable.'" Conjuring up a picture of his wife and seven children, he wrote that owing to a misunderstanding about municipal regulations, the Nazis' swastika flags had been flown on Cologne's suspension bridge. All he had done was express his willingness to have the flags hoisted outside the party meeting (the Nazis had accused him of having the flags torn down). The full letter has to be read to get the flavor. Its tortuous pleading is caught in this sentence: "Something which happened on one of the last Sundays before the Reichstag election aroused the impression that I was handling the NSDAP [Nazi] Party in a hostile manner amongst a certain part of the Cologne NSDAP which did not know the full facts." And, later: ". . . at these meetings I stated specifically that I thought that such a large party as the NSDAP must undoubtedly be represented in a leading capacity in the Government."

Konrad Adenauer became Chancellor shortly after Hjalmar Schacht was let go by the West German courts and his son-in-law, Skorzeny, escaped. Most of Schacht's subsequent travels abroad and Skorzeny's establishment of an agency in Madrid were made with the active support of Adenauer and the West German spy chief, General Gehlen. He had a separate arrangement with the new Circle of Friends, formed by industrialists who supported neo-Nazi political groups.

140

Schacht's movements were never easy to follow. If he wanted to fly to South America to give advice on expanding German business interlocked with the trading agencies financed through Brotherhood funds, the most discreet route was through Madrid and a direct flight to Buenos Aires and onward. He was well aware of the systematic interception of Nazis and their mail before and during World War II, but modern jet travel made this impossible, even if there had been any desire on the part of foreign governments to continue surveillance. Skorzeny commuted from Madrid to Cairo and to South America in complete security. As he said: "A jet is a sealed container flung across oceans, perhaps the most efficient method yet devised for moving men and objects in legitimate secrecy. The weakness in the system is only at exit and entry points. Therefore we need to have our comrades develop close and friendly relations with immigration and customs police in each locality."

Moreover, with Skorzeny's business office in Madrid, a house there and a farm estate in the republic of Eire, there were ways to avoid public attention. Friendly relations with Eire did not last long, however. The Irish, quixotic as ever, disliked Skorzeny's indiscreet tirades against England. He had expected a demand for his services as a guerrilla expert. Instead, he found the Irish farm workers on his land started a resistance movement of their own— against Skorzeny.

Schacht never could understand that the Hitler period was remembered still. His precautions became slacker as he grew older. While Adenauer held office, he knew he could count on discretion among officials. He disliked wasting time with detours between the Düsseldorf bank and the new financial and industrial web that he wanted to weave before he died.

He had influential friends, just as in the old days. The second most influential man after the Chancellor was Adenauer's State Secretary, Dr. Hans Globke. His job was reminiscent of Bormann's as Secretary to the Führer. And it was to Bormann that Globke had addressed a draft of the 1935 Nuremberg Laws, which provided the basis for liquidating the Jews. These racialist decrees were promulgated by Hitler at the Nazi party convention in Nuremberg. Thus, since the Jews were being massacred in accordance with German law, intervention on behalf of the victims was not legal.

Hans Globke was startled when, some twenty-five years later, his record was dragged out from the personal and confidential files of the old Reich Ministry of the Interior.

Globke had taken refuge in a Catholic monastery in 1945 after his chief, Heinrich Himmler, failed to win acceptance from General Eisenhower. Then he sought his own freedom by giving evidence at the Nuremberg trials against his former superior, Wilhelm Stuckart. He slipped back into civilian life and was brought to Bonn by Adenauer, for whom he worked thirteen years. In July 1963 the Supreme Court of East Germany found him guilty *in absentia* of crimes against humanity and sentenced him to life imprisonment. Globke resigned.

Did Globke help Bormann's friends? He certainly made life easier for Schacht. His resignation under Communist pressure was window-dressing to quell the anger of Western liberals. Five years later, in September 1968, a dinner was given in his honor by President Heinrich Lübke, accompanied by Chancellor Kurt Kiesinger.

The President, the Chancellor, and the former State Secretary thus publicly thumbed their noses at the verdict of history. In the old days, Lübke approved the blueprints for death camps; Kiesinger supervized Nazi radio propaganda. And Globke wrote, in an official commentary upon the Nuremberg Laws: "The two Nuremberg Laws together with the regulations based upon them contain the basic solution for this racial problem. . . . The Jewish problem is not just a racial-biological problem. It must be solved for centuries to come."

Were memories so short?

A young German girl thought not. Beata Klarsfeld was the daughter of a soldier who came back from the Russian front. He was broken in health but unshakable in his conviction that he had only done his duty. When she asked him why he did as Hitler ordered, he replied: "Because everyone else did." Her father had not been a member of the Nazi party, however, and his reward was not public dinners and honors but the pushing of a pen in the Ministry of Justice. He did not share the guilty knowledge and the fear of betrayal that seemed, to his impulsive daughter, the common bond that purchased power and position in the rich new Germany.

In outrage, she stood up in the Bundestag at Bonn and cried: "Kiesinger, Nazi!" It was her first protest.

CHAPTER 14

Hitler's burning corpse shared the rubble of Berlin with a six-year-old girl who was to haunt the Brotherhood, and especially three men who were escaping with loot that would establish prosperous trade in South America.

Beata Klarsfeld was an attractive redhead, a vital and good-humored young woman when she smoked out a former Gestapo killer in Bolivia early in 1972. I talked to her while she was in the process of being ushered out of Peru, but not before she forced the police to jail a former Nazi counterfeiter whose defense was that he acted under orders to produce the biggest bundle of forged banknotes in history.

Back in Paris, a few months later, she showed me what remained of a parcel-bomb addressed to her apartment. The label carried a symbol which she took to be the Brotherhood's trademark. The parcel was mailed from Lyons, scene of "punitive expeditions" conducted by SS Colonel Klaus Barbie, Gestapo chief who tortured to death one of the greatest French resistance heroes. Barbie was a man who reported proudly that he had arrested and deported all the children in the Jewish orphanage at Lyon. He was a man adroit enough to get on the American payroll of the West German intelligence agency when it was run by General Gehlen. And until Beata Klarsfeld arrived, he had turned himself into Señor Altmann, a respectable fifty-eight-year-old businessman of La Paz, Bolivia.

Beata Klarsfeld accused the German authorities, East and West, of tolerating former Nazis in high places and of doing little to remove from public life a mentality that seeks to conceal the past and refuses to draw any lessons. She had an annoying habit of being right. After West German officials had told her she was mad, she persisted in the case of Señor Altmann until he had to confess his real identity.

She also persisted in the case of another war criminal, known as Wenceslas Turi alias Wendig Alisax of Lima, Peru. Again, irritated

143

German officials said she was crazy. Bonn's Ambassador to Peru, Robert von Förster, had been a jurist in the Nazi courts; and his colleague in Bolivia, Georg Graf zu Pappenheim, had been in the Nazi diplomatic service and held Nazi party membership No. 3,733,-418. Both made it clear to the local authorities that the lady was an unmitigated nuisance.

The police in Peru looked harder at Turi/Alisax and charged him with smuggling fountain pens. They listed him correctly on the charge sheet as Frederic Schwend. He had done rather better than pens. He had helped float phony banknotes with a face value of $500 million, which, at the time Beata Klarsfeld was in kindergarten, had a purchasing power many times higher. His partner in turning out fake notes in a Nazi concentration camp was SS Major Bernhard Krüger. Now it also turned out that Krüger was on the managerial staff of Standard Electric AG, a subsidiary of International Telephone and Telegraph, the American company that had been caught in a scandal concerning an alleged attempt to sabotage a socialist government in Chile.

What chance did a young woman have against such forces, which must appear to wield unlimited power?

Beata Klarsfeld answered this question late in July in Paris. The banks of the Seine were quiet, the cobbled streets nearly empty. We walked to her apartment, in a new building—one that could be guarded.

She said her resources were limited, of course. But she had friends. She would even like to believe she had friends in Germany, because this was her whole motive: to oblige her countrymen to face the truth of their actions.

Was this her only motive?

She glanced up at me, with eyes that changed color with the light. "My parents were middle-class Protestants," she said softly. "I have no racial hangups. I was raised in a solid bourgeois quarter of Berlin. I have been arrested in Communist East Europe, so don't get wrong ideas—"

"Arrested for what?"

"Handing out leaflets demanding the release of political prisoners."

"Why?"

She paused, and shrugged. "Someone has to do it, surely?"

We came back to that answer time and again.

"You're German. Why live in Paris?"

144

"My husband is a lawyer here. I have small children. I'm not sure yet if I want them to grow up in Germany."

"Aren't you showing prejudice? Isn't this what you disliked about the past—the prejudice?"

"You may be right. Willy Brandt understands how I feel. He went into exile, but he had good reasons then. Of course one fights for justice *inside* society. Willy Brandt could not fight from inside because of the Gestapo."

"Are you afraid of something like a Gestapo today?"

"I know Bormann is protected by men of that mentality. Here, the police keep an eye on me. Why do you suppose I was not killed by that bomb?"

She turned to face the slight wind that rose with the heat of the sun on the stones and the asphalt. "I'm not some heroine, you know. One day you live quietly, mind your own business, plan to be a contented German housewife in the tradition of *Kinder, Kirche, Küche*—a few babies, the church on Sundays, the kitchen most of the week. And then by some accident you find yourself in the middle of a situation you don't like. And nobody else is in the same position you are to do something."

Martin Bormann can hardly have expected a woman to run against the wind. Women in his world were for procreation. There was so little place for women in the National Socialist system. There was an official image of the perfect German woman, pure and strong, and there was the reality of women treated as breeders or, among the homosexuals around Hitler, with contempt. Bormann's decree on "The Safeguarding of the Future of the German Nation" described the fertility of millions of women as the Nazis' most precious capital. Bormann, a pig grubbing in a potato field, in the eyes of his enemies, applied to the problem the ideas of a small-animal breeder. The war would leave three to four million women unmarried, at an age when they should be reproducing. A special procedure would make it possible for such women to become second and third wives. "All single and married women up to the age of thirty-five who do not already have four children," echoed the faithful Kaltenbrunner, "must be obliged to produce four children by racially pure German men. Whether these men are married is without significance."

Was this why Beata Klarsfeld had gone after Bormann, in some state of righteous wrath?

She laughed. "Look at me. I don't need women's lib to release me from some imaginary bondage. I like men. They have their roles, and we have ours. No, it simply happened that I wanted to know more about my country's history, and I became stubborn when people kept putting me off. My parents refuse to speak to me because they say I drag their good name in the dirt. My teachers at school always asked: Why bring all that up? And I began to ask questions. How could it be, I asked, that a civilized nation did these things? And always I was told not to ask. It had happened, that was all. Hitler had done it.

"And then I saw that Hitler was like . . . like, you would say, an image projected upon the screen. He meant nothing without large audiences. He was nothing except shadows dancing in the mind."

"Bormann managed the show?"

"Exactly. You have to be German to understand how this could happen. This is why I make my countrymen uncomfortable. Still, it can happen anywhere." She began walking toward a small park. "It can happen anywhere, when the men feel heroic—perhaps a better word is 'erotic'—about mass parades and exhibitions of power."

Her father had been one of the great crusade.

"All right," she said. "So naturally I think it's evil when men form an immense secret society, with smaller societies inside the larger, and exclude the pity and the compassion."

"Exclude *women,* you mean."

She smiled. "You are right. To the extent that I am driven by a fear of these things repeating themselves, I have a strong feeling about women. I will admit it, but this is part of the whole. Women's liberation movements deal with a tiny section of what is wrong."

Beata Klarsfeld had discovered that she was considered a nuisance, at best, and an unbalanced fool, at worst, for feeling concern. Yet she had chosen to peer below the surface of a country she believed had too easily dismissed its own guilt.

She had young friends like herself, students and a new generation of intellectuals, who joined her. They ferreted information from official files, dug through documents, and caught the attention of Interpol.

Interpol has difficulty dealing with war crimes, which are outside its jurisdiction. In some countries, pressure groups from the Brotherhood developed good relations with the local police. In others, especially in South America, the local security police were indebted to the Brotherhood and to German concerns, which place police chiefs and politicians on the local boards of directorship. Yet In-

146

terpol has to cope with the criminal results of actions by former Nazis, and sometimes it has to use unorthodox methods. It would subsidize small organizations—say, a league against racial discrimination. In France, the publisher of a newspaper or the producer of a public-affairs program on the state-run television network might be persuaded to conduct an investigative report. For many years Interpol filed copies of American and British secret-service reports on Nazi Germany's pre-1939 and wartime operations in regions like South America. These operations involved the smuggling of large amounts of gold, banknotes, art treasures, and guns. These were within Interpol's legitimate sphere of interest.

Beata Klarsfeld was not the willing stooge of any police organization. She did have access to files, however. She got help from researchers in East Germany, even though she had been declared unwelcome there. Several Jewish documentation agencies offered their facilities.

Her conclusions were that Bormann had followed the escape route on which there seemed to be general agreement, and that Operation Eagle's Flight covered the transfer of money and documents. She had gone on her latest trip to Latin America with the intention of forcing Barbie into the open by arousing public anger. This led in the summer of 1972 to yet another of the controversies about the war that regularly shake France. She had come back with what seemed to be evidence that Barbie was one of the many survivors who worked for the Brotherhood's business consortium, employing funds created by Krüger and Schwend, and also by a staggering quantity of missing gold.

The disposal of Nazi gold reserves had been briefly covered in the reparations section of the 1945 Potsdam Agreement, in which the Soviet Union made no claim to gold captured by Allied troops in Germany.

On September 26, 1946, the Tripartite Commission for the Restitution of Monetary Gold announced that nearly 280 tons of gold had been located. The price of that much gold was given by Interpol in 1972 as close to $500 million, depending on where it was sold. Yet even this huge amount was regarded as a fraction of the total quantity of gold hoarded by men working under Bormann's orders.

No report on the commission's work had been published by 1964. But Jacques Rueff, French Inspector-General of State Finances, who had served on the commission, did receive a letter on the commission's official notepaper, signed by the commission's

147

Secretary-General, John Watson, and mailed from the commission's office in Brussels. The letter stated: "No details of the composition of the mass of gold in its entirety have been made public to date, either by the three governments which are the depositaries, or by the Commission. . . . In the Secretariat I have very few details on the negotiations between the three governments and the neutral countries with regard to gold of German origin."

What had happened to the captured gold, let alone the missing gold? Why a total lack of information after twenty years? A natural conclusion would be that the commission would find it embarrassing to say.

Another conclusion is offered by Julius Mader, an East German researcher with an obvious loyalty to the Soviet point of view. Once the panic subsided in West Germany and the Cold War quickly obscured the recent activities of Nazi bigwigs, the captured gold went back to Bonn. The missing gold was never pursued, although it was known to have traveled by way of Spain and Italy to South America, because the Western governments had no desire to create tension or weaken a united anti-Communist front.

That this is a Communist view need not make it invalid. Mader had been right in the past, and it was his persistence in 1972 that helped to make the West German authorities look into the case of Bernhard Krüger, whose partner was then in a Lima jail.

Chief Inspector C. I. Rudkin and Detective Sergeant S. Chutburn were assigned by Scotland Yard to find Krüger and investigate what was probably the biggest forgery operation in history. They began their work at the end of the war, assisted by an American Secret Service man, Major George McNally. They knew that 212 master draftsmen, engravers, and printers had been extracted from the Nazi death camps and put to work counterfeiting millions of British currency notes. They knew this operation had been moved into the Alpine Fortress. They knew that twenty-three coffinlike boxes had been discovered, containing the equivalent of $60 million in Bank of England notes.

They did not know that American agents had been chasing distributors of the notes in South America, or that British agents had collected a sackful in Lisbon. In a combined operation that typified their close partnership, Donovan and Stephenson had been watching the political changes in Germany's spheres of influence, particularly Argentina, Brazil, and Bolivia. There seemed to be ready financing for tough right-wing politicians with pro-Nazi ideas. The money was traced back to Lisbon and Zurich. This early warning of financial adventures in South America made it possible later for Allied agents to pick up the trail of Frederic Schwend. But such is the peculiarity of shifting world alliances that when they were ready to move in 1950, it had become diplomatically unwise to bring about the arrest of Schwend in Peru.

The first hint of money flowing illegally into South America came early in the war. Of the account of the prolonged battle to discover this, one example is enough. The Italian airline LATI carried valuable cargoes directly from Fortress Europe to Brazil, where one of President Getulio Vargas's sons-in-law was chief technical director, standard fascist procedure to guarantee noninterference. The Brazilian government would not agree to stop the airline's operations or examine the cargoes. The President had too much to lose. Brazil was one end of a two-way flow. Diamonds, platinum, mica, and other raw materials went to Germany. Convertible currency and gold were flown back to provide reserve funds if Nazi leaders had to retreat to South America. British agents could find no way to stop the traffic except to sabotage the planes, which Stephenson refused to do. The U.S. State Department was asked to put a squeeze on the operation by preventing an American oil company from supplying fuel, but this failed, too. In the end, a brilliant forgery caused the Brazilian President to suppose that he was being double-crossed. He canceled LATI's landing rights and eventually broke off relations with the Axis Powers.

The forgery used against the Nazis was the work of a team gathered together in the safety of Canada, and working under cover of a nonexistent Canadian Broadcasting Corporation radio station known as "Station M."

The Nazi forgeries were the work of prisoners under suspended sentences of death. It was thought for a long time that the sole purpose of manufacturing fantastic sums of British money was to wreck the British economy. If the integrity of British money became questionable in neutral and Allied countries in the middle of a war, the results would be catastrophic. Only much later was it evident that the counterfeit money had been exchanged for valid currency by Bormann's agents, working through banks in Spain, Switzerland, and Sweden. The fake notes had been used to finance Nazi Germany's intelligence operations—notably the spy in the British Embassy in Turkey—"Cicero," who sold secret files to the Nazis for 300,000 British pounds sterling, all of them forged. But the sums used to help Germany's war effort were nothing to those misdirected to prepare nest eggs abroad for men on the run.

Bernhard Krüger was in 1942 the director of a department of the Central Security Office of the SS that had been faking British currency since 1940. It grew out of all recognition when Martin Bormann was confirmed as Secretary to the Führer and issued orders that went beyond anything the stiff-necked bankers and civil servants of the Reich Printing Office and the Reichsbank had envisaged.

Just outside Berlin, in one of the most closely guarded camps in the country, groups of highly skilled technicians were gathered. The paper for the forged British notes had to be manufactured from pure linen. Watermarks had to be introduced, and the paper then treated to defy expert inspection. Printing and engraving took place in Block 19, an isolated shed from which escape was not just impossible, but unthinkable.

Walter Schellenberg has described some of the problems: "The secret service forged banknotes and rubles to finance our work. Then it became a much bigger operation. It took two years to imitate the so-called greaseproof paper needed for English pound notes. We had two large paper mills devoted entirely to that work alone. Engraving was complicated by the fact that 160 identifying marks had to be discovered in each note and then copied by the most skilled engravers. Professors of mathematics worked out a complicated formula by which they could anticipate each new issue of Bank of England notes. This was done so that the registration number on each banknote was always just about one hundred to two hundred figures ahead of the real notes coming off the presses in London."

Schellenberg was instructed to purchase good currency with a proportion of the forged notes. He believed Bormann was putting the notes into categories by testing them in foreign banks; the grade-one notes were finally converted into American dollars. In theory, the operation came under Himmler, but he frequently had little say in these things and was often unaware of details of an operation so vast. Bormann, on the other hand, was expert in handling money and had a cast-iron memory.

The chief bookkeeper of the operation was a Czech political prisoner, Oskar Skala. He testified after the war that the "plant" produced 400,000 notes a month, and that Krüger and Schwend packed away a proportion of the grade-one notes in large wooden boxes. Another expert, a concentration-camp inmate who was awaiting the gas chamber because he was a gypsy, Solly Smolianoff, specialized in American dollar bills up to denominations of one hundred. His work had been known to J. Edgar Hoover for some years, it later turned out, because Smolianoff had been a forger by profession who specialized in U.S. currency. It was pure luck that Krüger and Schwend found him in a death camp.

Smolianoff told a story to Scotland Yard and American investigators that seemed fantastic, except that the evidence was there in Gallery 16 near the village of Redl Zipf, part of the Alpine Fortress. The gallery was in an underground network of storage corridors and workshops. Along the two-hundred-foot tunnel were the banknote presses and machinery which had been transferred from Berlin. Smolianoff said they had been moved, kit and caboodle, while Himmler was trying to make a deal through Count Bernadotte. (He had failed, by then, to secure his future by selling the lives of Jews to his American contacts. Schellenberg had come to the glum conclusion that the American rabbinate did not wish to discuss terms of such an obscene nature.) The factory for the manufacture of fake banknotes was discovered first when American intelligence men tripped over a truckload of counterfeit notes. The notes were in wooden boxes, each box with a manifest stapled inside. The discovery was made soon after Hitler's suicide, and the truck was trundling along a back road of his Bavarian fortress. The German Army captain driving the truck simply told his American captors where to look for the printing presses that had almost wrecked Allied fortunes while they were making the fortune of their sponsor, Bormann.

A version of events was made public. Krüger, it was said, had disappeared from Gallery 16 at the end of the war after giving orders that all the records were to be burned and the printing dies sunk in Lake Toplitz. The craftsmen had been sent to Ebensee concentration camp to be exterminated. Out of 9 million Bank of England notes with a face value of about $600 million, about $6 million worth went to the Mideast to support German activities among pro-Nazi Arab leaders and about $30 million worth went to neutral countries to pay German accounts.

This left a sizable amount still to strike off the books. Where was it?

The Bank of England withdrew from circulation its banknotes of most denominations and exchanged them for five-pound notes of a new design in which a fine metallic thread had been drawn through the fabric in a manner thought to be proof against the most clever forgers. No explanation was given for this decision to Parliament. It was a desperate measure to kill the fake currency already in circulation. It succeeded to a limited extent. Foreign banks were caught with large sums of money, which they were able to change for the new currency if they worked fast enough. A number of banks, however, chose to take a loss. These were the banks on which Allied intelligence focused its attention after the war.

Nothing is so secret as the world of finance; nothing so sacrosanct as money. The movements of forged currency and gold are probably at the top of the list of priorities when it comes to preserving secrecy. The real fate of the Nazis' funny money has never been disclosed in documents made public. A rough estimate, based on independent calculations, is that about $300 million worth of forged notes was converted into usable currency to finance postwar Nazi groups in the Mideast and South America; and that $500 million worth of gold was fed into circulation through South Africa, where it can be transshipped to that "eternal sink for gold," India, and through Hong Kong to China. In both instances, neither buyer nor seller is much concerned about origin.

The Lake Toplitz story of hidden gold, sunken trunks of documents, and a fortune tucked away on underwater ledges originated with an officially inspired account of how Krüger drove up to the mouth of Gallery 16 and ordered everything to be tossed into the nearby lake.

Lake Toplitz has since become the stuff of legend. Krüger is supposed to have taken off in a red Alfa Romeo convertible, accompanied by a striking blonde, in the direction of Switzerland. His orders to destroy the craftsmen as well as the machinery were never obeyed, however, and a number of the forgers escaped to tell a different tale. The fake currency was utilized for a while to buy protection for escaping persons. For some time after the Bank of England recalled its banknotes, the fake money was still accepted in remote stations along the escape routes. As for Krüger, he was back in Stuttgart in 1961, an energetic businessman "with experience in administration."

He had been described in 1945 as a man wanted for large-scale forgery and the murder of four concentration-camp inmates. American investigators said publicly in 1952, obviously in good faith, that Krüger obliterated all trace of the biggest act of forgery in history and then left with his Alfa Romeo crammed with genuine currency acquired through black-market operations in occupied capitals and a variety of beautifully forged passports. He had not been heard of since, despite the concentrated efforts of half a dozen police forces to catch him.

Rudkin and Chutburn, of Scotland Yard, went back to their normal pursuits, having been informed that they need not trouble themselves any further over a matter that now involved the British Treasury and something known as "Higher Authority." They were subject to the Official Secrets Act, and nothing has been heard from *them*.

The search for Nazi funds was left to those not stifled by legal devices designed to protect bureaucrats from the penalties of their own mistakes. Ernest Cuneo, who had kept his special status within White House circles after Truman took up residence, checked with Sir William Stephenson in the 1950's a series of reports from different sources in South America, all suggesting that Nazi funds were behind certain business activities. His information was independent confirmation of what Stephenson himself had heard.

Stephenson had a considerable knowledge of German routes for couriers, agents, and smugglers. During the war, his intelligence net included at least one reliable observer on every neutral vessel sailing between the American continent and Europe; and these observers, as a matter of course, reported on arrival in port to the local British secret-service agent. At every civilian airport, he had men among the ground technicians and occasionally aboard the aircraft. One reason for his obstinate refusal to sabotage aircraft or ships was that he was protective of his own men; but also, as a pilot, he could never bring himself to destroy a plane and crew by such methods. His operations were shared with the U.S. Office of Naval Intelligence. Between them, it was agreed in 1945 that dirty money and Nazis on the run might be expected to move along well-defined routes. But at some point, and for reasons that one can now speculate upon, the curiosity of the two "happy amateurs," Stephenson and Cuneo, was curbed.

They knew that Brazil and Venezuela were the chief sources of industrial diamonds, needed by Hitler's War Production Minister, Albert Speer; and they knew also that after the war the trade went on. Platinum had been a vital commodity, purchased with gold or convertible currency from Colombia and Ecuador; it was required for the magnetos of aircraft engines. Again, long after the war ended, German agents were paying as much as $500 an ounce against the regular world price, which fluctuated around one-tenth of that figure. They knew that five years after Krüger and Schwend allegedly vanished, marked banknotes were found in circulation in these South American states. The marked notes were *not* forged; they were notes whose registration numbers had been recorded at the time they were purchased in Swiss banks for the forged currency.

The FBI had always been denied authority to wage "special operations" of the kind conducted by Stephenson. In this postwar period, the normal police investigative agencies of Britain and the United States were also hamstrung. In countries that tolerate criminal activities affecting other nations, it had not been unknown for Allied agents to apply the law themselves. There was pressure from some British Treasury agents simply to wipe out the sources of the fake money. To the old professionals, it seemed as if the bureaucrats, the Establishment intelligence agencies, and the departments concerned with foreign affairs had intervened.

Perhaps they had. General Gehlen and his company of intelligence experts, within months of switching from Hitler's side to that of the United States, had convinced his new friends that almost anything was justified in the Cold War against Communism. His agents were called V-men. They were recruited from the Gestapo and the SS. Nazi records, in which Germans who voiced opposition were frequently labeled "Communists," were suddenly an Allied index to the worthiness of West German civilians. Values must have seemed upturned, for now the middle-level Nazis could boast discreetly of their virtue as enemies of Bolshevism. I think this explains the convenient evaporation of Krüger and the bulky apparatus known as Operation Bernhard. For the man who was Krüger's real chief in this counterfeiting enterprise was Frederic Schwend; and his partner in the business projects launched on smuggled funds was Klaus Barbie, alias the Bolivian businessman Señor Altmann. By the summer of 1972, Barbie-Altmann was splashed across the front pages of Paris newspapers as the notorious "Hangman of Lyon." He was talking to television interviewers and offering his memoirs; and he was saying repeatedly that he had done his duty as a German, and that he had performed his duty to democracy as a V-man in the Gehlen Org. He named Otto Skorzeny as the chief of the network called Die Spinne.

The mass-circulation newspaper *France-Soir* crammed its front pages through several days of May and June with Barbie-Altmann's self-justifications and the retorts of former resistance men who had suffered or lost comrades through his actions. Prominent Catholic churchmen were dragged into the controversy. Skorzeny's organization, identified with the Brotherhood, was reported to command the loyalty of 100,000 fascist sympathizers in twenty-two countries, and to be funded by Nazi investments. Capital was estimated at 500 million francs by informers in some of the ten Brotherhood offices operating as private companies in France, with assets valued at 200 million francs.

The conservative *Le Figaro* reported that Barbie-Altmann was being helped to evade justice by the West German ambassadors in Bolivia and Peru.

Finally, the "International Wanted List of Nazi Criminals" entry for the Gestapo man was cited: "*Barbie,* Klaus: Lt-Col. or Captain of the SS, head of Department IV (Gestapo) involved in actions in Lyon, Dijon, Strasbourg 1934-44, sought by France and Great Britain on murder charges." In March 1973, Barbie was arrested by Bolivian police because, said a government spokesman, it was thought he was trying to escape into a neighboring country and evade extradition.

An outcry among French wartime resistance organizations obliged the Munich authorities to release some details of their investigations. These, however, were published *before* Barbie-Altmann had been forced into the open by Beata Klarsfeld. The wording seemed to me significant. It referred first to an application for a residence permit in West Germany made out by a thirty-year-old woman calling herself Ute Altmann, daughter of Klaus Altmann, a resident of Bolivia. She stated she was born in Kassel, near Leipzig. The registry office there had no trace of such a person born on the date given; but there was an entry for Ute Barbie. The woman's brother was named: "Klaus-Georg Altmann, son of Klaus Altmann, stated to have been born at the village of Kasel [*sic*] near Leipzig. There is no such place. The wife of Klaus Barbie gave birth to a son in the clinic of Dr. Kuhn in Kassel. . . . First name and date of birth coincide."

It seemed an example of bureaucracy at its worst: the slow-grinding, unimaginative mind of the civil servant resenting the intervention of citizen clods. There is the prim and proper nit-picking: some poor fool had misspelled Kassel, and the functionary meant to make the most of it. There is also a defensive note. The whole statement has the familiar ring of an official cover-up; the few details offered are those dug up already by newsmen.

This statement, forced out of the reluctant Munich authorities, came after the following steps had been taken:

• *December 7, 1959:* The West German Association of Nazi Persecutees requested action from the Ludwigsburg Office in the case of Klaus Barbie. No reply. Ludwigsburg (handling over-all investigations into Nazi war crimes) was run at the time by Erwin Schüle, sentenced for Nazi war crimes; later amnestied and handed over to West German authorities.

• *May 16, 1967:* The same association patiently informed the Ludwigsburg Office that over seven years had passed and they would like an answer.

• *May 23, 1967:* The Ludwigsburg Office replied that preliminary investigations were handed over to the State Prosecutor's office in Kassel back in 1963. It developed that Barbie last lived in Augsburg, so the case was given to the State Prosecutor there in August 1965. Then the Augsburg court found it could not act because Barbie had been sentenced to death by a French military court, which made it impossible for a West German court to retry him on the same charges. *"In any case prosecution is impossible since Barbie is believed to be in Egypt and is not likely to return or be extradited."* (My italics.)

• *June 22, 1971:* The State Prosecutor's office in Munich said the case against Barbie had been closed. Although Barbie might have taken part in deporting Jews, "there is no proof that the suspect knew the fate awaiting them." As to the executions of French resistance fighters, it could not be proved Barbie took part in the killing, although he ordered the arrests. *"A clarification of the executions in the Lyons Gestapo office is no longer possible in view of the passage of time and the number of killings committed in the area of responsibility of the Lyons Gestapo office."* (My italics.)

Barbie commanded the Gestapo detachments that killed the Frenchmen. He telegraphed his headquarters in Paris confirming he had sent three-year-old Jewish orphans in 1944 to "labor camps" in Eastern Europe, and that boastful telegram is still on file. It was evident to Beata Klarsfeld that her countrymen were not at all anxious to see justice done.

Her aim in raising scandalized attention to the Barbie case was to shake Germany out of a mood she believed Bormann always counted upon. She knew, too, that there was more likelihood of justice being done in France, where the courts were not infiltrated by old sympathizers and friends of the past. She had no idea that she had also picked upon an offensive example of how killers had escaped by selling their talents to the intelligence agencies of East and West. Klaus Barbie had worked for an import-export agency

156

at Schillestrasse 38, in Augsburg. Such agencies are the favored fronts of spy rings. This one had been operated by the Gehlen Org.

Beata Klarsfeld was described to me as "paranoid" by an official of a Jewish international agency. She was working out some inner problems, said this official. She belonged to a group of mentally unstable personalities seeking martyrdom. She wanted to be another Joan of Arc. And so on. This outburst was puzzling. The speaker was qualified in several disciplines: as a psychologist, as an economist, as a professor in international affairs. The professor went to some length to demonstrate that West Germany had grown out of its Nazi past; that the courts had done their best in difficult circumstances to weed out the major offenders. Germans like Beata Klarsfeld only muddied the waters.

The girl's sin against propriety was that she slapped Chancellor Kurt Kiesinger in the face at a public function, "to draw public attention to the disgraceful emergence of Nazis on the political scene again."

Puzzled by the strength of this attack on Beata Klarsfeld, which seemed out of proportion to the incident, I looked through the official Hansard report on a debate in the British House of Lords soon after Kiesinger became Chancellor in 1966. Lord Montgomery, an archconservative, one would have said, warned the Peers of the Realm of the dangers of German militarism. A fellow right-winger, Viscount Bridgeman, said that twenty years ago nothing seemed to be farther from the German mind than a reversion to Nazi practices. Now it looked as if this was beginning to be altered. . . . The mind went back to the '30's and remembered how quickly the political scene could change in the night in a place like Germany.

The British Foreign Office had an obligation to deplore any hint of disenchantment with West Germany. But the debate spoke for itself. Montgomery had also voiced the fears of many: that a large withdrawal of British troops would leave the Germans in command of the northern army group at a time when there were few restraints on a revival of neo-Nazi attitudes. Montgomery had been accused of many things but it would be difficult to persuade even his worst enemies that he was paranoid.

CHAPTER 15

A series of murders followed Beata Klarsfeld's denunciation in 1972 of Gestapo Colonel Klaus Barbie. Suddenly the Bormann puzzle ceased to be a game. Each murder was linked with the Brotherhood. Interpol became involved when one of the killings was associated with the sale of arms to Arab guerrillas through one of the Bolivian agencies run by Barbie under his cover name. These investigations broadened to include the otherwise unexplained murder of the Bolivian Consul in Hamburg. Next a well-known Italian editor died in a dynamite explosion in Milan, and it became apparent that assassination teams were at work, although it was far from clear what the motives were.

The first clue was provided when a former Nazi collaborator of Barbie's was found strangled in a suburb of Rio de Janeiro. This was Count Jacques Charles Noel Duge de Bernonville, a friend of the Hangman of Lyon. He was found dead on April 27, 1972 in his apartment, a gag in his mouth; his hands and feet tied.

The Count was sentenced to death by a French military court for helping Barbie during the Nazi occupation. Death came violently, but a little late. The Count evaded it first by escaping to French Canada, where he remained until 1951, a distinguished figure among the Catholic aristocracy of Quebec. When the French government finally heard where he was, a formal request was made for his extradition. He flew with his family straight to Rio. The Brazilian government refused to extradite him, and by 1956 he was a prominent spokesman for extreme right-wing groups. His wife returned to Paris, and he made periodic transfers of money through the Banque Nationale de Paris under the code "Credit L Jouvait XF 495." He traveled frequently to Bolivia and Peru, the two countries where Nazi funds had been put to work in a variety of business enterprises. It was in Lima, Peru, that his partner, Luis Banchero Rossi, was murdered on January 1, 1972, after being identified as an associate of Barbie. Shortly afterward, the Nazi counterfeiter Schwend was put in a Peruvian jail. Schwend, it later appeared, might have been put there for his own safety.

The Count de Bernonville was reported by Brazilian police to have said it was time to publish his memoirs and to challenge the French people to judge for themselves if the Nazis and their sympathizers were really so very wrong. This must have alarmed the less self-confident members of the Brotherhood. The Count's history and the other murders were engulfed in such a smoke screen of rumor and half-truths that it would take time to disentangle fact from fantasy. Meanwhile, I checked with Stephenson, who said I was on the right track. So I struck, not too confidently, into the veterans of the British Special Operations Executive, which had built up the secret armies of Europe with arms and supplies from America. These were all quite extraordinary men, not men given to melodrama, whose peacetime occupations put them in areas where large financial deals are closed on the basis of a man's word of honor.

This sense of honor had kept such men silent about wartime operations until the provisions of the Official Secrets Act were relaxed in this same year of 1972. This had the effect of making available a version of events as seen by the Establishment intelligence agencies, whereas the Special Ops men had functioned often without written authorizations or official files. There was always rivalry between "scholarship and skullduggery," and officialdom liked to put itself among the scholars. I went in search of the skullduggery merchants and discovered that they held strong views about the blind way the West forgot all the lessons offered by the Nazis in its anxiety to tilt at Communist windmills. There was never a disposition to underestimate Russian plans to destroy our own system; but the survivors of SOE had a misleadingly casual approach to threats of this kind. These Baker Street Irregulars were accustomed to think out a problem after the manner of their elected patron, Sherlock Holmes, whose fictional address was on the same street as their wartime headquarters had been.

They recalled that Nazi Germany occupied other countries according to well-laid plans in which the SS and the Gestapo were to provide garrisons at key points to keep the native population under permanent subjection. Some of the natives would supply slave labor for the industry and agriculture of the German empire, and would remain in a state of total inferiority, without any educational or human rights, condemned to be treated literally as subhuman and entirely at the disposal of the master race.

Memories were so alarmingly short that in the reborn West German republic Chancellor Adenauer and other prominent figures had been forgiven already the fact that they had employed slave workers in their homes and gardens. This was less worrying than the feeling that had grown among Communists that, on the whole, the Western Allies felt no particular outrage because the chief victims of the New Order had been mostly from the working class anyway. It was significant, for instance, that the Hangman of Lyon had received support in his dispatch of French resistance workers from the "cream of Lyon society," led by the Count de Bernonville. Resistance fighters were mostly peasants or intellectuals with a strong left-wing bias.

The persistent rumor among the skullduggery experts, who had often worked closely with Communist anti-Nazi groups in occupied Europe, was that there had been a Russian informer close to Hitler. At first, Martin Bormann was regarded as the likeliest candidate; and for a while this set a hare running which drew off the pack of hounds. Now it was accepted that Bormann, although an operator in ideological waters of the same type as Stalin, was committed to Nazi racial concepts, and furthermore was in charge of funds intended to keep alive the Nazi creed although they could be converted to his own use. He would have gone to ground almost anywhere but Russia.

There was the proof, however, that the Russians knew much of Hitler's most private affairs and also knew of the plans for escape. A former British agent in Berlin drew my attention to the fact that the name of the Gestapo chief, Heinrich Müller, had been taken off the list of officials with Hitler at the end. So the finger of suspicion pointed at Gestapo Müller once again. And another piece of the puzzle began to find its place.

Bormann was scrupulous in detailing the trivia of each day. Nobody knows how accurate he was in reporting the Führer, when he was not stage-managing the jerky figure whose shrill and rasping voice had played on the emotions of great crowds. Hitler's words in the privacy of the dining room were something else, known during the last thirty months of the war to the two men alone. What Bormann chose to make of the midnight monologues is something even Hitler, by then in a state of controlled hysteria, probably never knew.

The little facts of life were set down with exactitude. Who came, at what hour, and why; appointments, books borrowed, movies

160

projected in Hitler's parlor; and always those meticulous lists of names. These were records whose accuracy can be relied upon.

This made it all the stranger that Gestapo Müller's name was taken off the final list of those who were with the Führer to the bitter end. The list was meant as a record, and it fell into Russian hands. It is conceivable that the Russians removed his name. If so, why? The matter escaped attention at the time. It seemed now to grow in significance as the final shape of the puzzle was vaguely perceived.

Gestapo Müller was in and out of the Führer's bunker all the time. He was the man most intimately engaged for legitimate reasons in all the affairs that went on around Hitler. It was his business to know all about everyone in the Third Reich. He disappeared with Bormann; and he might have had a great deal to do with the Soviet Union's subsequent suspicions about the West.

Bormann wrote for public consumption. Even his letters to Gerda reeked of sycophancy. He had to maintain to the end the pretense of being the Führer's obedient servant. When he scribbled a curious note to Ernst Kaltenbrunner, telling the scarred veteran of the SS murder railroad that he must not stand in the way of Nazi leaders who made plans to escape, it was calculated to create a certain impression. The letter was dated April 4, 1945, when about seven hundred of Hitler's staff crowded into the shelter in the Chancellery compound amidst arguments as to the wisdom of heading south to the Alpine Fortress. This, of course, was Bormann's private objective. He had no wish to see Hitler move there and bring down the full weight of the Russian armies on the great complex of mountain tunnels and hideaways.

Kaltenbrunner took the reprimand calmly. Before he was hanged, he told Allied interrogators that his escape plans were those of Bormann; and that the self-righteous note puzzled him only for a moment. Then he realized it had been dictated. It was intended to reinforce Bormann's masquerade as the faithful dog who would remain with the master to the end.

The mood is perfectly captured by Hanna Reitsch, the girl who test-piloted a V-1 rocket in her fanatical determination to destroy London even while Berlin was being destroyed. In the end, she flew a small plane out of a burning Berlin street and described her feelings to General Karl Koller: "We should kneel in reverence and prayer to the altar of the Fatherland." Asked what she meant, she looked surprised. "Why, the Führer's bunker . . ."

It was known as the "Führerhauptquartier." It contained Hitler's private suite, his bathroom, his dog's quarters, his bedroom and Eva Braun's dressing and dining rooms; servants' quarters; a clinic and operating theater; Goebbels's study; a telephone exchange, and a long central corridor. At the start of the Battle of Berlin, Bormann made a careful note of those in the bunker. His list was one of the few documents recovered when the Russians found the shelter, raising doubts as to its authenticity; for once again Bormann had been writing for the record. The list was used in the great manhunt that followed, and there were quarrels when the Russians accused the Western Allies of holding back information. Perhaps Bormann anticipated that his list would cause confusion. The thought is grimly diverting. On his list were: Eva Braun; Blondi, Hitler's Alsatian bitch and four puppies; Dr. Stumpfegger, Hitler's surgeon; Dr. Goebbels and his wife and six children; Fräulein Manzialy, the vegetarian cook; Heinz Lorenz of the Propaganda Ministry; Bormann's deputy, Zander; Eva Braun's brother-in-law, Herman Fegelein; Colonel Nicolaus von Below, Hitler's liaison officer; Admiral Voss, liaison officer to Grand Admiral Doenitz; Ambassador Walther Hewel, Ribbentrop's liaison officer; Major Willi Johannmeier, Hitler's aide-de-camp; two pilots, Hans Bauer and George Beetz; Werner Naumann of the Propaganda Ministry; General Burgdorf and his aide, Lieutenant Colonel Weiss; General Hans Krebs, Chief of Staff; Major Bernd von Freytag-Loringhoven, Krebs's aide; and an orderly officer who later described the last days, Captain Gerhard Boldt.

Stumpfegger was reported to have been killed in the last-minute attempt to escape. Naumann surfaced again some years later, when he was accused of leading a neo-Nazi revival. George Beetz, Hitler's own pilot, was killed; Major General Bauer was captured by the Russians. Few escaped from the Russians, in fact. One was Zander, who had been sent away after Hitler's suicide with two other survivors: Lorenz and Johannmeier. They had to work their way through two and a half million Russian troops who covered the Berlin area. What happened to them was for a long time to puzzle the Russians, who thought the Western Allies had somehow grabbed them. In fact, Zander had turned himself into a Bavarian market gardener called Frederich-Wilhelm Paustin, and the other two passed themselves off as liberated slaves. They ultimately worked their way to the Bavarian hide-outs, carrying copies of Hitler's last testament and other important documents, which were intended to provide a source of inspiration in the future.

The Russians captured the chief of Hitler's detective bodyguard,

SS Brigadier General Johann Rattenhuber. *His* name was not on Bormann's list.

On July 17, 1945, Stalin told the U.S. Secretary of State, James Byrnes, that he believed Hitler was alive and probably in Argentina or in Spain.

Obviously the Russians had got onto something. Their secret service had been functioning as if the Western Allies were enemies; and they had informers and agents everywhere, since much of the resistance against Hitler's occupying armies came from Communists. Stalin had some of the facts, but not all. He knew that plans had existed for a long time to get prominent Nazis away to "neutral" pro-Nazi territory (Argentina's entry into the war on the Allied side was expediently timed to precede the German surrender by a few days). Stalin was receiving reports of Nazi bigwigs whose safety had been guaranteed by Catholic churchmen anxious to salvage something from the wreckage. The Vatican Office of Stateless Persons had been issuing special identity cards, and Stalin evidently knew that his professional intelligence men had obtained the registration numbers of these cards and where and to whom they were issued.

How much he knew in midsummer of 1945 is hard to say. Years later, when Nikita Khrushchev proposed to Western leaders that it would cut costs and simplify matters if everyone stopped using each other's spies, he was not joking. By then, each side was disenchanted by the price of trading in the intelligence market. By then, the West knew just how thoroughly Stalin in his day was informed of certain events. He could not believe, perhaps, that we did not honestly know the whereabouts of some major war criminals.

Perhaps to remind us that they held some cards, too, the Russians issued a statement in September: "No trace of the bodies of Hitler or Eva Braun has been discovered. . . . It is established that Hitler, by means of false testimony, sought to hide his traces. Irrefutable proof exists that a small airplane left the Tiergarten at dawn on April 30 flying in the direction of Hamburg. Three men and a woman are known to have been on board. It has also been established that a large submarine left Hamburg before the arrival of the British forces. Mysterious persons were on board the submarine, among them a woman."

The mysterious submarine caused the British endless difficulties because the Hamburg-Kiel area of north Germany was a British responsibility. It caused the Canadians a problem, too. The Canadian Army wanted badly to get its hands on SS General

Mohnke, who was charged with executing prisoners of war on the spot. He was in Russian hands. But the Russians became unco-operative, reinforcing their demands that Western intelligence be more forthcoming about the missing Nazis.

Drawn into the controversy was a Canadian intelligence expert on Latin America who was thought to have special knowledge of U-boat traffic to the region. His name was Peter Dwyer. He had been Stephenson's man in Latin America before he moved to Washington to represent the British secret service there.

Stephenson had already provided advance warning of the new Walther-type U-boats, and this was passed along to Stalin at Yalta. There, Churchill told the Russian leader: "It will be difficult for us to combat these new submarines, which have high underwater speed and new devices." Stalin was told that thirty percent of these new U-boats were being constructed at Danzig. He was urged to have Marshal Konstantin Rokossovski capture the base. The following month, in early March, the Second White Russian front accordingly swung in an arc that prevented escape from Danzig except by sea. Clearly, Stalin understood the implications of fast long-range submarines, even two months before the war's end. Dwyer believed Stalin had based his reference to the "large sub-marine" on similar information given to his security people by Allied sources which then neglected to release the information to the public. This fed Stalin's mounting fears of secret arrangements between the Western Allies and selected Nazis. Yet the silence with regard to an escaping submarine would have been under-standable in the circumstances of the time. Major war criminals were at large. Some were thought to have arranged escape by submarine. An Allied announcement that one had got away would tip off the organizers of the escape routes. Publication of any information at this juncture would help fugitives who had missed their rendezvous or lost contact.

What was happening was that the Russians, retaliating against what they thought was Western perfidy, held back on what they knew about missing Nazis. The Cold War was already freezing the exchange of information. Stalin had received frank advice from Roosevelt and Churchill on the U-boat situation in particular, and now he was confronted by what he thought was a sinister silence. He told Harry Hopkins in Moscow that he believed Bormann had escaped. Now he went further, and said it was Bormann who got away in the fleeing U-boat. More than that Stalin refused to disclose. Quite soon, any exchange of information between the two

164

sides became a matter involving official secrets and verging on treachery. Even at the height of the war, survivors of the Murmansk supply convoys had been treated as if they were hostile neutrals, if not outright enemies of Russia. So the fault for the breakdown in trust cannot be laid at any one door.

Dwyer remembered, after he left Washington to resume a normal career with the Canadian National Research Council, that he was told offhandedly one day by a visiting Russian academic that Hitler had died in Berlin, and that Stalin now accepted this but could not bring himself to say so publicly. "The three men and the woman are known to us," said the Russian. "Bormann and Erich Koch [whom Rokossovski's army had hoped to catch in Danzig] missed the boat."

The Russian was not joking. He said, correctly as it turned out, that Koch adopted the identity of a Major Berger and was in the British Zone around Hamburg still. Bormann had been reported in the same area, near Lüneburger. He had then left, heading south. Dwyer had the impression that the Russians knew where Bormann had been going.

The Russian pursuit of Bormann was certainly hastened by their capture of SS Major General Wilhelm Mohnke, who was commander of the Führer's bodyguard. Just how Mohnke explained his failure to preserve Hitler is not recorded.

There seems a certain irony in this last glimpse of Mohnke. He ran off with an escape group, hid in a cellar in Schönhauser Allee, and was caught there by a Red Army detachment. He was identified as the commander of what had become known derisively as the "Ersatztruppen," an SS battalion defending Berlin. Later questioning made it clear that he spent more time inside the bunker with the Führer than outside with his self-styled battle group protecting the series of bomb shelters underneath the Old and New Reich Chancelleries, known collectively as the "Citadel."

Mohnke helped the Russians locate the remains of the Führer's bunker. He talked readily about the last few days, named the major figures among the seven hundred clerks, secretaries, drivers, orderlies, servants, and SS men who had surrounded Hitler, and was hauled away, still chattering.

What he said must have riveted Stalin's attention. Mohnke was not cut from some heroic mold, any more than the SS leaders falling into Allied hands. He knew the Canadians were demanding that he be handed over to them for trial, because the Russians took good care to tell him so. He volunteered all the information he could, and made up what he did not know. Stalin, after the flight of Hess to Britain, had been more deeply suspicious than ever of an alliance between the Anglo-American forces and the Germans against the Soviet Union. Mohnke fed his suspicions with an account of the secret communications during the previous months between Nazi leaders and the West.

He told Russian interrogators of plans for the escape of Nazis who might have to face war-crimes trials. He described the hide-outs in the Bavarian alps; the transfer of money and gold to neutral countries; the concealment of treasures, including a great deal of looted art from Russia; and the promises of help conveyed secretly by the Rector of Rome's Pontifical Teutonic College, Bishop Alois Hudal, whose name cropped up frequently in the years following.

He talked of the Brotherhood.

Mohnke's disclosures trickled to the West through Soviet intel-ligence leaks, but the Russians would not admit they had him. It seemed likely that he was proving invaluable as a way to check the accuracy of what few disclosures were being made by the Western Allies. An intelligence game had started that later brought the great powers to the verge of another war.

The difficulties sharpened on May 19, 1945 when the Russian commission at Flensberg demanded to see the German intelligence files on Russia. It was told that the only man who would have much knowledge of German intelligence on the Red Army was General Gehlen.

As this time, the U.S. Army's Counter-Intelligence Corps, which had only seven experts on Russian and East European affairs, was concentrating on hunting Nazi war criminals. It now decided to look for Gehlen. He was located in a special prison camp, and was questioned by Brigadier General Edwin L. Sibert, the American intelligence officer who had been reprimanded earlier for under-estimating German fighting morale. Sibert reported at once to Allen Dulles the substance of Gehlen's boastful description of his spy network and his spine-tingling account of Russia's territorial ambitions. In August 1945, Gehlen and his experts were flown to Washington.

On August 31, the Soviet-controlled radio in Berlin announced: "Bormann is in Allied hands." A living Bormann must have seemed to Stalin, as indeed he did to the West, as potentially the Führer of a Fourth Reich. The legalities had been attended to; and none knew better than the Russians how the German invaders had invoked the rules and regulations to justify their brutality. Bormann was the executor of Hitler's will and the leader of the Nazi party.

The Russians knew by then that Gehlen, the man recommended to them, was Hitler's spy chief dealing with Soviet military affairs. They knew through their own wartime intelligence sources, and through captured leaders like Mohnke, that it was part of the Nazi plan for survival to convince the Western Allies that Hitler had been wrong only in the way he ran the war, but not in his identification of the real enemy of all humanity: the Soviet Union. Enough German Army generals had been talking of the need to fight Russia with Anglo-American help; and there was enough on the Nazi record to justify Stalin's suspicion that the West might yet fall for this gambit. Nor had the Russians forgotten the strange case of Hess, whose unfortunate aide, Captain Karlheinz Pintsch, was in their hands. It had seemed to Stalin that Hess must have discussed a possible alliance against Russia; and his aide was interrogated and tortured.* It happened that Pintsch was, after Hess's flight to England, arrested by Martin Bormann and his brother Albert, so that he was doubly unlucky. Whatever he told the Russians, it must have seemed to justify their glowering mistrust, which was intensified when Gehlen was whisked away.

Mohnke was held in a Russian camp at Strausberg, and Allied intelligence knew that he was rattling his tongue off. His statements were quoted, without any Russian confirmation of his capture, whenever inquiries were made by the Canadians. His accomplice in the massacre of Canadian troops, Kurt ("Panzer") Meyer, had been tried and found guilty of butchery, but was released after the heat of public feeling had cooled. When yet another request was made for information leading to the capture of Mohnke, the Russians merely replied that they were noting the appointment of "Panzermeyer" to the North Atlantic Treaty Organization (NATO) forces in Europe. "These forces, as is well known, are directed against the democratic republics. . . . Imperialist warmongers have permitted Nazis to return to their former military and civic positions. . . ." It proved a little difficult to respond to these Russian growls with convincing smiles of innocence. Colleagues of Meyer, jealous of the highly paid jobs being dished out to such proven battle commanders as Meyer (who had been the youngest divisional commander in Nazi German forces), were proclaiming their own eligibility. SS General Gottlob Berger and

---

* Pintsch was beaten, starved, and his fingers broken, one by one. He was released in 1955 to return to Germany.

SS General Paul Hausser, far from being grateful for being free within a few years of the war-crimes trials, were urging NATO to consider the claims of the SS, who "trained the first army in the struggle against Bolshevism."

Then, in 1965, the Russians produced an astonishing version of what had happened to Martin Bormann.

CHAPTER 16

Martin Bormann had not been killed in Berlin, in the Soviet intelligence version. He tried to reach a fugitive escape U-boat near Flensburg, went underground with Brotherhood help, and made his way finally to where his eldest son, Adolf Martin, was being prepared for the priesthood by Bishop Hudal at the Teutonic College in Rome.

Propaganda? If it was, then Tito had forgotten his feud with Moscow enough to confirm it. The Yugoslav authorities supported the Russian story and added details of their own. Bishop Hudal was the leader of the pro-Nazi Croats in Yugoslavia, and his escape organization was well known to Tito's guerrillas. Furthermore, the Nazi mass murderer Franz Stangl had fought Tito near the end of the war when his presence in Berlin became an embarrassment and his enemies decided he qualified for *zum Verheitzen* (incineration). Stangl was sent to Yugoslavia because Tito's men never took German prisoners. But Stangl escaped from one minor skirmish and kept going. The Yugoslavs had followed his trail to South America, and their Ministry of the Interior had dossiers swollen with reports on the Brotherhood.

I found this out when I went to Belgrade, where I was given every help in searching for wartime film for a documentary I was making on Tito. The film was buried all over the place. Old film, some of it combustible, was stored in battered cans. Some newsreels had been shot by combat cameramen sent by Allied intelligence, and also by Germans. When I said there was film enough to document the whole war, a former Partisan leader said: "You should see the documents and diaries we've got buried away. Some we can't even find. They were hidden for safekeeping when we were escaping from the Nazi death squads."

The Russian version of Bormann's escape was based upon extensive research by a Soviet intelligence major, Lev Bezymenski, who gave the first full public report on the Russian autopsy conducted on Adolf Hitler's body, in *Documents from Soviet Archives*. He had interrogated Mohnke, who was so eager to co-operate that he provided the smallest details about old and close colleagues like Otto Skorzeny, his companion in Hitler's personal bodyguard. The Soviet Major had also interviewed everyone who knew Bormann and was available to a Russian intelligence man. He was, of course, cut off from direct contact with witnesses outside the Communist countries. It was a nuisance, no doubt, but in comparing his account with the material unearthed by Western Allied investigators, the disadvantage becomes a positive help. The lines of inquiry were perforce independently pursued. They were separated by the Cold War. Yet many of the details and conclusions overlap. Furthermore, investigations *within* the Communist bloc were divided by the quarrel between Stalin and Tito. The Yugoslavs had their own problems with escaping Nazis, and their reports therefore provide a third source of possible confirmation.

According to the Russian version, Bormann escaped from Berlin, having prepared for the future with the gold coins buried at Berchtesgaden, with hard currency purchased with forged banknotes, and with art treasures that could be sold safely. He had men like Otto Skorzeny in the Alpine Fortress, and the bombing of the Führer's retreat there in many ways was to make things easier for him. The German commander of Luftflotte 6, Air Force General Robert Ritter von Greim, had driven up from his headquarters in Munich to find the place a shambles the week before Bormann's escape, and had so reported to him.

Bormann knew, from what happened at Stalingrad, that heavy bombing actually *creates* defensive barriers; that an army trying to advance behind its own bombers is delayed and even stopped. He knew that the galleries that honeycombed the mountains around Hitler's alpine home would be more difficult to reach than ever; that the two-hundred-foot-long Gallery 16, for instance, with its printing presses and machinery for turning out forged banknotes, could well defy discovery.

He had sent Gerda and the children deeper into the mountains (as everyone else has agreed). But Frau Bormann, using the name Bergmann, took with her some other children. The bus painted with a red cross in which she traveled thus assumed a more convincing appearance. One of the children, unfortunately for her, was by no means an orphan. The father had reported to the U.S. Army's Counter-Intelligence Corps in Munich that his child had been kidnapped from Berchtesgaden by Bormann's wife, and he suspected that he knew where to find her. (Again, this is confirmed, by the CIC authorities, who assigned Alexander Raskin, a Belgian Jew who had been a slave worker, to try to locate Bormann's wife. Raskin traveled by mule through the remoter areas and could testify that if the Nazis had mounted a guerrilla war there, it would have been difficult to catch them.)

The Russians believed Bormann visited his wife briefly before Raskin could find her. More than a month earlier, on April 2, 1945, Bormann had proposed to Hitler that the latest notes of the Führer's monologues, all of course recorded by Bormann or his team of stenographers, should be transferred to Bad Gastein, in the Austrian part of the Alpine Fortress. On April 16, when the assault on Berlin began with 20,000 Red Army guns bombarding a bridgehead to the east, a senior Nazi official left with Bormann's notes covering the period February 4 to April 2. His instructions were also to have the Nazi gold reserves moved from Bad Gastein to a salt mine on the German side of the frontier. (This former Nazi official later vanished into the Gehlen Org, where his account, recorded for the Western Allies, has been accepted as true.) It seemed to the Russians that Bormann was so familiar with the routes from Berlin south to the mountains that he was easily able to reach Gerda. She was already at this time gravely ill, and died a few months later. The Bormanns knew that "Frau Bergmann" and the "kindergarten" she had established must come under observation. This did happen, and from the end of May 1945 until her death in March 1946 she was watched constantly by CIC agents on the off-chance that Bormann might return. She told one American who questioned her that Martin had cabled her an all-is-lost message. From what is known of her devotion to the Nazi cause, preserved in volumes of letters until the end, the Russian view that she was putting Bormann's pursuers off the scent is not hard to accept. Her conversion to Roman Catholicism after her own diatribes against Christianity may be explained on many grounds; a charitable view is that she was anxious about the children, knowing her own death was near, and capitulated to the priests.

Bishop Hudal seems to have found Bormann's wife and children with unusual speed. He had been enthusiastically quoted by the Nazi press in the 1930's, and he had conveyed from the Vatican to Hitler the kind of assurances that permitted the Führer to take actions he might have hesitated to launch if there was a danger of united Catholic opposition. On this matter, the Yugoslavs and the Poles have made interesting observations: in both instances, the

171

postwar Communist regimes have bitter recollections of collaboration between their local Catholic communities and the Nazi occupiers.

The Russian explanation is that Hudal was indebted to Bormann from the earliest days of Hitler's chancellorship. This was reciprocated, for it was Bormann who had gotten Catholic burial for Hitler's murdered niece Geli. The conventional Catholic funeral had been part of his job to stop public gossip, but he was under considerable obligation in consequence. There is no new evidence that Bormann was using his contacts, especially Hudal, as a channel to the Vatican, apart from statements by the SS military commander in Italy, General Karl Wolff, after his release from a war-crimes prison. On the other hand, many Catholic critics of Bormann's behavior were given brutal treatment. Father Bernhard Stempfle, for instance, who knew many details of Geli's death, was shot three times through the heart and his spine smashed for good measure, during the blood purge after the Führer took power. The priest left behind papers that escaped the Gestapo. These voiced Father Stempfle's view that no bargains could be struck with the Devil.

Whatever Bormann's bargain, he is said to have visited his wife's hide-out undetected, and to have then made his way north to Flensburg. There he was to meet his old friend Erich Koch. (Koch was captured by the British, handed over to Poland, and held in Russian interrogation centers for eight years before being sentenced to hang. Like Mohnke and other intimates of Bormann, he seems to have been squeezed dry of every tidbit of information. He does not appear to have been hanged by the Communists, who yet demand ruthless treatment of war criminals in Western jails. More probably, he was being used for whatever knowledge he had, in the same way as his old comrades were singing for *their* supper in the West.)

Koch had always been a fanatical Gauleiter, one of Bormann's barons; he made himself overlord of East Prussia with a total disregard for the military and police machinery there, which he treated with contempt. He had already proved, at least to his own satisfaction, that bullying tactics paid in his bestial treatment of the Ukrainians. When the vengeful Russians moved on East Prussia, and Koch boarded the icebreaker *Ostpreussen,* he made his staff prevent refugees from following him. As Gauleiter, he had forbidden any evacuation and took public delight in the news of an earlier refugee ship, the *Wilhelm Gustloff,* which had preceded the icebreaker by several weeks into the Baltic, where it struck a mine.

More than 8,000 passengers had perished, history's greatest sea disaster, and one that caught scant attention in those days of horror except, characteristically, from Gauleiter Koch. He thought only Nazis deserved to get away in this evolutionary period when, again, only the strong should survive.

Koch was to have linked up with other escapees in the naval-base areas around Flensburg and Hamburg. U-boats were thought to be victualing for the long journey to South America. But something went wrong. Koch ended up in a refugee camp in the always-accommodating province of Schleswig-Holstein and remained there undetected until May 1946, when he became a day laborer in a British Zone village. There he was recognized and eventually returned to Poland, early in 1950.

The Russians, adding Koch to their small stockpile of Nazi insiders, were cagey. An early warning of their secretive approach to the Bormann mystery had been given on June 9, 1945, more than five weeks after they discovered the inefficiently burned corpses of Hitler and Goebbels. Georgi Zhukov, speaking for the Russian military command in Berlin, said: "We have not identified the body of Hitler. . . . He could have flown away from Berlin at the very last moment."

Even when investigations had reached a stage where the Russians felt able to put forward an informed guess, the first version came out in the curious form of a book published first in Moscow and then in East Berlin in 1965. The book was credited to the Soviet intelligence major who had devoted so much time to piecing together the evidence: Bezymenski. The German title was *Auf den Spuren von Martin Bormann*. Since nothing is published and distributed in a Communist state without official approval, and since a matter as sensitive as this one had been attended by unusual secretiveness, the production of the report in this edited version was clearly calculated. It claimed that Bormann realized that Grand Admiral Doenitz's remaining U-boats were manned by Allied prize crews and, financed by some of the gold delivered by his financial adviser, Helmut von Hummel, went into hiding.

He was said to have crossed the border into Denmark near Flensburg in March 1946, a date coinciding with that given by Ronald Gray, who maintains that he helped Bormann enter Danish territory, although not really with the intention of letting him escape. Bormann stayed in Denmark with the help of the ODESSA network until the Nuremberg trials were over. He then traveled back to the Inn Valley, where frontiers meet. He could move into Switzerland,

Austria, or Italy; and near to hand were the galleries tunneled beneath Hitler's Berchtesgaden estates, where some of the Nazi gold reserves were still concealed.

Bormann decided to place himself under the protection of a Franciscan monastery in Genoa. He put out cautious feelers through the broadly based Kameradenwerk (another name for the Brotherhood), and some time late in 1947 met Bishop Alois Hudal. The Bishop suggested two possible avenues of escape: to Spain, where Otto Skorzeny was settled with other members of the Brotherhood, or, following Eichmann, to Argentina. The latter route offered attractive possibilities; there were funds already at work in various business enterprises run by Brotherhood groups in South America. This was the Russian speculation.

Bezymenski's private report in Russian does provide a list of the many sources he consulted during a period of several years' investigation. He writes self-deprecatingly and with humor. He disliked playing "Sherlock Holmes, that celebrated English detective," but he notes that the great Holmes did pioneer methods for the assembly of circumstantial evidence leading to conclusions from which it was then possible to work back until the final proof was found. Besymenski has not, so far as I know, gone beyond making his point that the trail of Bormann after Italy led to the same destination as Eichmann's.

SS Lieutenant Colonel Adolf Eichmann had been a Nazi fifth columnist in Austria with Otto Skorzeny. After that, his road led to the death and destruction of millions. He went to Palestine to visit Jewish settlements in 1937, when Skorzeny's father-in-law, Dr. Schacht, was charging blood money for each German migrant. He reported on these and other Jewish communities in terms which would be reflected in Bormann's 1942 decree on the "Jewish problem."

Eichmann was in Prague when Hitler died. His name was not yet on the wanted lists, and he knew from the gossip passed along the grapevine that American camps were the easiest on the nerves. He used these internment camps like guesthouses, moving steadily west and north until he reached the Danish border. There he made contact with Rudolf Höss.

Höss was in touch with Bormann, who, the Russians said, had visited briefly his old home at Halberstadt, now inside the East German border, and a couple of hours by car from Hamburg. The sudden appearance of Eichmann may not have been the most cheer-

174

ful event for Höss, who found himself very shortly standing trial for his life in Warsaw. But Bormann's influence was based upon fear, not necessarily of Bormann so much as of what he could do to expose people or cut off their sources of money. The Brotherhood existed on mutual aid and mutual apprehension. So it was suggested to Eichmann that he use the network's resources and visit the southeast corner of the Alpine Fortress and collect certain valuable documents and treasures.

Eichmann's adventures, where they crisscross the paths of Bormann and the Auschwitz gang, were reconstructed in 1970 by an enormous Montenegrin member of Tito's Cabinet, who swept into the Hotel Metropole in Belgrade one evening to talk to me of events not chronicled by the Russians. Tito had been involved in a direct and personal way with the story of Nazi war criminals, not only because he had seen atrocities committed against his own people, and not only because pro-Nazis had escaped from Yugoslavia to set up armed camps abroad. Tito's closest friend during the time he spent in prison as a young Communist had been a Jewish political writer and philosopher, Moshe Pijade. What happened to Jews as a result of Nazi Germany's policies, it seemed to Tito, had never been properly understood. He was further frustrated because, although Yugoslavia had suffered more than any other victim of Nazi atrocities (in terms of size), Tito had been treated as an outsider and his country as having nothing to say at the Nuremberg trials. Yugoslavia, caught in the Cold War, was regarded as a Russian satellite; and in view of the secret struggle between Tito and Stalin during the first four postwar years, this had been an unfair and a foolhardy judgment. So the Yugoslavs had kept their files to themselves.

In October 1942, the Yugoslav Communist party had captured copies of Bormann's decree "Preparatory Measures for the Solution of the Jewish Problem . . . Rumors about the Position of the Jews in the East." Little Moshe Pijade, a tough and resilient intellectual, was shaken by it. He was, as he proudly declared, a Communist theoretician. Still, he could hardly help feeling Jewish at that moment. The decree stated: "In the course of the work on the final solution of the Jewish problem discussions about 'very strict measures' especially against the Jews in the Eastern territories have lately taken place. . . ." The style was Bormann at his best and worst. The phrases wrapped terrible propositions in opaque language. "It is conceivable that not all 'Blood Germans' are capable of demonstrating sufficient understanding for the necessity of such measures, *especially those who do not have the opportunity to visualize Bolshevist atrocities."*

The italics were those of Tito's Jewish comrade. Bormann went on to say, in the impenetrable double talk of the virtuous official, that Jews currently being deported would be "transported still farther to the East." In Russia the transports were mobile gas trucks into which Jews were herded and killed with exhaust fumes while the vehicles were on the way to the burial pits. Extermination camps went into operation, and an enormous railroad system was organized for the transport of prisoners to the death chambers, where crystallized prussic acid was proving a more efficient killer. "It lies in the very nature of the matter," Bormann had decreed, "that these problems, which in part are very difficult, can be solved only with ruthless severity in the interest of the final security of the people." In such fine phrases lie hidden the terrible truths of life, as we continue to discover.

Tito's Partisans, having formed their own government, faced problems with the groups that had collaborated in the Nazi anti-Bolshevik crusade. It was claimed, and there is certainly ample evidence to confirm this, both in captured German newsreels and in Yugoslav government documents, that many of the recruits were Catholics, whose arms and Nazi-style uniforms were blessed by local priests. Some collaborators escaped into Italy, and the Yugoslavs drew up their own lists of wanted war criminals. (They have been plagued ever since by exile groups committing acts of terror against their diplomats and other officials abroad.) Among the Yugoslav documents were letters from Eichmann written, many of them, from his office in Vienna, in the former Rothschild palace. He was then pursuing the orders for the mass slaughter, and wrote to the German diplomatic representative in Croatia (treated by Hitler as a separate state, although part of Yugoslavia) confirming that the German authorities would pay thirty Reichsmarks per Jew delivered to the Zagreb railroad station. Eichmann had a large budget to build all the machinery of extermination, from the collection of live bodies to their final disposal.

Tito, with his extensive underground contacts among Communists who were not necessarily devoted to Stalin, had been informed that Eichmann had returned, on Bormann's instructions, to the eastern end of the Alpine Fortress and that a convoy of trucks had been seen climbing up to the mountain area of Bla Alm. This was an area well known to Tito, who, as a young Communist on

176

the run, had escaped through the Austrian alps. His own agents reported several curious developments. Eichmann had been seen supervising the unloading of twenty or more large boxes at a farm. The trucks bore the insigne of a German military unit based in Prague. The boxes were thought to contain melted-down gold taken from victims of the death camps in Czechoslovakia. All the boxes had been taken away later, nobody knew where.

For the Tito government, the most important result of these inquiries was the identification of the leaders of an escape organization set up during the rule of Ante Pavelić, whose Croatian puppet state was established in 1941 under fascist patronage. Here, Bishop Hudal's code of militant Catholicism and racial purity had been bundled together under an anti-Bolshevik flag and a three-fingered salute symbolizing the gun, the knife, and the cross. The Pavelić group was in close touch with Die Spinne, the "travel agency" run by the Brotherhood. It was established that Eichmann had been helped by the agency in Rome, issued a Vatican refugee passport with the name "Ricardo Klement," and sent to Buenos Aires. Eichmann, as the world now knows, was captured there by Israeli agents in 1960 and sent back to Israel for trial. There he told interrogators that Martin Bormann was alive. The Israeli prosecutor, Gideon Hausner, reported that Eichmann received a note on which appeared only the words: "Courage! Courage!" The prosecutor said that handwriting experts were satisfied the note was written by Bormann.

The view was held in Belgrade as recently as 1972 that a chain of monasteries, under Hudal's protection, was used by escaping Nazi Croats, and that this was at Bormann's disposal. Because of Yugoslavia's peculiar situation, being a part of neither the Soviet nor the Western bloc, and being therefore excluded from certain forms of international police co-operation (although much is done unofficially), Yugoslav police developed their own international organization. They are particularly well informed on the use of forged passports (Tito himself traveled before the Nazi invasion of his country on a fake Canadian passport). Their Minister of the Interior holds the view that Hudal took care of Bormann in Rome until he was sent by sea to Argentina.

Why did the Russians wait so long to disclose their own theory? They were inhibited for a time by Stalin's brooding suspicion of plots against himself by the Western Allies and Germany, and it was only after his death that the Soviet Union officially confirmed the discovery of Hitler's corpse. Curiously enough, their fraternal satellite East Germany has never officially endorsed Bezymenski's report.

The Yugoslavs had been in turmoil since the end of the war, but particularly since the break with Moscow in 1948. Discussing this with Tito's Cabinet Minister, squashed in a corner of a lively Belgrade night club, I was dismayed again by the evidence of excessive reactions on all sides once the Cold War began. "It made things easier for war criminals," he said. "The Allies against Nazi Germany were suddenly enemies. Russia was determined to secure its hold over East Germany and ourselves. The Americans and Britain wanted to set up their own kinds of political society in their own zones of influence. Manhunts were simply ridiculous against the background of nuclear forces building up across Europe."

He was echoing, unconsciously (and, I am sure, to his potential embarrassment), an observation made by a senior CIA officer of long experience and balanced judgment. Bormann had been tried and convicted in his absence by the International Military Tribunal, whose charter was never dissolved. The responsibility for finding Bormann was that of the charter's signatories. By 1950, they were close to a war among themselves, and Bormann became unimportant.

Unimportant, that is, except to those who shared his past. To quote the former British chief of "black radio" propaganda against Nazi Germany, Sefton Delmer: "It was the so-called reformed Nazis, the boys who became our allies against Communism the moment the fighting ended, who set a match to the Cold War. It was their salvation."

People are always talking about the "hidden treasures of Lake Toplitz," usually these days in cynical terms, for the phrase has come to represent what my friend in Jacob's Well Mews described as the "lure of the treasure hunt," the folly of chasing phantoms. Thrillers have been written about the search for Nazi loot.

And loot it was. Europe was stripped of everything valuable. When the technical details are swept from the board, and we see the Nazi period as something more than beautifully machined guns and tanks and planes, we are left with a handful of squalid men obsessed with greed. Art treasures, gold, and incriminating documents were their currency; terror, their weapon; a vulgar pretense of political philosophy, their protection against appeals to their humanity. None of these leaders behaved bravely when the end came. They crept into their holes, concealed their possessions, and hoped for the best.

The Yugoslavs had a great deal of experience in the concealment of documents in conditions where courage was always required. Their guerrillas defied Hitler as did nobody else in Europe, and they were subjected to massive attacks. With Tito from the beginning of Allied interest in his resistance movement was a middle-aged farmer from Welland, Ontario, a veteran of World War I: Major Billy Jones. This unconventional soldier, with a typical Canadian disregard for stuffed shirts, volunteered to parachute into the mountains of Yugoslavia long before Tito was taken seriously in London.

Jones's adventures have never been recorded, but he kept diaries, and so did his companions, including Tito. They all felt the need to preserve an accurate account of the long ordeal, in which one out of every nine men, women, and children was killed; in which, in a single German reprisal, a Serbian village was ordered to give up 8,000 persons to be shot (the number came to less even when every adult was hauled out, and so three hundred schoolchildren were marched in from outside to make up the required total).

Jones himself was shot through the head, but survived, with the bullet lodged near his brain. He had become skillful at wrapping documents in waterproof materials and hiding them—usually in lakes, under rocky shelves just below the waterline. So he did not scoff at the Lake Toplitz tales. Nor did Tito.

After the war, Jones returned to the mountains he had walked over in Tito's own Long March. With Yugoslav officials, he made several exploratory trips to the scenes of guerrilla fighting. Using maps, he went to each of the locations where he was once forced to hide important documents. These included lists of names that, in Nazi hands, could have brought tragedy to many families; copies of his messages radioed to London; and verbal instructions from Tito. He had kept precise notes, in code, of where the material was hidden. Yet he was never able to recover the documents that had been stowed away in lakes and streams and underground caves.

Tito awarded him the highest of Yugoslav military honors when Jones made his last journey back, and then ordered him to go straight into the hospital, so that surgeons could remove the bullet working its way toward his brain. Jones replied that he had to bring in the fall harvest at his Ontario farm. He died when the bullet, as Tito had predicted, entered a critical area of the skull.

Shortly after, in 1971, Tito went to Canada and consoled Jones's widow. He made the observation that men all through history have felt a need to preserve a record of their deeds. The worse the deeds, the more important it seemed for their perpetrators to keep for future generations a documented and doctored version. The honest versions, recording true courage, got lost, whereas the works of Hitler survived. Then he added in a quick aside: "But we haven't heard the last of them yet."

The problem in recovering the wartime diaries was that an underwater ledge is the hardest thing in the world to locate years later merely on the basis of coded notes. Jones had described to me the difficulties, and his belief that in the mountains of the Alpine Fortress there must still be large quantities of materials. His Yugoslav aide, a Partisan who is now a senior member of Tito's government, added that their own agents had reported the curious circumstance that on May 2, 1945 an armed German unit visited a salt mine near the Berchtesgaden fortress. Deep in one of the galleries were art objects from the Vienna Kunsthistorisches Museum and the Osterreichische Galerie. Some 184 paintings were selected, many of them impossible to evaluate, along with boxes of sculpture and fifty large containers for tapestries. The haul was carried away in trucks toward Switzerland.

Many of these treasures were recovered by American Monuments, Fine Arts and Archives teams. But Tito's man observed casually that a great deal more was never found. The treasure beyond price, he suggested, was the thick file of names linking the Brotherhood, Die Spinne, ODESSA, and other agencies, whose strength lay in the fact that membership lists were not circulated.

Were such lists known in Belgrade? The answer was yes. One of the largest neo-Nazi colonies of Yugoslavs was still led by Ante Pavelić, who at war's end had been forced to run. His trail had been followed by Tito's men to the Tyrolean town where Gerda Bormann had been received into the Catholic church before her death and where former Nazis have since built homes remote from the world. Pavelic had been picked up by ODESSA couriers, taken to Spain, and given a new identity and papers for Latin America. His Brotherhood contact was SS Colonel Walter Rauff, who designed and built mass gassing chambers for Auschwitz. Travel was arranged by La Araña, the Spanish name for Die Spinne. Pavelic had since withdrawn into an armed camp in Paraguay shared with German settlers in the restricted military zone northeast of Asunción. There he worked with Dr. Josef Mengele, the death-camp experimenter, and Rauff, who commuted between Spain and the neo-Nazi movement of his own invention: Das Reich.

How effective was Das Reich? I asked. There was an impression that these secret organizations were for men on the run, and divorced now from ideological pretense.

Tito's man shrugged. "We know it works for the Croat terrorists. They've assassinated our people, including one of our Ambassadors just this year. They have military training camps, in Latin America and now in Australia. But they have trouble traveling abroad. This is why they need to test the legality of their position, and public opinion. You will see. Mengele will try to justify his work in the death camps. Altmann-Barbie, the Gestapo man in France, is testing the wind with his memoirs. If they can come out of hiding, then Das Reich ceases to be a drab underground."

He paused. "Personally, I think the Franz Stangl case is being watched for this reason."

Franz Stangl was one of the SS killers sent to fight Yugoslav guerrillas. When caught, he was put into the American camp near Salzburg, Camp Marcus W. Orr, from which so many escaped. Like Otto Skorzeny, he walked away one day with the knowledge, passed along by fellow SS prisoners, that ODESSA would look after him. His route was through the former German secret-service net in the Mideast, and he lived in Syria until fear of reprisal drove him out. In Damascus he ran an import-export agency, a mark of the spy trade.

He was transported to Brazil, where he worked in the São Paulo Volkswagen factory. Then the "bomb" dropped in midsummer 1967. The governments of the Netherlands and Israel demanded his extradition in accordance with the international convention against genocide, which Brazil, unlike some Latin-American countries, had signed. It was another three years before he was brought to trial.

Stangl had been commander at Treblinka, near Warsaw, where 700,000 prisoners were sent, of which fewer than a hundred are known to be alive now. When he was posted to Yugoslavia, the Partisans got copies of his SS record. His Cross of Merit was awarded for "Secret Reichs Matter" involving "psychological discomfort." He had delivered to Berlin in the space of less than one year: 2,800,000 U.S. dollars, 400,000 pounds sterling, 12 million Soviet rubles, 145,000 kilograms of gold wedding rings, 4,000 karats of diamonds valued at more than two carats each, 25 freight cars of women's hair for industry, about 1,000 freight cars of used clothing, and so on.

When Stangl's job was done, Poland was officially regarded as *Judenfrei*, rid of Jews.

Asked how he would answer the charges when he went on trial at Düsseldorf (justice being a little delayed, it was altogether twenty-seven years later), he said: "My conscience is clear. I was simply doing my duty."

An observer at the trial on behalf of the Brotherhood was SS Colonel Hans-Ulrich Rudel, who became another piece in the puzzle.

CHAPTER 17

Beata Klarsfeld was one of many who thought the Soviet intelligence report was designed to smoke out Brotherhood members in the Spanish arena, where the first round between Communism and fascism had gone to Franco; and in Latin America, where the struggle was just beginning. Interpol and the Treasury agents of the United States and Britain were well aware of secret and counterfeit funds invested in businesses that fronted for Nazi survival groups. Bormann's party funds had amounted to $120 million and SS funds were the equivalent of another $60 million: considerable sums in the mid-1940's, converted into hard currency, and shrewdly invested. The money, as always, had been under Bormann's control.

The West German secret service, formerly the Gehlen Org, reacted to the Russian report that Bormann had run away in a curious fashion. General Gehlen made known the view, first only within his own and Allied security services, that Bormann was in fact a Russian agent. The Soviet Fourth Bureau was blamed for calculated deceit, part of an over-all plan to nourish fear in East Europe of a Nazi revival.

Two major scandals had engulfed Gehlen's agency. The General was shown to have played politics by forming an alliance with the periodical *Der Spiegel,* and the German public, aware at last of Gestapo and SS influence inside the secret service, became uneasy. The trial of Heinz Felfe, hired by Gehlen for his impeccably anti-Communist background, showed that the whole security apparatus had been penetrated by Russian agents, taking advantage of their Nazi wartime records. There had been, in addition, cyanide spray-gun killings of two Ukrainian leaders, which were at first blamed on Russian agents and then on Gehlen's men.

The extent to which Gehlen's empire was rotting away by 1964 was measured by Chancellor Ludwig Erhard, nearing the end of his first year in office. He had evicted from the attics a special staff of liaison officers placed there by Gehlen. "I refuse to live under the same roof as these people," he said after a prolonged campaign to get them out. Former disciples of the Order of the Death's Head were reported by responsible West German publications to have moved into key jobs under Gehlen; and it was widely reported that the sure way of finding employment in the new federal secret service was to recite the theories about Slavs being subhuman and Bolshevism the curse of civilization.

So when the Russians produced what was, for them, a restrained account of Bormann's probable adventures, only speculating upon what might have happened once he left for South America, General Gehlen's supporters began to lay a smoke screen of rumors that Bormann was really a Russian spy. The scandals involving the Gehlen Org were denounced by the General as "hogwash from the fairy-tale empire of the press." He had worked always in total secrecy, but after the transfer of his agency to the West German government, it became apparent that the public was the real victim of this secrecy. The Felfe trial demonstrated that Gehlen had kept nothing secret from the ideological enemy in Moscow.

During the war, Gehlen collected military intelligence on East Europe and Russia as head of Foreign Armies East (FHO). The man who first made it possible for Gehlen to build up those Russian files, General Franz Halder, now said Bormann was the only man who could have been the Russian agent known to be leaking top-secret information until the very end of the war. (Halder had appointed Gehlen to FHO in April 1942.) The military historian Dr. Wilhelm von Schramm disclosed that a regular interception of messages between Berlin and Moscow had been traced to Bormann's party chancellery. All the messages were signed PAKBO, which was the acronym for Parteikanzlei Bormann. A Berliner, Frau Gertrud von Heimerdinger, stated that she had been held in Russian custody when Bormann escaped and that shortly after she was taken to the Moabit Prison she saw "through an open doorway the Secretary to the Führer surrounded by armed Soviet soldiers."

Dignity was given to such stories by the high-ranking German officers Gehlen, as a matter of diplomatic policy, made a practice of hiring. My subjective observation is that these decorative figures were selected for the impression they made on the military amateurs of the West; I use the word "amateurs" in the complimentary sense. I was not alone in this impression by any means. It resulted from a healthy distrust of a certain kind of military pomp and circumstance. These distinguished soldiers dropped casual remarks at formal social occasions, reinforcing the view that Bormann had betrayed the Third Reich. Such a figure was Lieutenant General Friedrich Wilhelm von Mellethin, ex-Chief of Staff to the Fourth Panzer Army. Later he left for South Africa, where he became a director of Trek Airways, which undertook special charter operations for police agencies supervising the blacks. He was a friend of Otto Skorzeny, that adviser on racial problems, who commuted regularly from Madrid. Skorzeny at this time contributed his share to the spreading tales of Bormann the Russian spy.

Gehlen was faced with a small problem of his own credibility. He had produced for the CIA an earlier study of the Bormann case in which he concluded that Bormann was killed in Berlin. Since he was now claiming that Bormann was alive and well in Russia, he had to kill his earlier speculation. This he did. The park where Bormann was thought to have been buried in West Berlin was dug up during the night of July 20, 1965, and of course nothing was found.

This may seem an elaborate operation. General Gehlen was an elaborate man. He had been described as "ruthless in his determination to re-create the German Reich" by Major Hermann Baun. At one time Baun was regarded as the best Russian expert within German military intelligence. Baun was got rid of, dying so miserably that much hostility was created against Gehlen even among those who shared his nationalist ambitions. One reason for Baun's elimination was that in 1946 he had co-operated a little too closely with the British secret service for his own good. He had described the plans made during the war for escape. And his report linked Gehlen with such prominent figures as Skorzeny.

Otto Skorzeny first appeared at the side of General Gehlen late in 1944, when he was commissioned to set up resistance groups in the Soviet rear. Later, the two men worked on the grisly Werewolf concept and Hitler's imaginary Alpine Fortress.

There, in retirement, Gehlen told me in 1972 what he had said about the Russian report on Bormann. His retort was typical of a man I must confess I did not like. There was no way to confirm his statement that Bormann had been a Russian spy and escaped back into Russia. The story had the virtue of explaining away the humiliating defeat of the Germans; and of throwing suspicion on the motives of anyone who claimed Bormann *had* escaped more or less as the Russians had said.

"Beata Klarsfeld plays the Communist game," Gehlen told me. "Is it true she married a Jew?"

His secretary, Annelore (Alo) Krüger, inclined her head with the nodding motion of an old gray nag. "Doubtless that explains it." He tugged an ear. "Bormann was a Communist for different reasons. He worked for Moscow from the beginning. He made Hitler invade that part of Czechoslovakia which started all the fuss. He did it on Stalin's orders, you see. Stalin wanted us to go to war with England and America. Bormann did it all. We would have been united together otherwise, all firm against the Bolsheviks.

"Bormann alive in a South American jungle? Newspaper rubbish. My V-men would know if he went that way."

General Gehlen, code-named "Gray Fox" in the kindergarten of bureaucratic intelligence, was also called (one could wish it were just as much a childish joke) the "Spy of the Century." Now, with me, he approached the details of Bormann cautiously.

"Admiral Canaris compared notes with me and we found we came to the same conclusion independently. But I must be careful. I am no longer in the secret service," said Gray Fox gravely. "I am, however, still a general in the German Army, and a man has certain obligations, loyalties, duties. . . ." Since Canaris had become a symbol of the "good" German, Gehlen quoted extensively from conversations with him, implying his own virtue.

The Cold War had led the United States to hire him. *Time* had called him "a tight-lipped Prussian" fascinated by obsolete codes and invisible inks. Others labeled him the CIA's Nazi, throwing open the doors of his spy net to unemployed Gestapo men.

I found him a mild-mannered old man busy with evangelical church affairs and fighting the Catholics of Bavaria. Outside the iron gates surrounding the two villas he shared with his son's family was a notice listing the daily services at the local Lutheran church. It was later, when I checked again the incredible list of unrepentant Nazis in his employ, that he came into focus. He cooed as gently as any dove, as sweetly as Professor Johann von Leers, who had moved with such mysterious ease out of American war-crimes camps to Argentina and then to Cairo.

Gray Fox had given me detailed instructions on how to find his home on the Bavarian lake at Starnberg. Each time I phoned from overseas, the instructions were the same. Fly to Munich. Take the electric train to Starnberg. Pick up a taxi outside the station. He sounded affable, anxious to please, and solicitous about my health.

I landed at Munich on July 25, 1972 and broke all the rules. A taxi took me straight from the airport, southward twenty miles through a region thickly populated by strange leftovers from Hitler's war, to Berg, Waldstrasse 27/29. As a result, I was dropped on his doorstep without warning. The large expensive Mercedes slid away, back to the airport, the driver a little curious about my bags sitting on the sidewalk. There was no way through the fence around the two villas standing on land that sloped down to the lake. A sign warned me against the dog. Another offered me the choice of two bells: Gehlen Senior or Gehlen Junior. I tried them both. Nothing happened. I walked up the road and down again. Large, discreet villas. Neat as pins. Lots of trees. Very woodsy. This must be the place Walter Schellenberg had talked about. On some foreign intelligence job thirty years ago, he had driven here in a fast car to see Wilhelm Frick, who had placed the Jews outside the law and so turned them over to the Gestapo.

And this was where Frick had lived, drawing up his administrative charts, regulations, decrees, and laws so that nothing overlapped and loopholes were plugged. He had drafted the laws that gave a legalistic gloss to the "final solution," precisely setting forth the legal framework that permitted Germany to be purified of racial contagions. He had not broken the law, he said before being hanged. His conscience was clear. The law was the law. . . .

I remembered Schellenberg's detailed account of that drive to this leafy Bavarian estate. Over there, in the mountains, was Hitler's Berchtesgaden. All this region had been part of the Alpine Fortress and that great plan to cover the escape of Bormann's friends.

A pair of German Army helicopters sprang out of the trees and clattered across the lake. A man in a white linen jacket and a broad-brimmed white straw hat fiddled with the lock on the double gates, and courteously drew back.

The face seemed familiar. A face, I realized later, astonishingly like that of Hitler. The feeling grew when I talked with him later. A small man with curious pointed ears, slow-moving blue eyes, a neat little mustache. He shook my hand and walked me down the drive, past the larger villa, toward the lake and his own modest quarters. He had just been for a swim. Would I leave my bags in the small hallway? Sorry about the darkness of this room. The blinds were down, against the sun.

He pottered around the windows, slowly winding the metal blinds. A modest room, with the kitchen off to one side, a small patio, and a passage leading to a bedroom. A framed etching of some London clubs in Pall Mall; a tall embroidered screen from China; a rather handsome sword from an Arab sheikh; and a battered writing table. The bungalow seemed to be built of lathe and plaster. *Not* the palace the CIA should have built.

"All those stories about money"—Gray Fox caught my eye—"you see how humble we are. That bigger villa—my son and his family live there. This is enough for us." He motioned me to sit down. There was an old-fashioned sofa, with a chair near each end and a table. "No, not there." He moved me to the corner chair, and turned back to wind up another blind.

It was now an hour since my sudden arrival. About the length of time it would have taken if I had followed his route.

The front door banged open, and Miss Krüger came in. A grandfather clock struck the hour. A precise person, Miss Krüger. She sat down and pulled out a notebook. She had been with the General since 1942 and she had been protecting him ever since.

"Bormann," I began to say. They looked at me with quickened interest. "Bormann must have wielded great power."

"He was the power." Gray Fox glanced at Miss Krüger.

She got up, crossed the room, and sat on the sofa. I tried to return to a different chair.

"No," coaxed Gray Fox. "Not there. Here." He led me back to the corner, where, I could only suppose, the concealed microphone must function better.

Miss Krüger opened the notebook. The General sat opposite me.

"There is not much I am allowed to say about Bormann. The Bonn government asks me to wait."

"To wait . . . ?"

"Before selling the story."

I thought perhaps I had misheard him. "There is no arrangement . . . there's no fee attached," I said, and had a sudden memory of slipping one hundred dollars to another general, on compassionate leave from a war-crimes prison. The money, in that other case, had helped the General's young wife and children, living in half a miner's cottage. Gehlen, on the other hand, had asked for a quarter-million dollars from Lord Thomson's chain of newspapers for his memoirs. The Canadian publisher declined, muttering some appropriate comments.

"You see," the General said pleasantly, "much was known of Bormann, but not all of it could be told before. The first positive clue was when one of my men saw a newsreel in a Communist theater which included a big sports event in Moscow. The cameraman cut back to the spectators now and again. My man caught a glimpse of someone he recognized as Martin Bormann. We secured

188

the film and I am satisfied he was correct. But this is all I can say now.

"In my memoirs I am more concerned with the fight against Communism. These days it is not popular to talk against Communists. My political friends think it wiser to remain silent."

It was clear that the old man was a menace to right-wing friends trying to stop Willy Brandt's movement toward a *rapprochement* with East Germany. Our conversation took place on the eve of Chancellor Brandt's campaign for re-election, which was run on the basis of this policy to reduce barriers between East and West. Gehlen regarded the whole Brandt policy as essentially a Communist plot, and if he had been allowed to sound off in those terms, doubtless his more subtle colleagues feared he would drive the younger voters in the opposite direction.

He saw himself as the guardian of Germany's traditional institutions. He felt responsible for rescuing the only Nazi German organization and maintaining continuity almost unbroken from becoming head of Hitler's Foreign Armies East to chief of the Gehlen Org aimed at Russia. He quoted a politician of fifty years ago who had said: "Germany and Japan are the natural opponents of any Russian expansion. But the British Empire and the United States in the long run are the most threatened."

Now there, said Gray Fox, was true perception. If a man could see historical trends half a century ahead, how much more effectively this could be done with modern methods of analysis. . . . Absolute freedom of the press was dangerous. . . . There must be ways of screening officialdom from public scrutiny. . . .

My eyelids began to droop. Frick must have sounded like this.

If the war had turned out differently, Reinhard Gehlen's name would have been inscribed in the Thousand-Year Reich's Hall of Fame. His words showed no change of heart. SS men were put at the disposal of the Egyptian government "to inject expertise into the Egyptian secret service." He still betrayed indignation at the way the British during the war "pumped out propaganda against us through the BBC."

Miss Krüger scribbled away, and sometimes tore out a sheet with small notes for me, such as: "Read *Das Ende einer Legende* a collection of proofs that Otto John was not kidnapped but went over to Russians of own free will—With two interviews with Soviet Colonel Karpow who confirms this statement."

The grandfather clock bonged. Tea was brought, and sponge cake. The Gray Fox droned on. Willy Brandt's "Eastern policy" had been

189

plotted secretly at a meeting in Rome between West German so-cialists and Italian Communists. (Gehlen, I found later, repeated this accusation in his memoirs with no other documentation than unnamed intelligence sources.) No wonder Gray Fox's own political supporters wanted him to keep quiet. He could say unblinkingly that the secret service should be used to fight Willy Brandt, appease-ment, Communism, in fact everything that did not accord with his right-wing friends. It never occurred to him that a new generation of Germans might be put off by his authoritarian views.

If this sounds like an abuse of hospitality, I can only say that General Gehlen is a specimen worthy of study, in the way the previous resident in that place by the lake, Frick, considered some condemned prisoners warranted closer examination.

When Frick was Reich Minister of the Interior and Gray Fox was shadowboxing the Bolsheviks, this order went out: "The war against the Bolsheviks offers an opportunity of overcoming the shortage of skulls for the Heredity Research Center. The Jewish-Bolshevik commissars, embodying as they do a revolting but char-acteristic example of sub-humanity, give us the opportunity. . . . After the Jew has been done to death, whereby the head must not be damaged, the officer should sever the head from the body and dispatch it in preserving fluid."

It may be bad form to recall these things while taking tea and sponge cake with a general who boasts that, as a secret-service chief, he knew all about practically everything; and then adds, without visible embarrassment, that naturally his work did not concern itself with the bestial manifestations of Nazi security work. But Gray Fox was the kind of man who would never ever under-stand the effect upon ordinary people of what he was saying or what he had done. Not openly.

But somewhere a small worm of doubt must have wriggled into his conscience. He found it necessary to identify with the German resisters in a typically oblique way: "I took no part in the con-spiracy against Hitler but it would be false to deny that I knew one was afoot." He had the luck to be dismissed by Hitler three weeks before the war's end, when the Führer went into one of his tantrums and cut down anyone who happened to get in his way. It gave Gray Fox a drop of virtue, which, in the words of Hugh Trevor-Roper, "he greatly increased and used to lubri-cate his next and most difficult act of survival—his transforma-tion from Hitler's and Himmler's chief intelligence officer in the East into the Central European expert of the American CIA and afterwards the head of the secret service of the Federal Republic of Germany."

On September 21, 1971 three German officials called on Gray Fox. They were in charge of the Bormann case. General Gehlen had published a statement in the German edition of his memoirs claiming Martin Bormann spied for Russia and transmitted information on his own secret radio.

Judge Horst von Glasenapp, the Frankfurt investigating judge, who still hoped to track Bormann down, took a sworn deposition from Gray Fox, in the presence of Chief Prosecutor Wilhelm Maetzner. In this statement, Gehlen said what he repeated to me: that Canaris had arrived at the same conclusion as he had with regard to Bormann. He believed Bormann had been recruited in the 1920's, in that period when a polarization took place inside a wrecked Germany; "Discontented veterans went either to the extreme right or to the Bolsheviks." Bormann's method of rising within the Nazi hierarchy was based upon Stalin's example. His dedication was abnormal; it had nothing to do with Germany's national aspirations. Bormann manipulated Hitler in order to get results beneficial to Russia, and he destroyed all the men around the Führer in order to bring about the final collapse.

Gehlen was again adopting the familiar crabwise approach. Canaris "described to me his grounds for suspicion or supposition . . . two reliable informers in the 1950's convinced me that Martin Bormann was alive then and in the Soviet Union. . . . I am not able, even under oath, to divulge the identity of the two aforementioned informers since I am convinced that I am acting properly when I put the interests of security over the obligation to tell the full truth."

Let us put aside the temptation to speculate on the reliability of a man who says that security takes priority over truth. Put aside Lord Beaverbrook's headline in his *Daily Express:* HITLER'S GENERAL: SPIES FOR DOLLARS, which appeared in 1952 with the comment that Gehlen set a match to fires of hatred against Russia. Resist the temptation to wonder what would have happened if this man had indeed won control over all anti-Communist operations against the Soviet Union; and be thankful that there were many wiser heads directing Allied policy.

If Gehlen, whose entire military record is that of an armchair warrior, had played his games without any overriding control, the fat would have been in the fire. Russia had kept six million men,

50,000 tanks, and 20,000 aircraft in Europe. The United States, by contrast, began to reduce its forces as soon as the war ended, so that by 1947 they were down from twelve million to less than one and a half million. Gehlen was performing a dance of death, with provocative operations in Communist territory that involved the lives of men who little realized Gray Fox's deficiencies.

For the Russians were infiltrating the Gehlen Org. They put up for hire to Gehlen just the men he considered trustworthy: volunteer agents with the stamp of good Nazi stock on their rumps—ex-SS, ex-Gestapo, ex-Nazi intelligence; and Heinz Felfe, who became Gehlen's intimate companion and chief of counterespionage. The collapse of the Gehlen Org into a heap of ridicule came with the exposure of Higher Government Counsellor Felfe as a Russian spy, along with other V-men.

It has been argued that the Western Powers were fortunate in Gehlen's inefficiency. The Russians knew everything about his activities. And knowing all, they built up their strength but found it unnecessary to strike. He was not worth a war.

His Bormann story should have been discredited. But a study of his memos, reports, advice on formation of departments, and claims of intelligence coups around the world are couched in language that often does persuade other bureaucrats. He claimed, as a major accomplishment, the prediction by his Org of the 1967 Arab-Israeli war a few days before it began. Before the date of the Org's proclaimed prediction, I (and probably other correspondents) had phoned from Tel Aviv to warn my own employers, giving the day and time. In his memoirs, Gehlen quoted example after example of his supposed scoops, in reality based upon reading good newspapers specializing in world news. His determination to make Bormann a Russian spy is therefore odd. He knew public opinion was against him.

One explanation, given serious consideration by the investigating judge, was that Gray Fox had been asked to lend this story whatever prestige still remained to him. It would close the books on the Bormann case. It would discourage and perhaps even stop the hunt for Bormann in South America.

But the former chief of the Gehlen Org later named Werner Naumann, Secretary of State in Goebbels's Propaganda Ministry, as one of the witnesses whose identity he had previously refused to divulge. The British secret service arrested Naumann in 1953 for allegedly trying to revive secret neo-Nazi groups. He told interrogators that he left the Führer's bunker with Bormann, described the scene to which so many had already testified, but then added: "Bormann was rescued by the Russians. He was a Soviet spy and arranged where to meet the Red Army advance units. . . . Bormann now lives in Moscow."

The Naumann case arose because British intelligence believed it had proof of former Nazis conducting classes for youngsters. There was one eyewitness account of a Nazi youth camp addressed by Hans-Ulrich Rudel, a founder of the Brotherhood (or Kameradenwerk, as it is called in the British report). But for political reasons, the matter was brushed out of sight.

These political reasons had much to do with the Cold War. The West German republic was to be granted sovereignty. Chancellor Konrad Adenauer asked the British to let the federal authorities handle what the British called "the most serious neo-Nazi threat yet to surface."

Then Adenauer let the matter drop.

It was dropped on Gehlen's advice. Veterans of the Org have testified that Gehlen, while in American employ, ordered a full investigation into Adenauer's background. Then he committed himself. The man had served Hitler's Germany with a proper sense of duty. A former SS man who resigned from the Org because it seemed to him to duplicate his career under the Nazis said: "The rigid anti-Communism, the whole Org *mystique,* was attractive to political forces which were deciding then which way the new German state would go. Adenauer saw in Gehlen the perfect ally."

In brief, "Old Fox" Adenauer saw in Gray Fox a direct channel to Americans who could influence policy in Washington through the short circuit of intelligence. Misgivings might be voiced by diplomats in the Western alliance about neo-Nazi revivals or other forms of right-wing extremism. That didn't matter. The timid diplomats could be dismissed in private intelligence as crypto-Communists. It was still American military policy that prevailed.

The most important pawn in Gehlen's game was Adenauer's own "Bormann," the chief administrator, Dr. Hans Globke. He had been, as has been seen, the Nazi interpreter of anti-Jewish Nazi legislation, and one of Frick's men.

The Org became Globke's foreign intelligence service. Meanwhile, its agents went around the country investigating individuals and reporting the utmost trivia to headquarters. By putting himself on the side of the Americans in a common front against the Bolsheviks, the Chancellor felt safe against domestic critics. His Christian-Democratic government *was* the state. Anyone opposing it was a Communist or a neutral in the great ideological struggle.

A powerful opponent of that view was Dr. Otto John, who saw the whole story of Hitler and National Socialism unfolding again. He was sure Naumann was involved in neo-Nazi activities. He felt that Gray Fox encouraged the notion of Bormann's escape to Russia in order to divert attention from the Brotherhood, which he, too, knew by the name "Kameradenwerk."

Otto John was chief of the internal-security office. He was a lawyer who had been legal consultant to Lufthansa (and therefore knew a great deal about the traffic by commercial airliner in wanted men). He was a friend of Prince Louis Ferdinand, the head of the House of Hohenzollern, who for a short time had seemed a possible replacement for Hitler. By normal standards, John would have seemed the right man in the right job, if the Western Allies were really concerned to help build a democratic Germany. A few days after the plot to kill Hitler in 1944, he had escaped to Madrid in a Lufthansa plane, and from there he had gone to England.

But Otto John had helped the Allies at the trial of a German field marshal. That was disloyalty. That was what Gehlen was trying to destroy, root and branch.

Gray Fox was exceedingly industrious throughout his service. An inquiry into a private company's affairs was conducted with tremendous energy, and every bit of tittle-tattle was duly filed away. All this in the sacred name of freedom. A vast amount of industrial and economic intelligence must have been accumulated this way. The reports that have been made available are masterpieces of trivia or involve denunciations typical of the Third Reich.

At the same time, espionage was providing a means for groups of men to maintain contact. Gehlen's own brotherhood consisted of brother officers and sixteen relatives in top Org jobs. (They could be trusted, was the explanation.) There were secret societies all over the place, with impressive titles that sometimes reduced to the comic. The military-security service rejoiced in an acronym valid for Germans but which had Americans doubled up with laughter: MAD. Besides the Org, there were the BfV, Anti-Humanity Combat Group V, Industrial Warning Service Against Activities Damaging to the Economy, and any number of refugee and information services selling "secrets," so that at one stage in Berlin it was estimated that 47,000 adults made a full-time living as so-called spies. Many were middlemen selling to whatever side had the most to offer.

The climate was dangerously attractive for major war criminals. Not far from Gehlen's headquarters at the Org, and forty minutes' drive from his villa at Starnberg, was the flourishing town of Gunzberg, whose labor force was mostly employed by the family business of Dr. Josef Mengele, known at Auschwitz as the "Angel of Death." In 1959 he felt secure enough to fly from Argentina (where he was born and where the family has a large business) to visit the family and attend the funeral of his father. Gunzberg was dominated by the family enterprise: KARL MENGELE—MANUFACTURERS AND EXPORTERS OF FARM MACHINERY AND AGRICULTURAL IMPLEMENTS AND WITH SUBSIDIARIES IN SOUTH AMERICA: HEAD OFFICE/ARGENTINA.

Not the sort of place a V-man could miss. But General Gehlen had never thought Mengele's fate was any of his business, any more than the thought he had a duty, so he deposed to Judge Glasenapp, to convey information on Bormann to the Ludwigsburg Office, "in view of the fact I was not aware proceedings against Bormann were in progress."

His men saw no reason to pursue such figures, except under foreign pressure. The Gehlen Org took in the Hangman of Lyon, Klaus Barbie; SS Colonel-in-Chief Willy Krichbaum, former head of the Field Security Police, who put down the plotters against Hitler; SS Lieutenant Hans Sommer, who had planned in 1941 to blow up all the synagogues in Paris. The list goes on. After the treason trial of Felfe in 1963, there were public mutterings about the Org being too ready to hire "death's-head unemployables." The scandal led the Bonn government to retire Org agents with embarrassing histories.

Once in a while, the German public glimpsed the muted violence. A gas pistol was fired into the face of a man who led an anti-Communist Ukrainian group in Munich. The five cubic centimeters of hydrocyanic acid caused heart failure and left no trace. The gunman swallowed antipoison capsules for protection against the deadly vapor, which paralyzed the victim's heart if squirted at the mouth and nostrils.

The cause of death would not have been discovered if a Russian named Bogden Stashinsky had kept quiet. Instead, he told a West

Berlin police officer that he had killed on orders from the KGB. Furthermore, he had murdered the leader of another anti-Communist Ukrainian group in the same way.

Inquiries at Org headquarters were leaked to Moscow through Gehlen's trusted aide Felfe. At once the Communists set up a counter-propaganda attack. They held a press conference in East Berlin and invited Western correspondents. There, a former Org man told, with a wealth of unsubstantiated detail, how he had been instructed by Gehlen to perform one of the killings now credited to Stashinsky. He had refused, and defected to the Communists.

This public confession was made by Stefan Lippolz. He claimed that as an agent with the Gehlen Org, he was frightened. He could not perform the murder, which, he said, was required because the Org wished to foil British secret-service plans to train Ukrainians for espionage in the Soviet Union.

The bizarre story became too tangled for newsmen. One part of it did stick, however. Lippolz described the forged passports that were available for his escape. After deciding not to carry out the murder, he traveled along well-established spy routes through the Bavarian alps, into Austria and north Italy, routes based upon the old escape lines winding through mountain valleys. Then he became frightened again, and made his way, by another of the routes familiar to Org men, to Norway.

A curious habit of General Gehlen, I noticed, was that he copied one's gestures. It was unnerving at first. And then perhaps revealing. I would lean to one side of the chair and fold my arms, and so would he. If, in talking, I lifted a hand to make a point, his hand went up in response.

He was, it seemed, fit as a fiddle. Not uneasy. Not uncomfortable, as elderly people sometimes are, because they try to cover up some infirmity. Pouring a drink, his hand was steady, so it was just a curious habit—his hand twitching his ear when my hand twitched mine.

That first evening, I walked through the dimly lit streets, and then along the Seepromenade. The great white swans floated serenely on the dark waters. Strings of colored lights swung in a light summer's breeze above diners and dancers. I tried to analyze my own sense of anger. I had felt hostility toward the Germans, certainly, when my father was missing among the secret armies of Nazi-occupied Europe. I had felt hostile when, still a schoolboy and acting as head of a large family in my father's absence, I saw

196

one side of our small street destroyed by German bombs. But when it came my turn to fight, I had refused the alternative to becoming a combat pilot because I had no desire to bomb German civilians.

What I resented now was that once again, all these years later, I felt myself obliged to swallow my own rage. I did not want to hate these people. I did not want to believe that a group of human beings could arouse this hostility again.

It would be so much easier, more convenient, less troubling to the soul, to believe that a nation had reformed itself. I had been raised in the tradition that says the best way to heal is to forget. But how could one forget past evils perpetrated by a nation which so resolutely refused to examine its own conscience and which had never made a true confession of national error? The men hanged at Nuremberg had made it altogether too easy for Germany, East and West. All the wickedness could be blamed upon them. All the accomplishments so many Germans now claimed for the Nazi era—the discipline, industrial progress, great military victories—these were boasted about. How many times had I heard educated Germans, professional men and women, intellectuals, echo the same words: "If we had won the war, we would have been regarded as a great people. It's only because we lost that we're cast in the role of villains."

A friend from Munich met me, a professor who dabbles in journalism; not at all a young man, but much aware of trends. I find myself hesitant to give his name or even a clue to his identity. Why? Is it because he is a known protester against the reappearance of Nazis, even though they have grown old? He was a soldier at Stalingrad—a good soldier, I would think. There were 3,000 generals in Germany at the time of Stalingrad, and another 320,000 military officers. My friend was an ordinary soldier. That, for me, says a lot about him. He was one of the few thousand to survive captivity in Russia. He has no illusions.

"You look depressed," he said. I agreed that I was. This, in essence, is what he suggested was the cause: "You find it difficult to believe times haven't changed. You're also sensible enough to understand that the United States had no information on the Soviet Union when Gehlen came along with tons of material. He alone had the facilities to question prisoners—returning men like me. You know that he predicted the planning goals set for the East German Army, which wasn't picky about Nazis either. He reported there would be twenty-four regiments of infantry, seven artillery regiments, three tank regiments, and so on, to a total strength of 48,750 bodies. He was short by 103. That kind of precision cost you, cost the Western alliance, a lot. It also cost mistakes later. The Org made ghastly mistakes. It made those mistakes because secrecy protects men like Gehlen from the stimulus of criticism, and secrecy cuts them off from reality in the end, too. Reality is not in documents and reports and informers' tittle-tattle; it's in what people say to you over a drink or on the street. Gehlen's reality is a depressing return to the old obsessions, and the new German youth is looking back to *his* generation. They reject Nazism but they don't reject what led to the Nazis."

I peered gloomily into my beer.

"When I was a soldier," he said, "they discovered I was also a scholar. So they made me count bodies. *That* was called intelligence. I did it when I wasn't using a gun, hnnn? This makes me a member of an old boys' association of military intelligence. . . ."

And he told me about Gerolstrasse No. 39, in Munich. This was the office of AGEA—the Working Group of Former Abwehr Members. The name on the Director's door was Franz Seubert. He had been a Colonel in Hitler's military intelligence service. Then he worked for the Gehlen Org. AGEA published a magazine: *Rearguard*. It was distributed on a confidential basis.

A reunion of members took place at the residence of the Bishop of Würzburg. My friend's description of this gathering, which brought former agents from as far afield as the Tyrol and Italy, sounded like those Order of the Death's Head conspiratorial meetings under Himmler. My friend was not given to dramatics, however. He said they were addressed by a former general who had been in charge of a Nazi intelligence group: Gerhard Henke, chairman of AGEA. A record of the speech had been made and circulated. He said General Gehlen naturally could not allow official links with AGEA. But Gerhard Wessel, the successor of Gehlen, had received the AGEA managing committee for confidential talks. Wessel had been in Hitler's intelligence service and after the war carried on with the same work under American and then Bonn's orders. Before he succeeded Gehlen, he had been the permanent West German representative on the NATO military committee in Washington.

"In short," said my friend, "the price paid for highly questionable achievements over the long haul has been the Gehlen Org's cover for unsavory characters."

"That's a hard thing to say."

"Because you naturally counterbalance it with the thought of what They Do on the Other Side." He could speak at times in capitals, the way Germans do.

He got up. "But forget about the Communists. What have we been doing to ourselves?"

General Wessel had listened to the AGEA representations, as my friend had said. But the man who took over from Gehlen was more sure-footed. When Willy Brandt was Burgomaster of Berlin, every glass of whisky he drank had been reported to the Org's successor, the BND. But when Brandt became Chancellor, he was determined to get accurate information, not the kind of stuff dished up by the "froth-blowers" and "hydrocephalics" stuffing the ranks of his secret service.

Discontented veterans and aging officers talked freely about office secrets, hoping perhaps to change the situation. Their revelations confirmed the fears that Gehlen did in fact recruit Nazis; that his first ventures into the foreign field were in South America, where the best-informed men might be found. "He lived on the cold war," wrote Trevor-Roper, "and on the favor of those American and German governments which believed in the primacy of the cold war."

Gehlen's real criticism of Hitler was that he lost the war because he ignored professional advice. Gehlen remained philosophically a Nazi, though, like all army officers, he did not join the Nazi party. The Russians seized upon the Nazi backgrounds of his men, exploiting the doubts of Western moralists, who, voicing anxiety about a return to German authoritarianism, could not avoid feeding Communist propaganda mills, too.

This is what happened to Otto John. He was destroyed by Gehlen, ruthlessly. Gehlen used the secret files for a political purpose. He said about John's past: "He fled from Germany when the bomb plot failed and worked there for our enemies. He broadcast hate propaganda against our troops. Wearing German uniform, he interrogated many prominent German officers as prisoners, including many who later served under me in the Org. I said: 'Once a traitor, always a traitor.' "

If Gehlen felt so strongly about John, whose brother had been killed in the aftermath of their part in the attempt to kill Hitler, if "once a traitor, always a traitor" justified Gehlen's destruction of his rival, why did he tolerate the presence of Martin Bormann, the Russian spy, at the height of Germany's death struggle with Russia?

His answer was delivered in that calm and uncomprehending way I had learned to fear, because I knew now why Gehlen disturbed me and aroused the most profound sense of outrage. He had never fired a gun in anger but his room was hung with photographs of himself on the firing range, arm outstretched with pistol cocked, the stereotype of the figures one associates with the Nazi period, in ankle-length leather coat of black and black peaked cap.

He sat beside the grandfather clock, gold cuff links flashing, each link stamped with three tiny crowns in deference to his aristocratic connection, under a portrait of himself reviewing the poor doomed devils of the Russian "Liberation Army."

"I knew it was suicide to attack Bormann. It would have cost my life."

This was the reason for not exposing a man who was, according to Gehlen, in daily contact with the Kremlin, who reported daily the innermost secrets of the German high command locked in combat with Russia: there was too much danger to Gehlen himself.

The difference between attacking Bormann and denouncing Dr. John, one had to conclude, was that Gehlen knew the first had the power to destroy him whereas the second was helpless.

CHAPTER 18

Dr. John married a Jewish girl. When all other reasons are given for the enmity between the two West German spy chiefs, that fact remains. Otto John went to London after the plot to kill Hitler and met the Jewish singer Lucie Manén, of Berlin. As his wife, she was just too much for the German generals to swallow. In my talks with General Gehlen and Dr. John, I was aware of so much that went unsaid. This is one of those occasions when the writer has an obligation to state that he disbelieved one and not the other. John was in spiritual agony. He spent many hours with Catholic intellectuals trying to comprehend what had happened to his own people. Gehlen seemed never to question the values of his society.

There were other causes for jealousy, of course. John was determined to pull up every tiny Nazi weed when he took over the internal-security services in West Germany. He knew the Gehlen Org protected evildoers. He made several attempts to drag war criminals out of that shelter, and it was said by his enemies that he thought he was conducting a crusade of vengeance on behalf of the Jews. He never seemed, to me, to be anything more than a disarmingly honest man who found the realities of life almost too much to bear. He was accused of working far too closely with the British; and the Gehlen Org, despite all the nonsense about Bormann being a Russian spy, for a long time believed that John and his British friends knew where Bormann had gone and put agents on his trail.

Gehlen's men reported that Bormann was under observation from the time he crossed the frontier at Flensburg in the way described by Ronald Gray. The story of a body dropped into the fjord was either to discourage further inquiries, or Gray himself was not aware that other Allied intelligence men wished to see where Bormann would lead them, and staged the incident for his benefit.

These Gehlen reports were meant for internal consumption alone. They were circulated among the inner circle of his chieftains, whose anti-Communist bravado covered their own need to survive. In time, inevitably, such reports reached men who became either disaffected by the Nazi mentality preserved within the Gehlen Org or defected for other reasons. They were responsible for the first leak of this quite different version of events.

The theory was that Dr. John had proposed to the British secret service that it was worth letting Bormann escape. Support for this was provided by the strange way that Bormann's old comrade Erich Koch escaped. After he failed to make the rendezvous with Bormann at Flensburg, he went into hiding as a refugee, calling himself Major Berger. Was he known all the time to the British directors of the camp where he stayed? His face was well known, for he was hunted as the hateful Gauleiter of East Prussia. Yet he made speeches in the British-run refugee camp proclaiming his belief that "Erich Koch drowned in the Baltic." When he was finally denounced by another German officer, and taken away by the British, had the whole incident been prearranged? These were legitimate questions. Koch was handed over to the government of Poland under the agreements then in force among the Four Powers. He was not put on trial for eight more years. He was sentenced to death but there was never any evidence that the sentence was carried out. The Russians took no action against him either, although they had every reason to want him executed for his crimes in the Ukraine.

John denied, naturally enough, that Koch was allowed a short period of freedom while he and Bormann were under observation; or that later, in return for Koch's co-operation in disclosing Bormann's plans, the former Gauleiter became a prisoner-adviser on postwar Nazis to the Communists.

In the period between ex-Gauleiter Koch's exposure and his surrender to Poland, the scene in Europe had changed dramatically. The Soviet Union was reinforcing its position in East Germany, and the West had to concentrate on defense. Already by the winter of 1948 detailed reports were streaming into the Gehlen Org of the covert rearming of East German forces by the Russians, who did not scruple themselves to make use of former professional German officers. The so-called "People's Police" in the Soviet Zone was being built into a regular military machine of some dimensions. An exercise in military "extrapolation" was conducted in the best tradition of the German General Staff, which was the particular field in which General Gehlen excelled. By the end of 1949 Communist German forces were building toward the precise goal predicted by the Org. The search for Nazi fugitives seemed an eccentric pastime in the face of what was then considered to be a real and direct threat.

This atmosphere made it necessary to play down any under-the-counter deals with the Soviets. This was the period of such tension and crisis that on the North American continent bomb shelters were being dug again.

This would explain any secrecy about Allied use of Martin Bormann. It would explain any reluctance to talk about Bormann on the part of someone like Dr. John. The sharing of secrets was at an end.

Back in London after seeing General Gehlen again, I read more files on Dr. Otto John. He had recoiled from one political pole only to be repelled by the other. Inside Russia he had been questioned closely on wartime attempts to construct an alliance of Germany and the Western Allies against the Soviets, and he had said truthfully and with all the authority of a man who had acted as liaison between anti-Hitler elements and the British that quite definitely neither they nor the Americans had contemplated anything of the kind. The fear of conspiracy still lingered, as if the Kremlin had caught crumbs of conversation from Hitler's table. This feeling was strengthened by his encounter with Field Marshal Friedrich von Paulus, who was captured at the Battle of Stalingrad and became a kind of Communist showpiece. Although their meeting was engineered for the purposes of propaganda, John had been able to draw some conclusions.

The German Field Marshal believed that Martin Bormann or someone with similar access to Hitler had reported to Moscow throughout the war. John did not himself believe Bormann could have been that man.

An army commander beaten in the field is tempted to blame it on treachery or some other factor beyond his control. Paulus lost the entire Sixth Army in a trap which historians agree was most carefully baited and sprung at Stalingrad. He thought Stalin must have had some sinister influence in Berlin to persuade Hitler to pour his best troops into that trap against all the judgment of his military advisers; and that the Russians had been thus enabled to prepare and execute the lengthy and prodigious encircling movement that destroyed his forces.

John listened to this theory, and after he had escaped back again to the West, he commented that Paulus "no longer even had the strength to play the puppet role assigned him by the Russians."

There were other matters of which John had peculiar knowledge. He was cleaning out Nazi-minded public servants in the new and supposedly purged republic of West Germany when he tumbled into the hands of the KGB. There were few men with such an extraordinary breadth of harsh experience. Diplomats seldom rub against the gritty realities of an unprivileged life abroad. Agents seldom enjoy the fellowship of wealthy intellectuals. John had traveled in all these worlds. He had reported upon high-ranking officers who fled to Latin America. He had investigated, as Bonn's security chief, the case of the missing U-boats. He knew how Lufthansa might or might not have been utilized in Nazi times to run contraband and couriers into Spain and the Western Hemisphere, because he had been a key executive with the state-owned German airline. He had been a victim of betrayal in the treacherous arena of espionage and he had seen his own reports from inside the Nazi camp sidetracked by a traitor inside British intelligence.

I talked with him again when he was in London visiting the widow of the first Baron Vansittart, who gave his name to the doctrine that the military policies of German leaders had the support of the German people ever since the Franco-Prussian wars; and that Germany must undergo a program of demilitarization and corrective education to stop it happening again.

This time I was better briefed. The Public Record Office was a British institution that baffled me. But Ann Sharpley volunteered to help. As one of the most traveled foreign correspondents, she knew what to look for. Her account helps to explain why scholars take so long to produce their verdicts on recent history. She wrote in a memo:

"The Public Record Office is in that part of London that the Victorians put up when they tried to reconstruct Camelot. Between the traffic and the newspaper offices of Fleet Street and the sleepy Georgian quiet of the Inns of Court where lawyers browse beside green lawns and beds of roses, several ambitious Gothic buildings were flung up in a pinnacled declaration of the timelessness of things British, most notably the Law Courts and the Public Record Office. Here are housed many millions of documents *relating to the actions of the central government and the courts of law of England and Wales from the 11-th Century.*'

"Admission for more than one visit after a careful vetting by a clerk becomes of matter of giving references by 'a person of recognized position—i.e., a Minister of Religion, Medical or Legal Practitioner.' It is a place to make you weep for a computer. There is no comprehensive index so you make your way from clerk to clerk, from one scholarly, crammed, parchment-stuffed and paper-rustling room to another.

"Those who wish to consult the Foreign Office files have an indistinct little map pressed into their hands and must make their way through Dickensian streets to another Gothic pile (red brick instead of dressed stone) where the same sense of timelessness prevails. You are not allowed to use ink or ballpoint pen (in case, one supposes, you should deface the documents although more likely they prefer a pencil because it is quieter). There are requests posted on the walls to speak in a low voice, if at all: and warnings that requests for documents handed in after 3:30 pm cannot be dealt with that day, while 3 documents a day is the limit. It is a place where a deliberate pace in scholarship is enshrined and maintained and such are the formidable lessons of history that can be learned from its files that a reflective mood would be arrived at in any case, if it were not already insisted upon BY ORDER."

It was a rotten trick to leave Ann ferreting through those files. I consoled my conscience with the thought that she had more patience. Just once, in those cloisters, I had been lucky. I had wandered into one of the many cubicles to find a clerk in a black cotton smock of European design. On learning that I wanted the newly declassified files covering the war, he said: "Ah, you're after the Nazis who got away. Bormann and Company." He had overheard an earlier conversation with his boss. He glanced around cautiously and shifted his elbow. Underneath was a pile of index sheets related to the subject.

Dr. John had been kidnapped to take a Russian "cure" when he was still in charge of securing West Germany against Communists and neo-Nazis. Those who regarded him as a British agent claimed that by 1954 he was disgusted with the return to public life of the very Germans who kept Hitler in power. He had conspired against Hitler himself, and seen his comrades hanged or, like his own brother, denied even the dignity of a firing squad. Therefore, went the rumor, he had crossed to the Communist side in a mood of despair and embitterment. But veterans of British intelligence stated categorically that he had been abducted and placed under Russian pressure.

"There was a treason trial when I got back," John told me. "I was condemned by Nazi-minded judges who put me away for four years—when even the Prosecutor asked only for a two-year sentence."

He felt keenly the question of his own credibility. Yet he seemed philosophical and talked of the Dominican Father Laurentius Siemer, who during the war had helped the resistance against Hitler. He was not prepared to condemn the Vatican, although it was true that leading Nazis escaped along the route of monasteries. His own Evangelical church might have averted or at least delayed the Nazi terror back in the 1930's if it had joined forces with the small Catholic opposition. Clearly, he despised the German generals who changed sides or pretended to be anti-Nazi when war ended. He spoke scathingly of the apathy in West Germany today, and the same lack of civil courage that permitted the growth of dictatorship.

He seemed a man who had confronted situations that few of us can imagine, and who had emerged still clinging a little despairingly to some private belief. He was a German who had tried to fight those tendencies he regarded as dangerous within his own people, and now he was reviled by a great number of his countrymen from both camps. He reminded me of Beata Klarsfeld, who was disowned by her parents because she insisted on pursuing and exposing uncomfortable facts. Both of them had a certain serenity, as if there was nothing much left that their fellow humans could do to them or against them; and thus they were left with a private code of behavior.

Otto John was first known to British intelligence when he traveled from Berlin at great personal risk to Madrid to confide to their agents the details of a conspiracy to overthrow Hitler.

These contacts were one source of Russian concern, as he discovered during interrogation in 1955 by the KGB.

"Why was there this obsession?"

"Stalin was always afraid Germany would join the Western Allies against Russia." John paused, knitting his bushy eyebrows, bright-blue eyes fixed on me. "He was getting information all the time from Hitler's immediate circle. Someone must have told him, for example, that the flight of Deputy Führer Hess was part of such a plot. Someone who really believed this. In other words, an agent for Stalin who was not clever at interpreting political events but who did know a great deal in detail about most of Hitler's activities."

Bormann?

John looked away.

"Bormann was one of your problems . . ." I said.

"Bormann was one of the tough Nazis whose indoctrination would never be undone," he said after a pause.

"Was Bormann used in some way, after the war?"

"History may tell us that some day."

"Who *was* reporting to Stalin?"

"Someone close to Hitler. You know, after I was kidnapped, the Russians brought me to Paulus, who had lost his entire army at Stalingrad. I had seen him last when he was a witness for the Soviet prosecution at Nuremberg. He knew, of course, that he had lost some of Germany's best troops because of a trap. We talked about that, when I met him under Soviet supervision. We were both natives of Hesse and we could talk in a manner that was not embarrassing to him in front of his Communist controllers. Paulus thought all along there had been a leakage of top-level secrets from Hitler's circle."

I tried again to draw him on the subject of Bormann. It was obvious that he knew more than he wished, or perhaps was allowed, to say. Did the Russians know something about John himself that might have originated from their source in Hitler's court?

"They knew certainly from Kim Philby [the Soviet agent inside the British secret service]. Long after I escaped from Russian hands again, when I was back in London in 1967, I saw the proof that the Russians knew about secret contacts between myself and Philby during the war. This was why they kidnapped me. You see, in the war, I conveyed to London certain information about German resistance to Hitler. At the time, Kim Philby was the senior secret-service officer in charge of the Iberian desk, and my contacts were in Spain and Portugal, so of course he got my reports—and he stopped them right there. He refused to send them to higher authority and said they were nonsense. Philby could serve his Russian masters by stopping any attempt by the German resistance to use the British in a pact directed against Russia. During this period, Trevor-Roper, the historian, worked with Philby in SIS [Secret Intelligence Service], and he has written how my reports detailed the moves against Hitler, and how Philby stopped the reports going further. Trevor-Roper said the whole thing was inexplicable to him at the time. And now, in the light of what we know, I can see why the KGB abducted me and questioned me about my connections with the British secret service. They were checking on

Philby, who might be a double agent. And they were checking again the possibility that Britain secretly talked peace behind Stalin's back."

I asked John if, as legal adviser to Lufthansa before and during the war, he thought the airline had been used to move Nazi loot. He quoted the standing orders of the air transport command that the crews must not engage in espionage. But it was also true that during one of his wartime missions to Madrid, another German suspected of disloyalty to Hitler had been shipped back in a trunk.

He had been Director of Studies in the German Civil Airline Pilots' School in 1938 and was prepared to migrate to Ecuador, where Lufthansa had a subsidiary: SEDTA. But already the small group of resisters to Hitler was busy. "I decided I should stay and fight things out, but I refused to become involved with the military." He was in Berlin when Count Klaus Schenck von Stauffenberg tried to seize power, believing Hitler had been killed. In the blood bath that followed, he escaped and made his way to Lisbon. There, too, a suspected German officer was killed by SS agents and airfreighted home by Lufthansa.

The legend that Dr. John was always a British spy had been reinvigorated by his service toward the end of the war to the Allies. He advised on broadcasts to Germans, hoping to get some response from those who secretly hated what Hitler had accomplished. He screened German prisoners in the hope of finding genuine opponents of Nazism. He was the legal trustee of files on the German Eleventh Army, whose commander in Russia had been Field Marshal Fritz Erich von Manstein, and thus he attended Manstein's trial by a British military court.

Manstein insisted that he learned of the genocide of the Jews and other "subhumans" only after the war. John claimed this was an agreement made by all German generals he had questioned in the screening camps: that none should admit knowledge of atrocities.

Manstein, on the witness stand, repeated that he knew nothing of the mass murders. The Eleventh Army War Diary was opened to a passage which was read out in court: "A new Commander-in-Chief arrives. . . . He is an autocrat and somewhat difficult. However one can speak frankly to him." Then several lines had been, as John put it, "pasted out." The page was held up to the light, and John translated the censored passage: "The new Commander-in-Chief does not wish officers to be present at the shooting of Jews." Manstein signed the War Diary each day, and his credibility was thus lost. Just how bad this was for Manstein's self-esteem is demonstrated by the distortion in his book, *Lost Victories*. He says the pasted slip merely obscured the earlier sentences: "He is an autocrat . . . one can speak frankly to him."

There was no doubt in my mind, listening to Dr. John in 1972, that he was doomed from the moment he was appointed chief of the new West German security office. Old Nazis and pro-Nazis and the men of the Gehlen Org must all have regarded him with distaste. He was the man who had exposed Manstein, the great hero of Gehlen's youth, as a consummate liar. That alone offended the military caste and its ideals of a brotherhood that closed ranks against outsiders and concealed its sins.

Otto John used his period in office to lecture his own people, and in this way he lost a good deal of public confidence, too. He declared that a dangerous basis had been established for transforming the new federal republic into an authoritarian state on nineteenth-century lines. The Korean crisis and the fear of Communism had made possible the rearming of Germany. Men who had been Nazis in public service, including professional soldiers, could now apply for re-employment. Chancellor Adenauer was given the prerogative to lay down policy directives. To John, this looked alarmingly like a return to the past. Here was an old-style state administration based on the same old officialdom, with a federal chancellor who must be obeyed by ministers who were not his equal, and old-style generals back in the saddle with undemocratic powers over civilian life. Bringing back the Nazi-period civil servants was made acceptable to Germans with an automatic respect for craftsmen. Rearmament was made palatable by an American-financed newspaper, *Deutsche Soldatenzeitung,* which explained to young readers the need for a military program, and at one stage denounced Otto John as the man who had worn British Army uniform and called himself "Oscar Jurgens." (In fact, John did wear a British war correspondent's uniform on one occasion, to get fast permission to travel in a restricted zone.)

He found himself obliged to hire former police officers who, despite Nazi backgrounds, boasted they were the Indispensables, as indeed they were, since nobody else had their training. These were the only men John had available to investigate the Werewolves, SS men, and other old comrades. Obviously they were never going to take action against their own kind. When he cracked down on militant groups, he found former Nazis working as V-men for U.S. Army G-2 intelligence "fronts."

He realized these sudden changes were the political products of a tense world, but his dreams were shattered. He had planned an Albert Schweitzer Youth League to promote a democratic outlook and help youngsters develop a resistance to totalitarian influences of any kind. What he found instead were new youth groups of the extreme left and right, a polarization caused by the Cold War. But it satisfied what John feared were the instinctive responses to any kind of harsh authority.

Chancellor Adenauer was now receiving a stream of notes from Gehlen, delivered through intermediaries, denouncing John as a British stooge, an alcoholic, and a homosexual. Adenauer was hostile to this man chosen by the British, as much as he was hostile to the British, who had fired him as Burgomaster of Cologne for his arrogance.

Otto John was officially confirmed as President of the Federal Office for the Protection of the Constitution after a year in which Adenauer resisted the pressures of Germans who respected John's judgment. But the score was evened up when Adenauer also approved the appointment of a deputy to John who was one of the Gehlen Org appointees: Colonel Albert Radke, the wartime chief of security in Nazi-occupied Czechoslovakia.

John must have had few illusions left. He knew already how ruthlessly the Gehlen Org had disposed of Hermann Baun, the first head of the Gehlen Org's Acquisition Service. An honest intelligence man, Baun was outraged by Gehlen's obsession with sniffing out Reds, and he said so: "He wants to play Gestapo for the Americans." Baun was diverted into lesser work. One day, driving to an Org out-station to deliver money, he crashed. The money in his briefcase was said by his enemies to have been part of an embezzlement plan. He was called upon to resign because of "obscure aspects" to the case. Baun, who seems to have been a man of honor, broke down under Gehlen's accusations of fraud and "went morally to pieces like a whipped dog." He had thought Gehlen was his friend. He died a couple of years later, still an outcast.

A "protest by the generals" was delivered by Gehlen's friends asking that John be removed because he had interrogated German generals under what they regarded as degrading circumstances.

Then, on the tenth anniversary of the abortive attempt on Hitler's life, distinguished Germans gathered in West Berlin to honor the memory of the men executed by the Gestapo, and Dr. John vanished across the Communist border.

He had been invited to the gathering, and later had coffee with a surgeon he had known during the war. He remembered nothing more, he said later, until he woke up in East Berlin. The surgeon, Dr. Wolfgang Wohlgemuth, resided in East Berlin and was accused of lacing John's drink with dope.

Otto John was sentenced to four years' solitary confinement for treasonable activities when he finally got back to the West. One of the chief witnesses for the prosecution was tried for perjury sixteen years later.

Listening to John, I remembered the smug and self-righteous Gehlen and the strange affair of the cyanide-gun killings; and those incredible statements made in East Berlin by a former Gehlen Org agent who said he was ordered to perform the killings and make the Communists seem responsible. I remembered, too, that day at Pullach when the staff at last stripped away the cover title of South German Industries, along with their drab workaday titles and flowered again as colonels or major generals or "higher government counsellors" in the new federal intelligence agency. American dollars still sustained them, but they saluted the black-red-and-gold of the federal republic. And somewhere safely locked away in Russia was Gehlen's enemy, Dr. Otto John. And I remembered Gehlen talking of "vitriolic propaganda against Hitler's Germany" pumped out by John.

An acquaintance from East Germany who is quite openly an apologist for the Communist regime there said: "Otto John came over because he was desperately fed up with what was happening in the West. But then he fell apart and became a boring drunk. . . ."

John shrugged when I asked if the world had simply become too much for him. "It's pretty hard to be a German. On the Communist side, the regimentation is severe. In the West, well-meaning friends keep giving support to the Germans who shout loudest and longest against the wicked Reds. If you try to follow your conscience, you make an enemy of everyone."

Yes, he agreed, there had been a period when the authorities were eager to see justice done, but only because they wanted to convince the Allied occupation authorities that it was safe to give the Germans control of their own affairs again. Now, the old mentality was reviving in which clever lawyers found loopholes by which war criminals could slip back into public life. It was not a case of new Nazis, or neo-Nazis launching new movements, so much as a return to the lack of civic-mindedness and the absence of individuals willing to be stubborn about something in which they believed. It was a case of going back to the generation that fathered the Nazis, which was much riskier. Hitler you could identify as an evil figure; but the old authoritarian system simply encouraged an acceptance of a military caste, and there was no symbolic figure to arouse public alarm.

He was a lawyer, and he did not like the way the laws were being twisted to serve other ends than those of justice. Mass murderers of the Nazi era could now hope to escape scot-free. The men who masterminded the postwar survival of leading war criminals had achieved most of their objectives.

"All that prevents a new Greater Germany is the dividing line drawn by the Russians," he said with a bleak smile.

After the capture of Adolf Eichmann, the revitalized West German government, with its old hands back in positions of medium power and more, recognized that it should burnish its image abroad. The statute of limitations had come into effect so far as manslaughter and lesser offenses were concerned. But now, while giving a dazzling display of moral rectitude, the federal government got entangled in its own web. It had set up the so-called Ludwigsburg Office, whose chief was then himself investigated and found to have been sentenced to jail by a Soviet military court in 1949 for war crimes and crimes against humanity. He was fired. His successors dug up an embarrassingly large number of men and women who were candidates for trial. Hundreds of SS killers were identified in the police forces, and slowly the newly discovered guilty crept through the courts. The majority, however, were small fry, not those who drafted orders or signed decrees.

What happened was this. About the time John became President of the BfV security service, men like Gehlen and Adenauer were using the Korean war as a lever to get concessions from the Western Allies. An official of the U.S. High Commission in Bonn, Charles Thayer, described a typical incident in his book *The Unquiet Germans*. General Adolf Heusinger and General Hans Speidel visited the American diplomat secretly. They said that if prisoners awaiting the death sentence at Landsberg were hanged, Germany as an ally against Communism was an illusion. The Landsberg prisoners had been commanders of SS liquidation squads, and Thayer pointed out that *any* court would want such men hanged. What would happen if crime went unpunished? What assurance was there against a resurgence of barbaric German behavior? The generals retorted that Americans should assist the people toward repentance by tempering justice with mercy.

It was these interventions that had bothered John. Condemned men were reprieved under this kind of pressure. Almost all Nazi war criminals still in Allied and West German jails were released.

Most unsettling of all in these cynical bargains, an amnesty was declared for Germans who had assumed false identities after the war. It was then that John vanished in Berlin. The guilty began to feel safe. They saw, sitting on the right hand of Chancellor Adenauer (and gleefully assuming that John had gone for good) Hans Globke, who had drafted Hitler's anti-Semitic laws.*

The old German Penal Code said that cases of murder could not be prosecuted more than twenty years after. But the United Nations had resolved that "no statutory limitations shall apply to war crimes and crimes against humanity." Bonn subsequently introduced legislation that seemed to be concerned only with reducing criminal responsibility in *traffic accidents*. This said that culprits not actuated by base motives were guilty only of lesser offenses. The legislation attracted no great interest until the Supreme Court began to apply it to wartime mass murders. SS men who simply did their duty were no longer guilty of murder, but of manslaughter. The drafting of this loophole clause in an innocent-looking piece of traffic regulation was the work of ministerial directors in the Justice Ministry—Josef Schafheutle, who drafted most of Hitler's repressive legislation, and Walter Römer, who was Public Prosecutor in the Nazi special court at Munich, where he secured the death penalty for political offenders, which meant, in effect, those who opposed Hitler.

The situation now was one where the big offenders felt immune. Some would write their memoirs to prove their integrity, and others would creep back from exile with cranky versions of National Socialist philosophy.

Otto John was one of the many twilight-zone intellectuals who seem doomed to roam the earth and point out injustice in such implacable terms that nobody wants them around. He came out of that vindictive West German term in jail, having been interned or imprisoned in three other countries, quite resigned and yet incapable of remaining quiet. The Russians, obviously, must have offered him inducements to stay. So, too, the East Germans.

He went back to his old home in Cologne. No friends waited for

* Globke was kept by Adenauer as his key administrator until 1963, despite all the evidence of war crimes. Globke, for instance, had been Reich Commissioner for the Protection of German Blood and German Honor and organized the registration of those who were eventually liquidated.

213

him. He was neither pro-Communist nor pro-Nazi, and he did not seem to belong to any religious group. He was that most disturbing of men, an independent; and so they left him alone.

He moved out of Germany when Count von Kielmansegg took command of twenty-three NATO divisions, including the British Army of the Rhine, in 1966. General Kielmansegg had been a General Staff officer in the operations deparment of the army high command on July 23, 1941 when he signed an order to the Sixth Panzer Division, Section Ic: "Partisans who may be captured should not be shot but hanged in full view near the village. . . . In the case of attacks on German soldiers or units, all villages within a radius of four kilometers shall be razed to the ground and the male inhabitants sentenced to death by hanging."

CHAPTER 19

The guilty men were not only respectable again but also back in uniform. Decent men, honestly confused and not maliciously motivated, were pushed to the wall. The Dr. Johns were punished and the clever ones went free. Hitler's racist fantasies were back in circulation in foreign editions of *Mein Kampf*. His own propagandists were financed by responsible governments to broadcast the same racist poison as before. Israel got the full blast of Nazi vilification. Arab states received training from Nazi professionals. In Bolivia a Gestapo killer likened his massacre of French resistance fighters to the liquidation of Che Guevera's guerrillas. Nobody seemed astonished. Nobody cared.

The Nuremberg trials did not mark a sudden end to all evil. The Thousand-Year Reich had been going at full throttle and was only twelve years down the line when it switched tracks. There was still a tremendous amount of energy to drive the preachers of racial superiority. There was also a great reserve of expertise on fascism in all its forms.

An Allied army of all sorts of talents had been assembled by the end of the war. There were American and British writers, entertainers, fortunetellers, psychologists, safe-crackers, and other assorted brains. Those who reported to headquarters in New York included the famous mistress of a Nazi diplomat, champion heavyweight boxer Gene Tunney, European physicists, and graduates of spy schools established at a safe distance from prying Nazi eyes. Their orders were typed, their inoculations arranged, and their instructions given by young girls whose normal rendezvous for dates was "under Atlas" at Rockefeller Center on Fifth Avenue. Late in 1945 Noel Coward arrived to wind up his services for Allied intelligence. There, too, came the wartime Director of Propaganda in Enemy Countries, Campbell Stuart, and a young Royal Air Force fighter pilot whose children's stories were read by Eleanor Roosevelt to her family during the dark days of war: Roald Dahl. Out of this odd mixture of creative imaginations had been extracted brilliant schemes for espionage, subversion, and deception—anything to bring an end to Nazi slaughter. Then suddenly the whole organization broke up and the volunteers dispersed. Berlin had fallen. The Nazi U-boat chief had announced Germany's unconditional surrender.

Not everyone felt that this was the end of the struggle. General William Donovan, for one, feared the survival of men who would transplant the Nazi philosophy. He had asked for British co-operation in trying to predict the further actions of the potential Führer of a Fourth Reich. Work had been done on this on both sides of the Atlantic. Every Nazi leader had a proso profile. Martin Bormann's was updated, and into the dossier went an analysis of the party structure, the distribution abroad of secret funds, and thoughtful assessments of the effect upon his mind of Hitler's death.

"The Life Past & Future, Mind & Conduct of Nazi Party Reich Minister Martin Bormann" continued to accumulate stray bits of information over the years. The detective work appealed to Campbell Stuart, who had once gone on a special mission to the Pope and whose life was based upon grabbing the world by the throat, not in violence, but in a spirit of aggressive inquiry. He was a Montrealer who worked for better understanding between the United States and the United Kingdom. He had been Managing Director of the *Times* of London and he was just as much at home in Washington society as he was at the Palace of Versailles or Scotland Yard. Like so many others, he knew only too well the long wartime route between American intelligence, via Bermuda and the old Pan-American clippers, to Lisbon, thence to London's Baker Street or Churchill's bedroom for a consultation with the old man. The Bormann Life was under his general supervision, and when I asked him, what there was about it that fascinated him, he replied with one word: "Compassion."

"*Compassion?*"

"For all victims of this kind of evil. It never stopped with the collapse of Germany. It's with us now in one form or another. The Nazis grew out of racial prejudice. It really is just as simple as that. The whole drive of these people was in the direction of producing a superior race. We have to guard against this all the time, and Bormann is a useful reminder."

He tapped his long thin fingers on the side of his chair. "Bormann makes us examine our own consciences, if we're willing. The Pope was not, I suspect, willing . . . Pope Pius XII. Did you know his predecessor commissioned an encyclical 'The Unity of the Human Race'?"

"No."

"The draft was requested by Pius XI in 1938. It was written on racism and anti-Semitism. If it had been published it might have saved a great slaughter." Later, details of the draft encyclical ("Humani Generis Unitas") were made public.

Sir Campbell Stuart, at the time of this conversation, was out of public life, but he remained a governor of the Imperial College of Science and Technology and he continued to work, on and off, among the secret archives. When some of the wartime files became available at the Public Record Office in 1972, he suggested that I request the Bormann Life reports, if only on the basis that I could read through them. Some of the information was of recent date and still highly confidential. Many of the contributors to the later information, covering Bormann's distribution of wealth around the world, were prominent figures, and it would be embarrassing if their revelations were traced back to them.

Bormann's protectors appeared in the fitful gleam of the postwar twilight of Nazidom: assassinations, odd movements of stolen treasures, the blackmailing of a Jewish community in Paraguay, secret accounts in banking institutions where questions were never asked, and so on. This kind of knowledge is hedged about with legal restrictions, and it can be dangerous. Nonetheless, having been given access to the later files, I wondered just what did paralyze the civilized world? Forgiveness was one thing. But the West, so diligent in its pursuit of radicals, seemed to have done little to stem the flow of anti-Jewish bile from Cairo or interfere with racial pogroms initiated by Nazi-minded groups in Latin America.

"It's not *our* skins, that's why," Noel Coward told me late in 1972. His secret life as an agent had been a matter on which he could not speak until then. His first assignment had been the Latin-American beat, under Stephenson. His cover was the best. "I never had to *pretend* to be a silly ass," said Sir Noel. "I just played myself. The place crawled with Nazis, but, you see, those were times when we didn't pull our punches. Mind you—" he balanced a cigarette carefully in an ashtray—"don't make the mistake of supposing we let them get away with it now. The rules of the game have changed. Bormann got away, no doubt. I suspect he's never been lost though. He got away—but he did not get away with it."

This conformed with the suspicion gathering in my own mind. The Brotherhood had not been as clever as might be supposed. The valuable debris of the death camps, the jewelry and gold, the forged banknotes and stolen treasures, had financed business enterprises in faraway places. An examination of the commercial fortunes of these businesses, however, suggested that the Nazis were not good in trade. They were accustomed to bullying, not bargaining. Master forger Schwend wound up in jail when he bribed the wrong people. Others had died violently in lonely places. I had an impression that the slow strangulation of these people had been more painful than the Nuremberg hangings. Yet there still remained evidence of their lingering influence.

A summary of this influence in the 1970's, when I set it forth, produced an incomplete but not heartening picture. It was an accounting of Bormann and the Brotherhood gleaned from the most persuasive of intelligence digests then available. The pieces were the most striking in the puzzle, and worth recapitulating:

• *Ronald Gray's Story:* This was supported to some extent by Dr. Fritz Bauer, the West German State Attorney with over-all responsibility for the government's search for Bormann after 1964. Bauer believed he had escaped to the Flensburg exit route, missed the rendezvous with Erich Koch and an escape submarine, and followed Koch's example of lying low as a refugee during the period when Nazi sympathizers or Germans interested solely in making some money were able to bribe occupation troops to help fugitives cross the Danish border. "We believe Bormann stayed in the Danish Royal Castle at Gråsten, which was an SS military hospital. It became known that many high-ranking Nazi leaders hid there," Bauer reported. His testimony has been regarded as more reliable than that of most German officials dragooned into hunting war criminals in an atmosphere hostile to "disloyal" Germans. Bauer himself was a concentration-camp inmate who managed to escape.

• *Bormann's Personality:* This and the details of eyewitness reports of his escape were presented in contradictory ways by sources whose motives were often suspect. Comments that Bormann planned nothing, beyond service to Hitler, came from Germans eager to stop speculation that he got away. The psychological sections of the latest edition of his proso profile confirmed the observations of those who had studied his operations within the party machine. Bormann was a missionary intent upon leading the Nazi movement, and left Berlin when he was confirmed as the lawful successor to the Führer.

• *The New Führer:* In accordance with Nazi interpretation of German laws properly passed during the Hitler period, Martin Bormann was the appointed leader of a Fourth Reich. Those who subscribed to this belief sheltered in the "brotherhoods" of their particular crafts. Professional soldiers or policemen shared what they had and were helped by mutual-aid groups. Authority for this arrangement was the traditional German respect for each man's "trade-craft." Thousands of men skilled in the work of the party machine could be persuaded to collaborate. The first major step was to provide an anti-Bolshevik cover. General Reinhard Gehlen, chief of Hitler's Foreign Armies East (FHO), was delared to be the expert on Soviet military organization.

• *The Gehlen Org:* This put up a cloud of information and misinformation about the Communists; Hitler's former Finance Minister, Count Schwerin von Krosigk, having made a presurrender speech warning the Allies against a Bolshevized Europe. The Org was free to move its agents anywhere. Its chieftains found jobs and safe haven for Brotherhood members in need.

• *The Paper Chase:* Martin Bormann used his powers as the Führer's central authority to move documents and gold through German intelligence routes to Latin America before Hitler's death. The secret service had full authority to utilize Lufthansa and shipping routes, and cargo-carrying U-boats. Bormann selected key men in those military sections concerned with forging documents, transport of agents, unconventional warfare, evaluation of art treasures, and financial experts who were responsible for paying German agents abroad. The bankers by 1945 had spread many millions of dollars' worth of forged British currency around the world. The forged notes caused a major economic crisis in Britain. The subsequent "paper chase" by British Treasury investigators produced a pattern of Nazi operations. This led to discovery of:

• *Aktion Adlerflug* (Operation Eagle's Flight): This was the means by which blackmailing documents were distributed. The papers were concealed in three separate regions, guarded by leading fugitives.

• *Bolivia:* This was the residence of Bormann in 1948. The country's armed forces were trained by Hitler's men; and the postwar economy was dominated by friendly Germans. How Bormann reached Latin America was a matter of dispute. Some investigators thought he traveled on a forged Vatican passport issued by the Office of Stateless Persons on board the passenger vessel *Giovanni C,* from Italy. There were doubts among professionals like Sir William Stephenson. He emphasized the paramount weakness in many intelligence services. Agents lacking integrity could make up reports to cover themselves, with catastrophic results: "There is a

temptation to weave known facts into a generally fictitious report."
It was already known, however, that Adolf Eichmann traveled on
the *Giovanni* in 1950.

• *The Consortium:* This covered financial transactions for the
Brotherhood. Its branches were located in Latin-American capitals
and its affairs were directed from the Peruvian capital of Lima by
trusted chieftains: Klaus Barbie, sentenced to death by a French
court for war crimes; Adolf Hundhammer, alias Hubner, former
colleague of Scarface Skorzeny in Hitler's personal bodyguard;
Oskar Obrist, owner of an iron foundry named after the God of
Fire; Hernz Aeschbacher, a courier for Bormann. The Consortium
operated subsidiaries like:

• *SA Estrella:* It took exclusive care of Bormann's finances. Its
officers included relatives in Brazil of German Field Marshal Wil-
helm Ritter von Leeb (who nearly captured Leningrad) and of
German Armored Cavalry General Jochen Peiper, whose daughter
had looked after the Bormann children at Hitler's retreat, Eagle's
Nest. In Ecuador, the company's affairs were managed by former
SS man Alfons Sassen, sentenced to death in his absence by a
Dutch war-crimes tribunal.

• *Vatican Papers:* These were a collection of letters, reports of
conversations, and other documents said to have passed between
the Führer and Pope Pius XII. They were variously described as
demonstrating, perhaps confirming, the Pope's tacit agreement to
Hitler's proposal for a "final solution" to the Jewish question.
(Philip Toynbee has commented: "How typical that Pius XII made
vigorous protests against Nazi plans for 'mercy-killings' of the
feeble but no protest during the whole period of the extermination
of the Jews.") They included the copy of a report to which Hitler
had objected, written before World War II as the draft of a papal
encyclical attacking anti-Semitism.

• *Operation Bernhard:* This provided fake American and British
currency, and moved at least two experts to Peru. One, "Frederico"
Fritz Schwend, had been called into Brotherhood councils when
business operations ran into difficulties in 1965. Bormann was
asked what he had done with some ninety-five tons of gold worth
about 150 million U.S. dollars on the black market.

• *Brother Bormann:* He had adopted the role of a Catholic priest.
He called himself Monsignore Augustin von Lange-Lenbach (the
spelling was rendered as Lonbach in one report, and another recalled a line from Goethe: "They call me Friar Augustin von Lange
but my name is Brother Martin.") There was some confusion be-

220

cause his eldest son, also Martin, had been ordained a Catholic priest and became a missionary in a remote country. He left the priesthood in 1971 to marry a nun, and a year later was looking for work as a schoolmaster in Bavaria.

• *Bormann's Retreat:* This was described as "la monastère Rédemptoriste." He was said to move, as Father Augustin, between the cloisters of Rurrenabaque, in the northernmost part of Bolivia, and other sections of Redemptorist property in the fertile Yungas zone adjacent to the Mato Grosso.

Bormann's movements were given on the basis of reports from professional men—doctors, dignitaries, and politicians—who were critical of fascist tendencies in the countries where he was supposed to move. Photographs of Father Augustin were in the possession of Willy Reckhorn, in Warendorf, central Germany, who had been "married by Bormann, dressed as a priest, in the chapel of the German Nunnery of La Paz in November 1953." Reckhorn at the time worked as a teacher at the German School Mariscal Braun, and when the happy couple left to go home to Germany in October 1965, they were intercepted at the airport by Klaus Barbie and warned to keep silent about suspicions they had voiced about Father Augustin's true identity as Bormann.

• *Che Guevera:* He was quoted by Communist-front sources as having reported back to Cuba the presence of the Brotherhood in Bolivia, where he was killed. If this was true, it seemed odd that Communist propaganda failed to exploit the story.

• *Anti-Communist Groups:* These were trained by former German military figures, especially in Bolivia. A Major Westernhagen had been killed in Brazil. He was an intelligence adviser to the German Military Academy at São Paulo, and the son-in-law of an escaped SS general. He returned to West Germany when the federal government took full control of the country's affairs, and had been recruited by the secret service that succeeded the Gehlen Org.

• *Eva Perón:* She was described as having met Otto Skorzeny during a 1947 visit to Europe. There was no evidence that she had knowingly or otherwise helped Bormann get from Europe to Argentina, although Juan Perón, as military attaché, had lived and worked in Rome during the war and was a student and admirer of the Nazi German war machine. Eva had been welcomed by General Francisco Franco on her arrival in Spain and consulted a number of prominent Germans, including the former wizard of Hitler's early state finances, Hjalmar Schacht, father-in-law of Skorzeny. She had talked with the mistress of Gestapo killer Kaltenbrunner, Countess

Westrop. She had not visited Britain because of socialist protests against her reputedly neo-Nazi politics and the ruling Labour party's strong disapproval of Argentina's fascist tendencies. Since President Perón's downfall in 1955, Argentina had made it difficult for the Brotherhood to function except in legitimate business enterprises. (A footnote to one report here lists "smuggling into neighboring countries" as a pursuit not likely to fall afoul of the law.)

• *Die Spinne* (*The Spider*): This escape group functioned from the end of the war, for a time under the supreme command of the father of the Waffen SS, General Paul Hausser (who led public tributes to the last Germans to be hanged for war crimes, on June 8, 1951, as the "Seven Great Germans"), assisted by former Panzer General Hasso von Manteuffel, whose identity had been borrowed at one stage by Bormann. The Spider was known in Spain as La Araña and in France as L'Araignée. There was evidence to show that Bormann was helped by Die Spinne to reach Spain. One report stated he flew there on a Werewolf American Flying Fortress of the Luftwaffe squadron assigned to help guerrilla operations.

• *Revival of Nazism:* Sir Ivonne Kirkpatrick, an Irishman with a lifetime's study of Germany behind him, and onetime British High Commissioner in West Germany, believed Nazis and their successors would soon feel safest in their own country because they could appeal to German loyalties. He had interrogated Hess at length and knew the Nazi mentality. In 1953 he was convinced that some fugitives had crept back and were testing the wind. He had evidence of a neo-Nazi conspiracy but decided against informing German authorities "because the neo-Nazis had agents everywhere and might be warned in time to destroy documents." He ordered the arrest of Werner Naumann, who fled with Bormann from Berlin. Naumann had gone underground until the newly independent West German government announced an amnesty; then he went into partnership with the cousin of Belgian SS chief Léon Degrelle. The business: import-export. Overseas connections: Degrelle and Skorzeny in Madrid, and Brotherhood companies in Latin America. "One cannot betray an ideal in which one has believed since early days," he wrote. "The ruins of the Reich Chancellery held greater values. . . ." He had written about those values in Hitler's time: the necessity to destroy subhuman Slavs and Jews, and the virtues of keeping discipline through terror. Using the business as cover, he traveled to places of exile for wanted Nazis and conferred with Sir Oswald Mosley, the British fascist leader. He recommended a more subtle

222

political approach than that of neo-Nazi parties that copied Hitler's old slogans. He warned ex-generals who spoke too openly in public, including Gehlen, that the times required patience and stealth.

On the night of January 14, 1953, British agents raided his villa in a Düsseldorf suburb and collected slightly more than one ton of Nazi-type documents filling thirty large crates. His associates were arrested simultaneously, and the Minister of Justice in Bonn, Tomas Dehler, confronted with statements from Naumann and his comrades, said: "He was trying to fill key positions in the rightist parties with his supporters. The final goal was the restoration of the Nazi dictatorship with emphasis on the German race and its leadership role. [He] plotted to destroy the democratic system in Germany with considerable support from abroad." Kirkpatrick reported to the British Foreign Office that Naumann and his group were "like a Chinese pirate gang that plans to gain control of the bridge of one ship and then boards other ships until it collects a navy." The Naumann case happened at a bad time. The West German economy was booming, and the British were accused of jealously trying to create new difficulties. Chancellor Adenauer had his own reasons for playing down Nazi infiltration and saw an opportunity to prove that the British no longer had any voice in German affairs. The case had to go to a West German court, of course, and its spokesman announced a predictable verdict. The accused would be released because "there is no longer any justifiable suspicion that a genuine conspiracy existed."

Naumann, after his release, stated that Bormann had escaped but went straight to Russian military headquarters because he had always been a Soviet spy. Having regard to Naumann's known associations, his propaganda expertise throughout the Nazi regime, his analysis of why the Nazi movement after the war provoked Allied reactions and proved self-defeating, the chorus of Bormann-the-Russian-spy from his like-minded companions, his statements can be taken as a shrewd exploitation of the publicity surrounding his case. There were too many contradictions now in the reports that Bormann had been killed in Berlin, and too many indications that he had escaped to safety. It diverted attention to place him in Moscow.

The British move against the more obvious of neo-Nazi movements put the exiled fugitives on their guard again. Their operations abroad were difficult to prove. The views of men like Kirkpatrick and other authorities on German history were reliable, but it was

223

obvious that any countermeasures they took would have to be kept secret. Therefore, many official files had to be read with an eye for what they might also conceal.

I recorded a distillation of the more persuasive reports. Some, on closer examination, raised more questions than they answered. For instance, the reports from Bolivia collected by several different Western agencies, including Interpol, often gave as a primary source a man notorious for selling gossip to European newspapers. A Peruvian official with impressive credentials and an abundance of influential relatives told me a convincing story of armed Nazi camps and then undermined his whole credibility by telling me that Field Marshal Hermann Göring's widow worked in a Lima department store and that he would be glad to take me to see her. The woman was, of course, a fake. I had been in touch that same week with the real widow, ill in Munich.

I was inclined to agree with Simon Wiesenthal, of the Vienna Documentation Center, that a deliberate campaign was being conducted to confuse hunters of war criminals. He called it a "Nazi disinformation bureau," patterned on the KGB model. Somehow, that seemed too complex and sophisticated. And yet . . .

Bormann was the wealthiest man in the Third Reich by virtue of his control over party funds and Hitler's personal fortune. He had put in his own name all the Führer's "possessions" during Hitler's lifetime and presumably without Hitler's knowledge: all Hitler's properties, even the home of his parents, all the royalties, including those on postage stamps bearing Hitler's likeness, everything. It was estimated at the end of the war by Allied investigators that Bormann had personal control over $1,890 million by current American values. Nine years later, when a denazification court tried to confiscate Bormann's estate to pay compensation to victims of Nazi atrocities, a total of only $8,500 could be found. Then the Berchtesgaden County Court tried to settle Bormann's estate for his children. After a prolonged search, it found the equivalent of only $450, enough to pay legal costs.

Money in a hot climate buys privacy and an electrified fence around it. A Brotherhood without membership lists is impossible to pin down. In the London archives, among the thick volumes of declassified material, I browsed through the war's-end reports from British Foreign Office posts: "Military Groups of Nazis in South America" ran to several hundred pages; "Hitlerites and Falange in Uruguay"; "Looted Gold in German Hands" spread itself through several files; "Disposal of Undesirable Germans Abroad" was an intriguing bit of skullduggery; "Forged Bank-notes" filled more than a thousand pages; "Vatican Communications with Berlin."

There were obvious dangers to drawing upon this material exclusively. Intelligence agencies sucked up information and masticated it for tiny tummies. I had learned to be suspicious of obscure references, and especially the gleaming efficiency of West German agencies, with their neat assemblies of card indexes and mile upon mile of steel cabinets from which coded information was pumped into computers for immediate retrieval. Somehow I trusted the scruffy shirt-sleeved clerks wheeling British Foreign Office trollies behind beetle-coated old men with coal scuttles to keep the office fires burning; but I didn't trust them to the extent of swallowing their versions of events whole either. It was just too easy. I had seen how wrong conclusions were drawn by newsmen who relied too heavily on "informed sources" and military intelligence digests in places like Vietnam. I had seen propagandists who got into the habit of reprocessing information already processed by armies of intelligence clerks until the end result was totally unidentifiable with any reality.

I stumbled across one example of this. It was reported that members of the Brotherhood began to quarrel over money during the 1960's, and this seemed most probably true. But the leader of the rebellion against Bormann was described as the commander of U-235. He was said to have brought his vessel to Argentinian waters, discharged a cargo of stolen Nazi treasures, scuttled the U-boat, converted the cargo to money, and bought a large estate. U-235 had carried the bulk of Bormann's treasures and gold to Mar del Plata, according to this report, in the spring of 1945. But U-235, I found in German records, was logged as having been sunk in the Kattegat on April 14, 1945, about three months' sailing from where she was supposedly discharging cargo off the Latin-American coast. She had been mistakenly attacked by a German torpedo boat, T-17, so that it was not even a question of an Allied claim of a "kill." The sinking had resulted in a full naval inquiry, and Allied naval officers had made a careful check later to guard against any deliberate covering up of an escape. U-235 was an early Type VIIC submarine built at Kiel in 1942, and not the best vessel to shuttle across distances involving a round trip of 8,000 miles. Even traveling at top speed on the surface, the journey would have taken ten weeks out and return, at a time when U-boats were being sunk at a savage rate. Even then she would have had to refuel after each 6,000 miles. To make sure that the report had not perhaps confused the digits of U-235, I checked the records on other submarines in the series.

U-234 was surrendered and finished her service in the U.S. Navy. U-233 was depth-charged and sunk by U.S. Navy destroyer escorts in July 1944. U-236 was bombed by the RAF on May 4, 1945. And so on.

I was dealing on the one hand with impressive-looking reports in which facts piled upon facts tended to lead to wrong conclusions. On the other hand, there were reports from parts of the world where "official intelligence agencies" could run up any report for the right sum of money. The smell of crisp green dollars had started a race among persuasive gentlemen from foreign ports, all promising to produce Bormann or his memoirs or both.

The skepticism aroused by these tipsters and pimps would, of course, benefit real fugitives. This was the unforgivable ingredient. The public became bored. Governments became wary about issuing requests for extradition. The guilty could withdraw behind the smoke screen.

Just when it became hard to distinguish between truth and falsehood, and one became fatigued and disgusted, the fanatical element among old Nazis could be relied upon to revive all one's suspicions. It was Cairo all over again. One heard the rumors, listened to convincing tales, became cynical, and then suddenly a lunatic like Leers would spill the beans.

This happened while I was plowing through the reports that included volumes of economic studies on Latin America today. The Swiss newspaper *Die Weltwoche* reported "an extraordinary scandal . . . dealt with reluctantly in the West German press. Nazi war criminals have been warned not to visit certain countries because of the danger of prosecution."

Eight hundred Germans, rendered safe at home by new legal loopholes, had been reminded they were still wanted for wartime murders by the French courts. The legal-aid department of the Bonn Foreign Ministry under Dr. Johannes Gawlik (Inspector-Director for occupied Czechoslovakia during Nazi overlordship there) conveyed the list to the German Red Cross with the label: Very Confidential. While the Frankfurt State Procurator was searching for mass murderers, the Bonn Foreign Ministry was tipping them off.

The scandal broke because a bulletin published by Front-Line Fighters of the 45th Infantry Division in Linz, once considered by Hitler to be his home town, listed ten men who "for political reasons are urged not to visit France. . . ." Among the names was that of Alois Brunner (not to be confused with another of the Eichmann group, Anton Alois Brunner, who was executed in Vienna for war crimes). Brunner had represented the Eichmann extermination program in Greece and Czechoslovakia, where he was still on the "Wanted" list. He had worked for the postwar secret-service conducted by the Gehlen Org and was reported last in Syria. The Swiss paper commented: "This is not the first time that Bonn has hindered rather than helped the search for Nazi war criminals. It can find them to warn them, but it cannot find them to arrest them."

There were legal devices by which wanted men could evade justice within Germany, as Kirkpatrick had foreseen. Many dossiers I saw in Europe that summer of 1972 dwelt on the problems of extradition, and advocated that immigration officials at points of entry in countries like France should be continually reminded to watch for ex-Nazis traveling as businessmen. The French counter-espionage chief, Jean Rochet, of Direction de la Surveillance du Territoire, had no sympathy for Communists but expressed his concern at the way the West European nations tolerated war criminals sought in East Europe and Russia. Other agencies, like Amnesty International, had a bias the other way, and were more concerned with Nazi-type operations in Catholic countries against Che Guevera types and revolutionary priests.

Somewhere between cases representing the extremes of right and left, there were ordinary victims of German malfeasance. Russian officials from various art centers, for instance, won Western support for their complaints that Bonn was hiding looted treasures until the expiration of its own thirty-year statute of limitations with regard to stolen goods. Professor Kanetzka, of Leningrad University, went to West Germany to plead the case for returning art works looted from the imperial palaces, including the contents of the Tsar's "Amber Room." The hoard had been shipped to Germany on Bormann's orders. The Moscow Patriarch of the Russian Orthodox church began negotiating for the return of what he described as the largest and most valuable collections of art treasures and religious relics, handed over to the West German government by the United States in 1956. The Patriarch's attorney in Bonn, Dr. Georg Stein, said he believed the federal government would keep the collection hidden until 1974, when it would not have to be returned without official authority.

The stolen treasures were locked and sealed in the vaults of the municipal art museum in the Ruhr town of Recklinghausen. No precise list of the contents was ever made public. When the enterprising correspondent for the *Times* of London, Anthony Terry, discovered the location of the looted art in 1972, he was told the collections from Russian sources had been entrusted to German troops for safekeeping by a member of the Estonian church. This man proved to be a Nazi stooge appointed by Alfred Rosenberg, Hitler's Commissioner for the East European territories. "Nobody in their right mind," argued Stein, "could claim such a man was acting legally for the church." He was warned by the West German Foreign Office: "You are interfering in a matter of utmost priority. Chancellor Kiesinger made arrangements for the collections to be safely stored and the records sent where they could not be easily found."

The self-righteous position taken by West German officialdom exasperated some critics. To others, like Terry, it was evidence of long-term planning. "They believe their own lies," he said to me. "They're letting the major Nazis back into public life. The poor little bastards who did nothing more than guard the death camps are kept in jail as tokens." And he referred me to the scandal in France over Klaus Barbie-Altmann. While the Gestapo man prospered in Latin America, flying back to Munich when it suited him, the French were unable to get him extradited. Now another row had blown up, over his French collaborator, Paul Touvier. Touvier had been hidden by the Catholic Archbishop of Lyon in return, it was alleged, for Nazi funds obtained from looting. He was sentenced in his absence as a war criminal by a French tribunal and his presence in Lyon under church protection came to light only in 1972. An appeal to let him live out his remaining years in peace was made by the French philosopher Gadeon Marcel, who later issued an apology: "I was weak enough to believe Touvier's plea that he repented."

This question of repentance hangs over the reports that many important fugitives were sheltered by Catholic institutions. It is impossible to dismiss so many accounts from reasonably dependable sources. Protection was given, if not to Bormann himself, certainly to others during their flight and later survival.

The position taken by church dignitaries was not necessarily approved by the Pope of the time. Yet in all these accounts there is a recurrent theme, which found yet another echo in 1972 when Cardinal Duquaire, challenged to explain why he also sheltered Touvier, said: "I did not forget the Nazi atrocities but I was moved by sentiments of pity and charity."

Charity and pity . . . Papal silence on Nazi liquidation of "inferior" races, but loud papal condemnation of Communism; church blessings on the Nazi collaborators in annexed states like Croatia, but only ruthless suppression by Croatian thugs of Partisans fighting to expel German invaders. There are ugly contradictions here which need, indeed demand, an explanation.

What terrors might have been terminated if a pope had spoken out against Germany's well-publicized plans? The speculation was revived years later by American Catholics, disturbed by its relevance to current events. The draft encyclical protesting Hitler's policies was commented upon by the *National Catholic Reporter* in these terms:

"An encyclical, condemning racism and anti-semitism, was commissioned in 1938 by Pope Pius XI, but it was never published. . . . Considering that Hitler had only begun to move into fullscale persecution of the Jews, and had not yet begun planned extermination; considering that Italy had only begun to copy Germany's racial laws; considering the persecution of the Jews throughout history; considering the difficulty, especially in Europe, of launching a similar widescale attack on Catholics; and considering the moral weight of the papacy, especially at that point in history—considering all this, we must conclude that the publication of the encyclical draft at the time it was written may have saved hundreds of thousands, perhaps millions, of lives. . . . Such a statement would have been welcome then as today, particularly in America where Catholics, particularly Catholic working people, have been set against blacks. An earlier hard-hitting statement on racism might have meant that we should have less racially motivated strife in the U S today."

The magazine added that the encyclical appeared to have been suppressed because of the excessive anti-Communism of the Superior General, which blinded him to the dangers of Nazism. It concluded: "This type of anticommunism is too common among American Catholics who have fought the left so hard they have been taken in by the right in Germany, Italy, the U S and Vietnam."

CHAPTER 20

The past can teach lessons if we know with some precision what happened in the past. In the case of such a complete breakdown in civilized standards as that occurring within our lifetime in an area touching upon Western culture at all points and thus calling into question all our claims to moral and intellectual superiority, it is unlikely that we can get within even spitting distance of the truth. The large group of men and women who commanded such immense power that they came close to governing us by bestial rules did not and could not vanish overnight. If Germany had developed the atomic bomb before the U.S., as German scientists were first to develop jet warplanes and rockets and missiles, then the Nazi theories we dismiss today as lunatic would in fact have prevailed. The horror is still too close for proper examination. It is certainly far too close to living dignitaries for us to hope to discover even a little of the truth with regard to the Nazi fanatics who found ways to survive. A few facts leak out here and there, confused by a good deal of fantasy. Governments that once shared their knowledge have become secretive. Vested interests, in the prosperity of a nation or of a single commercial group, prevent the pooling of information. Yet there are large international institutions that, by their claim to moral detachment and divine guidance, have an obligation to open their books. This is especially true of the Catholic church. Seen at this distance, the church and fascist-type governments are too much of a coincidental partnership to be airily dismissed. The communal pastoral letter of June 1933 published by Germany's Catholic bishops expressed their desire "not to hinder the National Resurgence of the New Reich." An early innocence about the true nature of fascism cannot be quoted as a justification, for statements of this kind run like a leitmotiv through the political history of the first half of this century.

There were intrigues among foreign powers and between individuals that were part of the diplomacy practiced for centuries.

There were plots of such asininity that they could have been conceived only by real leaders outside of fiction, behaving as real leaders usually do in reality but not always in history textbooks.

Any curiosity about the Vatican's part in the postwar adventures of major Nazi war criminals is inevitable. Now, a quarter-century later or more, many Catholic critics within the church are asking more searching questions.

In the Bormann puzzle, there are too many pieces bearing the Catholic imprint to be ignored. If some of these pieces seem too dramatic even for fiction, this is the nature of the world we live in. Sometimes the fantasy does not confuse the facts quite as much as we might think.

Help was given to many escaping men and women by Catholic intermediaries. This seemingly odd generosity toward self-proclaimed enemies of the church should be balanced against the few but nevertheless brave German Catholic resistance groups. Young priests in Latin America nowadays often lead demands for social and economic change. In the controversy provoked in France by the case of the Gestapo hangman, the Bishop of Reims described how Cardinal Gerlier refused to incriminate "Communist" resistance agents although he was offered the lives of two priests in exchange. Klaus Barbie-Altmann had issued a statement from his 1972 hideout in Bolivia that he had enjoyed the protection of the church. But at least Cardinal Gerlier stood up to the killer's threats and announced publicly: "The Jews are my brothers."

This said, the number of escapees given sanctuary in Catholic institutions is yet stupefying. Martin Bormann appeared to find safe haven during the last months of Gerda's fatal illness in the pastoral valley between the Black Forest and the Swabian Alps. This region is strongly Catholic, and perhaps some thought had been given to the possibility of redemption. Gerda returned to the church in her last hours and placed her children with Catholic instructors.

Her letters, which are now matters of public record, earlier spat venom against Christianity as well as Jews. And her husband's first action on being appointed leader of the party chancellery had been the odious directive to the Gauleiter of June 6, 1941 with regard to relations between the Nazis and Christianity:

"National Socialist and Christian conceptions are incompatible. The Christian churches build upon men's ignorance. By contrast [National Socialism] rests upon scientific foundations. When we speak of belief in God, we do not mean, like the naïve Christians and their spiritual exploiters, a manlike being sitting around some-

231

where in the universe. The force governed by natural law by which all these countless planets move in the universe, we call omnipotence or God. The assertion that this universal force can trouble itself about the destiny of each individual being, every smallest earthly bacillus, can be influenced by so-called prayers or other surprising things, depends upon a requisite dose of naïvety or else upon shameless professional self-interest. . . . The people must be increasingly wrested from the churches, and their instruments the priests."

Bormann's declared intention was to crush the churches. Yet his children were placed in the church's care.

Bishop Alois Hudal, tutor of his oldest son, was a chief agent in escape organizations. When Adolf Eichmann, the stealthy butcher of millions, said he had escaped to South America with the Bishop's help, Hudal stated publicly: "It was my Christian duty to help all who were in need and danger." The agency, whose activities came under a Vatican refugee organization, seems to have limited itself to ex-fascists. The Vatican, for that matter, issued passports only to self-avowed Catholics.

Hudal's name cropped up in statements made by a number of captured war criminals. Dr. Gerhard Bohne, charged with 15,000 "euthanasia" killings, escaped to Argentina, and when arrested in Buenos Aires, in March 1964, said that he had got away through "the charitable help extended to many fugitives." Bishop Hudal died in 1966, and it may have been convenient to credit him with several escapes that were in fact the work of ODESSA, in this period held responsible for Operation Silence. This involved a series of killings, some described as suicides, among personalities thought to have too much knowledge of ODESSA's operations.

Bishop Hudal voiced his views on Nazism at an early stage in the movement, and a book of his, *The Groundwork of National Socialism,* published in 1937 in Leipzig and Vienna, was greeted with enthusiasm by the Nazi press. He was, he wrote, in full agreement with Nazi "defensive actions." He justified the Nazi movement as one that displayed a powerful Christian culture despite appearances to the contrary. It could be argued that in the 1930's he might have been unaware of the pagan nationalism of the leaders, or the wild tribal theories of lapsed Catholics who had reached positions of eminence within the party. Unhappily, one is forced to conclude from his writings that he was obsessed with the anti-Christ nature of Communism. What concerned him, beyond anything, was the destruction of the Bolshevik Devil. He sought an

232

accommodation between the church and the Nazis, who were, he wrote, "on the right track." In the predominantly Catholic city of Cologne, the local Nazi party newspaper, *Westdeutscher Beobachter,* on October 17, 1936 gave Hudal's ideas front-page attention. How many Germans were thus encouraged to close eyes and ears to the growing evidence of what happened in their own concentration camps? How many buttered their consciences just when they were preparing to question the Draconian laws springing up around them like a forest? How many, given different guidance, might have resisted the Nazis? For in 1936 it was impossible for any intelligent German—and many Catholic Germans tended to be intellectuals—to remain ignorant of what Hitler planned to do.

All Catholic diocesan publications, with the notable exception of the Berlin See, carried the anti-Semitic propaganda churned out by Goebbels and his "expert" in Jewish affairs, Johann von Leers. In the conferences leading to the concordat between the Vatican and Germany, reference was made consistently and *ad nauseam* to the Jews and lesser breeds as evildoers. "I am only doing what the church has been doing for fifteen hundred years," Hitler told Bishop Wilhelm Berning on April 26, 1933. The Protestant clergy were no less informed; they adopted as church leader Chaplain Ludwig Müller, the Führer's confidant. On Hitler's fiftieth birthday in 1939, Protestant and Catholic bishops, with the exception of those in two dioceses, urged the following prayer upon all Germans: "Remember O Lord our Führer whose secret wishes Thou knowest." By then, his secret wishes were perfectly well known to all and expressed in the Nuremberg Laws, which Bishop Hudal described as "unavoidable countermeasures against alien elements."

Bishop Hudal kept open the line between Hitler's court and the Vatican. It may have been unofficial, in the sense that nothing has been published yet to reinforce the many verbal statements that the Third Reich, on the eve of launching a full program to liquidate the Jews, was assured that the Pope would say nothing to provoke any outcry among German Catholics. The fact remains that he was trusted in the Führer's court because of his strong endorsement earlier of the Nazi creed. Therefore it would make practical sense to use him as a messenger on the Pope's behalf. Shortly after the start of World War II with the cold-blooded invasion of Catholic Poland in September 1939, the new Pope, Pius XII, issued an encyclical which avoided all the main issues raised by Nazi aggression. Instead, there was reference to "misguided souls, whether of the Jewish people or of other origin [who] ally themselves or actively promote revolutionary movements." This referred to Bolshevism, and encouraged Nazi ideologues who hammered at the theme of a sinister conspiracy between Jews and Communists. As Gordon Zahn, author of *German Catholics & Hitler's Wars,* observed in the *National Catholic Reporter* of December 15, 1972: "It was not just Pius XII's *failure* to protest the systematic elimination of the Jews but, rather, his apparent *refusal* to go along with the intention of his revered predecessor," Pius XI, who had shown a readiness to denounce racism and terror bombing.

The Vatican's policy has been a source of controversy ever since. Anyone who followed it was aware that many embarrassing documents relevant to Pius XII's relations with fascist governments were buried away after the war. The story is a book in itself. The facts are clear enough that the Vatican's many institutions, as a matter of deliberate policy or in the manner of absent-minded medieval monks, left undisturbed in basements and archives those papers that confirmed an unhealthy papal tolerance of Nazi actions.

Similar documents may have found their way into Bormann's hands. This cannot for the present be proved. As Secretary to the Führer he was responsible for correspondence with the Vatican, and some of this has been recovered, either in the original or in duplicate. He kept careful notes of conversations with Vatican emissaries, as he kept records of all potentially useful meetings. His collection of bits of paper earned him the title of "Herr Paper Picker," and his use of the party's teletype communications center made him notorious as the dispatcher of messages. The messages and the bits of paper always had a purpose, usually the undermining of a rival or the overthrow of an easy victim. His use of incriminating papers as a means of blackmail has been described by members of the court. What he kept on file cost jobs, lives, prestige. His love of power over individuals was explored in the Bormann Life, and the power was exercised in the bureaucratic style he knew best.

The Vatican viewed him with thoughtful caution. He certainly knew enough to be able to make demands later for papal protection, and there were many practical reasons why, as a fugitive, he might call on the church for help.

One reason, reliably documented, involved men of the caliber of the head of the House of Hohenzollern, Prince Louis Ferdinand, and prominent Allied dignitaries. This was in the so-called X Report, which appeared in American and British intelligence archives under that title. The report professed to be a Vatican assessment that said that Britain was ready to negotiate peace. German peace feelers were put out, to give the Nazi war machine the freedom to focus upon Russia. But the report contradicted Winston Churchill's minute of June 28, 1940 to Foreign Secretary Anthony Eden: "We do not desire to make any enquiries as to terms of peace with Hitler . . . all our Agents are strictly forbidden to entertain any such suggestion."

Any misjudgment of British resolve at this time would have been disastrous. Britain was braced against aerial bombardment, and soldiers were training with broomsticks. In America there was a campaign, assisted by members of the German friendship and culture groups, to convince President Roosevelt that Britain was finished. The campaign was aimed not just at keeping the United States out of the war, but also to stop any supply of urgently needed arms. The X Report might have convinced all who saw it that the British were wavering. It ascribed a willingness to negotiate on the part of the very "Agents" Churchill had in mind, so that Hitler could safely overrun the rest of Western Europe before turning his full attention against the Soviets.

The X Report was an account of the Pope's talks with secret German contacts after the invasion of Poland. The papers were placed in Bormann's private files and contributed to the widely held belief that Pius XII, fearful of Communism and sympathetic to autocratic regimes that proclaimed their vision of Russia as the Devil incarnate, could live with National Socialism.

The report arose after an anti-Nazi group in Germany asked what terms the British would consider if Hitler was overthrown. The reply, as conveyed from the Vatican, was that if a trustworthy Reich government replaced the Nazi regime, and if no hostilities had broken out on the Western front, the British would consider talking about the "Eastern frontiers." However, the report injected an interpretation that the British regarded, when they found out, as dangerously misleading. The Pope said the British would negotiate in a spirit favorable to German interests. The conquest of Poland, the enlargement of German territory along disputed eastern borders, and what was regarded as an occupation of Austria and part of Czechoslovakia would be left unchallenged.

When the X Report reached Field Marshal Walther von Brauchitsch, the German Army Commander in Chief, he said the suggestion that an anti-Nazi government could negotiate with Britain struck him as treason.

But which interpretation of British proposals did he receive? All these years later, British intelligence records show that London's terms were inflexible: restoration of Austria, Czechoslovakia, and Poland to their former status, and the renunciation of Germany's economic policies which hurt all other trading nations. These terms were dependent, of course, upon Hitler and the Nazis being tossed out of office, preferably on the end of a rope.

There is a considerable difference here between official British terms and the reports relayed from the Vatican to Berlin. In the hands of the Brotherhood, or anyone who wished to stir controversy and anger against the Vatican, a copy of the report could be damaging. It was in the same category as the informal communications between Pius XII and Hitler's contacts at the Vatican, in which the Nazis were encouraged to feel they could go forward with "administrative measures" in regard to the problem of the Jews. Indirect language, and the veiling of the real meaning of Hitler's proposals to liquidate all subhumans, made it possible for Pius XII to throw up a mental barrier against the reality.

The X Report was discovered by Gestapo Müller in 1940, whose own informer was a Benedictine monk, Father Keller. The report then went to Bormann. It recorded the Pope's concern to protect the German church, and it stated that the British would be reasonable about the Eastern territories. We know now that the Pope was deeply concerned about a Russian takeover in East Europe and possibly farther afield. He was anxious to bring about an accommodation that would result in a common Anglo-German front against Communism.

The British terms were delivered directly by another channel, however: the two British agents known as "Captain S. Payne Best" and "Major R. H. Stevens." They met the Nazi intelligence chief, Walter Schellenberg, in Holland. Schellenberg was disguised as "Hauptmann Schaemmel" of the military transport department, and his job was to persuade British intelligence of an anti-Hitler movement within the army. He was, in other words, an *agent provocateur*. He was also fishing on Hitler's behalf for evidence of some weakness in British resolve. The war with Britain was only a few weeks old.

The first contacts were made in October 1939, and conversations took place before Hitler's invasion of France and its neighbors. The talks began in a car driving along the German-Dutch border. The British agents were taking grave risks. They had heard Hitler's broadcasts calling on Britain to recognize his conquests in Poland and Czechoslovakia. They knew the likelihood of a lightning strike by German forces south. They could only repeat that Britain under no circumstances would accept Hitler's expanded empire. Their last major discussion took place in the offices of a company called N. V. Handels Dienst Veer Her Continent, Nieuwe Uitleg No. 15, in The Hague. This was a cover operation for British intelligence. Schellenberg was given a British radio transmitter and receiver, the call number 0N4, and a secret phone number: 556/331. He was also given yet again a firm statement contradicting the X Report on British flexibility. There would be no appeasement, even if Hitler flew into another rage and invaded south.

In November a meeting was arranged by Schellenberg in a Dutch border restaurant. The day coincided with the anniversary of the Munich Putsch of 1923, and Hitler was in the beer cellar for the usual celebration. A bomb exploded shortly after he left; several senior Nazis were killed. Orders were issued at once to Schellenberg to stop his charade as an anti-Nazi German and to take the British agents prisoner. His special SS detachments, waiting near the border, promptly kidnapped Stevens and Best. In the gunfight, a third secret-service man, known as "Lieutenant Coppens" but in reality an officer of the Dutch General Staff, was badly wounded and died soon after.

Hitler claimed the British agents were responsible for the cellar bomb. Despite all evidence to the contrary produced by Schellenberg, he persisted in this belief and was encouraged in it by Gestapo Müller. But the agents' refusal under torture to confirm the X Report claim of British readiness to negotiate was enough to counterbalance the Vatican's dangerous interference.

Even at a later date, the full text of the report stirred up old feelings of bitterness. According to Otto John, all copies of the report in resistance hands were destroyed. Bormann's copy was among the tons of material trucked out of Berlin and still not accounted for.

His communications on behalf of the Führer with the Vatican were couched in language that must have satisfied both sides, and knowing Bormann's ability to summarize and to use plain words that cut to the bone, one must assume that whenever he took refuge in oblique or fat phrases, it was to save the Pope embarrassment. Certainly the Nazis had nothing to gain from launching the "final solution to the Jewish problem" with a statement disguising the true nature of what was planned. Bormann phrased it deliberately to meet the Vatican's desire not to be forced to take note of genocide. "It lies in the very nature of the matter that these problems which in part are very difficult can be solved only with ruthless severity in the interest of the final security of the people." The Nazis themselves knew well what that meant. It meant the Jews of Poland, the Baltic states, and occupied Russia, the heart of the prewar Jewish communities in Europe. There were more than three million Jews in Poland and one and a quarter million in occupied Russia. It meant their destruction.

It must have meant as much to Pius XII. His concerns about events inside Russia, so far as they hurt the church, were widely broadcast. He cannot have been knowledgeable in one area and totally blind and deaf to the new technique just introduced into Russia. There the invading Nazis arranged that the doomed civilians were to be gassed on their way to the burial pits in vans whose exhaust fumes were fed back ingeniously into the passenger compartments. The gassing was no secret. The Nazis were proud of the efficiency involved. The prisoners were herded into the vans and were liquidated along the road to the trenches. It was a technical accomplishment of which the designers and manufacturers boasted.

The orders were simple enough when conveyed to the death squads. And a simple statement from the Vatican could have stopped those orders.

Beata Klarsfeld had said to me: "If only the Pope had come to Berlin in 1933 and told the Nazis 'Ich bin ein Jud,' millions might have been spared. Instead, it was a Catholic President [John F. Kennedy] who told the Communists he was a Berliner."

Any beginnings of Catholic opposition to Hitler were blunted in that year of 1933 by the German-Vatican Concordat. It was the first official recognition given the Hitler regime by a foreign power. It regulated the relationship between the Catholic church and the new Germany, and thenceforward the German church did little to obstruct the Nazis.

Franz von Papen, found guilty by a postwar denazification court of being "a major offender," had negotiated the concordat and declared: "The Third Reich under the leadership of Adolf Hitler is the first state in the world in which the higher principles of the Pope are not only recognized but carried out in practice." Papen was a devout Catholic, and possibly he serves as well as any figure to illustrate a certain lack of balance that numbed Catholic sensitivities to one form of inhumanity while acutely responsive to Communist oppression.

Four years after the concordat with Germany, Pope Pius XI

delivered the encyclical *Divini Redemptoris*. It was a papal denunciation of atheistic Communism, which was described as intrinsically wrong. "No one who would save Christian civilization may collaborate with it in any field whatsoever."

At the same time, however, the proposed encyclical attacking racism and anti-Semitism never got far. It was drafted by the late American Jesuit scholar Father John La Farge and was entitled "The Unity of the Human Race." In a memo dated July 1938, Father La Farge wrote that the Pontiff told him: "Say what you would say if you were Pope." He worked in Rome on the draft with a German Jesuit scholar, Father Gustav Gundlach. It has been generally supposed that the draft never reached Pius XI because the Superior General stopped La Farge's work from going beyond his own desk.

The aborted encyclical was ready fifteen months before war broke out. But the Vatican was absorbed in its battle with the Soviet Union, where Catholic priests were being denounced as spies. Foreign Affairs Commissar Vyacheslav Molotov had accused the Vatican of meddling in world affairs on the side of capitalist imperialism and "the incendiaries of war."

Stalin had spoken of "a clerical crusade led by the Pope" against the Soviet Union. When Pius XII was elected in the year war broke out, his rejection of Communism seemed to some observers to come very close to that crusade. He refused to condemn Nazi atrocities. He had inherited a pact with Mussolini, a policy of favor toward Franco, and a hierarchy sympathetic to fascism.

Attacks on Pius XII for his silence on Nazi atrocities and his general attitude did prompt the Vatican to publish two volumes of selected documents from its own archives in 1966 to support the Pope. These left unanswered the question of why Pius XII did *not* remain silent on the subject of Communism. And there was no way, of course, to judge just how selectively the documents were retrieved. Nobody outside the secret could know what had been omitted.

The continuing bias was commented upon in 1952 when Pius XII tried to impose on the Italian Prime Minister an alliance between his party and a neo-fascist group in local elections. This would have avoided the appointment of a Communist mayor. A full account by the Defense Minister of the time, Giulio Andreotti, described the Pope's confidence that the big battalions of Catholic Action would tip the balance. A Jesuit called on the Prime Minister's wife to persuade her to influence her husband, who resisted the plan because it made nonsense of national policy. The wife said: "We don't want Mussolini back." She quoted the priest's reply: "Better Mussolini than Stalin."

The story not only in itself is significant. The fact that it is accepted as true by Catholic laymen is also significant. It has never been denied. The American Jesuit scholar Father Robert Graham wrote that when there were denials by Vatican spokesmen, they created a complication for historians: "These denials are sometimes diplomatic in nature. . . ." This is a diplomatic way of saying that the Vatican has its own version of what is truth.

This is why any documentary proof of what passed between Pius XII and the Nazi party was likely to be regarded as important. If anything of potential embarrassment was to be conveyed by word of mouth, emissaries from Hitler were received in one of a series of waiting rooms, furnished and decorated in a combination of gloom and heavy sentimentality. "Dark walls covered with damask, chairs supplied with coverlets of lace made by devoted nuns, pictures of a maudlin sort with a rainbow over St. Peter's and the world around lashed by storms," reported SS General Karl Wolff, who late in the day tried to negotiate separately with the Americans. Like many high-ranking Germans, he kept open a prudent line to God and paid regular visits to the Cardinal Secretary, the Pope's chief minister, with confidential reports of plans to salvage something from the ruins of the Third Reich.

Documents of consequence were handled by the Chancellor for Apostolic Briefs, housed on the third floor of the Apostolic Palace. The location was a guarantee of privacy, and there is no record of Allied agents penetrating either the labyrinthian corridors or the bureaucratic mysteries of Pius XII, who managed administrative affairs for himself. The Pope was well known for his liking in general for the Germans and his feeling that the church was not directly persecuted by Hitler. The papacy had always been a completely autocratic body, with no pretensions to democracy, and its foreign policy was to seek to promote by diplomatic means a condition where souls might be saved. (Nevertheless, the Hungarian revolt in 1956 brought from the same wartime Pope, Pius XII, three encyclicals in three days—something no other pope had ever done—condemning the Russian action.) A franker statement of its policy would be that the church has sought always to follow, in relations with goverments, a policy of the greatest advantage to its own survival. And of course this is implicit in Catholic theology.

Escaping Germans were given sanctuary on the assumption that they were returning to the fold or were prepared to be converted. Georg von Konrat, a Nazi intelligence agent on Russian affairs, described later how he was helped along the "monastery chain" to Rome, where he became a postgraduate civil engineering student, assisted by the Teutonic College, where Bishop Hudal held office. Konrat testified that he crossed into Italy with Martin Bormann in 1947,* after Bormann felt he could risk traveling from the refugee camp and, later, the Danish SS hospital where he had gone underground.

Bormann with his bundles of papers had a claim on papal protection; and his character was such that he would be quite ready, for the sake of survival, to kiss a cardinal's ring or go through any other rituals that might convince the church of his readiness to be saved. His lackey Kaltenbrunner had sent his mistress, the Catholic Countess Gisela von Westrop, to Switzerland with the bulk of the documents. When she was stopped that one time by American counterintelligence, she was on a final errand with convertible jewelry.

The traffic into Switzerland reached astonishing proportions, as Schellenberg made clear during his most productive period of detention, in the debriefing center on the estate of the Duke of Bedford. By 1944, said Schellenberg, the Swiss traffic was worth already the equivalent of $600 million in stolen gold alone.

The Swiss demonstrated, at least for Schellenberg, that the double standards applied to Nazi victims were far from peculiar to Rome. He told the British: "The Swiss sacrificed thousands of human lives as their part in your victory. Not their lives. The lives of perhaps 100,000 Jews who made their way to the frontiers and were turned back—thrown back in our hands." The Swiss Federal Council commissioned a postwar report which showed that Jewish refugees were either pushed back or handed over to the German police. The author of this official report, Professor Karl Ludwig, wrote: "Some committed suicide at the feet of Swiss guards rather than fall into German hands."

The movement of looted Nazi treasure was on a large scale even by late 1942. Yet in October, said Schellenberg, he was astonished to hear through his agents that Switzerland had ordered the First and Fourth Army Corps to reinforce the frontiers and seal certain zones with a no man's land between. His Swiss intel-

* He mentioned this encounter again, almost in passing, in a personal account of political and racial oppression in South West Africa: *Passport to Truth,* published in 1972.

ligence contacts explained: "This is to prevent the Jews entering our country." The fear of reprisal was universal. In the Vatican, the rationalization was that if the Pope spoke on behalf of non-Catholics, it would be the Catholics who would go to the death camps instead.

The Swiss government, at least, was prepared to examine its own conscience in public. The federal report on wartime rejection of refugees also commented upon the readiness to place Swiss banking institutions, notorious for their secrecy, at Nazi disposal. Great quantities of documentary material were moved into Swiss vaults, including duplicate prints of most Nazi war films and the footage of executions, which officials thought would be of future marketable value. At war's end, papers marked with the special secrecy stamp used by Bormann's party chancellery began to arrive. These included negotiable bonds and mortgages raised on property which everyone (including Hitler) thought belonged to the Führer. The Swiss, with their elaborate and salable respect for privacy even in criminal matters, were not prepared to disclose more information. But Schellenberg, who worked closely with Swiss intelligence for the last three years of the war, was less reticent. Before he left the debriefing center, he mentioned that among Bormann's papers were the plans put forward at Hitler's insistence to kidnap the Pope. He thought that if anything had made Bormann acceptable to Rome, it was his thwarting of those plans.

CHAPTER 21

The plot to kidnap the Pope was on a par with other wild-eyed conspiracies, but it was not likely to amuse the Holy See, which had knowledge enough of Hitler's increasingly monstrous adventures. He had sent his best agents to Lisbon when the Duke of Windsor was visiting that neutral territory in 1940; and Schellenberg described later the ludicrous preparations they made to capture the former King of England.* On that occasion, the British secret service did not take the matter lightly either.

A warning that the Vatican risked invasion by "Skorzeny's gangsters" was sent through devious channels by Martin Bormann. Thus he rendered a redeeming service to the church of which he had been the most dedicated persecutor. His action, though it cost him little and indeed saved him a lot, would certainly have helped his journey, to which so many apparently honest eyewitnesses have testified.

His quixotic deed was intensely practical when examined closely. Bormann had been a lifelong and fanatical anti-Christian. Hitler, on the other hand, remained a Catholic.

The plan to remove Pope Pius XII to somewhere in occupied France was proposed in late 1943. "Under the influence of Goebbels, the Führer was seriously considering the deportation

---

* Ribbentrop told Schellenberg that the Duke of Windsor had been virtually a prisoner of the British secret service, and now that he was in the Iberian peninsula "Hitler thinks you should offer to deposit 50 million Swiss francs for his use if he will reject the British royal family." If the British secret service blocked this approach, Schellenberg was to take other steps. The Nazi spy chief told British interrogators later that he was shocked and asked if Ribbentrop was in fact requiring that the Duke be kidnapped. "We are interpreting the Duke's wishes," Ribbentrop replied. "He may want it to *look* like a kidnapping." This comic episode might have had tragic results. Schellenberg ended up hiring a gang to throw stones at the Duke's villa in Lisbon so that he could report the Duke was under heavy guard when the villa's occupants reacted. Finally, an elderly British police sergeant came out and told them to go away.

of the Pope into a kind of exile at Avignon," Schellenberg reported after the war. He was himself, even at this early stage, preparing escape routes and had been in secret contact with an American, Abraham Stevens Hewitt, in Stockholm, whom the Nazi spy chief believed to be a special representative of President Roosevelt.

Kidnapping the Pope was not likely to advance the interests of those Germans hoping to either change sides or get a peace settlement that would leave them some measure of power. Schellenberg was worried. He talked to Bormann, arguing with considerable force that Hitler had avoided a direct confrontation with the church and that this had proved to be good strategy. So long as church leaders felt there was a prospect of preserving some foothold within the Third Reich they kept out of politics and pacified their congregations.

Otto Skorzeny was called in. He was already planning the aerial rescue of Mussolini, held captive after the overthrow of his fascist regime in July. Skorzeny was aghast at the prospect of storming the Vatican, not because he thought it was militarily impossible, but because even he could foresee the repercussions. Nevertheless, a plan was drawn up, based upon a precise knowledge of the layout of Vatican City and the Pope's routine.

If that scheme seemed insane, there was more to come. Ribbentrop now revealed his project to send a large number of special agents by U-boat to the American coast. They would co-ordinate their distribution of propaganda with a great radio campaign directed toward "hyphenated Americans" of European origin to create opposition to Roosevelt's re-election. At once orders were sent out requiring an immediate estimate of the long-range sub-marines available for this enterprise.

"Then," said Schellenberg, "came the most astonishing suggestion. Ribbentrop stood up and said he had a matter of considerable gravity. The utmost secrecy was essential."

Stalin was to be assassinated. Only Hitler and Bormann knew the details. A conference would be arranged so that Ribbentrop himself could come face to face with the Russian leader: "The Führer said one man cannot do it alone. An accomplice is necessary." Schellenberg, in considerable apprehension as to who that accomplice was likely to be, trotted off to see if his technical experts could produce a tiny revolver that would look like a fountain pen. It had to be capable of firing a heavy-caliber bullet with reasonable accuracy at a range of between eighteen and twenty-five feet.

Schellenberg thought they were all mad. Bormann did not agree

244

with him in specific terms. "But Bormann never did commit himself in such delicate matters. He told me, however, that the proposal to kidnap the Pope would be sidetracked."

The attempt on Stalin's life did go forward, according to Schellenberg, but not along the lines of Ribbentrop's suicidal suggestion. That one was eased out of Hitler's mind by Bormann, using the standard procedure he had long ago explained to Skorzeny: "Agree! Report progress! Let time pass, and then gradually introduce obstacles. . . ."

Two agents were selected to place an adhesive charge of explosives on Stalin's car. "It was about the size of a fist and looked like a lump of mud," Schellenberg recalled later. "The fuse was controlled by short-wave radio, and the transmitter which automatically set it off was the size of a cigarette box and had a range of seven miles. We had two Red Army deserters, one of them friendly with mechanics in the Kremlin garage, or so *he* said. They were flown to the region where Stalin had his headquarters and there they parachuted down and were never heard from again."

All these insanities were duly noted on Bormann's small squares of cardboard, while he continued with his usual energy to build up his future contacts. One of these was Paul Leverkühn, of Admiral Canaris's Mideast intelligence section. He was chief of the central station at Istanbul, where the Papal Nuncio was Cardinal Roncalli. Leverkühn had been recalled briefly to discuss the desertions by German intelligence officers, which had already begun. The worst case was that of the Abwehr workers in Istanbul. They deserted to the British, who had them flown to Cairo.*

The Istanbul station spymaster, having explained privately to Bormann the general chaos that had overtaken all Mideast operations, was requested, upon his return, to give the Papal Nuncio a packet. It contained the detailed plan for removing the Pope from Rome to Avignon, together with Martin Bormann's assurance that the plan was not going to be executed. What he had in mind may never be known. On past performance, he was making sure that the Vatican escape hatch stayed open. Leverkühn, who lived after the war to tell the tale, returned at once and faithfully delivered the package.

---

* Countess Plettenburg and Erich Vermehren, the Abwehr pair, had been summoned by the Gestapo to come home. They sensed trouble and asked the British secret service to help. The price of their ticket to Cairo was the key to the Abwehr codes, which yielded or confirmed much of the information contained here.

In this strange way, Martin Bormann made Cardinal Roncalli, the gentle old man who eventually succeeded Pius XII, the channel for odd news. The Cardinal at once informed the Pope. He did more. He got in touch with Archbishop Francis Spellman, in New York. They had been corresponding for some time, and Spellman had reported to Roosevelt upon the Papal Nuncio's friendly and personal letters. Roosevelt, in turn, informed the British, through an apartment suite at the top of the Hotel Dorset, on New York's West 54th Street. Here Churchill's personal intelligence chief, William Stephenson, lived in quiet obscurity when he was not directing the large and well-camouflaged establishment around the corner known as British Security Coordination.

Stephenson flew regularly by bomber across the Atlantic. He checked with Cairo and obtained the required collateral. Intercepts of Abwehr messages confirmed that the Pope had been warned of what was in Hitler's mind and in what manner Bormann had temporarily, at least, distracted the Führer. A description of Hitler's condition at this time further established the general suspicion that Bormann was the real man in command, a fact not appreciated before and that even at this time was recognized by a tragically small number of Allied strategists. "Hitler's appearance was alarming," a confidential report from Canaris stated. "His left arm trembled with such violence he had to hold it down with his right hand, so that one had the impression of a puppet whose strings were being misused by its master, the left hand jerking up and the right hand pushing it back down. His manner of walking was jerky too. His eyes, which I remembered always as hypnotic and dominating, had lost any spark of life. It really seemed as if this was a walking doll out of which emerged another voice that remained as strong and clear as before. But even here, the sentences were now short and staccato. This mansize puppet was wearing out, and whoever crouched inside it with more messages still to deliver must have been preparing to leave."

Bormann, the man crouching inside, *was* preparing to leave. Stephenson had more urgent matters on his mind, for the death of the Third Reich was far from sure. Nevertheless, he and General William Donovan, of OSS, had their experts prepare an analysis of what might happen, partly in order to encourage more defections from German intelligence stations abroad. These defections were producing invaluable intelligence, which would be vital to the success of D-Day and the final onslaught of Allied invasion armies.

It seemed to the experts assigned the task of predicting the movements of escaping Nazis once the war was won that Latin America was still the logical place of refuge. With uncanny foresight, they suggested that leading Nazis would make use of established escape routes through the Bavarian alps and Italy, following a chain of monasteries. Others would attempt to leave by air through Spain and by submarine from the Hamburg area. Special attention would have to be given to coded messages transmitted from short-wave stations operating in Spain and Lisbon with substations in North and South Africa; all were vital to German air and undersea operations and could be expected to have a role in any subsequent escape plans.

Thus a great many eyes and ears were open and listening by the time the Nazis began to leave their sinking ship. Perhaps the watchers were prepared too soon. At all events, by the middle of 1945 there were few among the Western Allies who took action on the prediction that the movement to Latin America would become a flood once the war ended.

The service Bormann rendered the Vatican was repaid with mathematical precision, according to Franz Stangl and other fugitives, captured later. They claim Bormann made at least one visit to his dying wife. She had settled the children in the villa at Wolkenstein in the Grödnertal of the Austrian Tyrol, a place best reached by muleback because it was so remote. General George Patton had been informed of her whereabouts through Alexander Raskin, who, with extraordinary compassion in view of his own wartime sufferings, reported that the local doctor told him Mrs. Bormann was fatally ill with cancer. Patton then instructed counterintelligence agents to "let the poor woman die in peace." As a result, security around the villa was relaxed.

However, a woman, whose credibility was attested by British investigators, reported seeing Bormann on the Italian side of the border in September 1945. Her evidence came too late, for by then Bormann had vanished again. Her name was Hannelore Thalheimer, and she said she had known Bormann in Munich and could not be mistaken. She had come face to face with him on the main street in Bolzano, about twelve miles from where Gerda Bormann had been moved into a small hospital run by Americans for prisoners of war.

A balancing of accounts must have taken place between Bormann and the church if these reports, which fit remarkably well together, are true. Gerda knew her husband would surely hang if caught. She was also under the shadow of death. Her published letters indicate that the collapse of one god, Hitler, left her, but *not* Bormann, in need of spiritual sustenance. She doted on the children, and in her last months must have been comforted by the thought of some other institution taking care of them. She talked a great deal to a visiting priest, according to neighbors at the villa and the Americans working in the hospital. So she might also have asked the church's help for her husband.

Before he committed suicide, Hitler called in his private pilot, Major General Hans Bauer, and said: "I would like to take my leave of you."

Greatly agitated, as he said later, Bauer proposed flying the Führer to Argentina. It could be done, he said, using a captured American Flying Fortress and traveling by way of Spain.

Hitler agreed that escape was still possible. But he would be "just where I am now within a fortnight. The war is over now that Berlin is finished. I am putting an end to it. I know tomorrow millions of people will be cursing me. . . ."

The Führer referred to the Alpine Fortress, Bauer reported to his companions. It was quite obviously known by then to Hitler that many of his followers were heading there. That Argentina should have sprung at once to Bauer's mind is equally significant. That neither of these two regions appeared to spring immediately to the minds of the Nazi-hunters, however, may not be quite as odd as first appears.

CHAPTER 22

Police agencies can do only so much in dealing with international criminals. In the case of political gangsters, the limitations are made more difficult because of changes in the alliances between nations. There was evidence of several foreign agencies on the track of Bormann's friends, each unwilling to take action for different reasons. Bormann was not actively hunted by the Israeli government, for instance, because he was not directly involved in the "final solution" in the way Adolf Eichmann had been. The Soviet Union's agents in Latin America obviously would prefer to keep a Nazi Brotherhood under observation than destroy it for no visible advantage. The Communists in this period were likely to gain in the long run from the despotism of Nazi-minded regimes, and their arrogant disregard for local sensibilities in a part of the world awakening to social inequalities and injustice. Western Europe felt no compulsion to pursue the remnants of a nightmare. And if anyone was going to find Bormann in Argentina, say, it would be better from the viewpoint of Anglo-American business interests if the Argentinians did it themselves.

This might seem a cynical theory. But students of Nazi Germany believed that it was typical of the leaders to live their own fantasies, and that this led to their undoing. Commercial enterprises that were financed with crooked Nazi funds would overreach themselves. Guilty men would in time feel a need to crawl into the sunlight and justify themselves. Something like this began to happen in the 1960's. A libel action in London, which caused a great stir around the world at the time, involved a best-selling American writer and a German death-camp doctor. The significance of the case was missed because its background was unknown to most people. It illustrated the theory that guilty men hang themselves. They do it more quickly, though, if unnerved by a sense of being watched. This is the old policeman's trick of letting a suspect know he is being shadowed. If he is a wrongdoer, he will make the false move that leads to his arrest.

I knew from my own encounters with former SS mobsters and Gestapo-type bullies that they needed, more than anything, to prove their right-mindedness—not their innocence, for either they did not feel guilty, or else they refused to permit a sense of guilt to invade their conscious minds. They wanted to be accepted in what they regarded as polite society. They could not resist the impulse to prove themselves right.

This line of thought led later to the conclusion that Nazi exiles were never truly lost by Allied huntsmen. The suspicion that the British let Otto Skorzeny go in order to see where he went and what he did was not so outlandish. Bormann, too, might have been followed in the same way. These speculations began, for me, during the "euthanasia" trial of Hans Hevelmann in 1964. I had shortly before moved my family to London from Africa, where German business enterprise was flooding into areas vacated by "Anglo-American imperialism." As editor of Independent Television Newsfilm, I was despondent at watching the world at second hand. The job gave a sense of involvement without any of the discomfort, and this seemed dangerous. The feeling that our society was becoming too detached from reality, helped by television, came to a boil one night when the contents of a correspondent's camera came into the studios.

The film, taken from the camera of an old friend, George Clay, of the National Broadcasting Corporation, was shot while he was dying from bullets fired by armed Congolese. One of the editors commented that it was a pity the camera was shaking. It was an everyday piece of graveyard humor, but I had a sudden sense of anger. George was dead. He had always had a conscientious concern for honesty. People looked at television and had little time to read the background reports that tried to convey more than exploding pictures. George had suffered much agony because he understood black Africans too well and could not therefore simplify his material to satisfy the people back home. He could neither condemn nor condone the extremes of African political life. He was a white from South Africa, and it would have been easy to pose as a great liberal and deplore what happened in Johannesburg while applauding lunacy in Uganda. He could have withdrawn from Africa and put an end to his private torture. He stayed because he believed in what he was doing. He had a blind faith in some central intelligence that might make sense out of all the despair

250

and stupidity. He thought, as I had when abroad, that somewhere at the top were wise men who evaluated reports from the field and did something about them. Now I was one of the men at the top. George had done his job and got killed for it. A film editor had dismissed the report, the film, and the correspondent in a single cynical sentence.

Yet I let the matter pass. There wasn't time. More fighting in the Congo was nothing compared with disasters nearer home. The report from the trial of Hans Hevelmann, former member of Hitler's chancellery, passed notice in the same way. Civilization seemed to be going backward with the help of faster communications and new technology. A hundred years ago, a dispatch from the Congo sent by cleft stick and steam packet might not reach the outside world in time to change anything, but it would be studied with some reasonable care. Now, a war was dismissed in a flash; and twice as much time and money was spent on the commercials flanking it.

The trial of Hans Hevelmann never got on television. It got a paragraph, perhaps, in one or two European newspapers. The West German press was almost alone in recognizing the importance of the surrounding circumstances.

Two of the accused died mysteriously before the trial began, and our correspondent in Hamburg reported confidentially that ODESSA was blamed. Out of curiosity, I called State Prosecutor Karl-Heinz Zinnall, of the Hesse province prosecutor's office. He said a third prominent West German, accused of war crimes, had died violently. He confirmed that the dead men included Professor Werner Heyde, in charge of "euthanasia" killings; and that the trial of doctors accused of similar activities had been put in doubt. He said: "There are people, I believe, who want to prevent the trial. There are doctors who do not want to hear their names mentioned, nor details of their work in the Nazi period."

The two others who had died were Dr. Friedrich Tillmann and Ewald Peters, the personal security chief to Chancellor Ludwig Erhard. Heyde was said to have committed suicide in his cell. Tillmann "fell to his death." The security chief was said to have hanged himself after being arrested on charges that he had been an SS assassin.

It was suggested that ODESSA protected those connected with the "euthanasia" killings. Heyde had been living and prospering under a false name after escaping from an American military truck in 1947 and going to ground in Schleswig-Holstein. He surfaced as

Dr. Fritz Sawade, medical adviser for the state insurance administration and local courts, and in this capacity and under his new name he did rather well for himself, until the secret of his real identity became impossible to conceal. He was arrested. Then began the business of unraveling old evidence and investigating the new friends who had protected him.

In the middle of this, the Minister of Education for Schleswig-Holstein, Edo Osterloh, vanished, and after a twenty-four-hour search was found "drowned" in three feet of water. Osterloh had been a figure of some controversy when he sprang to the defense of Dr. Werner Catel, who had been a member of the Reich Commission for Disposal of Children. This was part of a larger organization for dealing with racially unworthy and otherwise useless mouths, who were to be fed into a new disposal system.

It turned out that Osterloh always knew the true identity of Dr. Sawade, now exposed as the notorious Dr. Heyde, who figured on all West German police "Wanted" lists, with the black triangle beside his name that means "Murderer." The Minister had, nonetheless, assured parents that their children could be placed without fear in the hands of the doctor.

The doctors' trial was collapsing. Four important personages were dead. A fifth, Dr. Gerhard Bohne, escaped to Latin America when Heyde's existence became known.

I had no compelling reason to look deeper. Professionally, it was taking me far out of my way. I was writing an account of a Communist takeover in Zanzibar, where I had just been; my mood was not sympathetic to Communist sources of information. But this information was confirmed by West Germans, too. "Still, it's none of my business . . ." I began to say to a Berlin colleague. And then I remembered the scorn we had for Germans who never resisted Hitler. The state became absolute and individual liberty was suppressed because the welfare of the family was given priority by the breadwinner. How charmingly old-fashioned that word sounded. *Breadwinner?* These days, with bread in abundant supply, had we all become overly concerned about losing the second car or, worse, lacking money for a vacation? It had been said about the Germans in Hitler's early period that they could not resign or be discharged without subjecting their wives, their children, and themselves to misery and squalor.

Mercy-killing arose in Nazi-dominated Europe from the least likable trait of citizens in the National Socialist state: their submissiveness and eager acceptance of institutional rules. It was left to the institutions to decide if a person was mentally defective or the bearer of an incurable disease. The language of the social-welfare worker, heard loud in the land to this day, glossed over all the atrocities.

Martin Bormann delighted in the camouflage of nonsense talk. He was getting his own back at the intellectuals who held him in such contempt. He put his name to decrees such as this one: "The administration of justice can only make a small contribution to the extermination of members of these groups [Jews, gypsies, Russians, and non-Germanized Poles]. No useful purpose is served keeping such persons in German prisons even if, as is done today on a large scale, they are utilized as labor for war purposes."

What this meant, of course, was that the procedures for ad-ministering justice were irrelevant. Inferior races were "uncondi-tionally exterminable." Bormann's gobbledygook satisfied the legal-minded citizens. It sounded authoritative. Its true purpose was sufficiently concealed that few Germans felt any prick of conscience. All they chose to read into it was that the normal court procedures were costly and time-consuming in cases where the judgment was already clear. Of course Jews and gypsies were unconditionally exterminable. It said so, right there, on an official order properly signed and sealed.

Bormann's method is recognizable today in a world that has refined the art of concealing ugly decisions within tortuous and high-minded phrases. Any citizen who felt like fighting a Bormann ordinance would feel, like many of us today, that he had neither time nor energy to flail through the flatulent phrases to get at the truth.

The Bormann method enabled Leonardo Conti, Secretary of State for Public Health, to dispose of 50,000 "useless mouths" in the first six months of the war. The blue-eyed Swiss had Bormann's ordinance as his authority to make his own decision on who was to be gassed and who was to get a lethal injection.

To fight such decisions was also to be disloyal to the party and a traitor to the country. For instance, illness was, in effect, a crime among Nazis, with their morbid insistence upon youth and health. So it was easy to phrase a decision to liquidate an entire group in the language of this report to the security authorities on a Russian-Jewish settlement: "Contagious diseases having broken out, a second action consisted in applying special treatment to 812 men and women—all persons without interest from the racial and intellectual point of view." In other words, 812 villagers were executed.

There were few reliable statistics on the numbers killed during the "euthanasia" campaign between 1939 and 1941, based on Nazi theories about purity of race, in which the vanishing doctors and officials had been involved. Similar details, however, were emerging in a libel case being prepared in London against the author of *Exodus,* Leon Uris, on behalf of Dr. Wladislaw Dering, who then had a successful practice at Seven Sisters Road in the London suburb of Finsbury Park. Dering had performed experimental sexual surgery without benefit of anesthetic on prisoners at Auschwitz. The publicity which must inevitably follow the Dering case was anticipated with a good deal of nervous anxiety by others with guilty consciences.

Dr. Heyde, around whom the West German trial would have revolved had he not conveniently died five days before it was due to begin, was responsible for certifying that certain people were unfit to live when he began his official duties in 1939 in connection with the mercy-killing program. This was to dispose of people with alleged mental ailments, or misshapen and imbecile children. They were, when properly registered and certified, sent to one of five gassing stations. The gassing in those days was clumsily done. Relatives of the victims were told nothing until it was completed, when notices were sent out regretting "unsuccessful appendix operations" and other sudden illnesses. The selection of mentally retarded was based upon a questionnaire, and in two weeks before Christmas 1940, Heyde received 2,209 of these questionnaires for certification. The forms explained that all patients must be reported who suffered from "weak-mindedness" or senile illnesses, and who did not have German citizenship or were not of German or related blood. There were other stipulations, of course, and footnotes gave a handy guide to the methods by which the question of race could be answered. There was no written suggestion at first that "Jewish half-breeds of 1st or 2nd degree, Negro half-breeds, Gypsies" should be automatically gassed for being half-witted. That is how, in the end, the system worked, however. It became known in the concentration camps as "Operation Heyde," and various postwar witnesses testified at the Nuremberg trials that a commission led by Heyde visited the camps and quickly separated prisoners who were unfit for hard work, certifying them "incurably insane." The commission was made up of psychiatrists, and the statistics of those inmates sent to Mauthausen for gassing make it clear that the commission had less than five minutes to conduct the medical examination of each prisoner.

After the war, when Heyde had escaped from American captivity and adopted the name of Sawade, he was recognized in 1954 by a fellow psychiatrist, Dr. Creutzfeldt, who reported what he knew to the Flensburg Public Prosecutor, Bruno Bourwieg. The advice given to Creutzfeldt was that he should forget the whole matter. This advice came from Judge Buresch, who had shared with Heyde a room in a British internment camp in 1945. A conspiracy of silence then engulfed leaders of the North German community. The general view was expressed by Dr. Dering: these wartime actions were justified by the conditions that prevailed at the time.

On February 13, 1964, having been arrested as the result of more protest from West Germans with a stronger sense of justice, Dr. Heyde was said to have hanged himself, although he was held in a maximum-security cell.

Further inquiry established that much earlier he had been helped, while in detention, to make an attempt to escape. The view was held among West German police at Frankfurt (where he was first arrested) that he had been for many years under special protection by ODESSA men. His false papers were professionally executed. He had been warned to go underground again, just before his arrest, and disappeared only to be caught while attempting to leave the country. Only one of the accused doctors appeared at the preliminary hearing: Dr. Hans Hevelmann. As Bohne was to say later, when detained in Buenos Aires: "Our brothers did their best. Hevelmann was the least dangerous to the rest of us." And Heyde, it would appear, knew too much to be trusted to protect his brothers if he should ever be confronted by a public prosecutor before a public tribunal.

Meanwhile, the libel action brought by Dr. Dering against Leon Uris was getting under way in London. The big question was why Dering had brought an action for damages against the author and publisher of *Exodus,* in which appeared a paragraph concerned with experiments having as their objective the sterilization en masse of people of Jewish blood—the genocidal Nazi "final solution." The plaintiff alleged that he had been libeled because he was featured in the novel as "Dr. Dehring." Was Dering backed by his old colleagues in attempting, by this voluntary step on his part, to prove that experiments on prisoners at Auschwitz and other camps were *not* crimes against humanity? Dering had a flourishing

255

practice in a respectable London neighborhood and he could gain nothing from this action except unwelcome publicity. (In fact, he was awarded the traditional "one ha'penny" damages, which meant that although the jury had found for him, it was a technical decision based on the fact that few eyewitnesses were likely to be available in a case involving mass murder. The innnocent were dead. The guilty were hardly likely to come forward and give evidence. The ha'penny was worth a fraction of a cent. Dering died soon afterward, in disgrace.) Who paid the heavy legal costs involved? Who or what prompted him? These legitimate questions have never been properly answered, but in 1964 there were many West Germans who believed that the Brotherhood, as well as ODESSA, hoped the London libel action would provide a public platform on which Dering could make the case for Nazi actions.

Incredible though this seems, Dering was not alone by any means in arguing that he was the victim of defamation. One of the German doctors mentioned in the Dering action was Josef Mengele, an SS captain who *volunteered* to work in Auschwitz, particularly on Jewish twins. Mengele's wealthy family had more than recovered its fortunes by 1964 as manufacturers in West Germany and in Argentina, where they acquired a fifty-percent interest in Fadro Farm KG, SA. The family was just as anxious as other wanted Nazis to get a clear verdict in an English court of law which would allow others to come out of hiding. The Auschwitz trial in West Germany was at long last getting under way, and Josef Mengele was the chief defendant. He wanted to make an appearance, but only if the Dering case demonstrated that people no longer cared.

Another doctor mentioned in the case, Horst Schumann, had experimented on male and female prisoners at Auschwitz, had managed to gain acceptance after the war in his own country, and then, having received a tip that he might be dragged before a denazification court, fled to Africa, where he remained, resisting attempts to have him extradited.* Dr. Werner Blankenburg was Hitler's administrative chief of the "euthanansia" program and figured prominently in the libel action. He had escaped.

The shadows were everywhere. Dr. Schumann in German Air Force uniform peering at the pseudo-scientific operations on terrified young girls brought from Greece to have ovaries excised without anesthetic; Krystyna Dering, who was still asking questions

* Schumann was finally cornered in Ghana after his redeemer, President Kwame Nkrumah (known officially, indeed, as the "Redeemer"), was deposed.

about her missing husband, the doctor, in a restaurant in Poland when the libel action was first announced; the prison inmates mentioned in the register of surgical operations in one block at Auschwitz who had survived: all of them phantoms conjured up by the sonorous legal argument that "Dr. Dering did without medical, physiological or other legitimate reason" *and* "when to his knowledge some of the girls had on their backs or abdomens, or both, irradiation burns such as were likely to render any wound inflicted on them difficult or impossible to heal" *record and perform* "operations by injections causing such great pain that the girls had to be held down."

The shadows were more disturbing because I had been to Auschwitz; and I remembered the young Communist official with me who said: "This is why Poland regards Russia as a friend and ally. The Russians do not forgive as easily."

Because Auschwitz is in Poland, I asked a member of the Polish Foreign Office who had studied law in England if they had theories on why Dering had taken this singularly ill-advised action. He replied that the government security services of Poland were not in the habit of disclosing information outside the "democratic republics," implying that unrepentant capitalists like me were incapable of making fair judgments. Nonetheless, Poland was deeply interested in the case, because, apart from the obviously horrendous disclosures, Dering was a Roman Catholic and a large percentage of the Polish people were Catholics.

Intellectuals in Poland saw an opportunity to smuggle past the more stiff-necked Communist functionaries an important commentary upon society in general. The Dering trial demonstrated how Catholics collaborated with the Nazis and this was, of course, an acceptable reminder for Communists. But the trial also spelled out the dangers of blind faith in a single superauthority, whether one called it the Communist party, Hitler, or God. The Polish newspapers reported the case in some detail, including a brief exchange between the English judge and the defendant over the question of taking an oath to tell the truth. It underlined, for citizens in a land where the party was supreme, the healthy skepticism of those who live in a society that questions and challenges every statement said to be infallible because it is based upon some absolute authority.

The Judge: Are you satisfied that you have taken the oath in a manner binding on you?

Dr Dering: Yes.

The Judge: On what testament?

Dr Dering: It does not matter. I am a Christian and a Roman Catholic.

The judge at this point observed austerely that perhaps "you had better be sworn properly—Take the Douai [Bible] version."

When the case had run its course, a Polish legal observer from Warsaw called on me before flying home. Had it occurred to anyone, he asked, that *Dering* versus *Uris & Others* might be an oblique way of testing public opinion? The West German Minister of Justice, Ewald Bucher, had stated that no further war-crimes prosecutions would be initiated in the courts after May 8, 1965. The law provided for a statute of limitations which laid down that no prosecution for murder could be started more than twenty years after the offense. The date of Nazi Germany's capitulation was taken as the starting point for the twenty-year period.

The Polish lawyer made some acid comments about the survival of *useful* Nazis in Communist East Germany, and it is better if he remains anonymous. He became involved much later in the case of a Polish Jew who directed a Communist spy ring inside Nazi Germany, celebrated after the war as a hero in Poland, but then denied freedom to go to Israel in 1972. By then, of course, the passage of Jews from Communist states to Israel had become a major issue with the Soviet Union, and the Poles fell into line. The lawyer was to prove helpful later in the reconstruction of Brotherhood operations, or, in his words: "The works of the Kameradenwerk." He provided details of the death sentence passed on another Auschwitz doctor by a Communist East German court some time after the Heyde fiasco, as if to counterbalance his comments about his own side's tolerance of Nazis when it suited them. This was the case of Dr. Horst Fischer, found guilty of helping to murder 70,000 prisoners in Auschwitz. He practiced as a country doctor in East Germany. His trial took place after the date suggested by the West German Justice Minister as ending the twenty-year statute of limitations.

The proposal to drop war-crimes prosecutions in West Germany would mean that Adolf Hitler could reappear quite safely. In the Führer's case, the public would take care of the matter. But what about lesser figures? They might have felt safe if the libel action brought by Dr. Dering had ended in a resounding victory. The fact that Dering's unseen friends actually believed he would be vindicated was disconcerting proof of their insensitivity. The fact that Dering was not vindicated was an indication of the horror felt by the ordinary citizens of a free country when confronted with crimes that seemed to have been buried with Hitler. Anglo-Saxon law recognizes this capacity on the part of the people to remember and be shocked by crimes against humanity. This law, observed in the United States and Britain, is based on the principle *tempus non occurrit regi* (the passage of time has no influence on the prosecution of the crime). In the United States, as in England, there is no statute of limitations for murder.

The People's Chamber of the (East) German Democratic Republic appealed to all nations to stop the West German government from declaring a moratorium on war crimes, claiming that the "inner-German law" was subordinate to international law. It pointed out that it had suspended the statute of limitations with regard to war crimes, whereas "in West Germany, Nazi criminals have either not been punished at all or given totally inadequate sentences. Some of them even occupy today responsible positions in the state and the economy."

The West German Justice Minister who had started the whole controversy, Ewald Bucher, was a former Hitler Youth member and a registered member of the Nazi party. Political observers in Bonn felt that Bucher was under pressure from his own rightist Free Democratic party.

Prosecutions at this time were pending against 13,000 suspects. There were no prosecutions pending against prominent West Germans, but these might yet find themselves identified and charged with wartime criminal offenses. There were thirty-six senior police officials in the province of Schleswig-Holstein, for instance, who were said by the Social Democrats to have been involved in Nazi murders.

Out of a total of 274 senior police officials in this province, which was notoriously the favored hide-out for war criminals unwilling or unable to go abroad, an unknown number lived under false names. The Schleswig-Holstein parliament, yielding to demands from a section of the press, appointed a special commission to investigate Nazi infiltration of the police force. The commission, like similar courts of inquiry, never seemed to get to the end of its investigations because of "legal impediments."

Three out of four letters from the general public sent to the Bundestag in Bonn favored letting the statute of limitations lapse, in the manner recommended by the Justice Minister. Finally it was decided by parliament to extend the statute until September 21, 1969 —the twentieth anniversary of the day West Germany began to manage its own affairs. By 1972, the law had been extended again.

The year 1980 was loudly touted as the date when the Central Office for the Elucidation of National Socialist Crimes would end its activities, since the chances of satisfactorily clearing up cases was steadily deteriorating.

The lawyer directing this office, Erwin Schuele, had good reason to want the "witch-hunting" to stop. He was identified in 1965, after five years in the job of token Nazi-hunter, as being himself a member of the Nazi party from 1935 and a former Brown Shirt storm trooper from 1933. The Nazi court President in Stuttgart in 1943 recommended his appointment as a judge because of his "political reliability," and the Nazi Minister of Justice in 1944 made him, with the approval of the Nazi party, a junior judge.

The Polish lawyer who kept track of war criminals later had a few hundred feet of 16-mm. film sent to me which showed, it was claimed, Dr. Mengele near the border between Argentina and Paraguay. The film clip had been accepted by Communist authorities as a genuine portrayal of the Auschwitz Angel of Death. The results of an investigation into this piece of film were interesting. We ran the footage through a Moviescope alongside authenticated photographs of Mengele, and there was no question that the man in the film resembled the Auschwitz doctor in every visible way. By then, there was plenty of evidence to show that Mengele moved freely in Paraguay and did live near the Argentine border. I began to receive more "documentation" on Nazi fugitives. This also came from the Polish lawyer. When I saw him again late in 1964 he said, with what I have no doubt was complete truthfulness on his part, that he believed a genuine re-education program had purged East Germany of fascist influences. But in October of that year, Nikita Khrushchev was stripped of power. Friendly contacts with Communist officials became more difficult. Suddenly one appreciated how greatly the old tensions had been relaxed, and how little one had used the opportunity to deal with honest patriots before the old suspicions rose up in the wake of Khrushchev's downfall.

Before we lost contact again, the lawyer sent me the names of a few criminals among the 6,000 SS men who had served as guards and technicians in the gas chambers, or as medical orderlies and registration clerks, all at Auschwitz. Only 900 out of that 6,000 were known by name. Of these, Poland had dealt with 300, and even in these cases they found it difficult to locate witnesses. "How," he asked, "can Nazi war criminals ever be prosecuted, whether or not the statute of limitations is ended? There are just too many of them."

From East Berlin came a revised Brown Book on Nazi war criminals which claimed that 1,800 major offenders were back in key West German posts, or drew large pensions for their work in Hitler's lifetime. It listed fifteen government ministers, one hundred generals and admirals of the revived German armed forces, 828 leading judges and judicial officials, 245 senior diplomats, and 297 police and security officials. There were details referring to men like Ludwig Hahn, Nazi party member No. 194,465, appointed Deputy Chief of the Gestapo in Hanover, promoted to SS Major and transferred to Gestapo / Berlin, and given the task, between 1941 and 1944, of running the Nazi security police in Warsaw, which in that period was the setting for one of history's worst reigns of terror. Official Nazi party documents were cited whose authenticity seemed beyond doubt. Hahn was in command of the security forces which "resettled" some 500,000 Jews in gas chambers at Treblinka and liquidated the Warsaw ghetto.

By this time I knew that the Polish lawyer's interest in the fate of the Warsaw Jews was very personal. He had studied in England, had absorbed liberal intellectual ideas, but he could not forget that his own parents were Jews who had died in Auschwitz.

To test the accuracy of his information, I looked more closely at the case of Ludwig Hahn. His profession was given as that of deputy director of a life insurance company based in Karlsruhe. The company was a cover for the West German intelligence service, and Hahn was a senior officer in that organization.

Any further inquiries were met with blank stares. And since this was again idle curiosity on my part, there seemed no justification for spending time and money on the mystery of some obscure fifty-six-year-old German.

Looking back, one sees why indifference of this kind must have driven the Poles to despair. To the East Germans, the refusal to believe their Brown Book must have seemed positively sinister; it had been dismissed as Communist propaganda by Bonn officials, who thus disposed of the matter. The West German government was still recovering from the shock of the Felfe trial in the Karlsruhe federal court, which demonstrated the real ineffectiveness of the Gehlen Org and intelligence operations inside the Communist countries. It had prompted *Die Welt* to conclude that, "owing to a catastrophic personnel policy," the Gehlen Org had provided "a comfortable retreat for both major and minor Nazis."

So, feeling defensive, no doubt, Bonn ridiculed the East German Brown Book.

Eight years later, former SS Colonel Ludwig Hahn went on trial for tolerating the murder of prisoners in Warsaw.

His wife, sister of a top-ranking West German military figure, had good connections during the war. Hahn's brother-in-law, General Johannes Steinhoff, was now the chief administrative officer for the reconstituted Luftwaffe and thus part of the NATO military establishment. It seemed evident that Hahn had enjoyed a long period of protection; that the persistent complaints about his wartime role had been impossible to ignore; and that the trial, which began May 2, 1972 in Hamburg, was in keeping with a decision to make justice appear to be done. He was accused of the comparatively minor offenses of ordering the deportation of some Warsaw citizens and not interfering in the killing of Warsaw Pawiak Prison inmates.

A West German weekly, *Die Tat,* commented: "We drew attention more than two years ago to documents showing that Hahn gave direct instructions for the liquidation of the Warsaw Ghetto. . . . The files of evidence amount to 133 volumes. Charges were finally filed last August after strong public criticism."

If the "minor" charges against Hahn failed to bring a conviction, investigation into all other cases in which he might be implicated would have to start all over again. This seemed to be the intention. The Hamburg courts (where Hahn now lived) had refused all applications made by the prosecuting authorities to have him taken into custody between December 1970 and August 1971, and when finally the police did search his villa, they found photostats of pretrial statements made to the prosecutor by witnesses in his case.

Ludwig Hahn had known he was under investigation for many years. He must have been aware of Communist reports published ten years before he was finally brought to trial. There was no evidence produced in public that he followed his old comrades from the Auschwitz days to South America. Yet this would have been the prudent action to take.

A Polish police report reached Interpol in Paris in 1972. It alleged that Hahn indeed had flown regularly to Argentina and Brazil with false papers prepared by the Gehlen Org. More curious still, if the same Polish sources were again right: Hahn visited Dr. Dering at his clinic in London in the spring of 1962. Shortly afterward, on June 22, 1962, Dering, a Member of the Order of the British Empire for his postwar services to the Colonial Medical Service, issued his writ against Uris for libel.

Nobody in his right mind, protected by the Order of the British Empire, which was like a certificate of virtue, would have launched such an action. He was practicing medicine within the socialist National Health Service. Nobody in London had spoken against him. Nothing had been published in that city to bring him into disrepute, and it would have been an eccentric reader who connected a passing reference to "Dehring" in a large novel with a live Dr. Dering. By taking this legal action, he put himself in the center of a spotlight which could have only catastrophic results. By the eighteenth day of the trial, every English-language newspaper had carried reports of the horrors of Auschwitz as recounted in the cool legal language of the court; and after judgment was given, almost every British newspaper and weekly journal carried special articles in which the moral issues received attention.

Within a few months, work began on the extradition of Franz Stangl, charged with killing at least 400,000 Jews at another camp near Warsaw. He had taken refuge in Brazil, and was an old friend of Hans-Ulrich Rudel, a founder of the Kameradenwerk. When he was brought to trial at last, he told the court that he had escaped with the help of Bishop Hudal, who "knew exactly who I was."

What Stangl and the Brotherhood did not know was that the British Home Office decided in 1948 that there was not sufficient evidence to support a *prima-facie* case for the surrender of Dering as a war criminal to the Polish government. The Poles had been trying to get him ever since. Dering was on the United Nations list of war criminals on the complaints of the French, Czech, and Polish governments; and application had been made for his extradition from England. On that basis alone he was held in an English prison for nineteen months, survived the interrogations and investigations, and secured a job as a doctor in the Colonial Service. The presumption that he could clear his name, and thus secure for other war criminals a kind of ticket back into polite society, was founded upon the fact that English law had worked earlier in his favor. His ill-informed advisers had demonstrated again their total lack of moral, let alone common, sense.

They learned one lesson, however. If they were certifiably "denazified" in law courts where pressure could be brought to bear, they might re-enter public life. By 1972, when it was difficult to rouse the public conscience in some parts of Germany and Austria, sentences for wartime acts were cut short, and men belatedly brought to trial were winning acquittals. A former Nazi architect

263

who designed and built the Auschwitz gas chambers and cremation furnaces, Walter Dejaca, was freed by an Austrian jury. The New York *Times* was moved to protest, on March 14: "There can hardly be question of Dejaca's complicity. . . . The court was shown blueprints for the gas chambers, for the furnaces and for electric elevators to transport corpses to the ovens, all bearing the architect's signature. While no penalty can atone for the horror of Auschwitz, it is a desecration of the dead to allow its perpetrators to go scot free even a generation later. Crimes of this enormity serve to undermine the very foundations of human society. How can they so soon be forgotten—or forgiven?"

One reason why editorial writers in New York felt outraged while West Germany for the most part accepted with equanimity these echoes of horror was the difference in public attitudes. When American policies lead to military adventures that offend the public conscience, there is a powerful outcry from one quarter or another. The critics of American policy abroad have always drawn their raw material from American sources.

Big business in West Germany took back into positions of wealth and prestige men whose wartime records qualified them to join the Brotherhood's operations overseas. Their peculiar advantage was that they had been tried and sentenced for war crimes, and then released; and thus they were certifiably acceptable in decent society again.

The mechanism at Auschwitz for disposing efficiently of human beings was managed and improved to a great extent by I. G. Farben. This was the world's largest chemical combine during Hitler's regime. The name of I. G. Farbenindustrie AG was behind a global network of some 500 differently titled companies in more than ninety countries. The combine represented a form of international power that was resistant to catastrophe in Germany and therefore attractive to Bormann and those planning to survive the coming defeat. While the company still managed the machinery of mass extermination, it also prepared for a world without Hitler. This was demonstrated most vividly at the so-called "Auschwitz trial" in Frankfurt during 1964. Freight and cattle trains were packed with Jews and directed to the death camps, where "shower rooms" exterminated the victims and crematories sent up columns of fatty dark smoke and spread the stench of burned bodies. An American military court in Nuremberg sentenced thirteen executives of I. G. Farben to jail on charges of murder and looting. That was in 1948. Twelve years later, many were back with the company, its subsidiaries, or other chemical firms. For instance, Fritz ter Meer, who was found personally responsible for poison-gas production and experiments on concentration-camp victims at Auschwitz, returned to respectability as Chairman of Bayer Leverkusen, an I. G. Farben successor firm. The manager of the I. G. Farben slave-labor factory at Auschwitz, Otto Ambros (also Chairman of Hitler's chemical-warfare committee) came out of jail to become director of two I. G. Farben associates: Scholven Chemie AG and Feldmuehle Papier AG. It was Otto Ambros who wrote an ingratiating little note on April 12, 1941 to Fritz ter Meer: "At a banquet given us by the management of the Auschwitz Concentration Camp we decided on all further measures affecting the really wonderful concentration camp organization for the benefit of [I. G. Farben's] Buna Plant."

The large chemical monopoly was not the only offender; and this seemed to be the main source of irritation to its officials. To make them feel better, presumably, some were given awards by the postwar federal government for their services after leaving jail. Heinrich Bütefisch, who had been production chief at the slave-labor factory, and an SS colonel, was sentenced to six years by a U.S. military court, was released when Bonn was in charge of its own affairs, became Deputy Chairman of the Board of Directors of Ruhrchemie AG, and received from West German President Lübke in 1964 the Federal Grand Cross for outstanding services.

The Farben combine had obtained permission to build a synthetic fuel oil and rubber factory in Upper Silesia in the neighborhood where slave labor could be obtained. Eager to please, Bormann's old chum from terrorist days, Rudolf Höss, hurried along. He had been six years running concentration camps and thought he could oblige.

He was a pious Catholic in his youth. A little simple, people said, but clearly destined for the priesthood. By the fall of 1941 he had decided not to be present at the selection of the sick for the lethal syringe, a weekly parade.

He decided to reserve the gas chambers for the Jews. It was, to his way of thinking, a kindness. He got the figures up to 10,000 a day on one occasion, and the chemical industry then gladly increased its supplies of cyanide gas. Höss had not been in good repute with them before this. Farben directors complained that he provided only 1,300 slave workers out of the 2,700 needed on one rush job.

A photograph and a personality profile of Höss shows that he was destined to take the rap. He had the dilated eyes and the drooping face of a man who found life difficult to understand. Before he was hanged, two years after the war, at the very place where he had juggled with the chemical industry's labor demands, he told a Reuters correspondent that it was very unfair, because he had never killed nearly the number of people that the judges said he did.

The power of large or monopolistic companies must be considered in relation to the growing confidence felt by such men as Dr. Josef Mengele, who selected his human guinea pigs from thousands on their way to the Auschwitz gas chambers. Mengele in 1972 was traveling from his new home in South America by air to Spain whenever the Brotherhood there felt it was safe for him to do so, sometimes using the name "Dr. Nadich." His family's large business with Latin America made him feel he was wasting time and depriving the booming West German economy of his talents.

This animal-like unawareness of the savage nature of his own behavior was demonstrated at the time of the Auschwitz trial, when his extradition was sought from Paraguay, still the most thoroughly totalitarian state in the world. The President-dictator, General Stroessner, the German brewer's son, roared his refusal. Mengele still went ahead with plans to revisit the family home.

The atmosphere in these German company towns does make such arrogance at least comprehensible. I had seen how the Mengele family dominated "their" Bavarian town, so that Dr. Josef could visit with impunity; and in a classic court action I had seen how a similar company with a load of guilt escaped justice because of local influence. A study of the proceedings in this case was published in 1972 by two Swedish researchers, based on a 972-page indictment compiled by the Public Prosecutor which charged a pharmaceutical firm in the small town of Alsdorf with commercial greed, indifference to suffering, criminal negligence leading to death and malformation of babies, and willfully offering for sale a medicament likely to cause harmful effects—to wit, thalidomide.

The drug, which was eventually to sell in other parts of the world, was the product of Chemie-Grünenthal. It caused untold tragedy, especially in malformation of unborn babies who were by 1972 a fearful burden. They had matured into young people with flipper hands instead of arms and other indescribable handicaps. The hearings, instead of taking place in the regional center, at Aachen, were moved instead to the company town. It is a small place, where the workers are spoken of as "the labor force," recruited from the young, who move with bovine submissiveness from school to the drug company's employ. The big legal guns lumbered in, crushing the local prosecutor's obviously inexperienced staff. Expert witnesses for the prosecution were vilified and the company's high-priced lawyers dragged out the proceedings in a way that seemed possible only because they were fighting on local territory. The end result was the use of a loophole in the federal government's constitution to suspend the trial. Then the company, knowing the parents of the crippled children could not afford more legal proceedings, offered to pay a modest settlement if each recipient of this largesse promised not to bring a civil action. The London *Sunday Telegraph,* viewing the trial as a comment on West Germany in the aftermath of Nazi atrocities, called it "a frightening glimpse of the unbelievably callous origins" of tragedy.

I discussed the case with Beata Klarsfeld. She felt most Germans were easily impressed by the law. This was why the courts were infiltrated by Nazi-minded lawyers, masters of tactics similar to the thalidomide proceedings, making it possible for exiled Nazis to return home or come out of hiding. The fact that they were growing older mattered less than the need to restore them into good favor, give them a legal right to take public-service jobs again, and thus permit the absorption back into the national consciousness of ideas previously identified with Nazism and officially "wrong." She felt, as a German, that her people would always take a submissive attitude to legal-sounding propositions. This was why Bormann waited to get documents from Hitler that established his primacy in the party. His legal mind was that of a medieval despot who makes the court witness the actual birth of the son and heir to an empire. The documents were his essential witnesses.

CHAPTER 23

In March 1972 I flew from New York to the capital city of Colombia on Avianca's Saturday night flight to Bogotá. An old man had been dragged out of a remote jungle settlement. He was the right nationality, age, and general build to fit the profile of Martin Bormann. This interested me less than the deliverance at regular intervals into police hands of men who were said to be Bormann. He seemed to be doomed to materialize in different guises for the rest of time. He was like the gods and the devils invented by human beings since the dawn of recorded history: invented by societies quite independent of one another, so that one suspected that we created these haunting spirits for the good of our souls.

Those who reinvented Bormann, or truly believed that they had seen him, were not, as far as I could tell, driven by the usual motives of greed for notoriety or revenge. They thought they had seen him.

This proved to be the case with Johann Ehrmann, the spelling of whose name was to change in the next few days, along with other details, until I had the feeling that I had tried to capture a wisp of fog between my hands. I checked into the hotel very late. The usual nightly drizzle of high mountain rain made the wide streets glisten. Here and there below my window, small figures were squatting in ponchos like cones of incense as cigarette smoke dribbled from invisible lips. Towering over all was a giant illuminated cross. The taxi driver had said it marked the place of My Lord of Monserrate. Tomorrow there would be a pilgrimage of cripples to kiss the altar.

The phone rang. Hernando Orozco, of Reuters, like all good agency men, ignored the night hours in his personal life although a clock in his head told him what time it was anywhere in the world. Right now, in London, the readers of the Sunday papers were drinking their prelunch beer over reports that Bormann had been found in the Colombian jungle. "Perhaps it is true," said Orozco. "All I did was report what the general of security police told me."

The Department of Administrative Services (DAS) secret police had arrested the old man at an Indian settlement on the river that forms part of the frontier between Colombia and Ecuador. The village was itself some days' trek from the town of Pasto, which itself was a matter of weeks by road, in this weather, from the capital. By air, it was three hundred miles over high twisting valleys. There was still a space for me on the police plane leaving early for Pasto, where the old man would be questioned. The German Embassy had said it expected Bormann's fingerprints by air from Frankfurt immediately. It had said this under the pressure of publicity created by a former henchman of Che Guevera, a Cuban Communist who disagreed with Castro's way of doing things. This man edited an influential magazine, which refused to fall into line with the rest of the Colombian press, and it was he who brought the affair to light. So the police and the Cabinet could not ignore the matter. However, said Orozco, the Pasto community was entirely German, and there was already a campaign to protect a poor old man grubbing it with the Indians. And the spokesman at the German Embassy had changed his story twice about the fingerprints. Also, the police were backing off. It seemed that the old man had rather conveniently removed the tips of two fingers and a thumb in a regrettable accident involving firearms. He fitted the scant description of Bormann: right age, and so on. But . . .

It was the middle of the night, and I should have caught a couple of hours' sleep, but Bogotá is nearly 9,000 feet above sea level and that altitude always did keep me awake. I went downstairs and into the wet streets again. Soldiers in white helmets, with guns, stood in the doorways and smiled politely. The center of the city rose in formidable cliffs, lit only when the moon broke through drifting cloud. The Club Argentino beckoned. A friendly bar. Good music. I had forgotten how good that Latin-American rhythm was. Girls danced in a tiny pool of light. I found a corner and ordered a drink.

Did I really want to go on with this? If I sat here long enough, I would shortly find it difficult to know if I was in Saigon or Cairo or Warsaw or Djakarta. If I sat here long enough, there would come the inevitable man with his inevitably intriguing story.

"You will have a cigarette?"

Here he was. Inevitable. Sleek. Slightly menacing.

269

"You cannot sleep?"

"No," I said.

He raised two fingers to the bar boy. "You were not sleeping on the plane."

"What plane?"

"From New York."

I took his cigarette in resignation.

"Hey, Joe!" he called to a bulky figure sitting beside the pool of light where the girls were still writhing.

An American this time: large and rather crumpled. Joe Something. Big wide smile and big wide hands. Saw me on the plane. That's how Gastón, here, knew. Smiles all round.

"Is there anything we can do to help?"

"I'm not sure what you mean."

"You want to get down to Pasto, right?" Joe leaned forward. "I saw you reading the news."

More big smiles.

"I think I've got transport, thanks."

"Funny place, Pasto. Eh, Gastón?"

The other man nodded.

"They had trouble with the guerrillas there again. This country's all mountains and valleys. Guerrilla country."

"Cardinal Concha Córdoba could tell you much about that," said Gastón. "He defrocked the priest—"

"The guerrillas don't stand much chance," Joe interrupted. "They got some fine people down there at Pasto. Every Saturday is Bavarian night at the Gasthaus Eric. Brew their own beer. Solid German stock. They can handle these nuts who wouldn't recognize one end of a gun from the other."

"You must know the place?"

"Fly there all the time. Got my own plane. I could take you down if you needed the ride." He gave me his card, which bore the name of an oil company. "Call me, anyway."

I promised I would, and excused myself. The music was suddenly getting on my nerves.

"Until tomorrow," said Gastón.

Gray light crept over the ring of mountains. The cross shone more brightly than before. Perhaps it caught the sun. I walked along the wide streets. Big showrooms with expensive cars and tall office blocks. The cars in the windows stood like floodlit monuments to the Mercedes company. And a mile away in any direction, the people lived in shacks.

270

Funny, that mention of the priest. There was a defrocked priest named Camilo who took to the mountains to lead a revolution. On February 15, 1966 the Colombian authorities announced that Father Camilo Torres had been killed by government troops. There had been a movement for a time, spreading to Uruguay and Venezuela, called Camilismo—in memory of a Catholic martyr.

The old man drank a very good local beer called Club Colombia. He had been pulled into the town of Pasto on the pretense, said the local Colonel of police, that his ID card was out of date. It gave an opportunity to check his background.

The Germans in Eric's were friendly and bluff. "Why persecute a poor old Jew?" "That's right; he came here to get away from persecution." "You can see he's simple in the head." "Why pick on German exiles; haven't we suffered enough?"

The old man was born in Germany in 1899, one year before the registered birth date of Bormann. He had a piece of paper which said so. The crumpled certificate was issued to him in 1952. It bore the imprint of an American refugee organization. His name was really Johannes Hartmann, and he didn't know how the confusion arose. He smiled uneasily at the suggestion that he was Jewish. No, he said finally. No, he was not a Jew.

There was another bit of paper, tattered and greasy, issued by the frontier police in 1926 recording that he had crossed from Ecuador with the declared intention of becoming a resident foreigner. He had come from Germany in the 1920's to make a new life. Germany was a place of anarchists and thugs. He grew a few root crops with his Indian family. He knew nothing about Nazis. He smiled apologetically. After all, he had been gone before they arrived, and he was not much for reading newspapers.

He said he would like the police to fly him back to Germany. The jungle was a lonely place. He would like to see what had happened to his own country. Let the police send him there for a holiday. He grinned, running his tongue along a toothless gum, glancing at the uniformed police lounging in the dusty street.

That night the old man was taken back to his Indian community. He belonged to a sect, it was said, that refused to touch anything mechanical or metallic. They wore potato sacks because ordinary clothes were stitched by machine and they called themselves *"costellados"* after the word for a potato bag. They called the Devil *"Cameoneta,"* which meant literally "little truck." That is what they thought of man-made things. The place where they lived

271

was called "Hormiga" in honor of the ant. The symbol of their religion was a crooked cross, but they did not worship anything; neither spirits nor idols.

Could we go to his village?

No, said the local police chief. Not without permission. It would be necessary to go back to Bogotá for the permission, and then how are you going to return? "The air service is for officials. You were lucky. Anyway, this place of the old man is in a protected area. And if you try to go by road, it is not easy. And the jungle is all around. You will have to sleep in hammocks and eat some kind of *yuca* made from cassava and bananas, which will only make your belly ache."

"Come and have some more beer," said Eric. "On the house!"

There was in fact a military air service—SATENA—to jungle communities within what the government called National Territories. The passenger depended on official good will. Flying back over that terrain, I was again astonished by the steep-sided mountains and deep valleys, the lush vegetation and the difficulty of travel on foot.

"Made more difficult by certain police agencies," said my Colombian companion. "The country is efficiently divided into squares, so far as policing goes. You cannot move without being observed."

"Forgive my saying so—"

"But we don't seem all that efficient?" He grinned. "We are not. The Germans taught us. A special mission from Madrid led by Hitler's expert." He snapped his fingers. "The man who rescued Mussolini and Franco's brother-in-law during your big war . . . Otto Skorzeny."

"He was here? When?"

My companion scratched his head. "Three years ago, the last time. But who knows how often? It is easy, when our national airline shoots the big shots from here to there like capsules. Skorzeny lives in Madrid, no?"

Yes, indeed he did. I began to quote Skorzeny on the use of sealed airliners between countries where immigration could be bribed, and then I thought better of it. Three years ago . . .

Out of idle curiosity, I checked the diplomatic list. The German Ambassador was Ernst Ludwig Ostermann von Roth, whose Nazi background was on record: joined the party in 1937, No. 3,810,743 . . . Nazi party representative with the German Army in the occupied territories of the Soviet Union. . . .

272

Official German disapproval of this latest "Bormann" story was soon made plain. Editorials and news "stories" reporting the indignation of local citizens appeared in several of the country's newspapers at the same time. The phrases were almost identical. The war had been over and forgotten. Journalists who dug up dirt of this kind were helping the Communists.

The German Embassy had first said Bormann's fingerprints would arrive on the morning flight from Frankfurt via Madrid that Saturday. Now, two days later, the embassy said there were no fingerprints on file of Martin Bormann anywhere. In *those* days, thumb prints were taken. No, there was no plan to fly thumb prints over because none existed either. But of course there were criminal fingerprints made in the 1920's when Bormann was involved in a murder—except *that* was in Leipzig, and of course that city was today under Communist control.

I remarked on the coincidence of the press reactions, and it was pointed out that the German community advertised heavily in those papers. This observation came from a Colombian who made his living as a journalist, whose children went to a German school subsidized by the West German government, and were picked up by a German school bus at no cost. He was a cultured man, living in a modern apartment with well-mannered children and a fine wife. And he pointed out something else. There was no tradition of a free and balanced press. The editor who started the police investigation, José Pardo Lamas, was "removed" from his post on the weekly magazine *Cromos* a month later.

The police Colonel in the headquarters of General Luis Ordonez Valderana said: "My colleague wrote to the suspect a letter of congratulation. He said: 'Now you can dance through the streets of Colombia and tell everyone you are Martin Bormann and they will laugh and buy you a drink.'"

General Ordonez, chief of DAS, had been very proud on discovering "Bormann." Then the uniformed police, supervised by a different minister, took over the interrogation. Ordonez, known on the local board of German companies, changed his mind overnight. The suspect was to be released.

Just before the suspect was brought into Pasto, the town was flooded with an unaccustomed number of steel-helmeted and armed regular police. I commented on their numbers and received surprised looks, as if I had shown naïveté, which indeed I had. The police were there to intimidate strangers. But individually they were open to negotiation. "We have tough currency restrictions; all in the name of socialism but, in reality, to give a few families the monopoly on our trade." "Here is documentation of higher authorities who have directorships on German companies, *por favor.* Of course I can make you a copy. I can even make an original."

With documents so easy to come by, why did the old man have nothing to cover the years between 1926 and 1952? Well, they said at police headquarters, the papers for 1926 were issued in Ecuador, and the old man's canoe had capsized crossing the river and all the papers between got lost. A bewildering explanation.

A bewildering city. The way to get around it was by *collectivo,* a small Volkswagen bus, if you could find one. The business center reminded me of those grandiose plans Albert Speer used to draw up, showing Berlin as the heart of an empire. Walking past the cemetery, I came to the sudden end of tarmac. There flashed into my mind the vast highway Mussolini started in the Horn of Africa, and the time I drove two miles along it, past triumphal columns, into the desert, where it expired, like another dusty dream of glory.

The police changed their minds about Ehrmann-Hartmann. After I had left, along with an odd collection of investigators, he disappeared back into the jungle. The Viennese hunter of war criminals Simon Wiesenthal said he was the dupe of the Brotherhood's deception agency. He had been catapulted into prominence to distract attention from Bormann's real hide-out in Paraguay. This did not explain the anxiety of the large German community to discourage further questions. It did not explain the police medical report, which claimed that the old man was not only scarred in places where prints or tattoo marks might have been found, but that a clumsy and undoubtedly painful attempt had been made late in his life to remove his foreskin in a belated circumcision. He was not, as he had said, Jewish.

If the old man was a pawn in some deception plan, certainly his papers could have been put into better order. There were SS experts who surprised their own leaders by their skill at this. Walter Schellenberg described, after the war, how American interrogators were convinced by a fake passport that he had visited the United States. He was annoyed at the charge that he, an SS general, chief of foreign intelligence, skulked through America in the middle of the war. The Americans then produced the passport made out in Schellenberg's name. It was an American passport, and it had all the relevant embarkation and debarkation stamps, a photograph of Schellenberg overprinted by U.S. immigration in New York. The fake passport had been found among Schellenberg's papers. Then finally he had recognized it as a small joke produced for his birthday in 1943 by the SS technicians in the department of forged documents.

That department continued to forge documents after the war. Schellenberg, reduced to a spiteful exile in the shabby gentility of his Swiss retreat, described how Klaus Barbie had escaped French retribution for Gestapo crimes and took the name of "Mertens" before joining ODESSA, which was operating in an Augsburg POW camp a large-scale counterfeiting agency. "They went across the Atlantic to teach those Latin-American natives to be good anti-Communists," Schellenberg said maliciously. "After all, I know enough about *that*. There is a region where you could create your own Nazi state and never be noticed. Of course this has its disadvantages. The purpose of reviving Nazism is to spread the gospel, and there is no purpose hiding a fine Fourth Reich in the jungle. Yet it would make a start," he added pedantically. "Latin America is a sixth of the world's land surface. How often I studied it!"

A secret German U-boat refueling base, tolerated during the war by Colombia, was a small island in the Caribbean within striking distance of vital Allied shipping routes. This island, San Andrés, is reached these days from Miami by the West German subsidiary of Lufthansa, Condor Flugdienst GmbH. I took another look at it on the way to discuss this latest Bormann manifestation with friends in Allied intelligence and with Sir William Stephenson, in Bermuda, nearby. It was useful to remind oneself that the Germans had an intimate knowledge of these waters, which did not end abruptly with the war.

Farther north, the small island of Bermuda had been shared by the British with American naval intelligence, and all their vast resources made it possible to oversee Nazi operations on a scale that, in those days, was remarkable for its global dimensions, Here, once again, I paused. It was like old times. Years earlier, Stephenson's man in charge of Latin America, Peter Dwyer, had helped me to reach the killer of Stalin's archenemy, Trotsky. This episode was not irrelevant to events today. The same questions had come up about documents, methods of getting into Latin America, the purposeful hunting down of a rival leader in a movement that had the same ideological and international pretensions as the National Socialists. (It was Goebbels who was quoted once as saying he had spun a coin as a young man: heads he would be a Nazi, tails a Communist.) There had been the same problem faced by police organizations: in the case of Trotsky's killer, a forged Canadian passport like the one used by the pro-Nazi fugitive the Count de Bernonville. The source of the forgeries was known, and Canadian passports were the favorite choice of international assassins; but the Royal Canadian Mounted Police had been hamstrung by consideration for national sovereignty—not a consideration that handicapped the forgers, working on passports taken from Canadians killed in the Spanish Civil War. I remembered that it had been necessary to bribe a distinguished member of the Mexican Cabinet to get proof of the true identity of Trotsky's killer; and then we were obliged to check every word of the documents. The story is a complete case history of the silent work of Russian agents in Latin America. After that case, nothing would seem too fantastic. This explains my mood of ambivalence after seeing Ehrmann-Hartmann in Colombia. The long trail ahead was daunting. Nothing would be what it seemed.

Stephenson and CIA men who had been on the alert at all the Latin-American stations for Bormann thought the Brotherhood had certainly broken up into squabbling groups. The fascination lay in the way the man himself stirred primeval feelings.

This was the man's power, even now. The rest was an adventure story. But the man moved among us at different levels. There was the comic-strip character who knew, long before these things became commonplace news reports, about shipping dead agents in the cargo holds of aircraft. In the center of his web, from Berlin he dispatched an admiral to Japan by submarine. He trained in war the men who would operate Die Spinne with money drawn from numbered accounts in Swiss banks. He had cave-dwelling artists produce superb examples of counterfeit money. In the early 1940's, his couriers were capable of reaching Buenos Aires from his headquarters more speedily than our own men from Washington. At his disposal was the financial wizard Schacht, who looked down upon the world as if from a satellite and viewed it in blobs of color that represented not continents but concentrations of capital.

His greatest strength was his bovine air of peasant dim-wittedness. His greatest upset would be the way the Irish farm workers forced Scarface Skorzeny to sell his estate near Cork. *That* was hard to take. Borman considered himself a peasant. If newcomers to the Brotherhood seized control and forced him to give up his wealth, or if foreign agents broke down his morale so that he ceased to move in large centers of population, he would be perfectly capable of returning to the simple life of a peasant.

Comic-strip figures reflect, after all, a kind of reality. This superman held attention because he had this underlying toughness of the soil. Ehrmann-Hartmann could be Bormann for reasons that were disturbing.

The gnarled old man in the jungle had left me with a sense of his infinite cunning. Months after the fuss died away, he dematerialized like a piece of ectoplasm. He vanished.

Stephenson, noting this, insisted that it was folly to suppose this was the end. His professional colleagues in Washington and London agreed, for philosophical reasons. They recalled that during the trial of Nazi leaders after the war, U.S. Prosecutor Robert E. Jackson rejected the plea that they were innocent because they followed orders: "We must never forget that the record on which we judge these defendants today is the record on which history will judge us tomorrow."

Tomorrow had become today, and the British judge at the trial, Sir Hartley Shawcross, might have been commenting upon the great crises of our own times when he said: "Political loyalty and military obedience are excellent things but they neither require nor do they justify the commission of patently wicked acts. There comes a point where a man must answer his leader if he is also to answer to his conscience."

CHAPTER 24

Hitler's death at the climax of the war could establish a legend in the minds of later generations of Germans that would take a dangerously long time to eradicate. This was evident to his only close companion in the final years, Bormann. It was also evident to pioneers in a method which brought together Allied historians and psychologists in analytical studies of human reactions under stress. The method, though of course it has its pitfalls, is now commonly used. It played a role in changing Western policies toward Chairman Mao, and a similar prosopographic technique is employed by the Russians in responding to the West's leaders.

Martin Bormann was one of those men who are uncannily sensitive to all the factors at work in a political situation. He knew Hitler's ability to play on unconscious tendencies of the German people; to speak for their unexpressed desires; to paralyze the critical functions of individual Germans and take over himself the making of decisions. He knew Hitler could do this in communion with the masses.

Hitler was not unique. The German people were not peculiarly susceptible. The interplay between them is in some ways more easily duplicated today than it was then. The frustrated hopes of millions in Latin America have not found expression through Martin Bormann, but this does not mean that nations will not rebel again, as Germany did, against all the rules by which civilized society is supposed to live.

Hitler's suicide was foreseen as a dangerous basis for a new mythology during the pioneer work of the psychoanalyst Dr. Walter Langer. This work was reinforced by Oxford dons and such disparate characters as Ivonne Kirkpatrick and Lord Beaverbrook, who had questioned Deputy Führer Rudolf Hess.

All the elements come together in the puzzle Bormann presents by the very persistence of his own odd legend. Hitler destroyed himself and tried to destroy the world he secretly hated, but so far

278

none of this has woven itself into a new mythology. Instead, the old Nazi diehards promote a view that is agreeable to many Germans: the political philosophy was good, the leader bad. It is Bormann who became the legend.

Bormann showed every intention of wishing to lead a Nazi revival. The studies conducted by Anglo-American teams reveal this. What about the Russians? There is evidence they have made similar deductions: that Bormann was more useful alive but unaware of being under observation. He could be driven into moral collapse later if necessary. The Russians had a long history of close practical collaboration with Germany in Hitler's early days. This tends to be forgotten because of the later gargantuan battles between Nazi and Soviet forces. This influenced Bormann's career, of course. Both the Russians and the West, I now believe, regard Bormann as the type of man who would do anything to exercise power; who would acquire *personal* wealth to satisfy a deep peasant urge for possession of land; who was nevertheless not dependent upon luxuries, and because of this ability to live simply and even in discomfort would always be, as Albert Speer said, "a born survivor." He loved possessing people rather than things. He ruled by terror. His strength lay in secrecy, and also in his administrative talents, his knowledge of how to make a system work to his advantage, his control over men like Hitler.

His postwar career was therefore likely to be a disposition of his forces. Intelligence research-and-analysis teams submitted the idea that Bormann was even perhaps worth leaving alive and licensed to roam. He was more interesting for what he would do than for what he had done already. The past could not be changed. The future might be improved if more was known about this kind of man, and the men attracted to him even while they feared him.

These were not sickly preoccupations. The men who studied Bormann felt that he might explain a lot about human behavior. If he got away, and they followed his tracks, he would be more likely to lead them toward solutions to problems of men's behavior than he was likely to lead to a Fourth Reich.

A proposal to let Bormann run free would not be some irresponsible caper. His actions could be projected with fair accuracy. If anything went wrong with the project, it was more likely to be the result of indifference on the part of government agencies. The British were retreating into their own national self-interests. Americans were preoccupied with rebuilding Europe and large parts of Asia. Only the Russians, probably, had time to spare for single-minded pursuit of one man, which would require a considerable number of experts. Hitler had demonstrated the validity of proso profiles. His revenge fantasies were described in details that were confirmed after the war by those who worked close to him. The peculiarities of his conduct had a direct bearing upon Martin Bormann; and it was encouraging for professional analysts of war information to find that Hitler's sexual malformation had been accurately foreshadowed long before a physical examination proved its existence. His erotic and megalomaniac daydreams were deduced only on the basis of careful intelligence studies. They turned out to be symptoms of a certain kind of man whose early childhood approximated that of Hitler, combined with the psychological effects of genital inadequacy.

The latter was established when Russian doctors performed an autopsy and failed to discover the left testicle, in either the scrotum, the spermatic cord inside the inguinal canal, or in the small pelvis. The lack of one testicle was not regarded as a serious or uncommon disorder, but it could become a problem in combination with other infantile disorders.

The research teams could not, obviously, have known they were defining a physical malformation which Hitler had kept secret. What they described were the manifestations, based upon many interviews with refugees, including his nephew William Patrick Hitler and others who had known him well. His first major political victim, Ernst Röhm, had said at about the time of the murder of Hitler's niece that "his sex life is looking at the big round bottoms of peasant girls as they bend over in the fields." The analysts had said that Hitler seemed preoccupied with eyes and breasts and buttocks as substitutes; and went on to describe castration fantasies without, of course, knowing how close they were to the truth.

Note was taken of Hitler's dependence upon approval by older women, his need to draw strength from massed audiences, whose seduction he compared with that of a woman, his nightmares, his self-punishing behavior in private and his vengeful outbursts in public.

He satisfied his sexual needs in a manner that left him open to blackmail. Bormann cleaned up the dirt.

Bormann made sure Hitler kept to schedules, which the Führer hated. Bormann concealed from others the Führer's frequent, manic depressions. Nothing was exposed of the feminine nature hidden inside the great orator who boasted: "The audience is just like a woman. Someone who does not understand the intrinsically feminine character of the masses will never be an effective speaker. A woman expects from a man . . . clearness, decision, power, and action."

Hitler's role was one Bormann could never have played and did not wish to play. He knew the other Führer, who woke up in the middle of night screaming. The Reich Minister for Church Affairs, Hans Kerrl, compared the Führer to the Holy Ghost: "There has arisen a new authority as to what Christianity and Christ really are—Adolf Hitler. He is the true Holy Ghost." The founder of a new social order for the whole world loved long and impressive titles. He conveniently forgot promises and screamed with rage when thwarted. He seemed to stiffen into masculinity with the stream of his own words, hypnotizing himself into the conviction that he really was the Father.

Only Bormann saw the small man with flabby muscles, short and spindly legs, and a chest so hollow that his uniforms were padded in front. His teeth were brown and rotten, and when he was not strutting between the ranks of cheering disciples, he had a dainty ladylike walk in which one shoulder twitched and the opposite leg snapped up.

What would the puppetmaster do when the marionette broke? The scholarly soothsayers in early 1945 guessed correctly that Martin Bormann had been mentally prepared a long time for this moment. He performed his last task for the Führer-doll when he called for gasoline to burn the remains. It was one of the rare times when he miscalculated. The sandy soil outside the bunker soaked up the fuel. The broken doll did not burn long. Bormann shrugged and walked away.

It was never supposed that Bormann would waste time hanging around his family unless he suffered a nervous breakdown. Then, possibly, he would need the soothing hand of the woman he called, on occasion, "Mommy." Then, too, he might seek refuge in the very Christianity he had scorned and scourged; for in that relationship, love and hate were closely interwoven. The broken doll of Hitler might need to be replaced by an abstract god. This would no more divert Bormann from his pursuit of power, political or material, than his dependence upon women, and especially Gerda, directed him away from his goals. He was and would remain a single-minded man.

"Why would his wife do a back somersault into the Pope's lap?" I asked Campbell Stuart after the conversion of Mrs. Bormann became known. Stuart had gone on a political mission to the Pope many years earlier, when Catholic Canadian troops were needed during World War I. "For that matter, why would the Vatican take her?"

He shook his head. "Don't blame the Vatican for everything. You don't curse the president of Pan Am if a ticket clerk sends you to the wrong destination."

"None of the Bormann children ever discussed their mother?"

"They've always refused. Martin Bormann, Jr., once said he would protect his father, or so he was quoted. He became a Catholic missionary. A reporter found him in the Congo and asked if he would hide his father and young Martin said: Yes, because in spite of everything, he was his father. There was no law that said he must deliver his own father to the hangman."

"That must have been the mother's attitude."

"Funny you should say 'mother.' Bormann—*the* Bormann—had a mommy complex. It was something he concealed because the Nazi style was blustering masculinity. He wrapped his 'weakness' in brutality."

The Brotherhood, with true Nazi spirit, had no place for women in its ranks. From time to time, reports had come out of Latin America from women who claimed to have had affairs with Bormann.

One woman who had really known Bormann was the widow of Hermann Göring. Before I flew to the Munich area to speak with her in the summer of 1972, I saw that part of the proso profile on Bormann which focused on his life with Gerda and the place of women in Nazi Germany. An accompanying note quoted the priest of the Jesuit Order which ordained Martin Bormann, Jr., in August 1958: "This is new confirmation that even among the godless evolved by totalitarianism, there is a way back."

Frau Göring shed no light on philosophical matters. She regarded Bormann as the evil genius behind Hitler and the man who destroyed her husband. "Bormann interfered from the very start," she said. "My husband never thought of starting a war with Britain. He would have gone to the coronation of King George VI, but it was really Bormann who stopped it!"

The coronation was in 1936, but Frau Göring gave a vivid account of how Göring, the most powerful figure next to Hitler so far as the public had been concerned, was even then unable to talk privately with Hitler. "Bormann was always present and wrote down every word."

The Nazis never permitted women to play an open political role.

In the year Göring missed the coronation, there was a woman speaker at the Reich Party Day of Honor in Nuremberg. She was a stocky blonde of uncertain age named Scholtz-Klink, who told the vast assembly that all German women should stand shoulder to shoulder with the Führer in order to fight the evil of Bolshevism. Hitler replied that woman's role was to raise the family and bear children; men protected the whole of society. There was tremendous applause. Frau Scholtz-Klink promised in the name of all German women to try to lighten the Führer's burden.

Frau Göring, a former opera singer, with some knowledge of stage management, had observed the orgasmic nature of Hitler's relationship with the crowd. "When it came to Nazi party nights, Bormann produced the whole show for Hitler, and nobody out front knew this was so. I had the feeling, watching the Führer perform, that he was just like any poor little showgirl, entirely in the hands of the promoter."

The widow of Hermann Göring unwittingly confirmed in 1972 what was speculated upon in the mid-1940's. Bormann used women to gain control over his rivals. He held complete sway over the prude Heinrich Himmler, who could sign away the lives of thousands with an absent-minded stroke of his pen, but who was tortured by his conscience. He had a mistress tucked away in the Alpine Fortress. He had already married a Protestant girl, to the dismay of his Catholic Bavarian parents. Then his personal secretary became his mistress and bore him a son and a daughter. He acknowledged paternity late in 1944, and put himself deep into Bormann's debt by borrowing the equivalent of $20,000 from party funds—a large enough amount, and, for the publicly virtuous Himmler, a nightmare obligation.

Like so many of Bormann's victims, Himmler was too late in taking the measure of the common and vulgar fellow who danced attendance on the Führer. He was easily manipulated by Bormann because the pretentious little secret-police killer was suspended like a pendulum between prude and persecutor. He was indecisive behind those cold eyes. An order snapped out to dispose of God knows how many lives did not indicate strength of purpose, but fear of self-revelation. Bormann knew this. He knew he could always dominate a man who, while standing trial at the age of nineteen for killing the prostitute for whom he had also pimped, wrote: "I shall always love God and remain faithful to the Catholic church." Later, he forced SS men to leave the church and recommended the public execution of the Pope. This same Himmler could encourage his childhood friend Karl Gebhardt to pursue human-guinea-pig experiments at the same time that he put himself totally into Bormann's conspiratorial hands in his effort to conceal an extramarital relationship which would set a bad example to the public.

Himmler was obsessed with romantic visions of a Wagnerian era filled with Germanic heroes and glorious women who were, above all things, *pure*. This vision, in Hitler's case, led easily enough to the Nordic German master race, with a sexual code that ruled out extramarital relations. Hence Bormann's grip on the weak Himmler, who spoke in high moral tones ("healthy clean-living," he recommended to his future sister-in-law, adding severely: "You will have to be ridden on a tight rein"). His wife, Margaretta, always egged him on, and may well have been the real source of his malice. What they had in common was their sexuality, and after the war, in 1952, she confessed that she had known about his commission to liquidate the Jews and had encouraged him. Heydrich, the subordinate to Himmler, was driven by a shrewish wife who carried her feud against Frau Himmler into the postwar period. "All there was to her," she said, "was size-fifty bloomers."

Bormann managed their affairs to his benefit, and managed his own affairs with such discretion that few discussed them. He managed Hitler for subtler reasons to do with his own masculinity and the Führer's inability to get sexual relief except in public situations which were emotionally charged. There was a repeated note of homosexuality in Hitler's exaggerated regard for self-sacrificing comrades. Bormann deliberately fed his appetite for erect blond youths exuding male sweat and nobility of soul.

"Every child brought into the world is a battle women win for our existence," cried Hitler, himself above procreation. His teacher in 1919, Dietrich Eckart, had prophesied that the future savior of Germany would be a bachelor. "And *then* we shall bring in the women."

Bormann put it more crudely. The women were not going to get impregnated by the Holy Ghost after the war "but only by those German men still left." The state must see to it that "the decent strong-minded, physically healthy men reproduce themselves increasingly." He would permit pure Germanic women to produce children outside marriage, in order to make up for losses in battle. Superman was to be created by selective breeding.

Gerda Bormann's enthusiasm to share baby production with her husband's mistress persisted to the end, evidence of her fidelity to "national biological measures," which she and Bormann had largely foisted upon Germany. She was not likely to betray Bormann if he should visit her postwar mountain retreat. She would accept a permanent separation for the sake of the cause, and an overnight and expedient conversion to Catholicism to secure a guarantee of safe-conduct for Martin.

Bormann had no time for religion except as a drug. He was managing director of a large corporation which prospered by feeding the masses a regular dose of Hitler. Others could rhapsodize, like Alfred Rosenberg, whose seven-hundred-page *Myth of the Twentieth Century* was twaddle and rubbish. In this respect, Bormann saw through the intellectual pretensions of those who treated him with contempt. He betrayed none of his contempt if the courtier still enjoyed Hitler's favor. "He is unbelievably energetic and tireless," said Rosenberg before he discovered what a buffoon he was in Bormann's eyes. "He makes notes of everything, dictates, keeps voluminous records in a vulgarized form and is always with the Führer."

Of course. Bormann had worked his way up from messenger boy. Germany was an enormous corporation disguised as a bureaucracy.

The Allied study team that produced the first Bormann Life in April 1945 came to the conclusion that Martin Bormann would escape from the ruins of that corporation.

The highly secret study recognized that the man had tailored himself into the monstrous bureaucracy of Germany. He limited his vision deliberately, although he was capable of moving to extremes of intellectual activity. He did not push an idea to its limit, leaving that to Hitler. He cultivated a coarse and vulgar manner to disarm opponents and to satisfy Hitler's need for a brutish companion. He gave an impression of blinkering himself so that he trod a narrow line and was prevented from showing a curiosity about those matters which did not immediately cross his path.

There was no disposition to see him frozen into immobility by the defeat of Germany. Keeping in mind that this report was completed before events in the early hours of May 2, it was remarkable in predicting that Bormann would not leave until he had absolute and written authority that he was Hitler's successor. He understood the political intrigues of the court. He was compared, as he has been many times since, to Stalin under Lenin. Stalin, too, maintained the pose of a plodding bureaucrat while the intellectuals around Lenin ignored the lout and destroyed each other. Bormann

285

looked a peasant, and when the time came for escape, it was back to being a peasant that he would go. This ability to merge into a rural landscape would stand him in good stead.

Yet Bormann was extremely sensitive to the weaknesses in others; quick to take advantage of indecisiveness; capable of displaying the right degree of unctuousness if that was what his quarry seemed to require, but equally able to play the bully. He screamed at generals, and fawned on Albert Speer, his most hated rival, so that the Minister for War Production mistook the nature of his enemy and called him "brutal and lacking the culture which might have put restraints upon him."

The Allied Supreme Command was warned that if Bormann should be caught, he was to be handled only by very senior officers and then with extreme care. His physical condition was rated as A-1: "He is 45 years old and appears to have the strength and stamina to go underground for a considerable period of time."

The preparations for escape were noted in this particular Bormann proso profile. Several sources were quoted. For example, the Madrid station for German military intelligence had 357 full-time agents on the payroll and a large permanent staff, together with provision to pay, on results, about 890 Spanish locals. In the crossfire of intelligence during this period, the British and Americans were separately picking up the same reports of disaffection. When they compared notes, they found that the center of trafficking in loot was Switzerland. Top SS men were trying to barter Jews for their own safety, and by the end of 1944 there were two accounts of the situation. One came from Schellenberg, who said he had arranged to "save the lives of 1,200 Jews every two weeks" by freighting them into Switzerland. The other version claimed that former Swiss President Jean-Marie Musy had been asked to name the terms on which 250 Nazi leaders could secure political asylum. It required no great insight to perceive where the truth lay.

Was Switzerland where Bormann would go? Allied intelligence early in 1944 knew he had proposed two exits in private conversation with Gauleiter Koch and Auschwitz commandant Rudolf Höss, who was by then inspector of death camps. The convertible by-products of the camps, jewelry and gold, were shipped back in otherwise empty freight cars, and there were details to be discussed about future disposal. Other commodities, like human hair and old clothes, were part of an industrial process in which Bormann was careful not to pry. He did not get along with the large self-confident barons of the Ruhr. His escape plans were confined to thugs who

286

did not conceal their avarice behind toothy smiles or in the folds of double chins. The wealth accumulating from the camps had been dispersed through the Gestapo and Abwehr networks to safe places abroad. Bormann was expected to make a break for the northern redoubt first. Switzerland was the more obvious exit and therefore to be avoided.

How he would escape depended on Hitler's decision either to go to his alpine retreat or to stay in Berlin. The analysts thought he would stay. They knew enough already about the chaos in the wake of the Allied invasion armies to guess that Bormann would merge with the refugees while he made his way toward the Kiel submarine pens. He was the one leading Nazi who could vanish in a pigsty. His needs were really few. He had what Speer called "dogged perseverance."

In the flood of orders, memos, background briefs, and confidential documents that plagued Allied fighting men, a scholarly study on Bormann, almost totally unknown to most soldiers, was, not unnaturally, pushed aside. Academics in uniform tried desperately to rescue information from the ruins, knowing that within a few years humanity would be asking: "How could it happen?" The fighting men were tired and wanted the war over. The final part of the report, dealing with methods of escape, did not exactly rivet attention even within the tiny circle of recipients.

It emphasized the hostility toward the Allies among certain Swedish military men, including some in charge of intelligence, a result of highhanded British action against the Swedish Navy. The Scandinavian region was pinpointed as a target for escapees, an alternative to the U-boats in the region of Hamburg and Kiel. There was anxiety about the new submarines being built at Danzig, but the Baltic was shallow and heavily mined. The new Walther-boat submarines were given a million-to-one chance of breaking out. One earlier type of U-boat, the U-77, was reported to have made the suicidal run. It reached Oslo, where other submarines had been moved, partly to escape aerial bombardment. But another reason for submarines moving to Nazi-occupied Norway was to pick up shipments of loot and high-ranking officers.

All submarine movements were under the control of Günther Hessler, a son-in-law of Admiral Doenitz, and this was regarded as significant. One of the first acts required of Doenitz when he was captured was the transmission of a radio message: "In accordance with the unconditional surrender of all German forces, all German ships will refrain from any act of war. The crews are forbidden to scuttle their ships or otherwise render them unserviceable. Infringements are direct violations of the Grand Admiral's order and will have severe repercussions on the German nation." The meaning was clear: take no chances of Allied retribution. There was no great optimism in Allied naval circles that there would be an honest reckoning. The U-boat was a symbol of deceit and treachery. And it was later noted that in his last message, Doenitz had never specifically forbidden escape.

The Germans had their intelligence "cliques" in the Mideast and in Latin America, but it was the latter region that caused the greatest anxiety. The Bormann Life stated: "Catholicism is the faith of 200 million Latin Americans. An authoritarian form of government is the tradition. [But] large German communities have become quiescent as the fortunes of war turned against the Fatherland. These same factors of religion and totalitarian habits, however, will create a climate of acceptance for Nazis. We cannot pretend to have done more [during anti-Axis intelligence operations] than disrupt secret communications and in general make it difficult for Hitler to make use of the resources he had available here. The Nazi design in the western hemisphere * has been frustrated. The Nazi-type mind will persist. . . .

"Should Martin Bormann and leading German personalities succeed in concealing themselves, it is more than likely that they will antagonize their host-countries. It may be necessary, having regard to the foreseeable difficulties in extradition, to keep Bormann under constant surveillance. . . . A situation could arise where escaping leaders may be induced to waste their energies and exhaust their resolve in the *machismo* of the region."

The realists who had to study possible future developments were taking the hard view that if Bormann did escape through an Allied net which was bound to be poorly drawn around Europe in chaos, then he might be more useful in the end as a stalking horse.

* President Roosevelt said in October 1941 that a map obtained from Nazi sources "confirmed the Nazi design in South America against the United States." It showed a net of communications that would link centers in a nazified South America. Colombia was the centerpiece of New Spain, which would be General Franco's reward for passively supporting Hitler. "This proposed reorganization of South America," said Roosevelt, "includes our great lifeline, the Panama Canal."

CHAPTER 25

As a figure who disturbs humanity's conscience, Bormann had his effect among the Soviets, too. In all the reviews of his life, apart from that one semiofficial report by Lev Bezymenski, scant attention has been paid to the Soviet and East German side of the story. The basic facts originated in the West during a period when Russian historians were not co-operative. The new material of more recent years tends to be overlooked. The leakage of Allied analytical reports, for instance, was never a possibility when the Bormann puzzle exercised a number of brilliant minds. Yet it is clear now that Stalin was informed of the "soft" attitude toward some escaping Nazis by Kim Philby, the Russian spy at the top who was promoted in 1945 to head the new British Secret Intelligence Service section for operations against the Soviet Union. Nothing seems incredible after that. Philby had been in charge of the Iberian desk of the wartime SIS. Dr. Otto John, a trusting German bearing messages from the plotters against Hitler, was frustrated when his reports through British agents in Lisbon and Madrid produced no action. John never understood until the mid-1960's that his dangerous missions were to no avail because the hidden chief in London was stuffing his reports where they would never be seen. Philby shared with the Soviets a deep distrust of any communication between the Germans and the British. He had no intention of permitting a secret alliance, even with German rebels against Hitler.

So there were missing links in the Bormann story until Philby broke cover and told the world that he had been all along a Soviet agent. Philby's particular contribution to the puzzle is that his British secret-service job *required* him to study the problem of postwar Nazis. He was one of the senior men permitted to read the major proso profile on Bormann, in which the possibility was raised that the Nazi leader might escape. Philby's new job, opening an intelligence offensive against Russia because of the Cold War, was even more ironical. It meant that he knew all the details of the hiring of General Gehlen and his crew of German specialists on Communist affairs.

There is another important piece in the puzzle to which earlier students would have given little heed. Gestapo Müller, whose grave was clearly marked and honored year after year in West Berlin, was never buried there at all. He was the most wanted war criminal after Bormann. We know now that it is more than probable he was in Russian hands within a few hours of leaving Bormann. Many of the facts and much of the circumstantial evidence pointing to Gestapo Müller as the highly placed informer for the Russians inside the Third Reich have revealed themselves in recent times.

These additional pieces, if accepted, alter the shape of the final picture. The Philby piece must be accepted. There is no further dispute about his loyalty to Stalin from long before the war. Müller is not a case history that has been examined before, yet it is fair to assume that what the chief of the Gestapo knew about the inner secrets of Hitler's court was also known to Stalin. This explains some oddities of Russian behavior, and it also suggests that Stalin had some reasons for his insistence that his wartime allies were not entirely frank about the fate of wanted men.

The breakdown in communication between the Soviets and the Western Allies required folly in both partners. The distrust led to the pursuit of narrow selfish aims. Today the West cannot be sure if some branches of Brotherhood and related agencies were made to function, knowingly or not, on behalf of the Soviets; any more than they can be sure if the reverse is true. It can be fairly argued, for instance, that the Nazis in Cairo helped Russia by creating, or at least increasing, dissensions in the Mideast. This, indeed, was the view of individual American, British, and French diplomats and political leaders, who were sufficiently appalled in some cases to resign during the first Suez crisis.

The public suffers from secrecy, as always. Looking back, it is hard to justify the treatment of postwar Nazi affairs as top secret. Secret from whom? The governments and religious agencies involved in humanitarian work in the wreckage of Europe, if they needed protection from some unpalatable facts, could have weathered the storm. As it was, we cut ourselves off from what little the Russians were willing to tell us and a good deal of information that other Communist forces in Europe then had. We seemed to think we had a monopoly of the really significant information.

There are certain facts beyond dispute about what Stalin knew at the end of the war, not all of them taken into consideration in

290

earlier speculation about Bormann's fate. He knew that serious Allied attention was given to the desirability of letting some Nazi figures run loose. His troops had found those "incredibly important party documents" that Bormann ordered Scarface Skorzeny to rescue from a forest. Skorzeny told the Western Allies that he arrived too late and that the files, together with high-ranking German officers captured in Berlin, informed the Red Army General Staff's Fourth Bureau—the most successful of Soviet intelligence agencies —about plans for escape into the West. Stalin was fully informed on secret negotiations between leading Nazis and the Allies before the war ended. He knew that the Vatican regarded his empire as by far a greater threat than the German Reich. He had German intelligence papers listing 20,000 "safe houses" in Switzerland alone where Nazi collaborators could catch their breath and plan the transfer of funds for a possible Fourth Reich. And it is known now, after the 1963 Felfe scandal, that from the very beginning of the Gehlen Org's spying activities against the Soviets, most information fed by Gehlen to the West during the Cold War was already known by Moscow to be reaching us.

So the secrecy of those days, difficult to recall now until we remember the tragic aftermath of the Un-American Activities Committee and the witch hunt of Senator Joseph McCarthy's boys, served nobody more than the Axis ideologues and those Nazi survivors who had always dreamed of war between "civilization," led by Germany, and the Bolsheviks.

American commanders in the field, on the other hand, had a strong sense of the need to get on good terms with their Communist allies. General Walter Bedell Smith told Eisenhower's intelligence chief, Sir Kenneth Strong, that the U.S. regarded Russia as the country of the future. "I was a little surprised," Strong confessed in his memoirs, "but he was only repeating what many Americans were thinking at the time." This impulse was quickly discouraged by the Russians themselves.

Of course the Russians bore a great responsibility for the multiplication of suspicions on both sides. Their record in *prewar* Germany was an ugly one, and worth looking at more closely because it prepared the way for Bormann's role as an unconscious source of information for the Russians. There might have been some foundation for a *postwar* alliance with Russia, all the same, if a breakdown in trust had not started all over again with the sudden and still-controversial suicide of Himmler. No record was ever published of the last-minute babbling of a man whose name was synonymous with the planned mass murder of whole populations in order to improve the human breed. This struck the Russians as odd at the time, this sudden burial in an unmarked grave of a man who knew so much. It coincided, in time and place, with the discovery that the Western Allies were buying the Nazi expert on Russian affairs, General Gehlen.

All through the war, the only terms offered to Germany were "unconditional surrender." The purpose of inflicting an unmistakable defeat was to show Germans the dimensions of their crimes, to demonstrate the outrage of civilized society, to emphasize that any nation guilty of such barbaric behavior must expect to be punished. President Roosevelt had spoken for all the Allies when he said that only in this way could Germans be stopped from reviving the old stab-in-the-back theory which made them feel betrayed by World War I and its aftermath, and justified in embarking upon the Nazi path to the second war. Yet already it must have seemed to the Russians that this stubborn refusal to make deals with Nazis had changed. Here was Himmler, one minute in British hands and ready to talk his head off, and the next minute apparently dead, with nothing confided about his disclosures of Nazi escape plans. He must have known those plans, the Russians would have reasoned; they themselves had a good idea of the continuing help given to fascist groups by those institutions with an almost paranoid hatred of Communism. Allowing for the confusion at the end of the war in Europe, the best that can be said is that the most disastrous event of all, the disappearance of Bormann, came at a bewildering time for everyone. Yet he was the legally appointed leader of the Nazi movement, entrusted with all the works of the prophet.

Stalin understood the significance of Bormann's position as leader of a party that required no territorial definition. The title was like that of a Communist party theoretician. There was no compulsion to put assassins on Bormann's trail, as Stalin had done with Trotsky. What the Russians could do, and had demonstrated their skill at doing in Trotsky's case, was put a tail on Bormann and other fugitives. Meanwhile, there must have been some sense of outrage when Stalin's agents read Philby's summary of the Bormann proso profile, which examined his chances of escape. There was no sinister design behind it. Stalin in isolation would not have seen it that way. The projection of Bormann's possible actions was only one of many documents of that time; but the Soviets had a traditional fear of, and therefore a selective eye for, conspiracy.

A brief chronology of events that span a period of Soviet interest in Bormann suggests some interesting possibilities.

- *1942:* A senior American diplomat, George F. Kennan, an expert on Russia, proposes that the Western Allies remove Nazi officials after the war but retain all the central authorities in order to unify Europe, a proposal that would revive all Stalin's fears. (Kennan later wrote in his memoirs that the "Russians, determined to exploit the economic potential of Western Germany and Western Europe and fearful of being excluded from having a voice in these regions, would not hear of anything along these lines.")
- *1943:* Nazi officials begin secret talks with Allied contacts about the possibility of overthrowing Hitler. This is wrongly interpreted as indicating to Stalin that within the Western Alliance there is readiness to consider treating with a new Germany against Russia.
- *1945, April:* President Roosevelt cables Stalin: "I cannot avoid a feeling of bitter resentment toward your informers, whoever they are, for such vile misrepresentations of my actions or those of my trusted subordinates." This is the stinging reply to a message from Stalin complaining about negotiations in Switzerland between Allen Dulles, General Karl Wolff, and others. Roosevelt says there is no question of any agreement with the Germans: "Your information must have come from German sources."
- *1945, July 17:* Stalin tells Secretary of State James Byrnes that he believes Hitler is alive in Argentina or Spain.
- *1945, August 31:* Russians broadcast a claim that Bormann is in Allied hands. Montgomery's British headquarters replies: "We have not got him. That is definite, and it is not believed that the Americans have him."
- *1945, September:* Russian commission of inquiry reports no trace of Hitler but insists there is irrefutable proof of a small plane flying in the direction of Hamburg on April 30, and departure of a submarine from Hamburg with "mysterious persons on board."
- *1947/48:* Martin Bormann is reported to have arrived under another name in Argentina.
- *1955:* General Gehlen reports confidentially that his men have evidence Bormann escaped. He is told to keep silent. Meanwhile, others, like the Nazi propagandist Werner Naumann, have changed their stories about Bormann's fate. Naumann now claims, having been with him on the fateful night, that Bormann was seen to rejoin his real masters, the Russians.
- *1963:* Kim Philby, once in line as overlord of all British secret-service operations, vanishes and turns up in Moscow.

- *1964:* A Russian intelligence major produces a report which is published, an unusual procedure, tracing Bormann's movements until his departure for Argentina.
- *1965:* West German authorities dig up a park in West Berlin, hoping to prove Bormann is dead.
- *1971:* General Gehlen, no longer chief of West German intelligence, publishes his statement that Bormann was known to be alive in the 1950's. However, he says Bormann was seen in Russia.

General Gehlen was probably right for the wrong reasons; or wrong for the right reasons, depending on your point of view. There was plenty of evidence available to him in the mid-1950's that Bormann had escaped; and later it became expedient to say that he went back to his spiritual home in Russia. When Gehlen made that statement, Kim Philby had returned to Moscow and, as is known, was advising the Soviet authorities on psychological warfare and the manipulation of the information media. Soon after Philby disclosed his real loyalty, the Russian account of Bormann's escape was published. Then Dr. Otto John, who had been deeply involved in 1945 in the questioning of major German military and political leaders, suddenly bethought himself of the real reason for his being kidnapped while working as the British-appointed chief of West German security. It had everything to do with Philby and the possibility of past alliances between the West and German militarists; and the potential for a future alliance of that sort.

This obsession with Germany's power, past and future, cannot be overestimated where the Russians are concerned. They placed Philby in the center of Anglo-German friendship associations even before the Spanish Civil War because they suspected an identity of purpose between Western industrialists and the Ruhr barons. Their involvement in Germany went deeper and had strong historical roots. Germany was once regarded as the future base of international Communist strength. Germany had produced Karl Marx. It is not a fantastic notion to suppose that if the British Establishment could be penetrated to its most secret heart by a Soviet agent with impeccable English credentials, this could be done in Germany. Indeed, it would be incredible to suppose that the Soviets were *not* successful in a country far less insular and clubbish, and far more vulnerable to political extremes of action.

The most vivid account of Gestapo Müller's qualifications as Stalin's eyes and ears in the heart of the Third Reich came from Walter Schellenberg, who had to consult frequently with Müller. They had destroyed the Rote Kapelle, the Red Orchestra. (This

Russian espionage group can be discounted so far as this particular aspect of Stalin's operations is concerned. It was involved in the daily drudgery of espionage and was broken up in 1943, which rules out its director, Leopold Trepper, despite claims that he was a kind of genius spy.) Schellenberg noted in his published diaries that he was discussing the intellectual aspects of treason when Gestapo Müller began an astonishing and self-revealing diatribe against Nazi half-heartedness. "National-Socialism is nothing more than a sort of dung on this spiritual desert. In Russia there's an uncompromising and unified spiritual and biological force. The communists' global aim of spiritual and material world revolution offers a positive electrical charge to our western negativism."

Schellenberg recorded that he thought Müller was drunk and talking too much, and yet was also fishing for some response from Schellenberg. They were alone. They had been talking all night. The war was approaching its end. Müller said: "Everything we do is half-attempted and half-done. Himmler is only strong when Hitler is behind him. Bormann is a man who knows what he wants. . . ."

Schellenberg was surprised. He had thought Müller regarded Bormann purely as a criminal. He said: "Comrade Mueller, let's all start saying 'Heil Stalin!'—and our little father Mueller will become head of the Russian secret police."

Gestapo Müller was a dour man. He gave the spy chief a long hard look. "And when that happens," he said, "you'll be for the long drop—you and your bourgeois friends."

If Müller was, as Schellenberg later decided, at least to his own satisfaction, the source of high-level leaks to Moscow, then the possibility is raised that the Brotherhood was made an instrument of long-range plans for a resurgent and reunited Germany under Soviet tutelage. The possibility of the German military caste drifting back to its old ties with Russia had always been recognized. Gestapo Müller, with the freedom to pry into every corner of the Third Reich, would have known where potential recruits might be found. He seems, at this distance, much the likelier candidate as the silent observer for Stalin. We know that the Kremlin's information was sometimes lopsided: a private conversation between the Führer and a top general, for instance, was reported on Moscow radio a few hours later with fair accuracy as a propaganda device. Sometimes there were woeful misinterpretations, as if the unseen watcher lacked some wider statesmanlike ability to assess events. The flight of Hess, for example, was grossly distorted, as Stalin made clear in his conversations with Beaverbrook; and this distortion would not have been Bormann's work, because he knew all the circumstances leading to that escapade.

Russian inside knowledge of Nazi affairs became more apparent when the tensions relaxed again. The Premier of Poland, Jozef Cyrankiewicz, following the hanging of Bormann's friend Rudolf Höss, talked knowledgeably to me of the Bormann clique and its plans to preserve Nazi philosophy.

When, unable to escape these shadows, I followed up this Polish lead, it was through the Red Orchestra's director, Leopold Trepper, who had used a doctored Canadian passport. It was issued to Michael Dzumaga, of Winnipeg, and was taken from a dead Canadian volunteer in Spain. The passport was altered, as usual, and in it appeared Trepper's cover name, Adam Miklas, and his photograph.

A record of the false passport had shown up in old Gestapo files. After the war, foreign documents were referred back to the country of origin. The Canadian security authorities had been asked if they knew this citizen, Miklas, who joined the Nazis. Investigators were puzzled when they found that the doctored passport and other papers that belonged to Trepper had been stored in the private safe of Müller.

Heinrich Müller, "the thick-headed Bavarian," was at one time head of the anti-Communist section of Göring's early Nazi secret police. He had the reputation of being a fanatical anti-Communist, but on closer scrutiny this proved to be a ruse to continue his professional career as a Munich police detective in the Third Reich. He had won Bormann's good will by disposing of the scandal surrounding Hitler's murdered niece; and his career then rocketed.

Müller progressed along with Bormann, their fates closely interwoven. He had the opportunity and authority, as nobody else had, to look over Bormann's shoulder. Even Hitler, by reason of his position as Führer, lacked the freedom to display an interest in every small detail of all that went on within the Third Reich.

Müller disappeared at the same time as Bormann. Someone went to a lot of trouble to borrow bones taken from three men and place them in the Berlin military cemetery, where the grave was marked with his name and brief history.

A knowledgeable source, Marshal Tito, in his unpublished diaries, has taken the view that Müller was the Russian informer whose presence was always suspected but never proved. Tito was a militant young man caught up in the great trade-union movements that swirled through Germany in those days. His later career as Partisan leader has tended to obscure the years he spent as a Russian agent; one so successful that, almost alone among foreign Communist leaders recalled to Moscow during Stalin's great purge, he escaped death there.

Tito's belief is supported nowadays by Western intelligence experts who studied the period. The view is that Gestapo Müller was recruited when the German Communist party was approaching its peak membership of a quarter-million in 1928. It had twenty-seven newspapers, 4,000 known cells, and an unknown number of underground agents.

Müller was dispatched to the Soviet Union to study the police system there. It seems significant that he was always accused of trying to model the Gestapo on the Soviet secret police, in whose hands he was during the period he spent (with the Nazi party's own approval) in Moscow. When he came back, Germany was the arena for the largest spy network in the world, according to Tito, who was then working as a Comintern agent in a German factory. He recalls that the workers were told they were not being disloyal in giving technical information to the Soviet Union because this would help in the struggle for the dictatorship of the proletariat.

Later, Müller led a drive against Communists from his post on the Communism desk of Section VI at Munich police headquarters. But this purge coincided with the great power struggle inside Moscow, and hundreds of leading agents were being recalled to the Soviet Union only to face execution squads. Müller thus gave a convincing demonstration of anti-Communist diligence to the Nazis by knocking off those Communists who would have been liquidated anyway. He became the tireless foe of Communists. His reports covered every detail from small cells to the organizational structure of Moscow's police agencies. Heydrich was so impressed that he put Müller in charge of the destruction of courier posts, fake passport rings, and other paraphernalia. From the Russian point of view, it would be worth sacrificing a few thousand doubtful comrades to build up the credibility of a very senior agent.

A similar performance was given in Britain by Kim Philby, who joined the Anglo-German Fellowship to prove *his* anti-Communism to his bosses, and went on to become the most highly placed Soviet agent in Britain. Both Müller, the rabid Gestapo man, and Philby, the supposedly dedicated anti-Communist, could thus maneuver themselves into positions where they took charge of secret operations that enabled them to dispose of incriminating evidence against top-level Soviet agents. The purge of the 1930's helped Müller strengthen his good name with the Nazi leadership, in the same manner that Philby was proving his worthiness to a section of the British ruling class which, pre-Munich, was on good terms with German industrialists and not actively hostile to the National Socialist philosophy. Philby went to the Spanish Civil War on the side of the fascists and was decorated by Franco with the Cross of the Order of Military Merit.

The Philby story was exploited by the Russians once it was known to the world at large. The story of Müller was *not* given to the psychological-warfare experts in Moscow. The Red Army Fourth Bureau, like any other police or intelligence agency, gives away nothing unless forced to do so, either by outside exposure of the facts or because it hopes to get something back in return. This was evident when the Warsaw government refused to let Leopold Trepper leave Poland. He was notorious as the "Soviet master spy" in Hitler's Germany. It seemed to explain how Stalin knew so much of events inside the Nazi court. Yet in fact Trepper's Red Orchestra was already destroyed by the time the war with Russia was under way. If Trepper had rendered such great services to Communism, why was he held virtually prisoner even by 1973? He was old, very sick, and by normal standards his dedication and service should have entitled him to be granted his last great wish: to go to Israel, where he could die among his own people.

"He could still talk too much," I was told. "He was caught in 1942 and his spy ring was destroyed by the winter of that year." The informant was a former French resistance man now with the DST counterespionage section in Paris. "Trepper was made a Soviet hero because it was a means to distract attention from the mystery of where Stalin *did* get his information. But Stalin was still getting that information *after* the Red Orchestra had been totally cleaned up."

Müller's secret role would help explain the strange business of former Deputy Führer Rudolf Hess. The Russians insisted, even in 1973, that he alone should be kept in the fortress prison of Spandau, one man and 599 empty cells; one man guarded in rotation by the Russians, the French, the Americans, and the British. In this island of eight acres in Berlin, surrounded by machine-gun posts and electrified fences, this solitary man, now age seventy-eight and very ill, this victim of Bormann's rapacity, was kept prisoner on the insistence of the Russians and in the face of humanitarian appeals from other governments. Winston Churchill, not noted for his generosity toward Nazis, had long ago written: "I am glad not to be responsible for the way in which Hess has been and is being treated. Whatever may be the moral guilt of a German who stood near to Hitler, Hess atoned for this by his completely devoted and fanatic deed of benevolence."

The Russians had agreed to release every other war criminal incarcerated in Spandau, but never Hess. The old man was allowed to see his family for half an hour at Christmas. The Russians insisted, over the objections of the other three powers responsible for Spandau, that Hess must not in any way have physical contact with his wife or son; that his family must be thoroughly searched; and that they must undertake to reveal nothing of what was said during the short conversation.

Hess might as well be dead. If the Soviet member of the tribunal that sentenced him, Major General I. T. Nikitchenko, had his way, the Deputy Führer would have been sentenced to death anyway. What did he know that the Russians feared? During his captivity in Britain he had talked of a secret treaty between Hitler and Stalin defining spheres of interest in the event of war. This was not the Nazi-Soviet Pact of August 1939, but an agreement, signed at the same time, an infamous conspiracy between the Soviet Union and its class enemies, to plunder small nations.* The protocol preceded the invasion of Poland, which started World War II. The pretext for that invasion was an operation personally conducted by Gestapo Müller.

Müller was to drive "canned goods," consisting of concentration-camp inmates, to the Polish border. The prisoners would be clothed in Polish uniforms and at the last moment given lethal injections. German troops would stage a frontier incident in which it would be made to seem that Poland's soldiers had crossed into German territory. The "canned goods" would be presented as Polish troops shot on German soil. Foreign correspondents would be brought to the "battlefield" to see for themselves the bodies.

As head of the Gestapo, Müller was to convey the doomed prisoners from the camps to the border. Few Nazi leaders knew the details. The code words to start the operation were "Grandma

* The secret pact was confirmed by Ribbentrop at Nuremberg under cross-examination by Hess's defense counsel, Dr. Alfred Seidl. But the Soviet prosecutor, General Roman Rudenko, successfully objected to the production of a copy of the protocol.

dead." Hitler settled on August 26, 1939 for the invasion of Poland as the result of the "unprovoked attack," the proof of which would be the murdered prisoners.

Gestapo Müller was the only Nazi leader in a position, through his own empire of secret police, to warn Stalin of what was afoot. Martin Bormann was closeted with the Führer throughout this period. Müller, on the other hand, was extremely mobile because the plan required live Germans dressed in Polish uniform to make a mock attack from the Polish side of the frontier. There were 150 Polish uniforms to be found, troops to be briefed on what was represented as a military exercise, and the "canned goods" to be selected from concentration camps. In the event, the incident was postponed at zero hour, and Hitler finally pulled the trigger at dawn on September 1, 1939. POLISH INSURGENTS CROSS GERMAN FRONTIER was the *Voelkischer Beobachter* headline. The war had begun.

Stalin had known, in advance, the pretext for invasion. Baron Ernst von Weizsäcker, a former foreign state secretary, testified at the trial of Hess that "the secret protocol [between Hitler and Stalin] explicitly or implicitly was to create a completely new order in Poland. When it came into operation, a line of demarcation was followed. In the Soviet sphere were included Finland, Estonia, Latvia, the eastern parts of Poland and certain parts of Roumania. Everything west of that line was left to Germany. . . ."

That was undoubtedly why Hess remained in jail in 1973 despite Allied pleas for mercy. He, too, could say too much.

SS Lieutenant General Heinrich Müller has been described in Allied intelligence studies as a cold and secretive personality: "A man with an imposing head and sharp features, curiously disfigured by a thin gash of a mouth that had no lips."

His name was not on the list the Russians recovered from the Führer's bunker after the Battle of Berlin. Yet survivors have testified that he was there until Hitler's suicide, reporting to the Führer each day from his office. When he vanished, he made a good job of it. All his files on the continuing investigation into Hitler's family history from 1934 to 1943 were missing, too. If the Russians collected them, they never said so.

After the British secret service, working in 1963 through a cooperative German official, had "Müller's" grave opened, and after pathologists agreed that none of the bones could have been those of Müller, certain matters were recalled that were overlooked before.

In the twilight of the Third Reich, discussions centered on making new overtures to the Western Allies in the hope of a last-minute front against Communism. Müller was vehement in opposing such proposals. Three survivors whose relationships with Müller were totally different have each described separately his attempts to stop negotiations with the West. These were Felix Kersten, the masseur; Count Schwerin von Krosigk, the Finance Minister, who became briefly the Foreign Minister in Admiral Doenitz's rump government, and spy chief Walter Schellenberg. The latter suspected Müller was delaying matters until the Russians had overrun Berlin.

Near Müller's office was that of Adolf Eichmann, Gestapo chief in charge of the "Jewish problem." Müller was handing out certificates, which many SS men used later, attesting that they had worked for civilian firms in the past few years. He was annoyed when Eichmann waved his Steyr army pistol and said that was a good enough pass to freedom or death. "This document," Müller is reported to have told Eichmann, "is more than a pass. *It will tell us where you are.*"

Was this Müller's new task—to follow the fortunes of the Brotherhood? He was one of the gang and knew the various plans for escape. When General Hans Krebs, Hitler's last Chief of Staff, tried to negotiate with General Vassili Chuikov, commander of the Eighth Guards Army, he was rebuffed and made his way back to the Führer's bunker, whose Führer was now dead. He rejected the role of fugitive, condemned to roam the world like a hunted criminal, and snarled at Werner Naumann that "civilians are welcome to dive into Müller's rathole." Much later, reversing his original story that he did not know where Bormann went after escaping from the bunker, Naumann said he believed the "Fourth Führer" had sheltered in Müller's cellar before setting off on the long road to safety.

The shelter used by Müller in the last days was not the Gestapo bunker but another one used by the secret-police chief in the complex around Bormann's party chancellery. There is something more than mere symbolism in this constant proximity between Müller and Bormann. It provides an explanation for the consistent doubts and suspicions directed at Bormann by Admiral Canaris, while he was still chief of military intelligence. Canaris was a technologist. He was not so much pro-Western, as anti-Communist; and in his practical way, he looked at what a powerful Soviet empire could do militarily and the prospect appalled him. One of his underlings was a counterespionage radioman, Wilhelm Flicke, who monitored illicit transmissions between Berlin, Switzerland, and Moscow. After two years' detective work, Flicke traced the source of radio transmissions to Moscow. It was the cluster of ministerial buildings in Berlin. He refined his findings and concluded that only Bormann's had the necessary transmitters. The party chancellery, in fact, had its own communication system linking Bormann's Gauleiter and other officials loyal to him personally. Flicke's death in 1957 is still a matter for conjecture in German police circles. At all events, he reported his suspicions in a dutiful manner, up through the chain of command to Canaris. The Admiral was recorded by his assistant, Paul Leverkühn, as saying soon afterward that he was extremely worried at the possibility of the Red Orchestra net having links inside Hitler's headquarters, "possibly to Bormann."

Others who concluded that Bormann was a "brown Bolshevik" may well have been confused in a similar way. They were making informed guesses, based on inexplicable events, of which Bormann seemed to be the center. It was understandable that they should overlook the chief of the secret police, whose job included that of ferreting out anti-Nazis and lukewarm supporters of Hitler. It was also dangerous to hint at doubts regarding Müller. His Gestapo had agents everywhere. Who would dare voice suspicion, let alone put his name to a piece of paper? Once the finger of suspicion pointed in the direction of the party chancellery, wishful thinking and fear of the secret police took over. Bormann was universally disliked, although he wielded great power. But in 1942, Canaris and others who felt uneasy about Bormann did not realize just how much more power he wielded than anyone else. They prudently put aside doubts about Müller's loyalty. Was he not the most rabid of anti-Communists in the early 1930's? Unhappily for Canaris, his comparatively loose talk against Bormann led to his execution before the war ended.

There were many prominent German figures after the war who joined the chorus of accusations against Bormann. Their backgrounds sometimes put their motives in question. There was SS Lieutenant General Gottlob Berger, who sought Allied patronage for his anti-Communist dedication. His was the office that issued the military handbooks describing Russians as subhuman. He told the Wilhelmstrasse trial (one of the war-crimes trials that followed the International Military Tribunal at Nuremberg) that he felt Bormann "did the greatest harm of anybody," and that Bormann would reappear at the proper time as the Soviet-backed commissar of a Communist Germany.

Men like Berger were just as easily fooled by anti-Communist talk as they themselves fooled others. Berger was one of many convicted war criminals who got early clemency; in his case, twenty-five years were cut down to three. The Gehlen Org had played host to the best Russian spies in the business because they paraded their Gestapo and SS backgrounds, and talked convincingly of their hatred for the Bolsheviks.

What were the advantages to anyone who manipulated the Brotherhood behind the scenes?

• *Propaganda:* Most of the old Nazis were not politically adjusted to the postwar need for subtlety. Their behavior was an embarrassment to Germans who wanted to let memories die. The Brotherhood encouraged them to overplay their hands and provided grist for Communist propaganda mills. The former Waffen SS, for instance, reorganized itself as the Mutual Aid Committee (HIAG) in the front line against Bolshevism. When Stalin proposed the reunification of Germany in 1952, he took the Western Powers by surprise. They were arming their Germany in a policy of strength. To have Hitler's old associates mobilized against Russia was distressing and confusing for young Germans indoctrinated by the West immediately after the war to believe remilitarization was bad. They were told on the one hand that Hitler's regime had been evil and discovered on the other hand that Hitler's crusade against Communism continued in a new guise.

• *Espionage:* The Brotherhood provided a network into solidly anti-Communist countries and into West Germany. The lists of former thugs, police bosses, and other guilty men under Hitler were invaluable to the Communists for purposes of blackmail. Death-camp officers received certificates "proving" they were innocently working elsewhere as a protection against arrest by the Allies. Blackmail victims included the ex-SS men who infiltrated the Gehlen Org. Heinz Felfe, Hans Clemens, and Erwin Tiebel, who for ten years sold the Soviets everything about federal intelligence, had been promised amnesty for their crimes by the KGB. There was also the overlap between former Nazis and SS men working both sides of the street. ("Professionals" who worked in the German secret services during the war were forbidden by the military governments to work for Allied intelligence. At the same time, they were being secretly recruited as spies by all sides. An attempt by Dr. Otto John to create a central register, to prevent the postwar crop of spies from simply selling information to all interested parties was quickly frustrated.)

Some members of the Brotherhood would collaborate with the Soviets while exploiting the capitalist system and taking American

303

money. There are many recorded examples of Germans who did this. The matter is not really in dispute. The military caste kept its own "brotherhood" links across the great divide between East and West Germany. Other ex-Nazis could be manipulated without their knowledge. Always, there was the prospect of a reunified Germany: desired for political reasons by many in Bonn, and for economic as well as political reasons in the East. Germans who looked beyond the Cold War foresaw a time when large financial interests in Latin America, and strong blood ties with German communities, would become part of a new drive toward a different kind of German imperialism. This was not necessarily, by the 1970's, a prospect that would distress the Soviets. In the early days of the Revolution, there had been a fruitful partnership between Bolshevik Russia and the German military caste and its industrial and aristocratic partners. That partnership foundered when the Soviet Union lost control of the situation. Nearly three decades of Communist government in East Germany after the war, however, had provided the Russians with a pretty fair knowledge of the direction in which young Germans were likely to go.

The earlier experiment in partnership began when Trotsky was still active in Russia. His friend was the chief of German military intelligence after World War I, Colonel Walter Nicolai. They agreed that the Soviet Union should make the arms forbidden Germany under the Treaty of Versailles. German officers, in exchange, placed their expertise at the disposal of the Red Armies. Germany had neither tanks, heavy guns, an air force, nor a navy. Its tiny army was limited by the Versailles agreements to 100,000 men. The Soviet Union lacked officers. After Trotsky vanished from the scene, Nicolai kept up his contacts through the Soviet secret service. Nicolai created a business corporation that cheated the treaty limitations and arranged for the production of German poison gas in Siberia, Junker bombers near the Urals, submarines and battleships at Leningrad. Until 1930, a third of the annual budget of the German government plus 120 million "stabilized marks" went into the secret cartel. The "Black" German Army trained a 20,000-man tank corps in the middle regions of the Volga. Before leaving for Russia, each soldier had his name erased from army lists. Prototypes of German planes and tanks, developed in German workshops, went in sections to the Soviet factories through the free port of Stettin. In this way the men and weapons that later reduced cities like Stalingrad to rubble were produced on Russian training grounds and in Russian factories.

Colonel Nicolai simply drew on past entanglements. The German Army had traditional ties with Russia. Even before the Bolsheviks were in the Russian saddle, it was German troops who watched over the sealed train that carried Lenin and his comrades from Switzerland to take control of the Revolution. Stalin's decision to give the Nazis secret support in 1929 when Hitler needed money was an attempt to keep up these good relations.

It was, of course, all much too cozy. Stalin and Hitler had a common interest in dividing Poland but they were not compatible. The secret partnership led inevitably to the great Red Army purges of 1937, when thousands of Russian officers were executed on suspicion of treason and espionage for Germany.

Hitler, on his side, had wanted to break the power of the German General Staff. He let the Russian bloodletting speak for itself. There had always been a pro-Russian faction within the German Army, in his opinion. The greatest anxiety after 1945 among German liberals was that the military caste would maintain its traditional sympathies. In East Germany, the career soldiers found jobs within the Communist regime and were integrated with Soviet forces. It raised another real possibility that there were successors to Colonel Nicolai whose sympathies were with Moscow, like Gestapo Müller. One of the forgotten footnotes to history which now takes on dramatic significance is that when Hitler wanted Nicolai interrogated for alleged pro-Soviet activities in 1943, it was Gestapo Müller who stopped the investigation on his own authority.

CHAPTER 26

The vital pieces in the puzzle had been in the rag bag of my memory a long time. As happens so often, they turned up unexpectedly and lay there unrecognized. They had to do with the protection given by SS General Heinrich Müller's Gestapo to another man now celebrated officially by the Soviet Union as Stalin's greatest spy.

First I must explain how a seemingly trivial series of conversations produced those odd bits of information, which possibly make everything else fit together. As a Canadian, I was able to fly to Hanoi during the early days of Communist occupation because this was part of Canadian membership on the international truce commission. I crossed swords in Hanoi with a brilliant member of the commission who represented Poland. She struck me, frankly, as a dragon. Then I met her on the long and tiresome flight between Hanoi, Peking, and Moscow, during which she turned out to be charming and extremely funny in her criticisms of Russian bureaucracy. How I came to make that flight is another story; how she came to be on it, I shall never know. Nevertheless, I was satisfied that it had no sinister implications, because the lady did most of the talking, and most of what she said would have raised the hair on the venerable heads of the Central Committee of the One True Party.

She had worked in Mexico as the correspondent for the Polish state-run news agency, using that country as a base to cover the whole of Latin America, much of which was of course closed to a Communist, however charmingly feminine. We talked about the man who assassinated Trotsky in Mexico, whom I had confronted in his cell. The dedication of the killer to his Communist gods struck me as fanatical to a terrifying degree. "It was positively medieval," I said.

We were trudging through the mud of a small airfield somewhere

306

in Siberia while the plane refueled. She smiled and looked away. "Russia *is* medieval," she said. "Stalin might be the last truly medieval tyrant. He commanded that kind of devotion because he was a replacement for God in the minds of people suddenly robbed of their religion. The killer's background was Spanish and Catholic, but he had rejected his national loyalties *and* his inherited beliefs."

"Did you know him?"

"Slightly. He was in that Mexican jail for a great many years. He never stopped being a fanatic. He was trained from childhood to carry out assignments of that nature for the Communist party and he transferred his loyalty to the party as if he was raised to become a missionary priest."

"Except missionaries save lives, surely?"

"He saw the destruction of Stalin's greatest enemy and philosophical rival as the saving of humanity."

"Trotsky was no great threat. Why concentrate all that effort on an old failure?"

"Stalin concentrated on every possible competitor. Against a real enemy like Hitler he was cunning and implacable."

"But he couldn't produce an assassin."

She stared across the field. "I think we're ready for take-off." She turned as quickly as she turned away from the subject.

Much later, I raised it again. This time she made no attempt to dodge the implied question. "Stalin had a potential assassin right inside Hitler's circle," she said. "What would be the point in killing Hitler?"

"He'd have saved a few million lives."

"And made Hitler a martyr. And revived the old German stab-in-the-back theory. If Hitler had been assassinated, believe me, the Nazis wouldn't have had to go into hiding. No, what was needed was a watchdog who would report back to Stalin and make it possible to bring about the *military* defeat of Germany and the destruction of German master-race ideas."

"Who was this watchdog?"

She shook her head. "Who knows."

In Warsaw, stopping over en route to New York, I had one more fling at the subject. Her husband also held a degree in international law. He had been involved in the trial of SS Colonel Josef Meisinger, the "Beast of Warsaw," a Gestapo butcher of the arrogant kind, crude, vulgar, bovine—a bastard. "He was," said the husband, "a great and long-standing friend of Gestapo Müller."

The lady who could be a dragon in North Vietnam was here the solicitous wife. She gave her husband an anxious glance.

"It's true," he insisted. "He was Müller's right-hand man from the start. I had to go through both their histories before Meisinger hanged. He was a detective on the same Munich crime squad. Imagine it! The secret police are all the same. They think they have a license to kill."

"But Gestapo Müller never did kill the man he should—"

"Hitler? Why murder the Führer? You make him a martyr and the Germans sorry for themselves again. Müller was there to destroy others and keep an eye on Hitler. You will find Müller systematically got rid of some monsters but he was careful with Bormann and the Führer. The first was his source of information, though Bormann never knew it. Hitler was the symbol of evil, someone we could resist. It's more difficult to resist an idea than it is to hate an individual. Gestapo Müller, if only the story could be told, was the hero—"

At this point his wife, very sensibly from their point of view, cut him short.

A fascinating new line of inquiry had been opened up by this conversation. Gestapo Müller now seemed to have covered the tracks of the most celebrated of Russian spies. This was Richard Sorge, a fully certified member of the Nazi party, who filed reports through the German News Agency from Tokyo.

But Richard Sorge informed Stalin in advance of every projected Japanese move since 1937. He gave the date of Hitler's invasion of Russia. He provided the vital information that Japan would not attack Russia's Far Eastern bases when Stalin was weighing his defenses and wondering if he could risk keeping Siberian troops for the protection of Moscow.*

Sorge's cover as a German newsman became suspect in Berlin. In the winter of 1940, Schellenberg was still only Deputy Chief of the Security Service's foreign intelligence section and he was checking the reliability of German embassies abroad. He sent Meisinger, the future Beast of Warsaw, to work on the case. Meisinger duly reported back that the Japanese agencies believed Sorge was a Russian spy.

---

* By 1972, Sorge was publicly recognized as a Soviet Union Hero, with his name on a Soviet tanker and a Moscow street and his profile (much improved by the artist) on a four-kopek postage stamp.

The report went to Gestapo Müller, who suppressed it. Then he persuaded Schellenberg, an eager listener, to forget the whole thing. It was absurd to suppose Sorge worked for anyone else. Besides, it would reflect badly on Schellenberg's department if such stupid gossip got around. The last thing Schellenberg needed, with one ambitious foot on the ladder of promotion, was to have an investigation that might demonstrate his own lack of good judgment.

Unhappily for Sorge, he was betrayed by one of his own Japanese subagents. He was hanged by the Japanese almost three years later. After his exposure, Ribbentrop asked Müller for the files on the case. All he got was the standard Gestapo card index. Müller had destroyed the rest. Gestapo Müller had never deviated from his original anti-Nazi position. This was erased from the record by his excessively conscientious work on behalf of Martin Bormann at the time Hitler murdered his niece in 1931. The inference is clear. Müller had been instructed to make every use of his special relationship with Bormann in order to report to his real masters in Moscow.

An official Soviet account of Sorge is curiously insistent that he was the greatest wartime spy—a posthumous award the Russians can afford, so long as others among their great agents are not exposed. More important and relevant here, the official history demonstrates the similarity in background of Sorge and Müller.

Richard Sorge fought bravely in the Kaiser's war and then floundered in the aftermath. Like Bormann and Müller and thousands of other young Germans, he found the chaos unbearable. And, like so many, he looked for extreme solutions. The choice between Communism and National Socialism for a thoughtful man was a choice between a system without heroes or the hero without a system. The Communist system promised order and loyalty to all men. Hitler demanded loyalty from all men and promised an organized system based upon totalitarian control.

Talent scouts were abroad in Germany, looking for men to fill a variety of jobs. This is known from innumerable sources today. At that time, it was not obvious. Sorge happened to fit one profile; Müller would have fitted another. Sorge was coal mining in the Ruhr for a time, and he became a founding member of the Communist party in Hamburg. He was different material from Müller. He was sent to Moscow for training and then dispatched abroad as a Comintern agent. He transferred to the Red Army's Fourth Bureau. The path he followed from this point onward was one that clearly ruled him out as an informer inside Hitler's circle.

Müller did not have obvious Communist connections. He had been active against the Nazis, it is true. But by 1930, when Sorge was tagged for operations abroad, what the talent spotters needed at home was a man who could work his way up through the central column of the Nazi party; a man who would have every excuse to gather material on the personalities of Hitler and his closest advisers. The Soviet Union already knew a great deal about the new military machine being forged in Germany, for it had played a large part in helping to produce it.

Looking back now, it is not so curious that my chance encounter in Hanoi should have started this reconstruction of events. Richard Sorge, on his way to build up the Russian spy ring in Japan, paused in Shanghai to acclimatize. There, his old comrades of the Comintern had been active. Shortly after he left, the British police tore apart the headquarters of the Comintern's Far East network, which was led by Hilaire Noulens, who carried the inevitable faked Canadian passport. One of his men was Nguyen Ai Quac, who surfaced much later and became a household word throughout the world as Ho Chi Minh. The British policeman who broke up the network later trained American OSS agents at the spy school in Canada set up by William Stephenson.

Both Bormann and Müller were out to destroy the one powerful man who might have changed the shape of postwar Europe. This was Admiral Canaris, who was in deep trouble by 1944. He had shifted suspicion from Bormann to Müller as the Russian informer. At the same time, he was resisting Bormann's efforts to make his military intelligence system a creature of Nazi party intrigues.

Admiral Wilhelm Franz Canaris had been a legend in both world wars. He was known as the "Grand Prince of Espionage," the "Admiral of Darkness." His intelligence net covered the globe. Bormann lusted after it. Its agents and collaborators in foreign police forces, its transport facilities, its communications, and its methods of distributing large funds in great secrecy, all these were vital to any future Brotherhood abroad. But it was necessary to break the hold that Canaris had upon it, and so the organization became the target of vicious rumors and gossip. It was said to be full of sexual perverts; Canaris was a masochist, a sadist, and an ambidextrous homosexual, too; his military intelligence system was full of traitors.

These accusations were nourished for different reasons by Gestapo

Müller. He probably at last recognized that Canaris, by a process of elimination, regarded him as the prime suspect. Flicke, the radioman who first detected signals from the party chancellery to Moscow, had started an investigation that could be stopped only by killing Canaris. The death warrant was signed in the chaos following the bomb plot against Hitler in 1944, although historians to this day argue about the Admiral's part in it. The balance of opinion is against Canaris having played a direct role, but the plot gave Kaltenbrunner an excuse to question the Admiral, for Bormann. That interrogation was brutal beyond description; an account of it was given by British agent Peter Churchill, held in the same Gestapo jail. Churchill escaped, and held the view that by the time Canaris was taken by the goon squads he was doomed. Bormann wanted control over the world-wide facilities of German military intelligence. Müller wanted to get rid of the man who was uncomfortably close to discovering where all the leaks to Stalin were coming from. Early in April 1945, Admiral Canaris, at the age of fifty-eight, was stripped naked and hoisted so that his head could be maneuvered through a loop of wire hanging from a butcher's hook on a pole in the prison yard. Movie cameras were set up, and the subsequent film was rushed to Hitler's personal labs, where Bormann supervised its processing in time for the nightly film show. The executioners made sure the looped wire was caught under the Admiral's chin and then they let him drop.

Two weeks later, German military intelligence itself died—officially. In a labyrinth of underground concrete-and-steel-lined tunnels, in the suburb of Wholdorf, outside Hamburg, the thud of Allied bombs had been muffled. Several thousand men and women had moved through these tunnels during the years, feeding information to foreign stations and decoding incoming messages. On April 26, 1945 the last signal went out: "Conditions compel us to suspend communications but please stand by on schedule once a week. Do not despair. We will look out for you and protect your interests as usual."

Someone else had taken over.

PART THREE

THE CONDEMNED

CHAPTER 27

The mystery of Martin Bormann is that nobody appears to care and yet so many are involved. For some, there is a primitive lust for revenge. Others, haunted by guilt or fear of exposure, are torn between a desire to bury the legend along with the corpse and an instinctive need to justify their role. Those who fought the Nazi terror before and during World War II sometimes wish to believe that it could happen only in one place and in one stage of man's history. Not too many of us are prepared to look into our own hearts and recognize pieces of the ultimate puzzle. This is not so much what happened to Bormann, instructive though this may be. The real puzzle is how a supposedly civilized society, not far removed from our own moral and material hopes and ambitions, nonetheless gave birth to Bormann's perverted vision of a brotherhood.

Nations, like individuals, suffer from the same mixed motives and fearful hesitations. Among the more enlightened, the rule of law is allowed to waver and bend but not to break. Idealism is never quite abandoned although it frequently needs the reassuring support of rationalization. There are other nations and organizations which do not feel the need for restraint because they have no declared burden of conscience.

For too many, self-interest is their estate, practicality the key to the gate. If there are exceptions, they are found among that half of the world's population today which was not even born when the Third Reich fell and Martin Bormann vanished. For them, this is history. And among a hopeful few, there is a need to know that transcends fear or meanness or self-justification or prejudiced revenge.

It is not too difficult to determine the motivation of those few private persons who seek to solve the riddle of Martin Bormann. One can ask and expect a reasonable reply. But what can one deduce about the motivations of nations and institutions? Do the efforts to prove that Bormann died in Berlin in 1945 have more to do with an entire society than they have to do with morbid curiosity? Do the dental mechanics, the forensic experts, the Berliners with sudden flashes of memory in the 1970's come to bury Bormann or to bury the past?

The nightmare will not stop. The Federal Frontier Force was authorized by the Bonn government in June 1972 to supervise demonstrations and strikes. Ex-SS General Paul Wilhelm Felix Boulay thus became entitled to order domestic searches, arrests on the spot, and confiscations. Boulay was a member of the Bandit-Fighting Units, which during the war had the power to conduct mass executions of villagers in Nazi-occupied Europe. He won the Iron Cross for his "untiring energy." The Bandit-Fighting Units were explained at Nuremberg by his colleague SS General Ernst Rode: "[Bandit Fighters] was another name for patriots. . . . The fight against bandits was an excuse for the systematic extermination of Jews."

The old German-American Bund, which used to propagandize Nazism in the United States in the 1930's was revived forty years later by a Bavarian Member of Parliament, Walter Becher, whose commentaries as a Nazi journalist dwelt upon the need to purify the Germanic peoples. Becher's new interests in his old age were the German-American Heritage Group and the Federation of American Citizens of German Descent. The latter, in its regular publication, the *Voice of Federation,* complained in 1972 that the West German press was in the hands of Jews and Reds.

Manifestations of patent eccentricity or examples of absent-minded bureaucracy? Then what about Judge Hans Heinsen, of the West Berlin Criminal Court, who was a Nazi party member and an SS officer? He solemnly affirmed that he had never been a member of the Nazi party when he was first appointed a judge. Now, say the legal authorities, he cannot be charged with fraud because five years have elapsed since he made his declaration.

Sara Neubeck was sent to a death camp because she was found guilty in 1941 of collecting money to help migrants in Brussels, presented as a treasonable activity by a Nazi state prosecutor named Hubert Schrübbers. Is this man qualified to be chief of the Federal Office for Protection of the Constitution, the job once held by Dr. Otto John?

And the nightmare grows.

It is plain that the great powers who fought together in the war against oppression have taken little trouble to clean up the pockets of Nazis and their sympathizers, who, in areas like the Mideast, have been free to pursue the same old hate campaigns as before. Arabic versions of *Mein Kampf,* for instance, were weapons in the war against Israel. The end of that dangerous book did not come with the end of its author. Kitbag editions of *Mein Kampf, Hitler & Nazism* were found among the personal possessions of Egyptian officers captured in the Sinai campaign. The Arab edition with its notes and commentaries is quoted as an authority on an alleged Zionist conspiracy. It continues to circulate because Brotherhood groups subsidize foreign printings. (*Mein Kampf* is banned in Germany, in effect, because the copyright is now held by the Bavarian state government, which consistently refuses a license even for a critically annotated edition.) Spanish editions circulate in Latin America, but Jewish organizations on the whole take this fairly calmly, arguing that few readers today are likely to take Hitler seriously. Nevertheless, the London *Jewish Chronicle* was sufficiently concerned in 1972 to run a column which said in part: "There are elements in the book—the promise of discipline, authority and order—which can be very attractive in our chaotic age, especially where the price paid for Hitler's new order is unknown or forgotten. Memories are short and the public remains oddly receptive to strange, even crazy ideas and to produce a book with the history of *Mein Kampf* at such a time is an act of moral abdication."

It is conceivable that pragmatic arguments have been put forward for tolerating the Brotherhood so long as it could be controlled and even utilized. It is hard to see what these arguments are, beyond the old police dictum of setting a thief to catch a thief. It may have led some searchers to secret sources of funds; and it is probable that the Brotherhood is loosely linked and each group concerned only with financial agreements and under-the-counter arrangements that defy public analysis. If the Western Powers have covertly made use of Brotherhood expertise in regions where they sought to counter Soviet influence, this can only lead to a debacle like that of the Gehlen Org. There disaster struck and the declared aims were totally frustrated because it was supposed that a fervent Nazi was necessarily an anti-Communist. A fervent Nazi is not necessarily anything but a fervent Nazi.

The return of many German exiles can be explained on the grounds of old age, nostalgia, and of course a growing sense of confidence that the courts are not really keen to punish the big offenders.

The return of confidence was evident in the activities of men like Colonel Hans-Ulrich Rudel, the Brotherhood's and ODESSA's great friend, known to all in need of help, and back in circulation and very active again by the 1970's. Rudel, who boasted of being the most highly decorated officer in the Wehrmacht, spread the gospel

317

according to Hitler and as interpreted by Udo Walendy. The latter rehashed most of the sophistries put forward by official Nazi propaganda in the 1930's to prove *Mein Kampf* was not an indictment of the Führer. A young neo-Nazi, he used the political testament that Bormann had waited in the Führer's bunker to get from Hitler, with the idea that after the collapse, the philosophy could be resurrected.

Rudel commanded the Folk-True Youth (Volkstreue Jugend), which he wedded to other militant youth groups. They were lectured on the thoughts of Adolf Hitler. These might have been subtitled "Afterthoughts," since they came at the end of the Führer's life. Some samples: Germany had no option; Our enemies hate National Socialism because it exults the qualities of the German people; Adversity is the indispensable prelude to a great renaissance where the German people are concerned; Germany's enemies forced the war upon us; I have opened the eyes of the whole world to the Jewish peril.

Rudel traveled a great deal between the respectable villas that constituted a Nazi-minded community in the South Tyrol and settlements in Latin America, encouraging fugitives to test the climate by returning to Frankfurt with him. Most declined. But with Rudel to push him, Walendy addressed youth camps, using Bormann's collection of papers sent out of Berlin at the last moment and recording Hitler's ideas in the last weeks.

In Munich, a German friend took me along to one of these camps. This was a Brotherhood revival meeting. The group represented the New European Youth, the Viking Youth, and the Federation of Homeland-True Youth. Their aims were described as "national resistance to subjugation" and "restoration of Germanic Folk Territory." The boys saluted with *"Heil Dir"* (Hail to you) and drilled with pellet-firing rifles. Their hero for a Greater Germany was Franz Josef Strauss, Bavarian head of the Christian Democrats, who has protested in the past that a nation cannot be forever treated like a naughty child.

And of course a nation cannot be treated that way. This particular movement was a collection of failures, as the mass-circulation West German weekly *Stern* pointed out: teachers who could not deal with young rebels; civil servants who were frustrated; and, especially, the sons and daughters of old Nazis either in self-exile or just returned.

Still, these youth groups illustrate the use to which Bormann intended the Hitler chronicles to be put. And there is something disturbing in *Stern*'s rationalization that the Munich revival was a collection of failures. That same description would easily fit the early Nazi meetings.

Perhaps the woodsy gatherings of children were not worth much serious attention. Yet it was apparent that some form of public opinon was at work, or else the West German judiciary was letting the most notorious Nazi war criminals literally get away with murder. The International Concentration Camp Committee, an authoritative source, accused the judges of going out of their way to accept defense excuses that had the effect of postponing trials for years on end. The Secretary of the committee, an Austrian Jew who survived Auschwitz, Hermann Langbein, a man of undisputed integrity, told me that he was not driven by a desire for revenge. All civilization suffered if the law in a powerful nation like the new Germany became perverted.

His examples of delayed justice would fill a book. One that caught my eyes was that of Dr. Werner Best, charged with taking part in the murder of 8,723 Polish intellectuals as chief of the Nazi Security Service. The case was dropped six months later because of Best's old age. So far as I could see, the reason for bringing him into court at all was to satisfy public agitation, led by East Germany and the Polish government. His background was well documented. He was sentenced to death in Denmark for his efforts there, as Reich Commissar, to destroy the whole Jewish population. It was Best's notion at the outset of the anti-Jewish purges in Germany to have all passports held by Jews marked with a large red "J." He gladly endorsed Bormann's proposal that to simplify identification, all Jews should be obliged to make use of the middle name "Yid."

But Best had been running an industrial intelligence organization after the war for I. G. Farben's associates and was legal adviser to the Stinnes Trust, one of the largest West German military-industrial complexes, which was forgiven its criminal involvement with Nazi atrocities because in the postwar hysteria it performed a dutiful role guarding the western bastions against Russia. Thus the wheels of justice were persuaded to grind exceeding slow. Best was hauled into court but got released when that ingenious loophole was discovered by which it could be shown that he did not act with malice aforethought during the war and was therefore guilty only of manslaughter. Then, by attrition, the case against him wore down to the point where Best's health could not stand up to another inquisition. By 1972 he was, in effect, a free man. To one of the killers was given a full measure of the mercy he had never shown others.

319

CHAPTER 28

On the Putumayo River lives an old man with a dugout canoe and an outboard motor. This gives him mobility along the rivers that divide those small countries, which, like the Amazon, broaden as they descend toward the sea until they merge with the immensities of Argentina and Brazil on the east side of the vastness of Latin America. Here it is hard to make use of words like "countries," for the boundaries are fuzzy.

Where the old man putters in his canoe may never be known. He regards the landscape differently from most of us. He sees trails and waterways. He has little need of roads. He has the same peasant cunning that enabled Bormann and so many others to move with relative ease through the Bavarian alps while Allied soldiers were confined to tanks and tarmac. He is familiar with the dark interior in the same way that the Communist agents of the 1920's and '30's were familiar with the brooding mountains where so many cultures met. The great escape artists of that prewar period, men like Marshal Tito, who was then a mechanic hurrying back and forth between one illegal group of unionists and another, hiding by day and traveling by night, these veterans of early revolution would know how the old man sees the world differently. He, and they, returned to the ways of the hunter and the hunted.

The Putumayo River permits the old man to visit Peru and Ecuador. In the first country is a banking institution that conceals, it is said, the Bormann Papers. The second country shelters Alfons Sassen, the representative of the Brotherhood business enterprise known as "Estrella." It is said, too, that Sassen is financed by Dr. Josef Mengele, who controls now such funds as remain liquid from the sale of European loot. Sassen was sentenced to death in his absence by a Dutch court for war crimes; the details are drearily familiar. He was once a police captain in Ecuador, which is where the old man was provided with identity papers in 1952 before he made his small nest of rubbish on the Colombian side of the river.

The old man can navigate to the Amazon and swing up another tributary and so in time arrive in Bolivia, where it is possible to buy, for $57,000 (the price has gone up since the Swiss manufacturer Josef Hieber bought one), an honorary title as Bolivian consul-general in some area where one wishes to make a social splash.

But these are vast distances for an old man in a canoe. They are vast distances for investigators. It is quicker and just as discreet to travel by light plane.

The Brotherhood and its manifold organs had planes and seagoing ships at their disposal. Landlocked Bolivia bought a Brotherhood vision of a navy, which in the end consisted of a freighter and then another freighter and then another, commanded by Rear Admiral Alberto Albarracin and trading under the grandiloquent title of "Transmarítima Boliviana," with finally a Grand Admiral and Commander in Chief, Horacio Ugarteche, who announced, "We shall carry the Bolivian flag through the free ports of the world." And indeed they did. For Bolivia is in essence run by German businessmen, and the Brotherhood found cargoes of arms without much difficulty. Then a scandal in 1971 forced the "official" Bolivian government to take action. The navy was a registered company in Panama and Hamburg. In both those places, its assets were seized to pay creditors. But few assets existed. The manager of this vast enterprise, chartering vessels to move guns and cocaine around the world, was none other than Klaus Barbie-Altmann, that slippery Bolivian businessman and erstwhile murderer who was tracked down and exposed by Beata Klarsfeld.

The probability that the Bormann Brotherhood has been quietly breaking up does not diminish the stature of Beata Klarsfeld. The probability that the Bormann conspiracy was known to the Soviet Union and separately to the West cannot diminish what this German girl accomplished by forcing a smug and prosperous society to look more deeply into its soul.

For some time there had been "sightings" of Bormann in many parts of Latin America, and it would be tedious to list and examine them all. The old man in the canoe could be Bormann. He was a man of disguises even when he was the secret ruler of the Third Reich. A country retreat on the Putumayo might look, to more sophisticated and perhaps arrogant eyes, like a rat's nest or the lair of a small and frightened fox.

It is not the dramatic end desired by many different people for different reasons. It would be tidier to have him publicly hanged; then we could parcel up our consciences and tie them tight with legal ribbons. Such an event seems most unlikely. And so the legends go on, and grow, and change. There seems something almost super-natural in the way he comes back again and again. Eichmann in the glass booth in Jerusalem talked much of the time about Bormann as if he were alive and almost with him during the trial. A Dutch ex-SS officer, Willem Sassen, claimed he had hours of tape recordings in his Argentina home. There, Eichmann talked, before his capture, about how he and Bormann escaped. A disturbing thought, that. The voice of the dead Eichmann echoing tinnily through the hide-away of that Dutch Nazi in Buenos Aires, re-creating the actions and the words of this elusive Bormann. . . .

All these stories led to nothing. Bormann was reported by a man who "escaped with him from Berlin" to govern a self-contained Nazi colony in the land of the dictator he so admired, President Stroessner. It was hidden in one of the world's great fortresses (of which Latin America is full), one kilometer west of the Paraná River and twenty-four kilometers north of the Brazil-Paraguay border. It was called Kolonie Waldner 555.

Who could disprove the detailed story of Erich Karl Wiedwald? He claimed that as a noncommissioned officer in the Waffen SS he was a prisoner in a Russian military hospital the morning after Bormann vanished in Berlin. Wiedwald escaped in the company of six men, including Rolf Schwent and a stocky middle-aged officer who led them eventually north to Flensburg. At the Danish border, they broke up. Wiedwald felt safe enough to take a job (and this is certainly true) with the U.S. Military Police. There in the "Hungry Winter" of 1946 he met Schwent, who proposed taking the ODESSA route to Argentina. They followed what is now the well-known Brenner Pass road to a monastery in Rome. From there they were conducted to the freighter that took them across the South Atlantic. During the crossing, Schwent revealed that the middle-aged officer in their escape group was Bormann. Two years later, Wiedwald found safety in Kolonie Waldner 555, forty miles wide and a hun-dred miles long, protected down one side by the immense breadth of the Paraná's muddy waters and on the other side by thick jungle. Yugoslav guards from the old pro-Nazi Croat army led a small force of tribal Indians. The colony was linked with fourteen similar fortresses in the area. If strangers tried to approach by river, they had to hire German pilots to negotiate the hazardous waters; only

German riverboat pilots were available, and all were recruited by Bormann. If strangers tried to come by land, they fell into the hands of the guards. Stroessner's air force kept an eye open for intruders in the sky. Bormann kept Piper Cub light planes. So said Wiedwald.

It was in 1967 that Wiedwald decided to go back to Germany and tell the so-called facts. He reported that Bormann's face was damaged by bad plastic surgery; that the Reich Minister drew the equivalent of $45,000 a month for expenses; that Kolonie Waldner 555 was a model state run on Nazi principles; that Dr. Mengele and other notorious war criminals lived in similar colonies; and that their "foreign policy" was to create impressive miniature states and then invite international commissions to come and see how harmless they all had become.

Nobody discovered any evidence to support Erich Wiedwald's story. The former Waffen SS corporal was dying of cancer when he related the details. He showed no interest in making money. He had used some known facts to produce a red herring. Nobody seemed to know why. But he had certainly caught the public imagination with a comic-strip tale that, like the two-dimensional figures of television, filtered out the nightmare realities of the past. It was a fine example of tendentious reportage: the details of the house in Berlin where they hid, which proved accurate; the crossing of the Danish border at Flensburg; the names of helpers along the ODESSA and Vatican lines; even the descriptions of the sea crossing and the journey into Paraguay.

The central figure, Bormann, comes and goes like a piece of ecto-plasm. If he was a wealthy man by the 1970's, he could have escaped from the confines of jungle life. The world was full of strange men who could buy privacy.

Interpol's files are stuffed with reports tracing the movements of Nazi funds, and the business enterprises they are supposed to fi-nance. But as a Paris investigator said to me: "I cannot march into a foreign country and arrest a man I know is the former Inspector General of Nazi death camps. He is no longer Herr Richard Gluecks, you see, but Senhor Something-or-Other, a citizen of that country and entitled to protection. Our only hope is publicity. And it is only in recent times that we have been able to get the informa-tion out of the secret-police files of the Latin-American countries that conceal these devils. They spent a lot of money buying citizen-ship. They spent a fortune corrupting their new governments. As they say in Bolivia, 'this country cost us enough—we'll kill anyone who tries to sell us out.'"

There have been plots galore to trap Bormann. But Latin America covers more than eight million square miles. It stretches from Tierra del Fuego in the south to the Rio Grande, which in the north provides the line between an overindustrialized world and an almost totally undeveloped one. There are a million places to hide, and false trails at every turn.

In the twenty countries of Latin America, 125 million persons were living under military dictatorship within a decade of President Kennedy's launching of the Alliance for Progress. Another 12 million lived under civilian dictatorships. About 104 million could be said to enjoy a comparatively democratic form of government. After Castro came to power in Cuba, it seemed to some observers that the real danger to individual freedom would be not Marxism so much as military technocracy. The talk, among young colonels overturning old regimes, centered upon what could be regarded as new versions of National Socialism.

A strange combination of ideologies and forces had been observed. Like an echo from the days when Nasser drew his advisers from Nazis in Argentina, there were "Nasserite" combinations in which control of production and land by the state had been promoted in the name of the workers. There was a surrealistic quality to the promotion of Anwar Sadat from Nazi intelligence agent to President of Egypt. The international agency concerned with securing justice for political prisoners—Amnesty International—produced thick dossiers on torture and police brutality reminiscent of the Nazi era.

No Brotherhood, no bands of decaying Nazis, no groups of political gangsters had brought about these circumstances. But the ghosts of the Brotherhood were forever whispering their echoes of the past. In Germany, it had been the absence of a large middle class that helped Hitler to terrorize the population and intimidate the public services, because the danger of losing one's job was comparable to endangering one's entire family. In Latin America a small middle class had formed in Argentina, Chile, Peru, Colombia, and Mexico, but this was a tiny proportion of the whole. And whereas the middle class in North America developed values and ideals of its own, this Latin middle class aspired only to become part of the small aristocracy which sent its children to Europe for education.

The dangers made evident in the early days of World War II were still present, but this time without the urgency of some great political crisis. The large German communities that offended the sensibilities of Beata Klarsfeld were not really much concerned with ideology of the political right or left. In this respect they were moving into the same mental climate as that which had overtaken Germany. In the German Club at La Paz in Bolivia, the Gestapo killer wanted by the French government for atrocious wartime crimes, Klaus Barbie-Altmann, could draw himself up before the German Embassy's chargé-d'affaires and accuse him of bringing a Jew into the club as his guest. The conversation, as reported by several observers, went like this:

"Why do you bring a Jew here?"

"My guest is cultural attaché to the U.S. Embassy."

"We shall never accept a dirty Jew in our club."

"I shall report this to my Ambassador."

"Nobody frightens me. I was an important Gestapo chief. One day the national party will revive and then you will settle accounts with me."

When the scene was over, people shrugged.

A small delegation of Jewish businessmen, according to Simon Wiesenthal, the tenacious director of the Vienna Documentation Center, came to him from Paraguay with a request not to press for the punishment of Dr. Josef Mengele. They had been warned that if Mengele was kidnapped "not one Jew in Paraguay will survive." They said an outsider would never understand the influence of the old Nazi German *sippenhaftung* of racial discrimination. "The old ideology of 1933 is still very strong," said their spokesman.

They lived in a country ruled by the German brewer's son, Stroessner, where the President could order the local television station to change a commercial in which appeared a clock that told the same time no matter what the hour. "I have to protect the people from being misled," said the President.

The same stories keep repeating themselves. Amnesty International's investigations in Paraguay include a version of a report that has appeared in other bulletins published by the various documentation centers, the Catholic Information Agency among them. This one concerns six young men tortured to death by the secret police and then tossed into the Paraná River. Amnesty says they were killed because they were Communists. Another version claims they were young Israelis out to execute Dr. Mengele.

The curtain rises on another act in the drama. It began almost half a century ago. Its real inspiration lies deeper in mankind's past. Martin Bormann's immediate purpose has been fulfilled. The Brotherhood, as he conceived it, is being transformed. But the dragon's teeth are sown. Whether Bormann is alive or dead is almost irrelevant. It is the legend that is important now. It forces us to think again about man's unthinkable depravity. What matters is that there are Beata Klarsfelds in our civilization who see a need to make our flesh crawl from time to time, to warn those who have had no direct experience of modern tyrannical insanity on the Hitlerian scale.

"Nazism is only one word for that kind of madness," Beata Klarsfeld said that day we walked along the peaceful banks of the Seine. "It was a logical climax to centuries of racial intolerance. Because the Nazis are dying doesn't surely mean that the human race has suddenly purged itself. On the contrary . . . Perhaps I do seem obsessed. I wish more people were. I was raised a Protestant, and all I remember, looking back, is my horrified recognition that in the churches were the monstrous ghosts. Nearly eight hundred years ago, the Fourth Lateran Council of the Catholic church directed Jews to wear yellow patches.

"Does nobody see any connection between that horror and this recent holocaust? . . . Doesn't anyone today care that these are the roots of that jungle shared by Hitler and Mussolini and Franco— and Stalin too? . . . Yet nothing is done to stop this attitude of mind, or to confront the realities of racialism. Perhaps the churches are only a manifestation. I cannot tell. To me, the inescapable fact is that mankind has within living memory done to death with careful calculation—not in the heat of war—millions who were guilty of being innocently, harmlessly different. It happened that the most identifiable, the most victimized, were Jews. Yet all they had was their law and their endless dialogue with God. They had lost all symbols of unity but these. But these set them apart. . . ."

We have traveled a long and tortuous path. My account is ended, although hardly complete. I regret that I could not supply the answer (or even *an* answer) to "the puzzle" and that there are so many missing pieces along the way. In the deepest sense, I regret most that the course of events in this most bloody of centuries has made the writing of this chronicle not merely possible, but necessary.

Out of the infinite possibilities open to humankind in seeking a good life, it seems to me we have not often chosen wisely. How and why this condition has become so manifest in our time I must leave to the historian, the sociologist, the psychologist, and, perhaps finally, the psychiatrist. If, in their pursuit of cause, they can evolve some practical suggestions for saner human conduct, they will have indeed opened the gates to hope for this troubled planet. I bless their efforts although, in candid appraisal of what the senses and the mind can currently perceive, I do not envy them their task. It will, at the very least, take long.

I have tried to record, interpret, and speculate upon some aspects of the most vicious and degrading period in the experience of any of us now alive. It can rival, indeed surpass, the depravity of any era in history. My account is a small part of a staggeringly huge and ghastly record. No one can sustain the effort to absorb all of it. Yet no one can afford to ignore its essence.

I hope I will not be considered deceptive if I reveal at so late a place in this narrative that I intended more than a comment on a historical mystery; I mean this as a cautionary note to us and to our inheritors. The despicable forces loosed by the Third Reich are not expunged, although, like some virulent virus, they may have changed to other forms and be difficult to identify. They remain malignant and as potentially dangerous as before. If there is any value to the persistence of the Bormann puzzle, let it be to remind us of the darkest side of human nature that he and his brothers so monstrously exemplify.

George Santayana, a contemporary American philosopher, made a statement in *The Life of Reason* that is profound and grimly applicable to the journey we've taken and to its point. He said: "Those who cannot remember the past are condemned to repeat it."

Are we to be condemned? Must we be? I hope not. So I make this my valedictory:

Remember.

327

INDEX OF PEOPLE

Adenauer, Konrad, 11, 129, 133, 139-40, 141, 142, 160, 193-94, 209, 210, 213, 213 n, 223
Aeschbacher, Hernz, 220
Alanbrooke, Viscount, 74
Albarracin, Alberto, 321
Alisax, Wendig, see Schwend, Frederic
Ambros, Otto, 265
Andreotti, Giulio, 239-40
Axmann, Artur, 81, 111-13

Barbie, Klaus ("Altmann," "Mertens," "Hangman of Lyon"), 19, 143, 147, 154-57 158, 160, 181, 195, 220, 221, 228, 231, 275, 321, 325
Barbie, Ute, 155
Bassler, Hilmar, 130
Bauch, Gerhard, 127
Bauer, Fritz, 218
Bauer, Hans, 162, 248
Baun, Hermann, 185, 210
Beaverbrook, Lord, 44, 45, 55, 56, 124, 191, 278, 295
Becher, Walter, 316
Bedford, Duke of, 241
Beetz, George, 162
Behrens, Manja ("M"), 40-43, 44
Below, Nicolaus von, 162
Berger, Gottlob, 167, 302-03
Bernadotte, Folke, 73, 151
Berning, Wilhelm, 233
Bernonville, Jacques Charles Noel Duge de, 158-59, 160, 276
"Best, S. Payne," 236-37
Best, Werner, 319
Bezymenski, Lev, 169-70, 173, 174, 178, 289
Blankenburg, Werner, 256
Bohne, Gerhard, 232, 252, 255
Bohr, Niels, xi
Boldt, Gerhard, 77, 78, 162

Bormann, Adolf Martin (Martin, Jr.), 29, 42, 100, 169, 221, 282
Bormann, Albert, 54, 55, 79, 80, 167
Bormann, Gerda Buch (Mrs. Martin Bormann), 28, 29, 41, 42, 43, 44, 78, 79, 89, 100, 170-71, 180, 231, 247-48, 281-82, 284-85
Bormann, Martin, ix, x, xii, xvi, xvii, 3, 4, 5-9, 10, 12, 13-15, 16, 17-19, 23-29, 30-34, 35, 36, 37, 38, 39, 40-42, 43, 44, 45-50, 48 n, 52, 53, 54, 55, 56, 57, 58-60, 61-65, 66-67, 68, 70-71, 72, 73, 74, 75, 76, 77-78, 79, 80, 81, 82-83, 84, 85, 86, 88, 89, 90, 91, 92, 93, 94, 96, 97, 98, 99, 101, 103, 104, 106, 107, 108, 109, 110, 111-12, 113, 116, 117, 118, 119, 128, 131, 133, 134-35, 136-38, 145, 146, 147, 149, 150, 151, 156, 158, 160-61, 162, 164, 165, 166-67, 168, 169, 170-71, 172, 173-74, 175-76, 177, 178, 183, 184-85, 186, 188-89, 191, 192, 193, 194, 200, 201, 202, 203, 205, 207, 216, 217, 218-19, 220-21, 222, 223, 224, 225, 226, 228, 231, 232, 234, 235, 236, 237-38, 241, 242, 243, 244-45, 246, 247-48, 249, 250, 253, 264, 267, 268-69, 271, 274, 276-77, 278-79, 280-82, 283, 285-87, 288, 289, 290, 291, 292, 293-94, 295, 296, 300, 301, 302, 308, 309, 310, 311, 315-16, 318, 320, 322-23, 324, 325-26, 327
Bose, S. Chandra, 74
Boulay, Paul Wilhelm Felix, 316
Bourwieg, Bruno, 255
Bradley, Omar, 108
Brandt, Willy, 6, 145, 189, 190, 199
Brauchitsch, Walther von, 235
Braun, Eva, 39, 40, 79, 80, 84, 110, 162, 163

Braun, Wernher von, 118
Bridgeman, Viscount, 157
Brookes, Robert, 7
Brunner, Alois ("George Fisher,"
"Georg Fischer"), 127, 226-27
Brunner, Anton Alois, 226-27
Bryce, Ivan, 129
Buch, Walter, 28, 46
Bucher, Ewald, 258, 259
Bütefisch, Heinrich, 265
Bünsch, Franz, 124, 127
Buresch, Judge, 255
Burgdorf, Wilhelm, 77, 78, 79, 162
Burgess, Guy, xii
Busch, Germán, 47
Byrnes, James F., 163, 293

Canaris, Wilhelm Franz, xii, xvi,
59, 83 n, 109-10, 117, 186, 191,
245, 246, 301, 302, 310-11
Castro, Fidel, 324
Catel, Werner, 252
Chuikov, Vassili, 301
Churchill, Peter, 311
Churchill, Winston, 18, 44, 45, 55,
76, 82, 93, 96, 100, 101, 107, 116,
135, 164, 235, 246, 299
Chutburn, S., 148, 153
"Cicero," 149-50
Clark, Norman, 57
Clay, George, 250-51
Clemens, Hans, 303
Conti, Leonardo, 253
"Coppens, Lieutenant," 237
Córdoba, Concha, 270
Coward, Noel, 215, 217
Creasy, George, 95
Creutzfeldt, Dr., 255
Cuneo, Ernest, 129, 153
Cyrankiewicz, Jozef, 296

Dahl, Roald, 215
Darwin, Charles, 25
Degrelle, Léon, 94, 102, 103, 222
Dehler, Thomas, 223
Dejaca, Walter, 264
Delmer, Sefton, 178
Dering, Krystyna, 256-57
Dering, Wladislaw, 254, 255-58,
262-63
Dewavrin, André, xi
Doenitz, Karl, 4, 81, 83, 84, 85, 95,
96, 97, 100, 110, 162, 173, 287-88
Dollfuss, Engelbert, 34, 35
Donovan, William J., xi, 18, 71, 98,

116, 117, 129, 148, 216, 246
Dulles Allen, 71, 72, 74, 108, 122,
166, 293
Dulles, John Foster, 122
Duquaire, Cardinal, 228
Dwyer, Peter, 164-65, 275

Eckart, Dietrich, 284
Eden, Anthony, 235
Ehrmann, Johann (Johannes Hart-
mann), 268-69, 271-72, 273-74,
276, 277
Eichmann, Adolf, 46 n, 59, 79, 80,
92, 119, 124, 127, 174-75, 176-77,
212, 220, 232, 249, 301, 322
Eichmann, Horst Adolf, 92
Eichmann, Klaus, 92
Eisenhower, Dwight D., 76, 85, 107,
109, 142
Ellis, Charles H. ("Dick"), 91-92
Erhard, Ludwig, 183-84, 251

Farnbacher, Wilhelm, 123
Farouk I, King of Egypt, 120, 127
Fegelein, Herman, 162
Felfe, Heinz, 183, 184, 192, 195,
196, 261, 303
Filbinger, Hans, 102, 103
Fischer, Horst, 258
Fischer, Peter ("Major Fiedler"),
114
Fisher, John, 93, 98
Fisher, Lieutenant Commander, 93,
98
Fleishhacker, Hans, 73, 73 n
Fleming, Ian, 97-98, 129
Fleming, Peter, 98
Flicke, Wilhelm, 301-02, 311
Foch, Ferdinand, 101
Foote, Alexander, xi
Förster, Robert von, 144
Franco, Francisco, 122, 221, 239,
288 n, 298, 326
Frank, Hans, 17
Freytag-Loringhoven, Bernd von,
162
Frick, Wilhelm, 187, 189, 190, 193
Funk, Walther Emanuel, 119, 131,
132

Gawlik, Johannes, 226
Gebhardt, Karl, 284
Gehlen, Reinhard, 10, 11, 24, 42,
81, 88, 89, 104, 106-07, 109, 113,
114, 115, 118, 119, 120, 122, 127,

Gehlen, Reinhard (*cont.*)
130, 140, 143, 154, 166, 167, 183,
184, 185-200, 201, 203, 209, 210,
211, 219, 223, 290, 291, 292, 293,
294
George VI, King of England, 50, 54,
282
Gerlier, Cardinal, 231
Glasenapp, Horst von, 191, 195
Globke, Hans, 141-42, 193, 213,
213 n
Gluecks, Richard, 324
Goebbels, Joseph, 5, 49, 50, 65, 79,
108-09, 110, 124, 162, 173, 233,
243, 275-76
Goebbels, Magda, 79, 162
Göring, Emmy, 39, 50, 138, 224,
282, 283
Göring, Hermann, 17-18, 39, 49, 50,
51, 65, 75, 78, 81, 83, 88, 110,
133, 138-39, 282, 283, 296
Gouzenko, Igor, xvii, 116
Graham, Robert, 240
"Gray Fox," *see* Gehlen, Reinhard
Gray, Ronald, 3-9, 14, 15, 173, 201,
218
Greim, Robert Ritter von, 170
Grothmann, Werner, 85
Grundy, Ronald, 6, 7
Guderian, Heinz, 65
Guevera, Che, 215, 221, 227, 269
Guinzbourg, Victor de, 88
Gundlach, Gustav, 239
Gutenberg, Karl, 104

Hahn, Ludwig, 261, 262
Halder, Franz, 184
Hamilton, Duke of, 51, 54
Hamitsch, Professor, 35
Hanfstaengl, Ernst ("Putzi"), 30,
31, 33
Hangen, Welles, xii
Harel, Iser, xii
Haushofer, Karl, 53, 54
Hausner, Gideon, 177
Hausser, Paul, 168, 222
Heiden, Konrad, 33
Heimerdinger, Gertrud von, 184
Heinsen, Hans, 316
Henke, Gerhard, 198
Hess, Ilse, 54, 55, 299
Hess, Rudolf, 28, 44, 45, 46, 49,
50-52, 53, 54-55, 56, 58, 59, 65,
98, 100, 113, 135, 166, 167, 206,
222, 278, 295, 298-99, 300

Hess, Wolf, 54, 55, 299
Hessler, Günther, 287
Heusinger, Adolf, 212
Hevelmann, Hans, 250, 251, 255
Hewel, Walther, 162
Hewitt, Abraham Stevens, 244
Heyde, Werner ("Fritz Sawade"),
251-52, 254-55
Heydrich, Reinhard ("Butcher of
Prague"), 50, 59, 60, 63, 65, 80,
139, 284, 297
Hieber, Josef, 322
Himmler, Heinrich, xvii, 24, 37, 38,
46 n, 48, 49, 50, 52, 58, 59, 64,
65, 73, 74, 75, 81, 84, 85-88, 89,
90, 91, 103, 104, 110, 124, 142,
150, 151, 198, 283-84, 291-92,
295
Himmler, Margaretta, 284
Hitler, Adolf, xiv, 4, 5, 8, 12, 18,
19, 23-24, 25, 27, 28, 29, 30-36,
37, 38, 39, 40, 41, 44, 45, 46, 47,
48, 48 n, 49, 50, 51, 52, 53, 54,
55, 57, 58, 59, 60, 61, 62, 63, 64,
65, 66, 67, 69, 71, 72, 73, 74, 75,
77, 78, 79, 80, 81, 82, 83, 84, 89,
91, 94, 99, 100, 102, 104, 105,
106, 107, 110, 111, 113, 117, 118,
125, 126, 128, 130, 131, 132, 133,
134, 135, 136, 137, 138, 139, 141,
143, 146, 151, 160, 161, 163, 165,
170, 171, 172, 173, 174, 176, 177,
180, 184, 185, 186, 187, 190, 191,
194, 199, 205, 206, 207, 208, 210,
213, 215, 219, 220, 223, 224, 229,
233, 235, 236, 237, 238, 240, 242,
243, 243 n, 244, 245, 246, 248,
257, 258, 259, 264, 267, 278-79,
280-81, 282, 283, 284, 285, 287,
288 n, 289, 293, 295, 296, 299,
300, 301, 303, 305, 307, 308, 309,
310, 311, 317, 318, 326
Hitler, Alois (father), 32
Hitler, Alois (half-brother), 31
Hitler, Brigid, 31
Hitler, Paula (Frau Wolff), 35
Hitler, William Patrick, 35, 280
Ho Chi Minh, 310
Hoffmann, Heinrich, 37, 65
Hoffmann, Henny, 37
Holstein, Duke of, 84
Hoover, J. Edgar, 116, 151
Hopkins, Harry, 164
Horsley, Terence, 97-98

Höss, Rudolf Franz, 27, 90, 174-75, 265-66, 286, 296
Hudal, Alois, 89, 166, 169, 171, 172, 174, 177, 232-33, 241, 263
Hughes, Richard, xii
Hull, Cordell, 101
Hummel, Helmut von, 69, 173
Hundhammer, Adolf ("Hubner"), 220

Jackson, Robert E., 277
Jodl, Alfred, 63
Johannmeier, Willi, 162
John, Otto, xii, 10-12, 189, 194, 199, 200, 201-02, 203-04, 205-07, 208-14, 237, 289, 294, 303, 316
John XXIII (Cardinal Roncalli), 245-46
Jones, Billy, 179-80

Kadow, Walter, 26, 37, 60
Kaltenbrunner, Ernst, xvii, 59, 60, 69, 76, 79, 80, 88, 89, 145, 161, 221, 241, 311
Kanetzka, V. I., 227
Karpow, Colonel, 189
Keitel, Wilhelm, 84
Keller, Father, 236
Kennan, George F., 293
Kennedy, John F., 238, 324
Kerrl, Hans, 281
Kersten, Felix, 88, 301
Kesselring, Albert, 88
Khrushchev, Nikita, 127, 163, 260
Kielmansegg, Count von, xi, 214
Kiesinger, Kurt, 142, 157, 228
Kirkpatrick, Ivonne, 222-23, 227, 278
Klarsfeld, Beata, 16, 142, 143-46, 147, 155, 156, 157, 158, 183, 185, 206, 238, 267, 321, 325, 326
Koch, Erich ("Major Berger"), 60, 84-85, 107, 165, 172-73, 202, 218, 286
Kojima, Iso, 74
Koller, Karl, 161
Konrat, Georg von, 241, 241 n
Krebs, Hans, 162, 301
Kretschmer, Otto, 95
Krichbaum, Willy, 195
Krüger, Annelore (Alo), 186, 188, 189
Krüger, Bernhard, 144, 147, 148, 150, 151, 152-53, 154
Krumnow, Albert, 42-43

Krupp, Gustav, 128, 137-38
Kuhn, Dr., 155
Kundt, Hans, 46, 48

La Farge, John, 239
Lang, Iain, 123
Langbein, Hermann, xii, 319
Lange-Lenbach, Augustin von, see Bormann, Martin
Langer, Walter, 278
Lauterbacher, Hermann, 127
Leeb, Wilhelm Ritter von, 220
Leers, Johann von, 124-27, 186, 226, 233
Lenin, Nikolai, 285, 305
Leverkühn, Paul, xii, 245, 302
Levy, Ben, 54 n
Ley, Robert, 89
Liebenfals, Lanz von, 25
Liebknecht, Karl, 47
Lippolz, Stefan, 196
Lorenz, Heinz, 162
Louis Ferdinand, Prince, 194, 234
Lübke, Heinrich, 142, 265
"Lucy," xi
Ludwig, Karl, 241
Luxemburg, Rosa, 47

McCarthy, Joseph, 291
Macher, Heinz, 85
Maclean, Donald, xii
McNally, George, 148
Mader, Julius, 148
Maetzner, Wilhelm, 191
Manén, Lucie (Mrs. Otto John), 201
Manstein, Fritz Erich von, xii, 208-09
Manteuffel, Hasso von, 222
Manzialy, Fräulein, 162
Mao Tse-tung, 278
Marcel, Gadeon, 228
Marcinkiewitz, Major General von, 108
Marshall, George C., 107
Marx, Karl, 294
Maurice, Emil, 48
Maurice, Ernst, 32, 48
Maxwell-Fyffe, David, 99
Meer, Fritz ter, 265
Meisinger, Josef ("Beast of Warsaw"), 307-08
Mellethin, Friedrich Wilhelm von, 185

Mengele, Josef ("Dr. Nadich"), 181, 195, 256, 260, 266, 320, 232, 325
Messerschmitt, Willy, 67
Meyer, Kurt ("Panzer"), 70, 130-31, 167
Mitford, Unity, 34
Mohnke, Wilhelm, 74, 79, 164, 165-66, 167, 170, 172
Molotov, Vyacheslav, 239
Montgomery, Bernard L., 85, 157
Morell, Theodore, 31-32
Morgenthau, Henry, 101, 106
Mosley, Oswald, 222
Müller, Heinrich ("Gestapo"), 30-31, 32, 33-34, 37, 38, 43-44, 55, 56, 58, 59, 63, 78, 79, 91, 160, 161, 236, 237, 290, 294-95, 296-302, 305, 306, 308, 309-11
Müller, Ludwig, 233
Müller, Rene, 32, 34
Murphy, Michael L., 86
Mussolini, Benito, 118, 119, 121, 239, 240, 244, 272, 274, 326
Musy, Jean-Marie, 286

Naguib, Mohammed, 122, 123
Nasser, Gamal Abdel, 122, 123, 124, 126, 127
Naumann, Werner, 73-74, 80, 162, 192-93, 194, 222, 223, 293, 301
Neubeck, Sara, 316
Nicolai, Walter, 304-05
Nikitchenko, I. T., 299
Nkrumah, Kwame, 256 n
Noulens, Hilaire, 310

Obrist, Oskar, 220
Oppenhoff, Franz, 105-06
Ordonez Valderana, Luis, 273
Orozco, Hernando, 268-69
Osterloh, Edo, 252

Pabst, Waldemar, 47, 47 n
Padover, Saul, 105, 106
Papen, Franz von, 238
Pappenheim, Georg Graf zu, 144
Pardo Lamas, José, 273
Patton, George, 247
Paulus, Friedrich von, 61, 203-04, 207
Pavelić, Ante, 70, 177, 180-81
Pearson, Lester, 126
Peiper, Jochen, 220
Perón, Eva, 221-22

Perón, Juan, 68, 121, 123, 126, 221, 222
Peters, Ewald, 251
Philby, Kim, 207-08, 289-90, 292, 293, 294, 297-98
Pijade, Moshe, 175, 176
Pintsch, Karlheinz, 55, 167, 167 n
Pius XI, 217, 229, 234, 238-39
Pius XII, 102, 216, 220, 233-34, 235, 236, 237, 238, 239, 240, 242, 243-44, 245
Plettenburg, Countess, 245 n
Preutzmann, Hans, 105, 106, 107
Pucherl, Josef, 69

Quisling, Vidkun, 102

Radke, Albert, 210
Raskin, Alexander, 171, 247
Rattenhuber, Johann, 163
Raubal, Angela, 34, 35
Raubal, Angela ("Geli"), 30, 31, 32, 33, 34, 35, 36-37, 38, 39, 40, 41, 44, 45, 47, 48, 172, 280, 296, 309
Raubal, Leo, 35
Rauff, Walter, 180, 181
Rauschning, Hermann, 33, 37
Reckhorn, Willy, 221
Reitsch, Hanna, 81-82, 110, 118, 161
Ribbentrop, Joachim von, 18, 49, 82, 162, 243, 244, 245, 299 n, 309
Richter, Joachim, 7
Rochet, Jean, 227
Rode, Ernst, 316
Roestel, Franz, 69
Röhl, Henning, xiii
Röhm, Ernst, 33, 37, 38, 45, 46-47, 48-49, 65, 280
Rokossovski, Konstantin, 164, 165
Römer, Walter, 213
Rommel, Erwin, 64, 78
Roosevelt, Eleanor, 215
Roosevelt, Franklin D., 45, 55, 76, 93, 116, 135, 136, 164, 235, 244, 246, 288 n, 292, 293
Rosenberg, Alfred, 18, 228, 285
Rossbach, Gerhard, 25, 26, 30-31
Rossi, Luis Banchero, 158
Roth, Ernst Ludwig Ostermann von, 272
Rothschild, Baron, 32, 34
Rudel, Hans-Ulrich, 122, 182, 193, 263, 317-18

332

Rudenko, Roman, 299 n
Rudkin, C. I., 148, 153
Rueff, Jacques, 147
Russell of Liverpool, Lord, x

Sadat, Anwar, 64, 324
Salazar, Leandro Sanchez, xiii
Santander, Sylvano, 68
Santayana, George, 327
Sarnoff, David, 135, 139
Sassen, Alfons (Willem), 220, 320, 322
Sauckel, Fritz, 60
Schacht, Hjalmar, 49, 120, 122, 128, 129, 130-39, 140, 141, 174, 221, 276
Schacht, Mrs. Hjalmar, 136
Schaeffer, Heinz, 94, 95, 102
Schafheutle, Josef, 213
Schellenberg, Walter, 23-24, 50, 53, 58, 59, 63, 64, 114-15, 116, 121, 150, 151, 187, 236-37, 241-42, 243-45, 243 n, 274-75, 286, 294-95, 301, 308, 309
Schicklgruber, Maria Anna, 32, 34
Schirach, Baldur von, 37, 112, 113
Schlageter, Leo, 26, 60
Schmidt, Ursula, 6, 7
Scholtz-Klink, Gertrud, 283
Schramm, Wilhelm von, 184
Schreieder, Josef, 114
Schrübbers, Hubert, 316
Schüle, Erwin, 156, 260
Schumann, Horst, 256, 256 n
Schwarzwalder, John C. L., 89
Schwend, Frederic, 143, 144, 147, 149, 150, 151, 154, 159, 218, 220
Schwent, Rolf, 322
Schwerin von Krosigk, Lutz, 85, 100, 101, 219, 301
Seidl, Alfred, 299 n
Selvester, Thomas, 85, 86
Serrano Suñer, Ramón, 121, 272
Seubert, Franz, 198
Sharpley, Ann, 124-26, 204-05
Shawcross, Hartley, 277
Shulman, Milton, xii
Sibert, Edwin L., 166
Siemer, Laurentius, 206
Skala, Oskar, 150
Smith, Walter Bedell, 291
Skorzeny, Otto ("Scarface"), 23, 59, 60, 80-81, 89, 97, 102, 104, 107, 109, 117-20, 121-22, 124, 127, 128, 130, 132, 140, 141, 154,

155, 170, 174, 181, 185, 220, 221, 222, 243, 244, 245, 250, 272, 276, 291
Smolianoff, Solly, 151
Sommer, Hans, 195
Sorge, Richard, xii, 308-10, 308 n
Soustelle, Jacques, xiii
Speer, Albert, 18, 49, 63, 91, 94, 103, 153, 274, 279, 286, 287
Speidel, Hans, 212
Spellman, Francis, 246
Spengler, Heinz, 13-14
Stalin, Jacob, 60
Stalin, Joseph, xiv, 5, 51, 56, 61, 64, 76, 93, 95, 96, 126, 133, 160, 163, 164, 165, 166, 170, 175, 176, 177, 186, 203, 206, 208, 239, 240, 244, 245, 285, 289, 290-91, 292, 293, 295, 297, 298, 299, 300, 303, 305, 307, 308, 311, 326
Stangl, Franz, 169, 181-82, 247, 263
Stashinsky, Bogden, 195-96
Stauffenberg, Klaus Schenck von, 208
Stein, Georg, 227, 228
Steinhoff, Johannes, 262
Stempfle, Bernhard, 172
Stephenson, William, xviii, 18, 71, 98, 116, 117, 129, 135, 148, 149, 153-54, 159, 164, 217, 219-20, 246, 275, 276, 277, 310
"Stevens, R. H.," 236-37
Strasser, Gregor, 38
Strasser, Otto, 31, 33, 38
Strauss, Franz Josef, 133 n, 318
Streicher, Julius, 28-29, 65, 88
Stroessner, Alfredo, 48, 266, 322, 323, 325
Strong, Kenneth, 101, 291
Stuart, Campbell, 215, 216-17, 281
Stuckart, Wilhelm, 142
Stumpfegger, Gertrud, 112
Stumpfegger, Ludwig, 111-12, 162
Sukarno, 129, 130
Sweet-Escott, Bickham, xiii
Syme, Ronald K., 40

Tank, Kurt, xiii-xiv
"Tate," 94
Terboven, Josef, 102-03
Terry, Anthony, 227-28
Thalheimer, Hannelore, 247
Thayer, Charles, 212
Thompson, Robert, xiv
Thomson, Roy, 188

Thümmler, Josef, xiii
Tiebel, Erwin, 303
Tillmann, Friedrich, 251
Tito (Josip Broz), 169, 170, 175, 176-77, 179-80, 296-97, 320
Torres, Camilo, 271
Touvier, Paul, 228
Toynbee, Philip, 220
Trepper, Leopold ("Adam Miklas"), 83 n, 295, 296, 298
Trevor-Roper, Hugh, 111, 190, 199, 207
Trotsky, Leon, 276, 292, 304, 306-07
Truman, Harry S, 100, 153
Tunney, Gene, 215
Turi, Wenceslas, see Schwend, Frederic

Ugarteche, Horacio, 321
Uris, Leon, 254, 255, 262

Van der Valden, Bishop, 105
Van Fleet, James, 4
Vansittart, Robert G., 204
Vargas, Getulio, 149
Vermehren, Erich, 245 n
Volmy, Prelate, 42
Voss, Hans, 162

Wagner, Friedelind, 33, 36
Wagner, Richard, 25, 35-36
Wagner, Siegfried, 36

Wagner, Winifred, 33, 35-37
Walendy, Udo, 318
Watson, John, 148
Weber, Christian, 48
Wei, James, xiv
Weiss, Lieutenant Colonel, 162
Weizsäcker, Ernst von, 300
Wells, C. J. L., 86, 87
Welters, Gunter, 106
Wermuth, Otto, 96
Wessel, Gerhard, 198, 199
Westernhagen, Major, 221
Westrop, Gisela von, 79, 88-89, 222, 241
Wiedwald, Erich Karl, 322-23
Wiener, Alfred, xvii
Wiesenthal, Simon, xvi, 224, 274
Windsor, Duke of, 32, 243, 243 n
Wise, Donald, 124
Wisliceny, Dieter, 73
Wohl, Louis de, 54
Wohlgemuth, Wolfgang, 211
Wolff, Karl, 74, 172, 240, 293
"Wood, George," 72
Worgitzky, Hans-Heinrich, 127
Wyatt, A. G. N., xiv

Zahn, Gordon, 234
Zander, Wilhelm ("Frederich-Wilhelm Paustin"), 81, 162
Zeitzler, Kurt, 32
Zhukov, Georgi, xiv, 173
Zinnall, Karl-Heinz, 251

THE LIBRARY
ST. MARY'S COLLEGE OF MARYLAND
ST. MARY'S CITY, MARYLAND 20686